Multipliers

To

Sir Michael Ogden QC

Multipliers

Rodney Nelson-Jones MA(Oxon)
Partner, Field Fisher Waterhouse, Solicitors

Butterworths
London, Dublin & Edinburgh
1998

United Kingdom	Butterworths a Division of Reed Elsevier (UK) Ltd, Halsbury House, 35 Chancery Lane, LONDON WC2A 1EL and 4 Hill Street, EDINBURGH EH2 3JZ
Australia	Butterworths, SYDNEY, ADELAIDE, BRISBANE, CANBERRA, MELBOURNE, and PERTH
Canada	Butterworths Canada Ltd, TORONTO and VANCOUVER
Ireland	Butterworth (Ireland) Ltd, DUBLIN
Malaysia	Malayan Law Journal Sdn Bhd, KUALA LUMPUR
New Zealand	Butterworths of New Zealand Ltd, WELLINGTON and AUCKLAND
Singapore	Butterworths Asia, SINGAPORE
South Africa	Butterworths Publishers (Pty) Ltd, DURBAN
USA	Lexis Law Publishing, CHARLOTTESVILLE, Virginia

A CIP Catalogue record for this book is available from the British Library.

ISBN 0 406 89620 8

Typeset by Columns Design Ltd, Reading
Printed by Butler and Tanner Ltd, Frome

Visit us at our website: http://www.butterworths.co.uk

Preface

The purpose of this book is to provide personal injury lawyers, insurers and other practitioners with the essential equipment for the selection of suitable multipliers. As such, it is a response to three main developments over the last year.

The first was the landmark judgment in July 1998 of the House of Lords in the linked cases of *Wells v Wells, Thomas v Brighton Health Authority* and *Page v Sheerness Steel Company Limited.* Subject to the Lord Chancellor's subsequent exercise of his power under s 1 of the Damages Act 1996, this has set for the foreseeable future an underlying discount rate for accelerated receipt at 3% pa, based on the Index-Linked Government Stock (ILGS), in place of the 4.5% pa that had prevailed before. This significantly, and in cases of young plaintiffs very substantially, increases multipliers for future loss. In addition, their Lordships gave valuable guidance on the subjects of discounts for contingencies and discounts in cases of agreed life expectancy. They also set at 3% pa the rate for calculating the cost of additional accommodation under the principle in *Roberts v Johnstone.*

The second main development was the publication in May 1998 of the third edition of what have become universally known as the *Ogden Tables.* These were prompted by the publication of *English Life Tables No 15*, based on data for 1990–92, and the increased longevity shown by these tables is reflected by the rather higher multipliers in the third edition. In *Wells v Wells*, the House of Lords effectively endorsed the principles underlying the *Ogden Tables* 1–10. Indeed Lord Lloyd observed that actuarial tables should now be regarded as the starting-point, rather than a check, and added that judges should be slow to depart from the relevant actuarial multiplier on impressionistic grounds. When s 10 of the Civil Evidence Act is brought into force, the *Ogden Tables* will be admissible in evidence without further proof.

The third development—and far be it for the author to compare it with the first two—was the publication in December 1997 of the sofware disk and associated book entitled *Computing Personal Injury Damages* (CPID). This took the same software program and data used by the Government Actuary's Department on the third edition of the *Ogden Tables* to the point where users can compute multipliers that match the exact dates of any particular case: eg a man with a normal life expectancy born on 10 April 1957 whose case is due to be heard on 25 November 1998 who but for his injury would have retired at the age of 62. While precision of this order must remain the preserve of CPID purchasers, it is nevertheless now possible to produce much more elaborate multiplier tables than before: entirely consistent with the *Ogden Tables*, but providing a detailed extension of them.

This book simply, but it is hoped usefully, presents these changes in a form designed for everyday use. Shortly after this preface, there appear short summaries of vital statistics from the *Ogden* and CPID tables. Then, after an introductory essay, come the three main parts.

(1) The full House of Lords judgment in the case of *Wells v Wells*, *Thomas v Brighton Health Authority* and *Page v Sheerness Steel Company Limited*.
(2) The full third edition of the *Ogden Tables*—the 'Government Actuary's Department Actuarial Tables with explanatory notes for use in Personal Injury and Fatal Accident cases'—with kind permission of Her Majesty's Stationery Office.
(3) The CPID tables which, inter alia, suppy detailed 'page for age' life, earnings loss, and pension loss multipliers for each age between 1 and 75 covering each retirement age between 50 and 75, together with multipliers for any fixed period up to 100 years.

I am most grateful for the kind co-operation of Adrian Gallop of the Government Actuary's Department who produced the *Ogden Tables*, software programmer Warren Leggatt who has produced the CPID tables, Frank Burton QC and my partner Paul McNeil who have provided valuable comments and suggestions, and Butterworths staff for their editorial and technical assistance. Responsibility for any errors that remain rests with me.

Finally I wish to pay tribute to the pioneering work of Sir Michael Ogden QC, to whom this book is dedicated. His early recognition of the solution presented by Index-Linked Government Stock, together with his enlightened espousal of actuarial tables, have been a beacon of light in an age of comparative darkness.

10 August 1998

Rodney Nelson-Jones
Field Fisher Waterhouse
41 Vine Street
London EC3N 2AA

Contents

Tables of statutes and cases

Statutes*

Cases*

* Referred to in the Introduction.

Main summary tables

Fixed term multipliers

For whole year; 3% pa discount

Years	*Multiplier*	*Years*	*Multiplier*	*Years*	*Multiplier*	*Years*	*Multiplier*
1	0.99	26	18.14	51	26.34	76	30.25
2	1.94	27	18.60	52	26.56	77	30.36
3	2.87	28	19.04	53	26.77	78	30.46
4	3.77	29	19.47	54	26.97	79	30.56
5	4.65	30	19.89	55	27.17	80	30.65
6	5.50	31	20.30	56	27.37	81	30.74
7	6.32	32	20.69	57	27.56	82	30.83
8	7.12	33	21.08	58	27.74	83	30.92
9	7.90	34	21.45	59	27.92	84	31.01
10	8.66	35	21.81	60	28.09	85	31.09
11	9.39	36	22.16	61	28.26	86	31.17
12	10.10	37	22.50	62	28.42	87	31.25
13	10.79	38	22.83	63	28.58	88	31.32
14	11.46	39	23.15	64	28.73	89	31.39
15	12.12	40	23.46	65	28.88	90	31.47
16	12.75	41	23.76	66	29.02	91	31.53
17	13.36	42	24.06	67	29.16	92	31.60
18	13.96	43	24.34	68	29.30	93	31.67
19	14.54	44	24.62	69	29.43	94	31.73
20	15.10	45	24.88	70	29.56	95	31.79
21	15.65	46	25.15	71	29.68	96	31.85
22	16.17	47	25.40	72	29.80	97	31.91
23	16.69	48	25.64	73	29.92	98	31.96
24	17.19	49	25.88	74	30.03	99	32.02
25	17.67	50	26.11	75	30.15	100	32.07

Male age multipliers

3% pa discount

Age	Life	Earnings *60*	Pension *60*	Earnings *65*	Pension *65*
16	27.22	24.07	3.15	25.14	2.08
17	27.04	23.79	3.25	24.89	2.15
18	26.86	23.51	3.35	24.65	2.21
19	26.67	23.22	3.45	24.39	2.28
20	26.48	22.92	3.56	24.13	2.35
21	26.28	22.61	3.67	23.86	2.42
22	26.08	22.30	3.78	23.58	2.50
23	25.87	21.97	3.90	23.29	2.57
24	25.65	21.64	4.02	23.00	2.65
25	25.43	21.29	4.14	22.69	2.74
26	25.20	20.93	4.27	22.38	2.82
27	24.96	20.56	4.40	22.05	2.91
28	24.72	20.18	4.54	21.72	3.00
29	24.47	19.79	4.68	21.38	3.09
30	24.21	19.39	4.82	21.02	3.19
31	23.94	18.97	4.97	20.66	3.28
32	23.67	18.54	5.12	20.28	3.39
33	23.38	18.10	5.28	19.89	3.49
34	23.09	17.65	5.45	19.50	3.60
35	22.80	17.18	5.62	19.09	3.71
36	22.49	16.70	5.79	18.67	3.83
37	22.18	16.21	5.97	18.24	3.95
38	21.86	15.70	6.16	17.79	4.07
39	21.54	15.18	6.36	17.34	4.20
40	21.20	14.65	6.56	16.87	4.33
41	20.86	14.10	6.76	16.39	4.47
42	20.51	13.53	6.98	15.90	4.61
43	20.15	12.95	7.20	15.39	4.76
44	19.79	12.35	7.44	14.87	4.91
45	19.41	11.94	7.68	14.34	5.07
46	19.03	11.10	7.93	13.79	5.24
47	18.65	10.45	8.19	13.23	5.41
48	18.25	9.79	8.47	12.66	5.59
49	17.85	9.10	8.75	12.07	5.78
50	17.45	8.40	9.05	11.47	5.98
51	17.04	7.67	9.37	10.85	6.19
52	16.62	6.93	9.70	10.22	6.41
53	16.20	6.16	10.05	9.56	6.64
54	15.78	5.36	10.42	8.90	6.88
55	15.35	4.55	10.81	8.21	7.14
56	14.92	3.70	11.22	7.51	7.41
57	14.49	2.83	11.66	6.78	7.70
58	14.05	1.92	12.13	6.04	8.02
59	13.61	0.98	12.63	5.27	8.35
60	13.18	—	13.18	4.47	8.71
61	12.74	—	—	3.65	9.10
62	12.31	—	—	2.79	9.52
63	11.88	—	—	1.91	9.98
64	11.46	—	—	0.97	10.48
65	11.04	—	—	—	11.04

Female age multipliers

3% pa discount

Age	Life	Earnings *60*	Pension *60*	Earnings *65*	Pension *65*
16	28.23	24.33	3.91	25.47	2.76
17	28.07	24.05	4.02	25.23	2.84
18	27.91	23.76	4.15	24.98	2.93
19	27.74	23.47	4.27	24.72	3.02
20	27.57	23.16	4.40	24.45	3.11
21	27.39	22.85	4.53	24.18	3.20
22	27.20	22.53	4.67	23.90	3.30
23	27.01	22.20	4.81	23.61	3.40
24	26.82	21.86	4.96	23.31	3.51
25	26.61	21.50	5.11	23.00	3.61
26	26.41	21.14	5.27	22.69	3.72
27	26.19	20.77	5.43	22.36	3.83
28	25.97	20.38	5.59	22.02	3.95
29	25.75	19.99	5.76	21.68	4.07
30	25.52	19.58	5.94	21.32	4.19
31	25.28	19.16	6.12	20.96	4.32
32	25.03	18.73	6.30	20.58	4.45
33	24.78	18.29	6.50	20.19	4.59
34	24.53	17.83	6.69	19.79	4.73
35	24.26	17.36	6.90	19.39	4.88
36	23.99	16.88	7.11	18.97	5.03
37	23.71	16.38	7.33	18.53	5.18
38	23.43	15.87	7.56	18.09	5.34
39	23.14	15.35	7.79	17.63	5.51
40	22.84	14.81	8.03	17.17	5.68
41	22.54	14.26	8.28	16.68	5.85
42	22.22	13.69	8.54	16.19	6.03
43	21.91	13.10	8.81	15.68	6.22
44	21.58	12.49	9.08	15.16	6.42
45	21.25	11.87	9.37	14.62	6.62
46	20.91	11.24	9.67	14.07	6.83
47	20.56	10.58	9.98	13.51	7.05
48	20.21	9.91	10.30	12.93	7.28
49	19.85	9.21	10.64	12.33	7.52
50	19.48	8.50	10.98	11.72	7.76
51	19.11	7.76	11.35	11.09	8.02
52	18.73	7.00	11.73	10.44	8.29
53	18.34	6.22	12.12	9.78	8.57
54	17.95	5.42	12.53	9.09	8.86
55	17.55	4.59	12.97	8.39	9.16
56	17.15	3.73	13.42	7.66	9.48
57	16.74	2.84	13.89	6.92	9.82
58	16.33	1.93	14.40	6.15	10.17
59	15.91	0.98	14.93	5.36	10.55
60	15.49	—	15.49	4.54	10.95
61	15.07	—	—	3.70	11.37
62	14.64	—	—	2.83	11.82
63	14.22	—	—	1.92	12.30
64	13.79	—	—	0.98	12.81
65	13.37	—	—	—	13.37

1 Introduction

PRINCIPLES OF LAW

So many summaries of the *Wells* judgment appeared after its publication that it is otiose to repeat them here. As an alternative, there is set out below a summary of principles of multiplier law including those established in *Wells*.

(1) 'Where any injury is to be compensated by damages, in settling the sum of money to be given ... you should as nearly as possible get at that sum of money which will put the person who has been injured ... in the same position as he would have been in if he had not sustained the wrong': per Lord Blackburn in *Livingstone v Rawyards Coal Co.*

(2) The principle of full compensation is paramount. 'There is no room here for considering the consequences of a high award upon the wrongdoer or those who finance him': per Lord Scarman in *Lim Poh Choo v Camden and Islington Area Health Authority.*

(3) The object in assessing future loss is to find the size of a fund which can be invested, so that if capital is gradually drawn to make up income to the level of the loss, the fund will last for precisely the period of the loss (*Taylor v O'Connor*).

(4) The future loss is calculated by applying to the annual loss a multiplier of a number of years' purchase. This multiplier depends on the rate of interest which it is assumed that money would earn during the period (*Cookson v Knowles*).

(5) It is desirable to select a single interest (discount) rate that will apply to the vast majority of cases, in order to facilitate settlements and to save the expense of expert evidence at trial (*Wells v Wells*).

(6) This rate should be based on investment in Index-Linked Government Stock (ILGS). What the plaintiff will actually do with the award is irrelevant. As it is undesirable that the guidelines should be changed too often, the average gross return should be ascertained by taking a broad view over a substantial period (*Wells v Wells*).

(7) In applying the discount rate to find the multiplier, actuarial 'tables should now be regarded as a starting point, rather than a check. A judge should be slow to depart from the relevant multiplier on impressionistic grounds ...': per Lord Lloyd in *Wells v Wells.*

(8) A figure for the discount rate 'should be selected which will match the rates of interest on which the multipliers in the Ogden Tables are based ... This means that the figure should be expressed to no greater degree of accuracy than one-half of a decimal point': per Lord Hope in *Wells v Wells*.

(9) The correct discount rate at present is 3% per annum. This should apply until the Lord Chancellor specifies a new rate under s 1 of the Damages Act 1996 (*Wells v Wells*).

(10) Damages Act 1996, s 1.

> '(1) In determining the return to be expected from the investment of a sum awarded as damages for future pecuniary loss in an action for personal injury the court shall, subject to and in accordance with rules of court made for the purposes of this section, take into account such rate of return (if any) as may from time to time be prescribed by an order made by the Lord Chancellor.
>
> (2) Subsection (1) above shall not however prevent the court taking a different rate of return into account if any part to the proceedings shows that it is more appropriate in the case in question.
>
> (3) An order under subsection (1) above may prescribe different rates of return for different classes of case.
>
> (4) Before making an order under subsection (1) above the Lord Chancellor shall consult the Government Actuary and the Treasury; and any order under that subsection shall be made by statutory instrument subject to annulment in pursuance of a resolution of either House of Parliament.'

(11) The recommended rate of 3% per annum is net of basic rate tax, after allowing for the impact of allowances and tax bands and the fact that the income element in the annual draw-down will reduce and the tax-free capital element will increase as time goes by (*Wells v Wells*).

(12) The position regarding higher tax rates should remain as stated by Lord Oliver in *Hodgson v Trapp*, that in very exceptional cases plaintiffs are free to place their arguments for a lower discount rate before the court (*Wells v Wells*).

(13) No separate allowance is made for inflation, instead 'Inflation is taken care of in a rough and ready way by the higher rates of interest obtainable as one of the consequences of it': per Lord Diplock in *Cookson v Knowles*.

(14) In the case of a living plaintiff, the period of future loss is calculated from the date of trial (*Pritchard v J H Cobden Ltd*).

(15) In a fatal case, the appropriate multiplier is selected as from the date of death. The actual period from death to trial is then deducted from this, in order to arrive at the future multiplier (*Cookson v Knowles*).

(16) Where in a fatal case there has been a long delay between death and trial, the multiplier from the date of death should be increased to allow for the removal of many uncertainties (eg the plaintiff's survival to trial) and much of the acceleration of receipt (*Corbett v Barking Havering and Brentwood Health Authority*).

(17) Where there is an agreed life expectancy, there is no rational basis for applying a further discount for contingencies since these have already

been incorporated. There is no room for any discount in the case of a whole life multiplier with an agreed or otherwise decided expectation of life (*Thomas v Brighton Health Authority*).

(18) When calculating loss of future earnings, the multiplier may be reduced to allow for adverse contingencies such as sickness or redundancy. The further ahead the contingency is, the less its effect should be (*Mallett v McNonagle*).

(19) Where the trial judge had reduced the loss of earnings multiplier for a 28 year old plaintiff by 8.65% from 20.28 to 19 in order to take account of the substantial risk that, due to the particular nature of his work, the plaintiff might not have continued working until his proposed retirement age of 62, there was no need for an appellate court to intervene (*Page v Sheerness Steel Company Limited*).

(20) Allowance for adverse contingencies is also to be made when fixing the loss of pensions multiplier (*Auty v National Coal Board*). On the facts above, there was no reason for increasing the discount on the pensions multiplier from the 10% reluctantly allowed by the trial judge (*Page v Sheerness Steel Company Limited*).

(21) Split multipliers may be awarded to cater for different anticipated losses or expenses arising during different future periods. In *Hunt v Severs*, an overall multiplier of 14 was split into three constituents of 1, 9 and 4.

(22) A system for using multipliers to calculate loss of pension in a scheme involving entitlement to a retirement lump sum and a widow's pension is to be found in *Auty v National Coal Board*. The outline of the approach remains valid, but many of the principles applied within it have been implicitly overruled by *Wells v Wells*.

(23) In a pension scheme providing for a lump sum on retirement, where a plaintiff receives a lesser lump sum on his early resignation due to injury credit should be given for part of the lesser lump sum in the ratio that the part of the multiplier attributable to the period after normal retirement age bears to the whole life multiplier from the date of trial (*Longden v British Coal Corporation*).

(24) Multipliers convert future annual amounts into a lump sum payable immediately. One alternative to this is periodical payments by consent, as allowed by s 2 of the Damages Act 1996.

> '(1) A court awarding damages in an action for personal injury may, with the consent of the parties, make an order under which the damages are wholly or partly to take the form of periodical payments.
>
> (2) In this section 'damages' includes an interim payment. ...'

(25) The other alternative to multipliers is the use of structured settlements, of which the earliest English example is *Kelly v Dawes*.

THE OGDEN TABLES

The Ogden Tables is the colloquial name for what is officially titled 'Actuarial Tables With Explanatory Notes for Use in Personal Injury and

Fatal Accident cases'. They are based on the life expectancy data contained in the English Life Tables which show, in particular, the proportion of the population who die in any particular year of life. Not only do these feed through into the Ogden whole life multiplier tables but also they constitute the sole contingency incorporated into the tables for loss of earnings and loss of pension respectively.

The reason for the publication of the third edition of the Ogden Tables in May 1998 was the appearance of English Life Tables No 15 in 1997, based on detailed data for 1990–92. No further data of this nature has become available since. Therefore, it is uncertain whether any fourth edition of the tables will be needed in the near future, especially as the effect of the House of Lords' judgment in *Wells v Wells* was not to invalidate the third edition but to endorse it.

After the preliminary pages, the Ogden Tables contain introductions to their editions in reverse order: third, second, first. Thereafter, the explanatory notes and tables that follow all belong to the third edition. Some of the notes deal with problems that, it is submitted, may be solved by use of the CPID tables. Thus it is not necessary to make the adjustments explained in notes 16–18 for retirement ages other than 60 or 65, because the CPID tables provide multipliers for each retirement age between 50 and 75. Nor is there any need to carry out the calculations suggested in notes 19 and 20 for plaintiffs under the age of 16, since the CPID tables cover plaintiffs of each age from one year old onwards.

The extra extensions provided by CPID in no way detract from the pioneering importance of the core Ogden Tables 1–10. These provide, for each half point of discount rate between $1\frac{1}{2}$ and 5% pa, multipliers for males and females respectively for:

(1) pecuniary loss for life;
(2) loss of earnings to pension age 65;
(3) loss of earnings to pension age 60;
(4) loss of pension from age 65;
(5) loss of pension from age 60.

In addition, there are two further traditional tables.

Table 21—Discounting factors for term certain—purports to show the 'discount value of multiplier for a period of deferment'. As is recognised in note 20, however, this is not precisely what Table 21 does because it ignores the impact of mortality. As such, it does not supply the exact multiplier for a 50 year old who has a loss due to start at the age of 58, because (unlike Tables 1–10) it is does not allow for the chances of death between the two ages. It is therefore submitted that, while the table is perfectly valid, this validity is limited to discounting a given figure, eg a retirement lump sum that would have been payable at age 58.

Table 22 requires neither introduction nor qualification. It states the multipliers for pecuniary loss for any fixed term between 1 and 40 years. Thus on a 3% pa discount rate the life multiplier for an agreed life expectancy of 20 years is 15.10. In the light of *Wells v Wells*, it is as simple as that.

Tables 11–20, which are counterparts of Tables 1–10, attempt to break new ground. Notes 7–8, which explain them, point out that, in view of steadily increasing longevity, the mortality rates that will be experienced in future by those who are alive today will probably be lower that those in English Life Table No 15, and increasingly so the further into the future one goes. Indeed, when preparing the official national population projections, the Government Actuary makes a considered estimate of future improvements in mortality. Tables 11–20 show the higher multipliers that result from the application of these projected mortality rates. The majority of the Working Party who have produced the Ogden Tables recommend the courts to use Tables 11–20 rather than Tables 1–10. This reconsideration will doubtless give rise to an important test case in the future. As an aid to those involved with this issue, the English Life Tables No 15 (based on data for 1990-92) and the Interim Life Tables (based on data for 1994–96) are reproduced as an appendix to this book.

The other contentious area of the Ogden Tables is Section B of the notes (26–43) which provides formulae for taking account of contingencies other than mortality. This was a response to the courts randomly reducing multipliers by as much as 20%. To counter this, the formulae provide methods of allowing for levels of economic activity and employment, lower intended pension ages, and variations by occupation and geographical region. However, they have not yet found favour with the courts. Furthermore, it is submitted that the need for them has been much reduced by the House of Lords' strict restoration of the trial judge's earnings loss multiplier discount of 8.65% in *Page v Sheerness Steel Company Ltd*, a case of a 28 year old plaintiff at trial who had planned to retire at the age of 62, where the trial judge had stated that he was giving a larger discount than average due to the hazardous nature of the plaintiff's work. When discounts are confined to a matter of several per cent, the problem addressed by the formulae largely disappears.

Section 10 of the Civil Evidence Act 1995, which it is hoped will now be brought into force, provides for the admissibility and proof of the Ogden Tables.

'(1) The actuarial tables (together with explanatory notes) for use in personal injury and fatal accident cases issued from time to time by the Government Actuary's Department are admissible in evidence for the purpose of assessing, in an action for personal injury, the sum to be awarded as general damages for future pecuniary loss.

(2) They may be provided by the production of a copy published by Her Majesty's Stationery Office.

(3) For the purposes of this section—

(a) 'personal injury' includes any disease and any impairment of a person's physical or mental condition; and

(b) 'action for personal injury' includes an action brought by virtue of the Law Reform (Miscellaneous Provisions) Act 1934 or the Fatal Accidents Act 1976.'

THE CPID TABLES

The CPID Tables are entirely consistent with the third edition of the Ogden Tables. They are based on precisely the same software program kindly shared between the programmers for the Government Actuary's

Department (Ogden) and Butterworths (CPID). Whenever the CPID tables cover exactly the same ground as the Ogden Tables, they return exactly the same answer. Consequently the CPID Tables should be seen, not as an alternative to the Ogden Tables, but rather as an extension to them.

Their purpose is to take advantage of the available computer software, and of the extra space furnished by this book, to provide a detailed range of multipliers that could not be compressed into the compass of the Ogden Tables booklet. This is perhaps all the more important in the new post *Wells v Wells* area in which not only has the use of actuarial tables been approved but also the elaborate network of judicial precedents based on the former 4.5% pa discount rate has been almost totally invalidated. Nor can lawyers draw on their own accumulated experience of appropriate multipliers, which now belongs to a bygone era. The only proper course at present is to look up multipliers in one of the available tables and then to consider what discount if any to apply to them.

The main differences between the CPID Tables and the Ogden Tables are as follows:

(1) In order to save readers looking at three different pages for the life multipliers, earnings loss multipliers and pensions loss multipliers respectively, CPID adopts a 'page for age' approach in which, on a page devoted to each year of life up to 75, all the possible multipliers in each category are shown.
(2) CPID utilises its new Child Earnings Multiplier program to provide earnings loss and pensions loss multipliers for each age between 1 and 15, not just starting at 16. These allow for entry to the workplace at the four main standard ages of 16 (GCSE), 18 ('A' level), 21 (first degree) and 24 (post-graduate).
(3) CPID provides multipliers, not just for the traditional retirement ages of 60 and 65, but also for each possible retirement age between 50 and 75.
(4) In its tables of fixed term multipliers and consolidated compound interest, CPID provides figures for each month between 1 month and 100 years.
(5) After *Wells v Wells*, CPID only covers the relatively central discount rates of 2.5% pa, 3% pa and 3.5% pa, with the columns based on the current recommendation of 3% pa duly highlighted.
(6) CPID contains no parallel to the Ogden method of discounting for contingencies other than mortality, since there has been no sign of this receiving judicial endorsement.
(7) Nor do the CPID Tables contain any counterpart to the Ogden Tables 11-20 which are based on the Government Actuary's Department's projections of increasing national longevity., The question of whether modern multipliers should be based on these will, no doubt, be decided in a major test case some time in the future.

Given the wealth of detail that the CPID Tables already contain, it has been deemed undesirable to lengthen and thicken the present edition to cater for alternative ranges of multipliers that are not currently in use. Instead the preferred option, assuming sufficient demand, would be promptly to produce a fresh edition if any change occurs to invalidate the present one. Thus the Ogden Tables and the CPID Tables can constructively complement each other: the Ogden Tables providing the main multipliers under the present and proposed alternative systems and acting as an authoritative catalyst for change, while the CPID Tables supply detailed sets of multipliers on the basis of the current law.

2 House of Lords judgment in *Wells v Wells* etc

WELLS v WELLS
THOMAS v BRIGHTON HEALTH AUTHORITY
PAGE v SHEERNESS STEEL CO PLC

[1998] 3 All ER 481

HOUSE OF LORDS
LORD LLOYD OF BERWICK, LORD STEYN, LORD HOPE OF CRAIGHEAD, LORD CLYDE AND LORD HUTTON
5–7, 11–13 MAY, 16 JULY 1998

Damages—Personal injury—Amount of damages—Assessment—Anticipated future losses and expenses—Appropriate test.

When assessing damages for anticipated future losses and expenses in personal injury cases, the court should fix the award by assuming that the plaintiffs will invest their damages in index-linked government stock (ILGS), since this is the most accurate way of calculating the present value of the loss which they will actually suffer in real terms. Although this approach will result in a heavier burden on the defendants and the insurance industry in general, it is not unjust. Moreover, the search for a prudent investor will always depend on the circumstances of the particular investor. For a plaintiff who is not in a position to take risks, and who wishes to protect himself against inflation in the short term of up to ten years, it is clearly prudent to invest in ILGS. It cannot therefore be assumed that he will invest in equities and gilts; still less is it his duty to invest in equities and gilts in order to mitigate his loss. Logically the same applies to a plaintiff investing for the long term. In any event, it is desirable to have a single rate applying across the board, in order to facilitate settlements and to save the expense of expert evidence at the trial. How the plaintiff in fact invests his money is irrelevant. Further an investment in ILGS will save up to 1% will be saved per annum by obviating the need for continuing investment advice (see p 492 *j* to p 493 *h*, p 504 *c* to p 505 *a*, p 506 *j*, p 510 *e*, p 513 *e*, p 520 *h j* and p 521 *g h*[*†]).

Decision of the Court of Appeal [1997] 1 All ER 673 reversed.

* Original All ER page references.
† Ie pp 21–22, pp 33–34, p 36, p 40, p 43, p 51 and p 52 of this book.

Notes

For the measure of damages in personal injury cases, see 34 *Halsbury's Laws* (4th edn) paras 78–87, and for cases on the subject, see 36(1) *Digest* (2nd reissue) 479–504, *4159–4266*.

Cases referred to in opinions

Admiralty Comrs v Valeria (owners) [1922] 2 AC 242, [1922] All ER Rep 463, HL.
Auty v National Coal Board [1985] 1 All ER 930, [1985] 1 WLR 784, CA.
Birkett v Hayes [1982] 2 All ER 710, [1982] 1 WLR 816, CA.
Cookson v Knowles [1978] 2 All ER 604, [1979] AC 556, [1978] 2 WLR 978, HL.
Croke v Wiseman [1981] 3 All ER 852, [1982] 1 WLR 71, CA.
Cunningham v Camberwell Health Authority [1990] 2 Med LR 49, CA.
Duxbury v Duxbury [1990] 2 All ER 77, [1992] Fam 62, [1991] 3 WLR 639, CA.
Every v Miles [1964] CA Transcript 261.
George v Pinnock [1973] 1 All ER 926, [1973] 1 WLR 118, CA.
Hawkins v Lindsley (1974) 49 ALJR 5, Aust HC.
Hodgson v Trapp [1988] 3 All ER 870, [1989] AC 807, [1988] 3 WLR 1281, HL.
Hunt v Severs [1994] 2 All ER 385, [1994] 2 AC 350, [1994] 2 WLR 602, HL; *rvsg* [1993] 4 All ER 180, [1993] QB 815, [1993] 3 WLR 558, CA.
Hussain v New Taplow Paper Mills Ltd [1988] 1 All ER 541, [1988] AC 514, [1988] 2 WLR 266, HL.
Janardan v East Berkshire Health Authority [1990] 2 Med LR 1.
Lim Poh Choo v Camden and Islington Area Health Authority [1979] 2 All ER 910, [1980] AC 174, [1979] 3 WLR 44, HL.
Livingstone v Rawyards Coal Co (1880) 5 App Cas 25, HL.
McIlgrew v Devon CC [1995] PIQR Q66, CA.
McKechnie v James Henderson & Son (1858) 20 D 551, Ct of Sess.
Mallett v McMonagle [1969] 2 All ER 178, [1970] AC 166, [1969] 2 WLR 767, HL.
O'Brien's Curator Bonis v British Steel plc 1991 SC 315, Ct of Sess.
Pickett v British Rail Engineering Ltd [1979] 1 All ER 774, [1980] AC 136, [1978] 3 WLR 955, HL.
Roberts v Johnstone [1989] QB 878, [1988] 3 WLR 1247, CA.
Smith v Manchester Corp (1974) 17 KIR 1, CA.
Taylor v O'Connor [1970] 1 All ER 365, [1971] AC 115, [1970] 2 WLR 472, HL.
Todorovic v Waller (1981) 150 CLR 402, Aust HC.
Wright v British Railways Board [1983] 2 All ER 698, [1983] 2 AC 773, [1983] 3 WLR 211, HL.

Appeals

Wells v Wells

The plaintiff, Margaret Thelma Wells, suing by her daughter and next friend Susan Smith, appealed with leave of the Appeal Committee of the House of

Lords given on 3 June 1998 from the decision of the Court of Appeal (Hirst, Auld and Thorpe LJJ) ([1997] 1 All ER 673, [1997] 1 WLR 652) delivered on 23 October 1996 allowing the appeal of the defendant, Derek Sydney Wells, from the decision of Judge Wilcox, sitting as a judge of the High Court on 13 June 1995 ([1996] PIQR Q62), whereby he awarded the plaintiff the sum of £1,619,332 in damages and interest in respect of his admitted liability for injuries suffered by her in a road accident. The facts are set out in the opinion of Lord Lloyd of Berwick.

Thomas v Brighton Health Authority

The plaintiff, James Oliver Thomas, suing by his mother and next friend Susan Thomas, appealed with leave of the Appeal Committee of the House of Lords given on 3 June 1998 from the decision of the Court of Appeal (Hirst, Auld and Thorpe LJJ) ([1997] 1 All ER 673, [1997] 1 WLR 652) delivered on 23 October 1996 allowing the appeal of the defendant, Brighton Health Authority, from the decision of Collins J on 7 November 1995 ([1996] PIQR Q44), whereby he awarded the plaintiff the sum of £1,307,963 in damages in respect of its admitted liability for injuries sustained by the plaintiff as a result of maladministration of a drug to the plaintiff's mother during labour. The facts are set out in the opinion of Lord Lloyd of Berwick.

Page v Sheerness Steel Co plc

The plaintiff, Kelvin Page, appealed with leave of the Appeal Committee of the House of Lords given on 3 June 1998 from the decision of the Court of Appeal (Hirst, Auld and Thorpe LJJ) ([1997] 1 All ER 673, [1997] 1 WLR 652) delivered on 23 October 1996 allowing the appeal of the defendant, Sheerness Steel Co plc, from the decision of Dyson J on 4 December 1995 ([1996] PIQR Q26), whereby he awarded the plaintiff the sum of £906,000 in damages in respect of the defendant's admitted liability, as the plaintiff's employer, for injuries sustained in the course of his employment. The facts are set out in the opinion of Lord Lloyd of Berwick.

Christopher Purchas QC and *George Gadney* (instructed by *Russell Jones & Walker*) for Mrs Wells.
John Leighton Williams QC and *Richard Methuen QC* (instructed by *Lawrence Graham*, agents for *Linda Y Oliver*, Worthing) for Mr Wells.
Robert Owen QC and *Philip Havers QC* (instructed by *Charles Russell*) for Mr Thomas.
Kieran Coonan QC and *Christina Lambert* (instructed by *Hempsons*) for the Brighton Health Authority.
Christopher Purchas QC and *Matthias Kelly* (instructed by *Russell Jones & Walker*) for Mr Page.
John Leighton Williams QC and *Richard Methuen QC* (instructed by *Lawrence Graham*) for Sheerness Steel.

Their Lordships took time for consideration.

16 July 1998. The following opinions were delivered.

Lord Lloyd of Berwick

My Lords,

Introduction

There are before the House appeals in three actions for personal injuries, all raising the same question, namely, the correct method of calculating lump sum damages for the loss of future earnings and the cost of future care. Negligence was admitted in all three cases.

In *Wells v Wells* the plaintiff, a part-time nurse, aged nearly 58, was very severely injured in a traffic accident when she was travelling as a passenger in a car driven by her husband. She suffered serious brain damage. As a consequence she is no longer capable of working, or caring for herself or her family. She will require care for the rest of her life. Judge David Wilcox sitting as a judge of the High Court in the Queen's Bench Division ([1996] PIQR Q62) awarded her £120,000 for pain and suffering. The total award, including loss of future earnings and cost of future care on a life expectancy of 15 years, came to £1,619,332. The Court of Appeal ([1997] 1 All ER 673, [1997] 1 WLR 652) reduced the figure for pain and suffering to £100,000 and substituted a life expectancy of 10 years 3 months. They arrived at a total of £1,086,959. The main reason for the sharp reduction was that the Court of Appeal took a discount rate of 4·5% in calculating the lump sum for future loss, whereas the judge had taken 2·5%.

In *Thomas v Brighton Health Authority* the plaintiff was six years old at the date of the trial. He sues by his mother and next friend. He was injured before birth by the maladministration of a drug intended to induce labour. He suffers from cerebral palsy, and is very severely physically handicapped. Collins J ([1996] PIQR Q44) awarded £110,000 for general damages. The total award on a life expectancy to the age of 60 came to £1,307,963. The Court of Appeal ([1997] 1 All ER 673, [1997] 1 WLR 652) reduced the figure to £994,592. The reason was the same as in *Wells v Wells*, save that Collins J took a discount rate of 3%, not 2·5%. The judge took the same rate of 3% in arriving at a figure of £72,592 for additional housing costs. The Court of Appeal reduced this item by taking the conventional rate of 2%: see *Roberts v Johnstone* [1989] 1 QB 878. The reason why the Court of Appeal took a rate of 4·5% for discounting future loss, but only 2% for the cost of additional housing will appear later.

In *Page v Sheerness Steel Co Ltd* the plaintiff, then aged 24, was working in a steel mill alongside a cooling bed when a white-hot steel bar buckled and struck him in the head. It entered the right side of his skull, penetrated his brain and emerged on the left side. A workmate cut the bar short. The plaintiff then pulled the bar out with his own hands. He was conscious throughout. It is hard to imagine how he could still be alive. Dyson J ([1996] PIQR Q26) awarded £80,000 for general damages. The total award, including loss of future earnings to a normal retiring age of 62 and the cost of future care on a normal life expectancy came to £997,345.64. The judge took the same discount rate as Collins J, namely 3%. The Court of Appeal ([1997] 1 All ER 673, [1997] 1 WLR 652) substituted an award of £702,773·20. The reason for the reduction was the same as in the other two cases.

A number of separate points arise in relation to the individual cases. They would not by themselves have justified leave to appeal. However, the point which is common to all three appeals is of considerable importance, both for the plaintiffs themselves and for the insurance industry in general. It is convenient to deal with that point first.

It was common ground between all parties that the task of the court in assessing damages for personal injuries is to arrive at a lump sum which represents as nearly as possible full compensation for the injury which the plaintiff has suffered. This is not therefore the place to discuss other methods of compensation, such as the structured settlement. By s 2(1) of the Damages Act 1996, a court may make an order for the whole or part of the damages to take the form of periodical payments, provided the parties agree. This was in accordance with the recommendation of *Structured Settlements and Interim and Provisional Damages* (Law Com No 224) (1994). I note that the Law Commission recommended that in the absence of agreement there should be no judicial power to impose a structured settlement for the reasons which they set out in paras 3.37 to 3.53 of their report.

It is of the nature of a lump sum payment that it may, in respect of future pecuniary loss, prove to be either too little or too much. So far as the multiplier is concerned, the plaintiff may die the next day, or he may live beyond his normal expectation of life. So far as the multiplicand is concerned, the cost of future care may exceed everyone's best estimate. Or a new cure or less expensive form of treatment may be discovered. But these uncertainties do not affect the basic principle. The purpose of the award is to put the plaintiff in the same position, financially, as if he had not been injured. The sum should be calculated as accurately as possible, making just allowance, where this is appropriate, for contingencies. But once the calculation is done, there is no justification for imposing an artificial cap on the multiplier. There is no room for a judicial scaling down. Current awards in the most serious cases may seem high. The present appeals may be taken as examples. But there is no more reason to reduce the awards, if properly calculated, because they seem high than there is to increase the awards because the injuries are very severe.

The approach to the basic calculation of the lump sum has been explained in many cases, but never better than by Stephen J in the High Court of Australia in *Todorovic v Waller* (1981) 150 CLR 402 at 427 ff (see Kemp and Kemp *The Quantum of Damages* (looseleaf edn (1997)) vol 1, para 7–010), by Lord Pearson in *Taylor v O'Connor* [1970] 1 All ER 365 at 377, [1971] AC 115 at 140, and by Lord Oliver of Aylmerton in *Hodgson v Trapp* [1988] 3 All ER 870 at 879, [1989] AC 807 at 826.

The starting point is the multiplicand, that is to say the annual loss of earnings or the annual cost of care, as the case may be. (I put so-called *Smith v Manchester* damages (*Smith v Manchester Corp* (1974) 17 KIR 1) on one side.) The medical evidence may be that the need for care will increase or decrease as the years go by, in which case it may be necessary to take different multiplicands for different periods covered by the award. But to simplify the illustration, one can take an average annual cost of care of £10,000 on a life expectancy of 20 years. If one assumes a constant value for money, then if the court were to award 20 times £10,000 it is obvious that the plaintiff would be overcompensated. For the £10,000 needed to purchase care in the 20th year should have been earning interest for 19 years. The purpose of the discount is to eliminate this element of overcompensation. The objective is to arrive at a lump sum which by drawing down both interest and capital will provide exactly £10,000 a year for 20 years, and no more. This is known as the annuity approach. It is a simple enough matter to find the answer by reference to standard tables. The higher the assumed return on capital, net of tax, the lower the lump sum. If one assumes a net return of 5% the discounted figure would be £124,600 instead of £200,000. If one assumes a net return of 3% the figure would be £148,800.

The same point can be put the other way round. £200,000 invested at 5% will produce £10,000 a year for 20 years. But there would still be £200,000 left at the end.

So far there is no problem. The difficulty arises because, contrary to the assumption made above, money does not retain its value. How is the court to ensure that the plaintiff receives the money he will need to purchase the care he needs as the years go by despite the impact of inflation? In the past the courts have solved this problem by assuming that the plaintiff can take care of future inflation in a rough and ready way by investing the lump sum sensibly in a mixed 'basket' of equities and gilts. But the advent of the index-linked government stock (they were first issued in 1981) has provided an alternative. The return of income and capital on index-linked government stock (ILGS) is fully protected against inflation. Thus the purchaser of £100 of ILGS with a maturity date of 2020 knows that his investment will then be worth £100 plus x % of £100, where x represents the percentage increase in the retail price index between the date of issue and the date of maturity (or, more accurately, eight months before the two dates). Of course if the plaintiff were to invest his £100 in equities it might then be worth much more. But it might also be worth less. The virtue of ILGS is that it provides a risk-free investment.

The first instance judges in these appeals have broken with the past. They have each assumed for the purpose of the calculation that the plaintiffs will go into the market, and purchase the required amount of ILGS so as to provide for his or her future needs with the minimum risk of their damages being eroded by inflation. How the plaintiffs will in fact invest their damages is, of course, irrelevant. That is a question for them. It cannot affect the calculation. The question for decision therefore is whether the judges were right to assume that the plaintiffs would invest in ILGS with a low average net return of 2·5%, instead of a mixed portfolio of equities and gilts. The Court of Appeal has held not. They have reverted to the traditional 4 to 5% with the consequential reduction in the sums awarded.

The argument

Mr Leighton Williams QC and Mr Coonan QC for the defendants pointed out that those who receive large awards are likely to be given professional investment advice. All but one of the accountants called as experts at the three trials gave as their opinion that lump sum awards should be invested in a mixed portfolio of 70% equities and 30% gilts. This is what the ordinary prudent investor would do. For experience shows that equities provide the best long-term security. Thus Mr Topping, the accountant called on behalf of the defendant in *Wells v Wells*, produced a table which showed the real rate of return on equities to 31 December 1992 on an investment made on

1 January in each year from 1973 to 1992. In only two of those years has the return been less than 4·5% net of tax. If the ordinary prudent investor would invest substantially in equities, it was to be assumed that the plaintiffs would do the same.

The point is put well in the following passages from the judgment of the Court of Appeal ([1997] 1 All ER 673 at 696, [1997] 1 WLR 652 at 677):

> 'It is for the court to hold the balance evenly between both sides, and just as the plaintiff is entitled to an award which achieves as nearly as possible full compensation for the injuries sustained, so also we think the defendant is entitled to take advantage of the presumption that the former will adopt a prudent investment strategy once he receives his award. Furthermore, the court, which, as already noted, is dealing with probabilities when fixing the multiplier, can and should pay regard to the high probability that the plaintiff will invest prudently; any other approach would be artificial.
>
> Undoubtedly, equities are more risky than ILGS. Undoubtedly in some individual years investing in equities would have yielded a negative return in the ensuing period (the same applies albeit less severely to ILGS). However the figures produced by the appellants' experts, and in particular the BZW [Barclays de Zoote Wedd] tables, seem to us to demonstrate that, over longer periods of years, equity investment has been sound.'

Mr Leighton Williams went so far as to argue that it was the plaintiff's duty to invest in equities in order to mitigate his damage.

But the matter is not quite so simple as that. It now appears that Mr Topping's figures, which are reproduced in the Court of Appeal's judgment, and are an important link in the chain of reasoning, are misleading. Mr Topping has failed to observe that his figures are extracted from a table in the BZW Equity and Gilt Study in which all the income is assumed to be reinvested. But in the case of these plaintiffs the income is, ex hypothesi, assumed to be spent year by year. Unfortunately Mr Purchas QC and his experts failed to spot this error at the trial, although it seems obvious enough now. So Mr Topping was not cross-examined on the point.

Mr Purchas sought to fill in the gap by producing tables from the updated BZW (now Barclays Capital Equity and Gilt Study), showing the net real return on equities without reinvesting the income. He hoped to demonstrate that the real return on equities is little, if anything, above the return on ILGS, especially if one takes into account the difference in the cost of investment advice, which might amount to as much as 1% per annum. But Mr Leighton Williams and his experts were unable to agree Mr Purchas's figures. So I say no more about them, save that the difference between the two sides does not appear to be all that great. On Mr Purchas's figures the average annual return net of tax on a 20-year investment in equities over the period 1960 to 1997, without reinvesting the income, was 3·4%. On Mr Topping's revised calculation the figure was 4·12%.

The inability of the experts to reach agreement on the figures is not, in the end, of great consequence. For the problem with equities lies elsewhere. Granted that a substantial proportion of equities is the best long term investment for the ordinary prudent investor, the question is whether the same is true for these plaintiffs. The ordinary investor may be presumed to have enough to live on. He can meet his day-to-day requirements. If the equity market suffers a catastrophic fall, as it did in 1972, he has no immediate need to sell. He can abide his time, and wait until the equity market eventually recovers.

The plaintiffs are not in the same happy position. They are not 'ordinary investors' in the sense that they can wait for long-term recovery, remembering that it was not until 1989 that equity prices regained their old pre-1972 level in real terms. For they need the income, and a portion of their capital, every year to meet their current cost of care. A plaintiff who invested the whole of his award in equities in 1972 would have found that their real value had fallen by 41% in 1973 and by a further 62% in 1974. The real value of the income on his equities had also fallen.

So it does not follow that a prudent investment for the ordinary investor is a prudent investment for the plaintiffs. Equities may well prove the best long-term investment. But their volatility over the short term creates a serious risk. This risk was well understood by the experts. Indeed Mr Coonan conceded that if you are investing so as to meet a plaintiff's needs over a period of five years, or even 10 years, it would be foolish to invest in equities. But that concession, properly made as it was on the evidence, is fatal to the defendants' case. For, as Mr Purchas pointed out in reply, every long period starts with a short period. If there is a substantial fall in equities in the first five or 10 years, during which the plaintiff will have had to call on part of his capital to meet his needs, and will have had to realise that part of his capital in a depressed market, the depleted fund may never recover.

While therefore I agree with the Court of Appeal that, in calculating the lump sum, courts are entitled to assume that the plaintiff will behave prudently, I do not agree that what is prudent for the ordinary investor is necessarily prudent for the plaintiff. Indeed the opposite may be the case. What the prudent plaintiff needs is an investment which will bring him the income he requires without the risks inherent in the equity market; which brings us back to ILGS.

There are currently 11 stocks available, issued at various dates between July 1981 and September 1992, and maturing at various dates between 2001 and 2030. They are criticised by Mr Leighton Williams on a number of investment grounds.

First it is said that if index-linked stocks are sold before maturity they will suffer like other securities from the vagaries of the market. True. But it misses the point. The assumption is that the stocks will not be sold before maturity. For it is to be assumed that stocks will be purchased with maturity dates which match the plaintiff's future needs over the period covered by the award. Since the plaintiff will be holding all the stocks to maturity, there is no risk (or minimum risk) of him having to sell before maturity at depressed prices.

Secondly, it is said that there are gaps in the maturity dates. Thus there is no stock maturing in 2002, 2005, 2007, 2008 or 2010. Nor is there any stock maturing later than 2030. As for the gaps, they may be filled by new issues. According to the Debt Management Report for 1998–1999 issued by HM Treasury, the authorities are committed to a minimum annual level of 2·5 billion index-linked stock in 1998–99 and for the foreseeable future thereafter; and the aim is to maintain liquidity 'in all maturity areas across the curve'. But even if gaps remain, there is no problem. The plaintiff will be assumed to purchase enough stock maturing in 2001 to cover his needs for that year as well as 2002. And so on.

As for the period after 2030, again there is no reason to suppose that there will not be further issues. But even if there are not, the plaintiff knows that he will have an inflation-proof lump sum at that date which will reflect his needs for the rest of his life more accurately than any other available investment. Mr Owen QC put it well during argument: the court now has at its disposal a tool for calculating damages which enables it to assume a stable currency until at least 2030.

Thirdly, it was pointed out that the inflation-proofing of ILGS is based on movements in the retail price index, whereas nursing costs have, historically, risen faster than the RPI. This may be true. But it is hardly a point which helps the defendants. If account were to be taken of this factor it would be an argument for rounding up the lump sum rather than rounding down.

The Court of Protection

I have left to last the argument on which the defendants placed the greatest reliance, and which weighed heavily with the Court of Appeal. Two of the three plaintiffs are patients. Their affairs are being administered by the Court of Protection. One of the witnesses called for the defence was Mr Bruce Denman, who is in charge of the investment branch of the Public Trust Office dealing with Court of Protection cases. His evidence was that in the case of a long term investment for an individual patient the portfolio would consist of about 70% UK equities with the balance in gilts and cash. The Court of Appeal ([1997] 1 All ER 673 at 696, [1997] 1 WLR 652 at 677) said that they were 'strongly influenced' by the policy of the Court of Protection.

But in the case of short term investment (five years or under) the policy of the Court of Protection is very different. The fact sheet published by the Court of Protection shows that in such a case 'very little risk is acceptable'. Equities should be excluded altogether. This corresponds with the expert evidence in the present case, and with Mr Coonan's concession. What is not explained in the policy statement is why risk is any more acceptable in the long term than in the short term. I can understand an argument that in the case of a long-term fund the equities will have had time to recover after a fall such as occurred in 1972 and October 1987. But as already explained it may by then be too late. The gilts may have been sold and the cash may all have been spent.

In the end it comes back to the question of risk. Ex hypothesi equities are riskier than gilts. That is the very reason why the return on equities is likely to be greater. The plaintiffs say that they are not obliged to bear that extra risk for the benefit of the defendants. Others like them, with fixed outgoings at stated intervals, take the same view as to prudent investment policy. So the plaintiffs are not alone. Thus Mr Prevett's evidence [for the plaintiff in *Wells v Wells*] was that, since index-linked stocks have been available, it has become the general practice for closed pension funds to be invested in ILGS, so as to be sure of being able to meet their liabilities as they fall due. I would not be surprised to find others in the same position, but on a smaller scale, taking the same view, such as school governors investing a prepaid fees fund. The Court of Appeal rejected this part of Mr Prevett's evidence, but without giving any very satisfactory reason, other than the need for an investment which affords some flexibility in view of the inevitable uncertainty in estimating the multiplicand. I agree, of course, that there is bound to be some uncertainty in fixing the multiplicand. But that does not seem to me to be a good reason for introducing an unnecessary uncertainty in fixing the multiplier. Two wrongs may make a right. But they are just as likely to make a double wrong.

As for the Court of Protection's current policy, it may be that they feel obliged to invest in equities so long as the sums available for investment are calculated on the basis of a 4·5% return. In spite of the risks, it may be the only way of making the money go round. But it does not tell us how large the fund should have been in the first place. In a letter written since the decision of the Court of Appeal Mr Denman records the advice given by the Lord Chancellor's Honorary Investment Advisory Committee to the Master of the Court of Protection in the event of awards being calculated by reference to the return on ILGS. The advice is given in guarded terms. He should 'seriously consider' a minimum-risk index-linked portfolio. The master has accepted this advice. It is at least clear, therefore, that the present policy is not set in stone.

Recommendations

I turn next to the commentators and textbook writers. It was the working party under the chairmanship of Sir Michael Ogden QC which blazed the trail. In the introduction to the first edition of the *Actuarial Tables with explanatory notes for use in Personal Injury and Fatal Accident cases* (1984) Sir Michael Ogden refers to the then recent introduction of index-linked government stocks in 1981. They had already become an established part of the investment market. Sir Michael (p 8) describes the advantages of ILGS:

> 'Investment policy, however prudent, involves risks and it is not difficult to draw up a list of blue chip equities or reliable unit trusts which have performed poorly and, in some cases, disastrously. Index-linked government stocks eliminate the risks. Whereas, in the past, a plaintiff has had to speculate in the form of prudent investment by buying equities, or a 'basket' of equities and gilts or a selection of unit trusts, he need speculate no longer if he buys index-linked government stock. If the loss is, say, £5,000 per annum, he can be awarded damages which, if invested in such stocks, will provide him with almost exactly that sum in real terms.'

In the second edition (1994) (Explanatory Notes, s A: General, para 8) Sir Michael Ogden repeats the views expressed in the introduction to the first edition:

> 'However, there are now available index-linked government stocks and it is accordingly no longer necessary to speculate about either the future rates of inflation or the real rate of return obtainable on an investment. The redemption value and dividends of these stocks are adjusted from time to time so as to maintain the real value of the stock in the face of inflation. The current rates of interest on such stocks are published daily in the

> 'Financial Times' and hitherto have fallen into the range of about 2·5 % to 4·5 % (gross).'

A little later he says:

> '… the return on such index-linked government stocks is the most accurate reflection of the real rate of interest available to plaintiffs seeking the prudent investment of awards …'

The third edition of the Ogden Tables was published in 1998, after the decision of the Court of Appeal in the present case, but before the hearing in the House. Sir Michael anticipates a fourth edition when the decision of the House is made known, and when the Lord Chancellor has had an opportunity to fix the rate of return under s 1 of the 1996 Act. Sir Michael will then be able, as he says, to retire from the task which he was first asked to undertake 15 years ago, and which he has performed with such conspicuous success.

The Court of Appeal ([1997] 1 All ER 673 at 698–699, [1997] 1 WLR 652 at 680) expressed their concern at departing from the recommendation of the Ogden Working Party, but added that the working party suffered from the disadvantage that the membership did not include any accountants or investment advisers. The plaintiffs challenged the truth of that observation; but in any event I would not regard it as weakening the force of the working party's recommendation.

In between the first and second editions of the Ogden Tables, the Law Commission published Consultation Paper No 125, *Structured Settlements and Interim and Provisional Damages* (Consultation Paper No 125) (1992), to which there was a large response from a variety of sources, including investment advisers. The consultation paper led to Law Commission Report No 224 (1994). The following passages are relevant:

> '2.25 … Our provisional view was that courts should make more use of information from the financial markets in discounting lump sums to take account of the fact that they are paid today. One way of doing this would be to enable courts to refer to the rate of return on ILGS as a means of establishing an appropriate rate of discount. The purpose of this would be to obtain the best reflection of market opinion as to what real interest rates will be in future. The question upon which we sought the views of consultees was whether it would be reasonable to use the return on ILGS as a guide to the appropriate discount.
>
> 2.26 Almost two-thirds of those who responded to this question supported the use of the ILGS rates to determine more accurate discounts. These consultees agreed that the assumption of a 4–5% rate of return over time is crude and inflexible and can lead to over- or under-compensation and hence to injustice …
>
> 2.28 We share the views of the majority of those who responded to us, that a practice of discounting by reference to returns on ILGS would be preferable to the present arbitrary presumption. The 4–5% discount which emerged from the case law was established at a time when ILGS did not exist. ILGS now constitute the best evidence of the real return on any investment where the risk element is minimal, because they take account

of inflation, rather than attempt to predict it as conventional investments do.'

This is a very strong recommendation indeed. Once again the Court of Appeal expressed concern at departing from such a recommendation, but commented that the recommendation was based on implicit assumptions as to the objective to be achieved, which they did not accept.

There is a sustained criticism of the Court of Appeal's decision in *Kemp and Kemp* vol 1, paras 6–003/9–13, and in David Kemp QC's article, *Discounting Damages for Future Loss* (1997) 113 LQR 195. I have derived much assistance from Mr Kemp's commentary, for which I am grateful.

In the current edition of *McGregor on Damages* (16th edn, 1997) para 1601, pp 1047–1048, Mr Harvey McGregor QC hazarded a guess that the House would indorse a rate somewhat less than the Court of Appeal's 4·5% but would not adopt the ILGS rate. In Mr McGregor's view that would have been the right solution, because he regarded it as highly unlikely that a plaintiff with substantial damages would invest it all in ILGS. He would be more likely to accept investment advice, and end up with a portfolio largely of equities. This would lead to over- compensation, if equities continue their upward progression.

For reasons which I have already given I would not agree with this approach. The suggestion that plaintiffs with a substantial award of damages are likely to invest in a portfolio consisting largely of equities is not supported by the research carried out for the Law Commission: see *Personal Injury Compensation: How Much is Enough?* (Law Com No 225) (1994), para 10.2. In any event what an individual does with his damages is a matter for him. If he invests in equities, he may be lucky and end up by being overcompensated. But the question is whether his damages should be calculated on the basis that he is obliged to invest in equities.

Apart from *McGregor on Damages,* we were not referred to any other commentary or textbook which disagrees with the recommendations of the Ogden Working Party and the Law Commission.

The authorities

I turn last to see whether the approach which I favour is inhibited by any previous decision of the House. Early cases, such as *Taylor v O'Connor* [1970] 1 All ER 365, [1971] AC 115, are not of any real assistance, since they were decided before the advent of ILGS, the collapse of the equity market in 1972, and the rapid inflation which lasted until the end of that decade. By the time *Cookson v Knowles* [1978] 2 All ER 604, [1979] AC 556 was decided the theory that one could protect an award of damages against inflation by investing in equities had been exploded. If protection was to be had at all, it was by the higher rates of interest available on fixed interest securities.

Wright v British Railways Board [1983] 2 All ER 698, [1983] 2 AC 773 is an important authority, although not directly in point on the present issue. The question in that case was what is the appropriate rate of interest to award on general damages for the period between the date of service of the writ and the date of judgment. The Court of Appeal in *Birkett v Hayes* [1982] 2 All ER 710, [1982] 1 WLR 816 had awarded 2%. The House declined to interfere with that rate. Lord Diplock's speech is important for a number of reasons.

It was the first and, so far as I know, the only occasion on which he has expressed himself on the subject of ILGS. He pointed out ([1983] 2 All ER 698 at 704, [1983] 2 AC 773 at 783) that the—

> 'rate of interest accepted by investors in index-linked government securities should provide a broad indication of what is the appropriate rate of interest to be awarded'

for non-pecuniary loss. It provided 'powerful confirmation' for the rate of 2% adopted by the Court of Appeal in *Birkett v Hayes*.

Lord Diplock's use of ILGS in *Wright v British Railways Board* convinces me that if ILGS had existed at the time of *Cookson v Knowles* Lord Diplock would have been the first to see that they provided the answer for which he was looking.

Wright v British Railways Board is also important because of Lord Diplock's observation ([1983] 2 All ER 698 at 705, [1983] 2 AC 773 at 784) that guidelines as to the rate of interest for economic and non-economic loss should be simple to apply, and broad enough to allow for the special features of individual cases. Such guidelines are not to be regarded as rules of law or even rules of practice. They set no binding precedent, and can be altered as circumstances alter. It follows that a new approach to setting the appropriate discount rate, differing from that adopted in *Mallett v McMonagle* [1969] 2 All ER 178, [1970] AC 166 and *Cookson v Knowles*, does not have to be justified under the 1966 practice statement (see [1966] 3 All ER 77, [1966] 1 WLR 1234). Lord Salmon made the same point in *Cookson v Knowles* [1978] 2 All ER 604 at 613, [1979] AC 556 at 574.

Mr Leighton Williams rightly relied on *Lim Poh Choo v Camden and Islington Area Health Authority* [1979] 2 All ER 910, [1980] AC 174. It is the strongest authority in his favour. Lord Scarman ([1979] 2 All ER 910 at 923, [1980] AC 174 at 193) acknowledged the wisdom of Lord Reid's dictum in *Taylor v O'Connor* [1970] 1 All ER 365 at 368, [1971] AC 115 at 130 that it would be unrealistic to ignore inflation in calculating lump sum damages for future loss. He nevertheless held that it was 'the better course' to disregard inflation in the great majority of cases. Among the reasons he gave was that it was inherent in any lump sum system of compensation, and just, that the sum be calculated at current market values, leaving plaintiffs in the same position as others who have to rely on capital for their support. To attempt to protect them against inflation 'would be to put them into a privileged position at the expense of the tortfeasor, and so to impose upon him an excessive burden, which might go far beyond compensation for loss' ([1979] 2 All ER 910 at 923, [1980] AC 174 at 194).

No doubt it was this passage which the Court of Appeal ([1997] 1 All ER 673 at 696, [1997] 1 WLR 652 at 677) had in mind when they said that it was necessary 'to hold the balance evenly between both sides'. I have to say that I do not find Lord Scarman's reasoning persuasive. If the object of an award of damages is to put the plaintiff in the same position as he would have been in if he had not been injured by the negligence of the defendant (as was common ground) then one ought, in principle, to get as near as one can to the wages which he would actually have earned but for the injury and the cost of the needs which he will actually incur. In other words, one ought so far as possible to take account of inflation, as Lord Reid had said.

What then did Lord Scarman mean by saying that this would put the plaintiff in a privileged position in comparison with others who have to rely on capital for their support? Once the lump sum has been calculated and paid, he is in exactly the same position as others, such as those who have saved or inherited a lump sum. But in calculating the sum his position is in no way comparable. For the plaintiff is entitled to be protected against future inflation at the expense of the tortfeasor; otherwise he does not receive full compensation. The others are not so entitled. It is only in that sense that the plaintiff is in a privileged position. I cannot for my part see anything unjust in requiring the defendant to compensate the plaintiff in full, however burdensome that may prove. Lord Scarman recognised this himself when he said ([1979] 2 All ER 910 at 917–918, [1980] AC 174 at 187):

> 'There is no room here for considering the consequences of a high award upon the wrongdoer or those who finance him. And, if there were room for any such consideration, upon what principle, or by what criterion, is the judge to determine the extent to which he is to diminish upon this ground the compensation payable?'

Conclusion

My conclusion is that the judges in these three cases were right to assume for the purpose of their calculations that the plaintiffs would invest their damages in ILGS for the following reasons.

(1) Investment in ILGS is the most accurate way of calculating the present value of the loss which the plaintiffs will actually suffer in real terms.
(2) Although this will result in a heavier burden on these defendants, and, if the principle is applied across the board, on the insurance industry in general, I can see nothing unjust. It is true that insurance premiums may have been fixed on the basis of the 4 to 5% discount rate indicated in *Cookson v Knowles* [1978] 2 All ER 604, [1979] AC 556 and the earlier authorities. But this was only because there was then no better way of allowing for future inflation. The objective was always the same. No doubt insurance premiums will have to increase in order to take account of the new lower rate of discount. Whether this is something which the country can afford is not a subject on which your Lordships were addressed. So we are not in a position to form any view as to the wider consequences.
(3) The search for a prudent investment will always depend on the circumstances of the particular investor. Some are able to take a measure of risk, others are not. For a plaintiff who is not in a position to take risks, and who wishes to protect himself against inflation in the short term of up to ten years, it is clearly prudent to invest in ILGS It cannot therefore be assumed that he will invest in equities and gilts. Still less is it his duty to invest in equities and gilts in order to mitigate his loss.
(4) Logically the same applies to a plaintiff investing for the long term. In any event it is desirable to have a single rate applying across the board, in order to facilitate settlements and to save the expense of expert evidence at the trial. I take this view even though it is open to the Lord Chancellor under s 1(3) of the 1996 Act to prescribe different rates of return for

different classes of case. Mr Leighton Williams conceded that it is not desirable in practice to distinguish between different classes of plaintiff when assessing the multiplier.

(5) How the plaintiff, or the majority of plaintiffs, in fact invest their money is irrelevant. The research carried out by the Law Commission does not suggest that the majority of plaintiffs in fact invest in equities and gilts, but rather in a building society or a bank deposit.

(6) There was no agreement between the parties as to how much greater, if at all, the return on equities is likely to be in the short or long term. But it is at least clear that an investment in ILGS will save up to 1% per annum by obviating the need for continuing investment advice.

(7) The practice of the Court of Protection when investing for the long term affords little guidance. In any event the policy may change when lump sums are calculated at a lower rate of return.

(8) The views of the Ogden Working Party, the Law Commission and the author of *Kemp and Kemp* in favour of an investment in ILGS are entitled to great weight.

(9) There is nothing in the previous decisions of the House which inhibits a new approach. It is therefore unnecessary to have resort to the 1966 practice statement ([1966] 3 All ER 77, [1966] 1 WLR 1234).

Consequences

Once it is accepted that the lump sum should be calculated on the basis of the rate of return available on ILGS, then an assessment of the average rate of return at the relevant date presents no problem. The rates are published daily in the Financial Times. A table of average rates for the period June 1990 to December 1994 ('Gross Return on Index-Linked Government Securities') is included in *Kemp and Kemp* vol 1, para 8–068. No doubt the table will be brought up to date from time to time.

The average gross redemption yield in June 1995 when Mr Prevett gave his evidence was 3·78%. If one takes the average over the previous six months it was 3·8%, and if over the previous 12 months it was 3·83%. The equivalent figures for November and December 1995 when Collins and Dyson JJ gave judgment were marginally lower at 3·53% and 3·52%. There must then be a deduction for tax on income. In his valuable appendix to the judgment below, Thorpe LJ scorns the assumption of a 25% flat rate of tax as 'crude, unrealistic, and favourable to plaintiffs' (see [1997] 1 All ER 673 at 699, 703, [1997] 1 WLR 652 at 680, 884). I agree. In the first place it ignores the impact of allowances and tax bands. Secondly, it assumes a constant rate of income throughout the period to be covered, whereas in reality the income element in the annual draw-down will reduce and the tax-free capital element will increase as time goes by. The *Duxbury* Tables (*Duxbury v Duxbury* [1990] 2 All ER 77, [1992] Fam 62; 'At a Glance,' Family Law Bar Association (1991 and annually)) attempt a much more accurate calculation of the incidence of tax. Figures put before us show that on a fund of £1m invested to produce 3% over 20 years the actual incidence of tax would be no more that 15·37%.

It is not altogether clear how Judge Wilcox arrived at his 2·5% as the appropriate discount on an average gross return of 3·8%. If he deducted tax at 25%, he would have arrived at 2·8% net, not 2·5%. But for reasons already mentioned 25% is certainly too high, quite apart from the fact that it is no longer the standard rate of tax. Judge Wilcox's figure of 2·5% cannot stand.

In its place I would substitute 3%, which is the net discount rate adopted by Collins J and Dyson J, representing a deduction of 14% for the impact of taxation on a gross return of 3·5%. This sounds about right. I appreciate that such an approach is less precise than what is available by using the *Duxbury* Tables, which was Thorpe LJ's preferred approach. On the other hand it is important to keep the calculations simple as well as accurate, as Thorpe LJ was the first to recognise. So far as the three appeals currently before the House are concerned I would regard 3% as the appropriate net return. It follows that the award in *Wells v Wells* will have to be recalculated on that basis.

Guidelines

Section 1 of the 1996 Act provides:

> '(1) In determining the return to be expected from the investment of a sum awarded as damages for future pecuniary loss in an action for personal injury the court shall, subject to and in accordance with rules of court made for the purposes of this section, take into account such rate of return (if any) as may from time to time be prescribed by an order made by the Lord Chancellor ...'

The section came into force on 24 September 1996, but no rate has yet been prescribed. Lord Mackay of Clashfern, the previous Lord Chancellor, was said to be awaiting the decision of the Court of Appeal in the instant cases. It goes without saying that the sooner the Lord Chancellor sets the rate the better. The present uncertainty does not make the settling of claims any easier.

In the meantime it is for your Lordships to set guidelines to replace the old 4 to 5% bracket. There is something to be said for a bracket, since it allows some flexibility in exceptional cases, as where, for example, the impact of higher-rate tax would result in substantial under-compensation. Thus on an award of £2m higher rate tax payable over the first half of a 20-year period would alone amount to nearly £75,000. But the majority of your Lordships prefer a single figure. I do not disagree provided it is subject to the same flexibility as is to be found in s 1(2) of the 1996 Act.

What then should the figure be? The average gross redemption yield on ILGS has fallen steadily over the last year. In May 1997 it was 3·68%, by May 1998 it was only 2·8%. Less tax at, say, 15%, this would give a net return of 2·38%. Logically, therefore, we should take 2·5% as the guideline figure, since the assumption is that the plaintiff will purchase in the market at that price. The higher-yielding stock is no longer available. If therefore the calculation is done at 3% instead of 2·5%, he would be substantially under-compensated.

But since it is undesirable that the guidelines should be changed too often, it may be better that the average gross return should be ascertained over a period of months rather than on a particular day; and since, as I have said, the average return has been falling over the last year, one would expect the average return over that period to be higher than the current return. Such proves to be the case. Over the last six months and 12 months to March 1998 the average return has been 3·02% and 3·28% respectively. These figures justify a guideline rate of return of 3% net rather than 2·5%, and this is the rate which I would propose for general use until the Lord Chancellor has specified a new rate under s 1 of the 1996 Act.

I would not, however, accept that the average should be taken over as long a period as three years. For if the rate of return had been falling steadily over the whole period (in fact this has not been the case) it would work very unfavourably to the plaintiffs; and vice versa if it had been rising steadily over three years. A year would seem to be the best compromise period. Once the net return has been established to the nearest 0·5%, it is a simple enough matter to find the correct multiplier from the Ogden Tables.

Wells v Wells

I come now to the miscellaneous points. They do not call for extensive discussion, since they were argued only briefly. The underlying question is whether the defendants in each case succeeded in showing that damages awarded by the judges at first instance in respect of any particular head of damage (see *George v Pinnock* [1973] 1 All ER 926 at 934, [1973] 1 WLR 118 at 126 per Sachs LJ) are outside the appropriate bracket (see *Every v Miles* [1964] CA Transcript 261 per Diplock LJ; *Kemp and Kemp* vol 1, para 19–006), or else represented a 'wholly erroneous estimate', whether due to mistake of law or a misapprehension of the facts (see *Pickett v British Rail Engineering Ltd* [1979] 1 All ER 774 at 782, 799, [1980] AC 136, at 151, 172 per Lord Wilberforce and Lord Scarman respectively).

As already mentioned, Judge Wilcox awarded Mrs Wells £120,000 for pain and suffering. The Court of Appeal reduced the figure to £100,000. On behalf of the defendant it is said that the case falls at the upper end of the moderately severe brain-damage bracket as described in the Judicial Studies Board's *Guidelines for the Assessment of General Damages in Personal Injury Cases* (2nd edn, 1994) (£77,500 to £95,000), and not within the most severe brain-damage bracket (£105,000 to £125,000). Mrs Wells is severely disabled and will remain so for the rest of her life. But I agree with the Court of Appeal that the sum of £120,000 awarded by the judge falls well above the bracket for her type of case. The Court of Appeal was therefore right to intervene for the reasons set out convincingly in their judgment, which I need not repeat. As for *Cunningham v Camberwell Health Authority* [1990] 2 Med LR 49, on which the plaintiff relied, Mr Leighton Williams pointed out that the plaintiff in that case was 12 years younger than Mrs Wells, and it looks as though her injuries may have been rather more serious. In any event the award in that case may have been on the high side. I would uphold the Court of Appeal's figure of £100,000.

On the other hand I am unable to agree with the Court of Appeal's reduction in Mrs Wells's life expectancy from 15 years to ten years. Dr Peter Harvey's evidence was that her life expectancy is not affected by her present condition in view of the intensive care which she now receives. He would therefore predict a normal life expectancy for a woman of her age, namely 20 years. Mr Alan Richardson, on the other hand, predicted a life expectancy of ten years, or 13 at the most. The judge ([1996] PIQR Q62 at Q65) expressed his conclusion as follows:

'I prefer the considered and more closely reasoned approach of Mr Alan Richardson and doing the best I can upon the medical evidence and all the other evidence I am persuaded that the life expectancy in this case more likely than not is 15 years.'

The Court of Appeal fastened on the judge's preference for Mr Richardson's evidence, and held that he was therefore wrong to split the difference (if that is what he did) by taking 15 years. But this is to misunderstand the judge's approach. Even though he preferred Mr Richardson's evidence, he was not obliged to accept the lower of his two figures uncritically. Nor was he obliged to reject Dr Harvey's views out of hand. In arriving at a life expectancy of 15 years the judge took all the medical evidence into account, and all the other evidence besides. In my view the Court of Appeal should not have interfered. I would therefore restore the judge's figure of 15 years' life expectancy.

The third point relates to the multiplicand. The Court of Appeal rightly rejected a number of Mr Leighton Williams's criticisms of the judge's findings. But in one respect they found his criticism justified. At the time of the trial the care regime consisted of a residential carer and a day carer by day, and the residential carer and a night carer by night. Miss Teresa Gough, who gave evidence at the trial for the defendant, urged strongly that a night sleeper could be substituted for the night carer, with a saving of £10,539 per year. But the judge (at Q67) preferred the evidence of Mrs Statham and Mrs Clarke-Wilson, who had, as he put it 'the direct hands-on experience'. If, as they said, Mrs Wells needed to be seen three times a night, then Miss Gough accepted that that was a task for a night carer rather than a night sleeper.

In my view the Court of Appeal was right to scrutinise the individual items which went to make up the multiplicand. Since the effect of reducing the rate of discount will be to increase the multiplier in every case, it is all the more important to keep firm control of the multiplicand. Plaintiffs are entitled to a reasonable standard of care to meet their requirements, but that is all. Having said that, however, and having heard all that Mr Leighton Williams had to say, I am not persuaded that the Court of Appeal was entitled to substitute their own view of the evidence to that formed by the judge. They gave no reason other than it was another instance of the judge over-providing. I would therefore restore the judge's finding under this head.

Thomas v Brighton Health Authority

The agreed medical evidence was that the plaintiff has a life expectancy to the age of 60. Collins J ([1996] PIQR Q44 at Q57) held, however, that he ought to reduce the arithmetical multiplier by about 20% 'to cater for the hazards of life in such cases'. In the result he took a multiplier of 23. The Court of Appeal agreed with the judge's approach but started from a different starting point. With a 4·5% discount rate the arithmetical multiplier came to 20. Reduced by 15%, rather than 20%, they arrived at a multiplier of 17.

Was it correct for the judge and the Court of Appeal to reduce the arithmetical multiplier, and therefore, in effect, override the expectation of life agreed by the doctors? Mr Owen submitted that there could be no rational basis for applying a further discount for 'contingencies', since the doctors had already taken account of all the contingencies that might affect the plaintiff, such as the increased risk of accident, chest infection, and so on. The only reason given by the judge was that the courts had 'tended to reduce multipliers by about 20%'. The Court of Appeal took the same line.

I can see no answer to Mr Owen's argument. The inevitable result of reducing the multiplier to 17, as Mr Havers pointed out, will be that the plaintiff's damages will run out when he is 39. He will have nothing to cover his needs for the remaining 21 years of his life.

Mr Havers conceded that there is room for a judicial discount when calculating the loss of future earnings, when contingencies may indeed affect the result. But there is no room for any discount in the case of a whole life multiplier with an agreed expectation of life. In the case of loss of earnings the contingencies can work in only one direction—in favour of the defendant. But in the case of life expectancy, the contingency can work in either direction. The plaintiff may exceed his normal expectation of life, or he may fall short of it.

There is no purpose in the courts making as accurate a prediction as they can of the plaintiff's future needs if the resulting sum is arbitrarily reduced for no better reason than that the prediction might be wrong. A prediction remains a prediction. Contingencies should be taken into account where they work in one direction, but not where they cancel out. There is no more logic or justice in reducing the whole life multiplier by 15% or 20% on an agreed expectation of life than there would be in increasing it by the same amount.

It follows from what I have said that I do not agree with the discount which McCullough J allowed in *Janardan v East Berkshire Health Authority* [1990] 2 Med LR 1. In that case the plaintiff, aged five at the time of trial, had a life expectancy to 55. This indicated a multiplier of just under 20 by reference to a 4·5% discount rate (see [1990] 2 Med LR 1 at 8). McCullough J (at 7) held that a discount was required to allow for the possibility that the plaintiff might not survive to 55. I do not accept this; and it may be that McCullough J would not have accepted it either, if he had not felt constrained by previous authority. Left to himself, he said (at 9) he would have taken a whole life multiplier of 17.5 to 18. But the multiplier chosen by the Court of Appeal in *Croke v Wiseman* [1981] 3 All ER 852, [1982] 1 WLR 71 and by the House in *Lim Poh Choo v Camden and Islington Area Health Authority* [1979] 2 All ER 910, [1980] AC 174 required him to choose 17 instead. But this meant, as Mr Havers pointed out, that the plaintiff in *Janardan*'s case would have run out of damages at the age of 33, although he was expected to live to 55.

In *Hunt v Severs* [1994] 2 All ER 385, [1994] 2 AC 350 the plaintiff had a life expectancy of 25 years. The appropriate multiplier by reference to a 4·5% discount rate was 14·821. But the judge reduced this figure to 14 because 14 seemed more in line with the multiplier applied in other comparable cases. The Court of Appeal, correctly in my view, substituted a multiplier of 15, as being the nearest round figure to 14·821. Bingham MR ([1993] 4 All ER 180 at 201, [1993] QB 815 at 841) observed that an allowance for contingencies may sometimes be appropriate. But he continued:

> 'Such an allowance is not appropriate in the present case, where the agreed life expectancy of the plaintiff is 25 years. That is a fact, or rather an agreed assumption, upon which the damages payable for future care must be based.'

But the House disagreed. Lord Bridge of Harwich said ([1994] 2 All ER 385 at 396–397, [1994] 2 AC 350 at 365):

> 'The passage I have cited from the judgment of the Court of Appeal appears to show the court as treating the circumstance that both doctors in evidence estimated the plaintiff's expectation of life at 25 years as establishing the "fact" or "assumption" that she would live for 25 years and thus converting the process of assessing future loss into "a simple arithmetical calculation". I cannot think that this was the correct approach to the evidence. A man or woman in normal health, at a given age, no doubt has an ascertainable statistical life expectancy. But in using such a figure as the basis for assessment of damages with respect to future losses, some discount in respect of life's manifold contingencies is invariably made.'

I have some difficulty with this passage. The plaintiff's life expectancy was not derived from any tables. It was the agreed life expectancy of this particular plaintiff, taking her individual characteristics into account. I cannot for my part see what further room there was for 'life's manifold contingencies'. The whole point of agreeing a life expectancy, if it can be done, is to exclude any further speculation. With respect therefore I prefer the approach of Bingham MR and the Court of Appeal.

The explanation for the different approach of the House in *Hunt v Severs* may be a continuing hesitation to embrace the actuarial tables. I do not suggest that the judge should be a slave to the tables. There may well be special factors in particular cases. But the tables should now be regarded as the starting point, rather than a check. A judge should be slow to depart from the relevant actuarial multiplier on impressionistic grounds, or by reference to 'a spread of multipliers in comparable cases' especially when the multipliers were fixed before actuarial tables were widely used. This may be the explanation for the relatively low multiplier chosen by the House in *Lim Poh Choo*'s case.

For the reasons I have given, I consider that the Court of Appeal in the present case were wrong to substitute a multiplier of 17 for the judge's 23. But the judge himself was also too low. The appropriate multiplier derived from the tables on the agreed life expectancy was 26.58.

I can deal with the second of the two miscellaneous points in *Thomas v Brighton Health Authority* quite shortly. In October 1990, 15 months after the plaintiff's birth, and five years before the trial, the plaintiff's parents moved into a larger house. They needed more space, because of his disability. The additional cost was some £60,000 which they raised by way of a mortgage. The question is how the additional cost should be reflected in the award of damages.

Obviously the plaintiff is not entitled to the additional capital cost, since the larger house is a permanent addition to the family's assets. It will be there, and could be realised, at the end of the period covered by the award. How then should this head of damages be calculated? Should it be the interest on the mortgage? Or interest calculated in some other way?

The answer to this question, described in *Kemp and Kemp*, vol 1, para 5–044 as 'a satisfactory and elegant solution' was provided by the Court of Appeal in *Roberts v Johnstone* [1989] QB 878. It is to be assumed that the plaintiff will pay for the additional accommodation out of his own capital.

It is further to be assumed that the capital input will be risk free over the period of the award, and protected against inflation, by a corresponding increase in the value of the house. What the plaintiff has therefore lost is the income which the capital would have earned over the period of the award after deduction of tax.

But the lost income is not to be calculated by reference to a normal commercial rate of interest. For interest, as Lord Diplock explained in *Wright v British Railways Board* [1983] 2 All ER 698 at 703, [1983] 2 AC 773 at 781, normally includes two elements, 'a reward for taking a risk of loss or reduction of capital', and 'a reward for forgoing the use of the capital sum for the time being'. Since the capital input in the new accommodation is free of risk, or virtually free of risk, it is only the second of the two elements of interest that the plaintiff has lost, namely the 'going rate' for forgoing the use of money. The Court of Appeal in *Roberts v Johnstone* took 2% as the 'going rate'. This was the figure originally chosen by Lord Denning MR in *Birkett v Hayes* [1982] 2 All ER 710, [1982] 1 WLR 816 and accepted by Lord Diplock in *Wright v British Railways Board*. *Birkett v Hayes* and *Wright v British Railways Board* were both cases of non-pecuniary loss, but the point is the same.

Both sides accept that the correct approach is that adopted by the Court of Appeal in *Roberts v Johnstone*. The only question is how that approach should be applied. Collins J arrived at the 'going rate' by taking the average return on ILGS as the best possible indicator of the real return on a risk-free investment over the period of the award. In other words, he took the same discount of 3% net of tax as he had taken for the calculation of future loss. The Court of Appeal disagreed. They took the 'conventional rate' of 2%, pointing out that Stocker LJ had not tied his 2% to the return on any particular form of investment.

It is true that there is no reference to ILGS in *Roberts v Johnstone*. But in *Wright v British Railways Board* Lord Diplock chose the return on ILGS as the first (and in my view simpler) of the two routes by which courts can arrive at the appropriate or 'conventional' rate of interest for foregoing the use of capital. At that time the net return on 15-year and 25-year index-linked stocks was 2%. I can see no reason for regarding 2% as sacrosanct now that the average net return on ILGS has changed. The current rate is 3%. This therefore is the rate which should now be taken for calculating the cost of additional accommodation. It has two advantages. In the first place it is the same as the rate for calculating future loss. Secondly it will be kept up to date by the Lord Chancellor when exercising his powers under s 1 of the Act of 1996. On this point I would restore the order of Collins J.

Page v Sheerness Steel Co plc

The judge took a loss of earnings multiplier of 20·28, which he reduced by 8·65% to 19 in order to take account of the substantial risk that the plaintiff would not have continued working until the age of 62. The Court of Appeal took a multiplier of 14 including a discount of 17·9%, on the ground that there was merit in Mr Leighton Williams' submission that the discount should be at least 12·5%. But the judge had already said that he was giving a larger discount than average, because of the nature of the plaintiff's work. There was no need for the Court of Appeal to intervene.

The judge took a whole life multiplier of 24 based on a rate of return of 3% net on a normal life expectancy. The Court of Appeal started with a multiplier of 19 and reduced it to 17. For the reasons already mentioned there was no justification for a discount on the whole life multiplier. I would therefore restore the judge's multiplier of 24 as the correct starting-point.

But as the plaintiff is currently being looked after by his wife, the judge sensibly and correctly split the multiplier in two. He applied a multiplier of 12 to the additional cost currently incurred while Mrs Page is the prime carer, and the same multiplier for the further costs when she is no longer able to act as the prime carer. There is no dispute on that score.

Part of the current cost of care is to provide the services of an 'enabler', that is to say 'someone who will take the plaintiff out of the house, stimulate his interest in sporting and other activities and generally seek to motivate him and improve the quality of his life' (see [1996] PIQR Q26 at Q40). Mrs Gipson said that four sessions a week would be appropriate, but the judge reduced this to three sessions or 12 hours a week for the reasons he gave, and calculated the damages on the basis of a 52-week year. The Court of Appeal accepted that the cost of an enabler was justified, but reduced the period from 52 weeks a year to 40 weeks, on the ground that there would be breaks in the period of employment, as when the plaintiff is on holiday. It may be that some account should have been taken of holiday periods. But the judge's estimate was not so far wrong as to justify the Court of Appeal's interference.

Nor was there any sound reason for increasing the discount on damages for loss of pension rights from 10% allowed (reluctantly) by the judge in the light of *Auty v National Coal Board* [1985] 1 All ER 930, [1985] 1 WLR 784 to 15% allowed by the Court of Appeal.

Finally Mr Purchas argued that there ought not to be a reduction for the proceeds of permanent health insurance, on the ground that the plaintiff has contributed 4·5% of his earnings to the scheme. Mr Purchas sought to distinguish *Hussain v New Taplow Paper Mills Ltd* [1988] 1 All ER 541, [1988] AC 514 on that ground. The judge did not accept Mr Purchas's argument. He dealt with this point at some length and his views were upheld in the Court of Appeal. In my view they were right.

For the reasons I have given I would allow all three appeals.

Lord Steyn

My Lords, I confine my observations to the principal issue about the discount rate to be applied.

The conventional rate

It has for many years been settled practice, indorsed by decisions of the House of Lords, that the lump sum to be awarded in a personal injury action for the present value of a plaintiff's future losses of earnings, and the present cost of his future expenses, ought to be determined by using in the calculations a discount rate of 4 to 5%. The rationale was that there was no other practicable basis of calculation that is capable of dealing with so conjectural a factor as inflation with greater precision: see *Cookson v Knowles* [1978] 2 All

ER 604 at 611, [1979] AC 556 at 571, per Lord Diplock; see also the earlier and subsequent decisions of the House of Lords in *Mallett v McMonagle* [1969] 2 All ER 178, [1970] AC 166 and *Lim Poh Choo v Camden and Islington Area Health Authority* [1979] 2 All ER 910, [1980] AC 174. The question before the House is whether this practice should now be modified in changed economic circumstances by adopting a discount figure assessed by reference to index-linked government securities, the suggested figure being 3%.

The importance of the issue

The importance of the issue is shown by a comparison of the awards of the three trial judges, who relied on index-linked government securities to fix the discount rate, and the figures substituted by the Court of Appeal, who used the conventional rate. Ignoring for present purposes that in *Wells v Wells* the trial judge adopted a discount rate of 2·5%, the use of a 3% discount rate instead of 4·5% would increase the awards by very roughly the following sums:

Margaret Wells (a 58-year-old nurse)	£108,000
Page (a 28-year-old steelworker)	£186,000
Thomas (aged six years)	£300,000

These figures show the impact of the reduction of the discount rate in cases where damages are calculated over many years. But, since a judicial decision ought to take into account general as well as particular consequences, it is important to realise that the proposed modification of the discount rate would lead to an enormous general increase in the size of awards for future losses. Nobody has ventured a prediction of the likely cost. The sums involved would undoubtedly be huge. The implications of a modification of the conventional rate for the insurance industry would be considerable. Inevitably, it would be reflected in increased premiums. The one certain thing is that if the right decision is to make the suggested modification of the discount rate the public would by and large have to pay for the increase in awards.

The premise of the debate

The premise of the debate was that as a matter of law a victim of a tort is entitled to be compensated as nearly as possible in full for all pecuniary losses. For present purposes this mainly means compensation for loss of earnings and medical care, both past and future. Subject to the obvious qualification that perfection in the assessment of future compensation is unattainable, the 100% principle is well established and based on high authority: see *Livingstone v Rawyards Coal Co* (1880) 5 App Cas 25 at 39 and *Lim Poh Choo v Camden and Islington Area Health Authority* [1979] 2 All ER 910 at 917, [1980] AC 174 at 187 per Lord Scarman. The technique employed to achieve this result is to provide an annuity of an annual amount equivalent to the streams of future losses of earnings and cost of future expenses: *Hodgson v Trapp* [1988] 3 All ER 870 at 879, [1989] AC 807 at 826 per Lord Oliver of Aylmerton.

It must not be assumed that the 100% principle is self evidently the only sensible compensation system. Judges have to a limited extent tried to control the size of awards for pecuniary losses in personal injury cases. Thus judges have in practice imposed a limit of 18 years in fixing a multiplier and, having done their sums in the context of the facts of a case, they have resorted to the so-called judicial discount for uncertainties. The first tendency is illustrated by *McIlgrew v Devon CC* [1995] PIQR Q66 at Q74 per Sir John May, and the second by the judicial discount applied in *Thomas v Brighton Health Authority*. Moreover, the 100% principle has been criticised by commentators, notably in *Atiyah's Accidents, Compensation and the Law* (5th edn, 1993) edited by Peter Cane. About the 100% principle, Professor Atiyah states (p 131):

> '... most other compensation systems, especially social security systems (and in other countries, worker's compensation laws) generally reject the 100% principle. Our own social security system generally pays benefits well below the full amount of lost earnings. Similarly, the New Zealand Accident Compensation Act provides for benefits of 80% of lost earnings; and the Australian Committee of Inquiry recommended benefits equal to 85% of lost earnings. Moreover, in most compensation systems there are minimum loss qualifications. Thus, no social security benefits are payable in this country for the first three days' loss of earnings; no criminal injuries compensation benefits are payable if the compensation would amount to less than £1,000, and so on.'

Clearly, such arguments are stronger in the case of loss of future earnings than in respect of the cost of future medical care. Rhetorically, Professor Atiyah asks: 'why should different accident victims be compensated for the same type of injury on a scale which varies according to their previous level of earnings?' and 'if ... two people are killed in similar accidents, what justification is there for compensating their dependants at different rates?' (pp 127, 128). The author gives two main reasons for rejecting the 100% principle. The first is the cost involved. The second is that it reduces the victim's incentive to return to work. The second consideration is not relevant to the appellants in the present appeals but may arguably be relevant in other personal injury cases. Not only do these arguments contemplate a radical departure from established principle, but controversial issues regarding resources and social policy would be at stake. Such policy arguments are a matter for Parliament and not the judiciary.

Leaving to one side the policy arguments for and against the 100% principle, there is a major structural flaw in the present system. It is the inflexibility of the lump sum system which requires an assessment of damages once and for all of future pecuniary losses. In the case of the great majority of relatively minor injuries, the plaintiff will have recovered before his damages are assessed and the lump sum system works satisfactorily. But the lump sum system causes acute problems in cases of serious injuries with consequences enduring after the assessment of damages. In such cases, the judge must often resort to guesswork about the future. Inevitably, judges will strain to ensure that a seriously injured plaintiff is properly cared for whatever the future may have in store for him. It is a wasteful system since the courts are sometimes compelled to award large sums that turn out not to be needed. It is true, of course, that there is statutory provision for periodic payments: see s 2 of the Damages Act 1996. But the court only has this power if both parties agree. Such agreement is never, or virtually never, forthcoming. The present power to order periodic payments is a dead letter. The solution is relatively straightforward. The court ought to be given the power of its own motion to make an award for periodic payments rather than a lump sum in appropriate cases. Such a power is perfectly consistent with the principle of full compensation for pecuniary loss. Except perhaps for the distaste of personal injury lawyers for change to a familiar system, I can think of no substantial argument to the contrary. But the judges cannot make the change. Only Parliament can solve the problem.

The basis of the conventional rate

Although decisions of the House of Lords adopted the 4 to 5% discount rate, those decisions did not single out equities as the appropriate investment vehicle justifying that rate. Negatively this is clear from a study of the judgments in *Mallett v McMonagle* [1969] 2 All ER 178, [1970] AC 166, *Cookson v Knowles* [1978] 2 All ER 604, [1979] AC 556 and *Lim Poh Choo v Camden and Islington Area Health Authority* [1979] 2 All ER 910, [1980] AC 174. Moreover, although the issue in *Wright v British Railways Board* [1983] 2 All ER 698, [1983] 2 AC 773 was different, Lord Diplock's discussion in the context of *Cookson v Knowles* [1983] 2 All ER 698 at 703, [1983] 2 AC 773 at 781–782 of government stock as giving the 'going rate' makes clear that he did not have in mind equities as the appropriate investment vehicle. But in the present cases the Court of Appeal, relying on general observations in earlier decisions about prudent investment and the need for advice, has sought to justify a rate of 4 to 5% on the basis of plaintiffs investing in a spread of equities.

The changed economic landscape

In 1981 the government introduced index-linked government securities which are tied to the retail price index and hence protected against inflation. In 1982 these forms of financial instrument became freely available to individuals. Since that date a market in such instruments has developed and expanded. This has radically altered the investment scene. It is now practicable for a plaintiff to protect himself against inflation by investing in index-linked government securities. This form of investment guarantees that the sums invested will retain their real value. It is tailor-made for investors who want a safe investment: see Bootle *Index-Linked Gilts* (2nd edn, 1991) pp 94–104. It is in practical terms a virtually risk-free investment guaranteeing a return based on the market's view of inflationary trends. In its reports published in 1984 and 1994 the working party chaired by Sir Michael Ogden QC recommended that in future the discount rate should be based on availability of an investment in index-linked government stock. The working party observed that whereas in the past a plaintiff had to speculate by investing in equities, or in a basket of equities and gilts or a selection of unit trusts, he need speculate no longer if he buys index-linked government stock. After in-depth research the Law Commission took a similar view: see *Structured Settlements and Interim and Provisional Damages* (Law Com No 224) (1994), para 2.28. This is the changed landscape in which three trial judges felt free to depart from the conventional rate of 4 to 5%: see Mr Kemp's full and helpful discussion and analysis: Discounting Compensation for Future Loss (1985) 101 LQR 556 and Discounting Damages for Future Loss (1997)

113 LQR 195; Kemp and Kemp, *The Quantum of Damages* (looseleaf edn (1997) vol 1, paras 6–003 ff.

The critical issue

In a careful judgment Hirst LJ, giving the judgment of the Court of Appeal ([1997] 1 All ER 673, [1997] 1 WLR 652), held that a plaintiff should be treated in the same way as an ordinary investor. In one sense one can quibble and say that the ordinary investor is a rather elusive figure. For my part I regard the concept as meaningful: by its use Hirst LJ indicated that he declined to have regard to the special circumstances of plaintiffs who must be compensated in respect of future consequences of the injuries they suffered. That is a perfectly rational position to adopt. And it is one which counsel for the defendants urged on the House. In short, they argued that it would be wrong to put such a plaintiff in a privileged position. That, they argued, would not be holding the scales fairly between the two sides. On the supposition that the plaintiff must be treated like an ordinary investor, counsel for the defendants argued that in determining the discount rate the Court of Appeal was right to proceed on the basis that a plaintiff should invest in a diversified portfolio of shares, gilts, unit trusts and so forth.

It is necessary to consider how this issue should be approached. Hirst LJ said ([1997] 1 All ER 673 at 696, [1997] 1 WLR 652 at 677):

> 'the court, which … is dealing with probabilities when fixing the multiplier, can and should pay regard to the high probability that the plaintiff will invest prudently …'

The Court of Appeal assumed that such plaintiffs have in the past usually invested in a portfolio of equities. The only evidence was the Law Commission's research which yielded the answer that the majority of plaintiffs are 'risk-averse' and tend to deposit their damages with banks and building societies: see *Personal Injury Compensation: How Much is Enough?* (Law Com No 225) (1994) para 10.2, table 1001, pp 162–164. More importantly, the court cannot be expected to investigate what plaintiffs, who are not a homogenous group, will or will not do with their damages. The correct approach is to concentrate on the objective question, namely what is the type of investment that plaintiffs can reasonably be expected to make.

My Lords, the Court of Appeal have also approached the inquiry in the objective way required. But the Court of Appeal have assumed that the same investment policy would be suitable for all investors, regardless of any special needs. The premise that plaintiffs, who have perhaps been very seriously injured, are in the same position as ordinary investors is not one that I can accept. Such plaintiffs have not chosen to invest: the tort and its consequences compel them to do so. For plaintiffs, an investment in equities is inherently risky, notably in regard to the timing of the investment. The annuity method contemplates sales of capital from time to time. With equities there is the risk that planned sales of capital will have to be made during a slump, thereby eroding capital and depleting the fund. As the Ogden Working Party observed, it is not difficult to draw up a list of blue chip equities or reliable unit trusts which have performed poorly, or, in some cases, disastrously. The stock market slump of 1973 took substantially more than a decade to recover. Less dramatically, a slump in equities in December 1993 would have caused a loss of 10% (subsequently recovered) in a single year. The truth is that stock markets are seldom tranquil for long. Periodically, they rise and fall quite unexpectedly. Typically, by investing in equities an ordinary investor takes a calculated risk which he can bear in order to improve his financial position. On the other hand, the typical plaintiff requires the return from an award of damages to provide the necessities of life. For such a plaintiff it is not possible to cut back on medical and nursing care as well as other essential services. His objective must be to ensure that the damages awarded do not run out. It is money that he cannot afford to lose. The ordinary investor does not have the same concerns. It is therefore unrealistic to treat such a plaintiff as an ordinary investor. It seems to me entirely reasonable for such a plaintiff to be cautious and conservative. He does not have the freedom of choice available to the ordinary investor. If a comparison is to be made—and in this field all comparisons are inexact—the position of plaintiffs are much closer to elderly, retired individuals who have limited savings which they want to invest safely to provide for their declining years. Such individuals would generally not invest in equities. But for plaintiffs the need for safety may often be more compelling. In any event, it seems to me difficult to say that an investment in index-linked securities by plaintiffs would be *unreasonable*. After all, life companies are now accustomed to investing their annuity funds in index-linked gilts to meet index-linked annuities. Similarly, when the only liabilities of a pension fund are to pay index-linked pensions, the pension fund will invest entirely in index-linked government securities. Plainly insurers and pension fund managers, in so investing, are acting prudently. In these circumstances one cannot realistically say that an injured plaintiff who invests in index-linked government securities is acting imprudently. I therefore share the views of the Ogden Working Party and the Law Commission that it is reasonable for such a plaintiff to take the safe course of investing in index-linked government stock. From this it follows that the discount rate ought to be fixed on this assumption.

The satellite issues

It is possible for me to deal with the satellite issues quite briefly. First, there was much controversy about the real return on equities. Both sides put their case too high. For my part I am content to approach the matter on the basis that a diversified portfolio of equities would yield over a substantial period a better return than index-linked government securities. But I am not satisfied that even on this basis, and ignoring the availability of index-linked government securities, a net rate as high as 4·5% was justified. Bearing in mind the surprisingly high cost of advice that would be needed by a plaintiff to invest in a portfolio of equities my view is that the Court of Appeal took a rather optimistic view. Secondly, my impression is reinforced by the instructive Appendix on the *Duxbury Tables* prepared by Thorpe LJ. He observed ([1997] 1 All ER 673 at 704, [1997] 1 WLR 652 at 685):

> '(2) The 6% gross yield conventionally assumed in the multiplier/multiplicand method is probably currently too high. The rate of yield from ILGS is perhaps too low, although if expressed as 3% net it is only mar-

ginally below the current Duxbury assumption of 4·25% gross or 3·18% net were 25% to be deducted for tax.'

This observation goes a considerable way towards undermining the reasoning in the judgment of the Court of Appeal. That Thorpe LJ should be a party to both texts is not surprising: compromises are an inevitability in appellate judging. Thirdly, much was made of the fact that the Court of Protection presently works on a discount rate based on an investment in a diversified portfolio of equities. The Court of Protection acts on the basis that the damages are currently calculated by using a 4 to 5% rate and that it must try to achieve this net real rate even if it involves taking some risks. What the Court of Protection will do if the House adopts a discount rate based on investment in index-linked government securities is uncertain. It is putting it too high to say, as Hirst LJ did, that even if the rate is modified the Court of Protection 'would probably stick to their normal investment strategy of setting up a segregated portfolio [(of equities)]'. The witness from the Court of Protection in fact said:

> 'If you are looking to have no risk, then the advice to the court would have to be to use index-linked gilts because they are the only vehicle of that nature that will guarantee you a return over and above whatever inflation is. That we know can fluctuate dramatically.'

The past practice of the Court of Protection does not assist on the principal issue, and its future decisions are uncertain and, in any event, are a matter for its independent judgment. Fourthly, the Court of Appeal accepted an argument on behalf of the defendants that an investment in index-linked government securities was not risk free. That is a proposition that would surprise the market: being government backed such stock is surely virtually risk free. The principal point made was the alleged lack of availability of appropriate issues of index-linked government securities. This is unrealistic. According to the *Debt Management Report* 1998–99, Treasury (1997), the UK central government marketable sterling debt stood at £308 bn at the end of February 1998, of which £59 bn (including accrued interest) was in index-linked gilts. In the government's remit to the National Savings and Debt Management Office, the target proportions of index-linked gilts as a proportion of all gilt sales is 25%. In presently foreseeable circumstances the issue of index-linked government securities must be regarded as an integral and permanent feature of the investment scene. Moreover, if the Lord Chancellor in acting under his powers under s 1 of the 1996 Act were to be guided by the unanimous judgment of the House, and accept index-linked government securities as the best guide to the appropriate discount rate, this would no doubt be an added reason for the government to ensure that appropriate index-linked government securities are issued.

The guideline

My Lords, until the Lord Chancellor takes action under his statutory powers it is essential that there should be a firm and workable principle. It should be general and simple in order to enable settlement negotiations and litigation to be conducted with the benefit of a reasonable degree of predictability of the likely outcome of a case. While acknowledging an element of arbitrariness in any figure, I am content to adopt about 3% as the best present net figure. For my part I would derive that rate from the net average return of index-linked government securities over the past three years. While this figure of about 3% should not be regarded as immutable, I would suggest that only a marked change in economic circumstances should entitle any party to reopen the debate in advance of a decision by the Lord Chancellor. The effect of the decision of the House on the discount rate, together with the availability of the Ogden Tables, should be to eliminate the need in future to call actuaries, accountants and economists in such cases.

Tax

The rate of 3% takes into account tax at standard rates. But counsel for the plaintiffs argued that the rate should be lowered for individuals subject to higher rates of tax. The position is that index-linked government securities are free of capital gains tax held for more than a year. My understanding is that an unusually high proportion of returns from index-linked government securities comes from capital gains rather than income: see Bootle *Index-Linked Gilts* (2nd edn) p 99. But the income is taxable. For my part I am content that the position regarding higher tax rates should remain as Lord Oliver of Aylmerton in *Hodgson v Trapp* [1988] 3 All ER 870 at 885, [1989] 1 AC 807 at 835 described it, viz that in such exceptional cases plaintiffs would be free to place their arguments for a lower rate before the court.

The effect on the appeals

On the principal point I would uphold the judgments of Dyson and Collins JJ in *Page v Sheerness Steel Co plc* and *Thomas v Brighton Health Authority*. In *Wells v Wells* Judge Wilcox adopted a discount rate of 2·5% by reference to index-linked government securities. This award should be altered so as to reflect a 3% discount rate. The necessary adjustment in the calculation of damages can readily be agreed between the parties.

The remaining points

I agree with the speech of my noble and learned friend Lord Lloyd of Berwick on the remaining points in the case.

I would allow the appeal.

Lord Hope of Craighead

My Lords, the plaintiff in each of these three cases sustained very serious injuries of the kind which are normally classified as injuries of the maximum severity. The circumstances of each case are entirely different. But they all raise a common question which is of great importance to the assessment of damages generally.

The law requires that an award of damages must take the form of a single lump sum award which takes account of all the elements of future loss as well as all the loss for the past. The inevitable delay in the provision of compensation for past losses can be made good by the award of interest at an appropriate rate on those elements of the lump sum which relate to the past. The payment as part of the lump sum of losses to be incurred in the future gives rise to a different problem. A discount must be given for the fact that money is being paid now for a loss which will not arise until some date in the future. The rate to be applied in calculating that discount will affect the amount of the total sum to be paid as damages. In the majority of cases a difference of a point or two in the rate of discount will not have a very large impact on the total award. But in cases where the injury is one of maximum severity, and in any other case where the element of future loss forms a major part of the award, a difference of a point or two in the rate of discount will make a very great difference to the result. It may make all the difference between the adequacy and the inadequacy of the award as compensation for the losses which the plaintiff will sustain.

It has often been said that the assessment of damages is not an exact science—that all the law can do is to work out as best it can, in a rough and ready way, the sum to be paid to the plaintiff as compensation for the loss and injury. There remains much truth in these statements, despite the important advances which have been made in the search for greater accuracy. The amount of the award to be made for pain, suffering and loss of amenity cannot be precisely calculated. All that can be done is to award such sum, within the broad criterion of what is reasonable and in line with similar awards in comparable cases, as represents the court's best estimate of the plaintiff's general damages. Nor can the accuracy which can usually be achieved in the assessment of past loss of wages and of other past losses and expense which fall under the broad heading of special damages be matched when it comes to the future. The court cannot say precisely what will happen. It can only proceed by means of assumptions. The calculations which it then makes will involve the use of arithmetic as the multiplier is applied to the multiplicand. To that extent the exercise will give the impression of accuracy. But the accuracy of the result achieved by arithmetic will depend on the assumptions on which it has been based. In making these assumptions the court must do the best it can on the available evidence.

Nevertheless the object of the award of damages for future expenditure is to place the injured party as nearly as possible in the same financial position as he or she would have been in but for the accident. The aim is to award such a sum of money as will amount to no more, and at the same time no less, than the net loss. As Lord Oliver of Aylmerton said in *Hodgson v Trapp* [1988] 3 All ER 870 at 879, [1989] AC 807 at 826:

> 'Essentially what the court has to do is to calculate as best it can the sum of money which will on the one hand be adequate, by its capital and income, to provide annually for the injured person a sum equal to his estimated annual loss over the whole of the period during which that loss is likely to continue, but which, on the other hand, will not, at the end of that period, leave him in a better financial position than he would have been apart from the accident. Hence the conventional approach is to assess the amount notionally required to be laid out in the purchase of an annuity which will provide the annual amount needed for the whole period of loss.'

The annuity approach requires that, once the necessary assumptions have been made, the calculation of the award will result in an amount which matches as accurately as possible the sum required over the entire period of the assumed loss. Whatever policy reasons there might have been for regarding it as acceptable that there may be less than a full recovery in regard to wage loss—and I should make it clear that I do not subscribe to that policy—there can be no good reason for a shortfall in the amount required for future care or to meet all the other outlays which have been rendered necessary by the disability. The calculation should make the best use of such tools to assist that process as are available.

Some of the assumptions which have to be made in the assessment of future loss are made at the stage of arriving at the multiplicand for each head of the claim. The selection of the right multiplier requires that further assumptions be made, so that the calculation can be related to the period of the annual loss or expense which is to be compensated for. The general point of principle which is raised in all three cases relates to the final stage in the selection of the multiplier. This is the choice of the interest rate, which represents the discount for the payment now of a lump sum to compensate for loss to be sustained over a period of years in the future.

The measure of the discount is the rate of return which can reasonably be expected on that sum if invested in such a way as to enable the plaintiff to meet the whole amount of the loss during the entire period which has been assumed for it by the expenditure of income together with capital. It was suggested for the defendants in the course of the argument that the plaintiff was under a duty to minimise the loss to be borne by the defendants by investing the lump sum prudently, that is to say with a view to obtaining a reasonable return for it. The duty to invest prudently was an important part of the reasoning which was designed to show that this meant a duty to invest in equities, and that the discount rate to be applied was that appropriate to the return to be expected on equities. But I do not think that the duty to minimise loss has anything to do with the selection of the appropriate discount rate. The stage at which the duty to minimise loss is to be applied is at the earlier stage when the court has to identify the amount of the annual sum to be compensated for and the period over which it is to be compensated. That exercise is over and done with when the time comes to select and apply the discount rate.

The assumptions to be made at the stage of selecting the discount rate are simply these. First, it is to be assumed that the lump sum will be invested in such a way as to enable the plaintiff to meet the whole amount of the losses or costs as they arise during the entire period while protecting the award against inflation, which can thus be left out of account. Secondly, it is to be assumed that that investment will produce a return which represents the market's view of the reward to be given for foregoing the use of the money in the meantime. This is the rate of interest to be expected where the investment is without risk, there being no question about the availability of the money when the investor requires repayment of the capital and there being no question of loss due to inflation.

In the past it does not appear to have been too difficult to find a sufficiently reliable guide to the rate of return to be expected by the application of these principles. It was thought that a rough and ready approach could be taken, and it was generally accepted that the rate to be applied was the rate of interest which could be obtained on the lump sum during periods of stable currency. Mention was made of the use in practice of the interest rates of 4% to 5% in times of stable currency by Lord Diplock in *Mallett v McMonagle* [1969] 2 All ER 178 at 190, [1970] AC 166 at 176 and by both Lord Diplock and Lord Fraser of Tullybelton in *Cookson v Knowles* [1978] 2 All ER 604 at 611 and 615, [1979] AC 556 at 571 and 576–577. In *O'Brien's Curator Bonis v British Steel Plc* 1991 SC 315 at 320 I referred to an early example in Scotland of the use of the same two interest rates. That was *McKechnie v James Henderson & Son* (1858) 20 D 551 at 553, where the sheriff said that he had arrived at the conclusion that the sum which he proposed to award for future wage loss was a reasonable compensation having regard to the yield which could be obtained on that sum at 4% and at 5% per annum.

It seems unlikely that the yield which was being used 140 years ago was related to the return which was to be expected from what we would now understand by investment in equities. It was more probably related to the rates of interest which were currently available in the market for depositing the money in a bank. In modern times interest rates have had to provide for inflation as well as a return by way of a reward to the lender or depositor. So the rate of interest which he can obtain is not a reliable guide to the rate to be obtained in times of stable currency. But the fact that index-linked government securities (ILGS) are now available to the ordinary investor has altered the position fundamentally. In my opinion it would be wrong for the court to fail to take account of this form of investment. Indeed there are good grounds for regarding it as the most reliable guide to the return which, after allowing for inflation, a person who forgoes the use of his money by placing it in a secure investment can expect to receive. Both capital and income are protected against inflation, the investment is secure because it is underwritten by the government and after one year the capital gain which is obtained by index-linking is tax-free.

This form of investment is, it should be added, not entirely without risk. The prices at which ILGS are available on the market from time to time rise and fall according to the market's expectation of the future pattern of inflation as against the movement of interest rates. If they are bought and sold in the short term these price movements may result in a gain or a loss of capital. In the long term however, particularly if held to the redemption date, they produce a return which is inflation-proof and can be relied upon. The same cannot be said, to the same degree of confidence, of investment in equities.

There is much to be said for the view that a better return can be obtained by the ordinary investor who invests his money in equities. But the rises and falls in the market value of equities are unpredictable both as to their timing and as to their amount. Further problems are presented by the cost of investment advice and by the possible impact of capital gains tax if reliance has to be placed on the capital gains which can be achieved to deal with inflation and to supplement the income return by way of dividend. Moreover the plaintiff who is receiving the amount of his future loss in the form of a lump sum is not an ordinary investor. The amount awarded under each head of his claim is calculated on the assumption that this part of his loss will have to be met entirely out of the relevant portion of the lump sum. So in his case the only form of investment which could be described as a prudent investment is one which will as nearly as possible guarantee the availability of the money as and when it is required. He cannot afford to wait until the market moves in his favour, or to sustain the loss of capital which would result if he was forced to sell at a price which did not match the inflation rate. In any event the discount rate is to be selected not by forecasting what the plaintiff will actually do with the money but by identifying the return which the market will give for forgoing the use of capital. The availability of ILGS provides the best guide to what is required. It is the best tool for this exercise which is available.

The strongest arguments which were advanced against the use of ILGS were their inflexibility and the possible lack of their availability in the long term. It was said that the precise calculations which this form of investment assumed left nothing over to meet the possibility that the plaintiff might survive for longer than had been assumed or might need to meet costs over a longer period. Reference was also made to the fact that the longest dated ILGS which is currently available will mature in 2030, which is too soon to meet the entire period of James Thomas's assumed lifespan. I think that there is no force in either of these objections. As for the first, the whole exercise is carried out upon an assumption that the period of the loss and the amount of it throughout that period has already been ascertained by the court. The only question is the rate of the discount for paying that amount in the form of a lump sum. It may be that in practice the plaintiff will decide to invest part of the award in equities to meet the risk of a shortfall in the long term, but that is a matter for the plaintiff not for the court. As for the second point, the evidence strongly favours the view that ILGS will continue to be issued for the foreseeable future in view of their utility in the market where a secure form of investment is required for inflation-linked claims.

For these reasons I consider that the conventional discount rate of 4 to 5%, which the Court of Appeal held was appropriate having regard to the return to be expected from investment in equities, can no longer be regarded as appropriate. The discount rate should now be more closely related to the return to be expected from investment in ILGS. As to what that rate should be, I think that there are three points which should be made. First, I think that it would be wrong to link the discount rate too precisely to the figures showing the average gross redemption yield on ILGS which are published each day in the financial press. These figures fluctuate almost daily, albeit within a relatively narrow band. Frequent changes in the discount rate are undesirable. In the interests of maintaining a reasonable element of stability to assist settlements, a broad view needs to be taken having regard to the range of figures over a substantial period. Secondly, a figure should be selected which will match the rates of interest on which the multipliers in the Ogden Tables are based, as the admissibility and relevance of the information contained in these Tables is now generally recognised. This means that the figure should be expressed to no greater a degree of accuracy than one-half of a decimal point. Thirdly, the rate should be one which has regard in a general way to taxation on the index-linked income return on the investment, after the appropriate allowances, up to and including the standard rate. This is to avoid the need for further calculations to take account of this factor, which can ordinarily be assumed to have been taken care of. The impact of higher rate tax on particular awards in exceptional cases should be dealt with in the manner described by Lord Oliver of Aylmerton in *Hodgson v Trapp* [1988] 3 All ER 870 at 886, [1989] AC 807 at 835.

In my opinion the evidence as to the average gross redemption yield for the last three years on ILGS with lives over five years, assuming an inflation rate of 5%, indicates that for the time being 3% is the appropriate rate of net return to be expected from the investment of the sums to be awarded to the plaintiffs as damages for their future pecuniary loss. Adjustments may have to be made to that rate in the light of significant changes in the yield on ILGS in the future. But these adjustments and the timing of them should now be left to the Lord Chancellor and, for Scotland, the Secretary of State for Scotland in the exercise of the power which was conferred on them by s 1 of the Damages Act 1996. I would apply the rate of 3% to the awards in each of the three cases which are before the House. This means that on this point I also would uphold the judgments of Dyson J and Collins J in the *Page v Sheerness Steel Co plc* and *Thomas v Brighton Health Authority*, and that I would alter the multiplier of 12.5 applied by Judge Wilcox in *Wells v Wells*, which appears to have assumed a discount rate of 2·3%, to the appropriate multiplier at a discount rate of 3% for the period of 15 years which he took as the period of the plaintiff's life expectancy.

On the remaining points I agree with the speech by my noble and learned friend Lord Lloyd of Berwick which I have had the benefit of reading in draft. I would make the same order as he has proposed.

Lord Clyde

My Lords, it has for a long time been a settled rule that in respect of any one cause of action a plaintiff, if he sues for damages, must sue in one action for all his loss, whether it be past, present or future, and whether it be certain or contingent. The rule is established both in England and in Scotland. No doubt it has some practical advantages. It puts some termination to litigation, an end which must be in the public interest. It conclusively severs any continuing obligation on the defendant towards the plaintiff, so that the former may regard the episode as closed and the latter is left free to dispose of his award as he may choose. But the finality which is achieved by the adoption of the rule carries with it an inevitable element of imprecision, particularly in respect of those elements in the claim which relate to periods in the future. A structured settlement may to some extent enable that problem to be overcome; but that solution can only be achieved by consent of the parties. It is not, however, suggested in the present case that the traditional method of calculating the award on the basis of a lump sum should be departed from, and the arguments for and against such a development have not been explored.

The purpose of the award for an injured plaintiff is, in so far as a sum of money can do so, to put him as nearly as possible in the same position as he was in before he was injured. One has to accept that the calculation will not altogether be exact, but one has to do the best one can to achieve as close an approximation as may be possible. The tendency over recent years has been to pursue with increasing sophistication a greater degree of particularity and precision. For quantifiable past financial loss that object may be achieved with some accuracy. In respect of pain and suffering money can only be a conventional medium of compensation and the assessment of it to cover the past and the future must necessarily be imprecise and open to differences of view. But the accumulation of precedent and experience and the careful analysis of the nature and effects of particular injuries can go a long way towards establishing levels of award which may be generally recognised and accepted as reasonable in particular circumstances. If necessary those levels may be open to adjustment or even correction from time to time by those courts which are best qualified to review what must in essence be a factual assessment of the kind sometimes referred to as a jury question. In relation to future pecuniary losses and expenses the uncertainties in the calculation are at their most severe. Here particularly means have been devised to minimise the imprecision. But despite the development of detailed tables and actuarial calculations there will always remain an element of uncertainty in prediction which may only in a rough and ready way satisfy the desire that justice should be done between both parties. The problem of sufficiently providing for the future care of the very severely disabled plaintiff gives rise to particular concern, since any inadequacy of the award in that respect could be particularly serious.

One clear principle is that what the successful plaintiff will in the event actually do with the award is irrelevant. As Lord Fraser of Tullybelton observed in *Cookson v Knowles* [1978] 2 All ER 604 at 615, [1979] AC 556 at 577 it is for the plaintiff to decide how the award is to be applied. Whether he is proposing to invest it or spend it, or, more particularly, exactly how he is going to invest it or spend it, does not affect the calculation of the award. No distinction is recognised here between misers and spendthrifts. While it may be evident that there are certain ways in which he could prudently invest the award and other ways in which he could be imperilling his own future comfort by his employment of the award, the quantification of the sum to which he is entitled in compensation takes no account of the course which he may in the event choose to adopt.

The lump sum award which has to be made is in most cases a composition of several distinct elements. Each requires to be assessed as a single sum and the total represents the compensation. But while in the course of the exercise the judge's task may involve an exercise of a discretion based on his experience coloured by the particular facts of the case, the totality of the elements should not be a matter open to increase or modification merely on account of a feeling that the total seems unduly large or small. If each of the elements has individually achieved the best approximation possible to the proper compensation for each particular aspect of the claim, then the total figure should correspondingly represent the best assessment possible for the total claim. If at the conclusion of the exercise the judge is uneasy at the total result he should not seek to make any overall adjustment in either direction to the total award to meet his unease; he should return to reconsider each element in the calculation and secure that there is no need for revision at that level.

The present appeals are concerned with the calculation of lump sums in respect of future recurring expenses and losses which have been brought about as a result of the injuries which the respective plaintiffs have sustained. It is common ground that that lump sum in each case may be seen as funding a notional annuity from which both capital and income may be derived sufficient to secure the appropriate annual amounts over the likely future period or periods to which they relate. In practice the sum is calculated as the product of a multiplier representing an appropriate number of year's purchase and a multiplicand representing the amount of the annual loss or expense. The assessment of the latter will necessarily depend significantly on the facts of the particular case. But it calls for careful calculation particularly in relation to claims for future expenses incurred by the plaintiff, such as nursing care, where there may be a number of contingencies which ought to be reflected in the figure or the figures selected.

The exercise of calculating the lump sum which will produce the annual figure proceeds upon certain assumptions which strive to achieve a precision but necessarily involve an element of artificiality. One assumption is that the plaintiff will live for an expected number of years, no more and no less. The period will be based on an actuarial calculation, modified or not to meet any special considerations appropriate to the particular case. It will no doubt be the best approximation which can be achieved by such methods, but nevertheless the assumption may not eventually turn out to have been correct. Then again it is to be assumed that the whole of the income will be consumed each year, that it will be sufficient for its purpose and that there will be neither accumulation nor reinvestment throughout the whole of the period. Further it is to be assumed that constantly throughout the period in addition to the income a balancing sum of capital is being used each year to make up the annual amount required so that the capital will steadily decrease and will eventually be exhausted at the end of the period. It may well be that this is not the way in which the plaintiff will in fact deploy the award but these are the hypothetical requirements which the notional annuity requires to meet. The question is not one of asking what the ordinary prudent investor would do but rather what form of investment will most nearly secure the notional annuity able to meet these hypothetical requirements. Such an investment may well not be one which an ordinary investor would choose, but the exercise is not concerned with an ordinary investor nor indeed, as I have already observed, with any intentions of the particular plaintiff. Thus the general duty on a plaintiff to minimise his or her loss is not relevant to the calculation of this notional annuity. That duty relates to the nature and extent of the items which he or she may claim as arising from the injury. It does not extend to the way in which he or she may dispose of the award. The present exercise is simply concerned with the quantification of loss after it has been established as a reasonable loss flowing from the injury.

In order to calculate the appropriate capital sum which will secure such an annuity one has to ascertain the appropriate rate of return which is appropriate for such a notional annuity. That depends upon the choice of investment to be adopted. Here one can only look to the markets for a solution. Between the rival suggestions put forward in the present appeals, namely investment in equities or investment in index-linked government stocks, it seems to me plain that the latter are the preferred choice. The problem which has been of concern in past years of meeting the risk of inflation, a problem which cannot reasonably be wholly disregarded for the future, is substantially met by the nature of an index-linked investment. A confident understanding of the performance of equity investments was made more difficult by the belated realisation that some of the more important tables intended to show the performance of equity investments proceeded on an assumption that the income would be annually reinvested, which did not meet the hypothesis of the notional annuity. There remained a lack of agreement on any precise analysis on a basis closer to the requirements of the present study. However it could be readily concluded from the material before us that, despite considerable fluctuations in certain years, over the longer term the equity market could survive the effects of inflation. But it is also evident that its volatility in respect both of income and of capital makes it a less likely investment to satisfy the requirements of the notional annuity than the government-backed stocks, which, while they may not be completely immune from the effects of inflation, can at least minimise those effects and more constantly hold their value. For the purpose of the exercise on which one is engaged here it seems to me that the continuity of demand from the investment cannot be met by an investment which may recover in the long term but is subject to very considerable fluctuation in the intervening years. It was, in my view quite properly, recognised by counsel for the third defendant that the index-linked stocks were to be preferred for a short-term investment, which he put at about ten years. But once that is accepted it is not easy to see what particular merit remains in a preference for equity investments in respect of a longer period. The situation of a closed pension fund does not seem to me to provide too remote a comparison with the fund assumed to provide the hypothetical annuity and it appears that investment of such a fund in index-linked government stock is in practice not an unreasonable course to adopt. It was suggested that the present issues of index-linked government stock could not cover all the various periods which might be required in different cases. But the shortfall on an early maturity could reasonably be supposed to be covered by a cash investment from the remaining proceeds of the notional investment and in any event it may well be that future issues of index-linked stock will be made so that a greater variety of periods can be covered more precisely.

On this approach the problem which was raised of the need to allow for the costs and charges involved in the management of an investment portfolio substantially disappears. There is certainly no likelihood of costs and charges being regularly involved on the scale which would probably apply to the management of a portfolio of equities. The assumption would be that the index-linked investment would be held to maturity. In relation to such investments such costs and charges as there would be may for practical purposes be ignored.

While the risk of future inflation can be substantially overcome for the purpose of the notional annuity by investment in index-linked government securities, one other uncertainty of a general application remains and that is the future incidence of taxation. The levels of future taxation, let alone the tax thresholds and tax allowances, cannot be predicted with any certainty. Higher rates of tax may or may not be applicable to the receipts of the notional annuity. In my view one can only take a broad approach to this problem and proceed upon an allowance which embodies an appropriate modification of the ordinary level of tax. Of course in particular cases where the incidence of income tax can be shown to be out of the normal range for one reason or another an appropriate adjustment may be made. The calculation cannot be exact and some rounding off should be acceptable.

In principle I agree with your Lordships that the Court of Appeal erred in preferring what has come to be seen as the usual rate of 4·5% based on the equity market. Two questions arise. One is what rate should be adopted at least for the immediate future, pending a reconsideration of the problem by the Lord Chancellor. In that regard there are clear advantages in the recognition of a single formula which can be universally adopted for the calculation of recurring losses and expenses over any future tract of time. While simplicity may carry with it the risk of imprecision, that risk should be offset by the advantage of saving the time and expense which might otherwise be spent in the necessity for elaborate inquiry with expert witnesses. A conventional formula may seem artificial but now that detailed calculations and tables founded on reasonably reliable bases are available full advantage ought to be taken of them. The certainty of the result should produce economies in achieving agreement and settlement which should outweigh any rough edges of imprecision. Of course such a formula should not be seen as set in stone. It can serve as a general guide, open to modification and adjustment to meet the demands of particular cases. I would favour a rate at the present time of 3% net. More than one route was presented to us which could justify that result but the one which particularly commended itself to me was a calculation of the average rate on index-linked government stock over the past three years net of tax.

The other question is whether in the three particular cases before us the rates adopted by the judges who heard them should be accepted. In my view the material before them in each of the three cases was sufficient to support the rate of 3% which still seems to me appropriate today. I would accordingly agree with the calculations in *Page v Sheerness Steel Co plc* and *Thomas v Brighton Health Authority*. So far as *Wells v Wells* is concerned, I consider that the judge made too generous an allowance for tax and that the deduction from the gross rate which he took should be reduced so as to round off the rate also at 3%. The damages will require to be recalculated to allow for that correction.

It can be inferred from the result which the evidence in the present appeals has produced that in the past awards in respect of future losses and expenses may well have been unduly low. The figures brought out in the present cases may seem high in comparison but they seek to represent a fair compensation for the particular heads of claim to which they relate and underline the severity of the consequences which may be caused to the future lives of particular individuals who have suffered loss and expense as a consequence of negligent conduct.

On the particular points which were raised in relation to the claims I agree entirely with the views expressed by my noble and learned friend Lord Lloyd of Berwick. The appeals should in my view be allowed and the cases remitted for the necessary adjustment of the awards.

Lord Hutton

My Lords, in these three cases each plaintiff sustained very grave injuries by reason of the negligence of the respective defendants. The fundamental principle which governs the assessment of the damages to which each plaintiff is entitled is that an injured plaintiff should recover full compensation. In *Admiralty Comrs v Valeria (owners)* [1922] 2 AC 242 at 248, [1922] All ER Rep 463 at 465 Lord Dunedin stated:

> 'The true method of expression I think is that in calculating damages you are to consider what is the pecuniary sum which will make good to the

> sufferer, so far as money can do so, the loss which he has suffered as the natural result of the wrong done to him.'

The injuries caused to the plaintiffs have left each of them so gravely and permanently incapacitated that they will require constant nursing care for the remainder of their lives and they are entitled to compensation for the future costs of such care. James Thomas sustained his injuries at the time of his birth and was aged six at the time of the trial. Mr Page was aged 24 at the time of the accident at work that injured him and was aged 28 at the time of trial. Therefore, in addition to receiving compensation for the cost of future nursing care, James and Mr Page were also entitled to recover compensation for the wages or salary which they would have earned for many years in the future if their earning capacity had not been taken away by their injuries. At the time of the road accident in which she sustained her injuries, Mrs Wells was aged almost 58. She was therefore close to retirement from her work as a nurse and it was agreed between the parties that she had a working life of 2.5 years from the date of the trial.

Under our present system of law the compensation to which each plaintiff is entitled must, unless the parties agree otherwise, be paid in a lump sum and there is no power for the courts to award periodical payments. Therefore each plaintiff must receive a lump sum to provide compensation for the annual cost of lifetime nursing care and for the loss of future earning capacity. The method adopted by the courts to calculate such compensation was described by Lord Oliver of Aylmerton in *Hodgson v Trapp* [1988] 3 All ER 870 at 879, [1989] AC 807 at 826:

> 'Essentially what the court has to do is to calculate as best it can the sum of money which will on the one hand be adequate, by its capital and income, to provide annually for the injured person a sum equal to his estimated annual loss over the whole of the period during which that loss is likely to continue, but which, on the other hand, will not, at the end of that period, leave him in a better financial position than he would have been apart from the accident. Hence the conventional approach is to assess the amount notionally required to be laid out in the purchase of an annuity which will provide the annual amount needed for the whole period of loss.'

The multiplier which the courts apply to the annual cost of nursing care and the annual loss of earning capacity to produce the lump sum of compensation is determined by reference to the respective periods in the future for which the cost will be incurred and the loss will be sustained, but discounted to allow for the immediate receipt of the lump sum rather than the receipt of periodical payments over a number of years. The discount is assessed by reference to the assumed rate of return on the lump sum when invested, so that the higher the rate of interest assumed the smaller the multiplier.

Two principal questions have been debated in this appeal. One question is whether allowance should be made for future inflation to take account of the fact that in future years the cost of nursing care will rise and that the earnings of the plaintiff would have increased. The other question relates to the rate of interest which the courts should assume the capital sum awarded will earn in order to arrive at the multiplier.

In judgments given in this House in the decade between 1970 and 1980 it was held that the courts should not make allowance for inflation in the assessment of future loss. In the last of these cases, *Lim Poh Choo v Camden and Islington Area Health Authority* [1979] 2 All ER 910 at 923, [1980] AC 174 at 193, in a speech in which the other members of the House concurred, Lord Scarman said:

> 'The law appears to me to be now settled that only in exceptional cases, where justice can be shown to require it, will the risk of future inflation be brought into account in the assessment of damages for future loss.'

But it is important to recognise that this approach was not based on the view that the risk of inflation should be ignored. In *Taylor v O'Connor* [1970] 1 All ER 365 at 368, [1971] AC 115 at 130, referring to future inflation, Lord Reid said: '... it would, I think, be quite unrealistic to refuse to take it into account at all.' The approach that allowance should not be made for inflation in assessing future loss was based on the view that prudent investment of the capital sum awarded would protect the plaintiff against the effects of inflation. In *Taylor v O'Connor* [1970] 1 All ER 365 at 378–379, [1971] AC 115 at 142–143 Lord Pearson said:

> 'Certainly it is right to have regard to the prospect of continuing inflation as an important factor in the situation, but I do not think a mere increase in the multiplier is a suitable method for protecting against inflation, although it achieves something. I think protection against inflation is to be sought by investment policy, and that the lump sum of damages should be assessed on the basis that it will be invested with the aim of obtaining some capital appreciation to offset the probable rise in the cost of living.'

And in *Cookson v Knowles* [1978] 2 All ER 604 at 611, [1979] AC 556 at 571–572 Lord Diplock said:

> 'Inflation is taken care of in a rough and ready way by the higher rates of interest obtainable as one of the consequences of it and no other practical basis of calculation has been suggested that is capable of dealing with so conjectural a factor with greater precision.'

(See also [1978] 2 All ER 604 at 615, [1979] AC 556 at 577 per Lord Fraser of Tullybelton.)

The principal submission advanced in this appeal on behalf of the appellants is that the issue for the first time in 1981 by the government of index-linked government securities (ILGS) has changed the economic background against which the courts assess damages for future loss. If a plaintiff invests the damages awarded to him in ILGS the interest paid to him each year will rise in accordance with the retail price index as will the payment made on maturity. Therefore the appellants contend that the court should now fix the multiplier by reference to the net return of about 3% per annum on ILGS rather than by following the conventional approach of taking a multiplier by reference to a net return of 4 to 5% per annum from a mixed basket of equities and gilts. Such an approach has the consequence, as shown in the present cases, of increasing the multiplier with a resultant very large increase in the damages.

The plaintiffs advanced two principal arguments in support of their submission. The first is that fixing the multiplier by reference to the return on ILGS ensures with much greater precision that over the years ahead the plaintiff will receive the annual sum which he requires to pay for nursing costs and to compensate him for the wages which he would have received. The second submission is that an assessment of damages based on the return on ILGS protects the plaintiff against the risks inherent in investment in equities, such risks being much greater than the risks in investing in ILGS. These arguments on behalf of the plaintiffs mirror the arguments succinctly stated in the introduction to the 1984 Report, *Advarial Tables with explanatory notes for use in Personal Injury and Fatal Accident cases* of the working party chaired by Sir Michael Ogden QC at p 8:

> 'The working party concluded that the following arguments could not be faulted. The courts seek to put the wage-earner, or, if he has been killed, his dependant, into the same financial position as if the accident had not happened. Investment policy, however prudent, involves risks and it is not difficult to draw up a list of blue chip equities or reliable unit trusts which have performed poorly and, in some cases, disastrously. Index-linked government stocks eliminate the risk. Whereas, in the past, a plaintiff has had to speculate in the form of prudent investment by buying equities, or a "basket" of equities and gilts or a selection of unit trusts, he need speculate no longer if he buys index-linked government stock. If the loss is, say, £5,000 per annum, he can be awarded damages which, if invested in such stocks, will provide him with almost exactly that sum in real terms.'

These arguments were accepted by the judges in the High Court who tried the respective actions, and in *Page v Sheerness Steel Co plc* [1996] PIQR Q26 at Q36 Dyson J stated:

> 'In summary therefore, the advantages of calculating the discount rate on the basis of the ILGS are that inflation is taken care of precisely and not in a rough and ready way, and the net return is the actual net return on investments rather than a net return that it is assumed by the court is enjoyed on notional prudent investments made at a time of stable currency.'

The approach adopted by this House in *Lim Poh Choo v Camden and Islington Area Health Authority* [1979] 2 All ER 910, [1980] AC 174 and the cases preceding it was influenced to a large extent by the recognition that at those times, when ILGS did not exist, there was no way in which a court could, with accuracy, estimate the rate of inflation in future years and make an assessment of the allowance which should be made for it in the assessment of damages. In *Cookson v Knowles* [1978] 2 All ER 604 at 611, [1979] AC 556 at 571–572, after stating that: 'Inflation is taken care of in a rough and ready way by the higher rates of interest obtainable as one of the consequences of it', Lord Diplock concluded that statement by saying 'and no other practical basis of calculation has been suggested that is capable of dealing with so conjectural a factor with greater precision'. And in *Lim*'s case [1979] 2 All ER 910 at 923, [1980] AC 174 at 193 Lord Scarman said:

> 'An attempt to build into [lump sum compensation] a protection against future inflation is seeking after a perfection which is beyond the inherent limitations of the system.'

Moreover the speeches in those cases made it clear that the House was not laying down that allowance should not be made for inflation as a principle of law which would continue to govern cases for all time. In *Cookson v Knowles* [1978] 2 All ER 604 at 613, [1979] AC 556 at 574 Lord Salmon stated:

> 'There is one matter that I should like to emphasise, namely that in my view it is impossible to lay down any principles of law which will govern the assessment of damages for all time. We can only lay down broad guidelines for assessing damages in cases where the facts are similar to those of the instant case and where economic factors remain similar to those now prevailing.'

And in *Lim*'s case [1979] 2 All ER 910 at 923, [1980] AC 174 at 193, after stating that the law appeared to be settled that, save in exceptional cases, the risk of inflation should not be brought into account in the assessment of damages for future loss, Lord Scarman said: 'It is perhaps incorrect to call this rule a rule of law. It is better described as a sensible rule of practice, a matter of common sense.'

Therefore, in the changed circumstances where damages can now be invested in ILGS which will protect against future inflation, I consider that it is open to this House to consider whether the approach adopted in earlier cases should now be changed and the multiplier should be fixed by reference to the return on ILGS.

The argument now advanced on behalf of the plaintiffs is, in essence, the same as the argument succinctly stated in *Structural Settlements and Interim and Provisional Damages* (Law Com No 224) (1994) para 2.28:

> 'We share the views of the majority of those who responded to us, that a practice of discounting by reference to returns on ILGS would be preferable to the present arbitrary presumption. The 4–5% discount which emerged from the case law was established at a time when ILGS did not exist. ILGS now constitute the best evidence of the real return on any investment where the risk element is minimal, because they take account of inflation, rather than attempt to predict it as conventional investments do. Capital is redeemed under ILGS at par and index-linked to the change in the retail price index (RPI) since issue. Income remains constant in real terms, rising with increases in the RPI. There is no premium available for risk because there is no risk.'

This is a powerful argument, and I turn to consider the submissions advanced against it by the defendants.

One of those submissions is that in assessing damages, the court should assume that the plaintiff will invest the damages prudently and that, when he receives a large sum, the plaintiff will take competent investment advice and that advice will be that it would be prudent to invest in a mixed basket of equities and gilts. Closely linked to this submission is the further submission that the court must hold a fair balance between the plaintiff and the defendant, and that the plaintiff is entitled to no better protection against inflation than others who have to rely on capital for future support and who seek to protect themselves against inflation by investing in equities.

These submissions were accepted by the Court of Appeal and were the grounds on which the appeals of the defendants were allowed (see [1997] 1 All ER 673 at 694–695 and 696, [1997] 1 WLR 652 at 675 and 677). Support for these submissions and for the grounds of the Court of Appeal's decision is to be found in the speech of Lord Scarman in *Lim Poh Choo v Camden and Islington Area Health Authority* [1979] 2 All ER 910 at 923, [1980] AC 174 at 193–194 (cited by the Court of Appeal [1997] 1 All ER 673 at 681–682, [1997] 1 WLR 652 at 661–662), where he said:

> '... as Lord Pearson said in *Taylor v O'Connor* [1970] 1 All ER 365 at 378, [1971] AC 115 at 143, inflation is best left to be dealt with by investment policy. It is not unrealistic in modern social conditions, nor is it unjust, to assume that the recipient of a large capital sum by way of damages will take advice as to its investment and use. Thirdly, it is inherent in a system of compensation by way of a lump sum immediately payable, and, I would think, just, that the sum be calculated at current money values, leaving the recipient in the same position as others, who have to rely on capital for their support to face the future ... the victims of tort who receive a lump sum award are entitled to no better protection against inflation than others who have to rely on capital for their future support. To attempt such protection would be to put them into a privileged position at the expense of the tortfeasor, and so to impose on him an excessive burden, which might go far beyond compensation for loss.'

My Lords, I consider that the introduction of ILGS providing an income which is protected against inflation has changed the problem which Lord Scarman was addressing in *Lim*'s case and that the passages from his judgment cited above should not prevent your Lordships from holding that it is now appropriate to make allowance for the risk of future inflation by fixing the multiplier by reference to the rate of return on ILGS. I think the reality is that the plaintiffs in the present cases are not in the same position as other persons who have to rely on capital for future support. Unlike the great majority of persons who invest their capital, it is vital for the plaintiffs that they receive constant and costly nursing care for the remainder of their lives and that they should be able to pay for it, and any fall in income or depreciation in the capital value of their investments will affect them much more severely than persons in better health who depend on their investments for support. Moreover, a plaintiff who claims damages for loss of future earnings should, in my opinion, not be placed in the same position as a person who relies on capital for his future support. Such a plaintiff, but for the injuries which have taken away his earning capacity, would have been better protected against inflation by the rise in his wages in future years than the person who has to rely on a sound investment policy to protect him in the years ahead. In *Livingstone v Rawyards Coal Co* (1880) 5 App Cas 25 at 39 Lord Blackburn stated:

'... where any injury is to be compensated by damages, in settling the sum of money to be given for reparation of damages you should as nearly as possible get at that sum of money which will put the party who has been injured, or who has suffered, in the same position as he would have been in if he had not sustained the wrong for which he is now getting his compensation or reparation.'

I consider that an award assessed by reference to the index-linked return on ILGS will give protection against inflation closer to the protection which would have been given by the rise in the plaintiff's wages, and will give better effect to the principle stated by Lord Blackburn, than will an award assessed by reference to the return on equities.

Moreover I think that a plaintiff, as gravely injured as these plaintiffs, who seeks advice as to the investment of his damages is entitled to receive guidance as to the degree of risk involved in investing in ILGS as compared to investing in equities, and having regard to the necessity of ensuring that income and capital will always be available to pay for his nursing costs, I consider that a plaintiff who decides to invest his damages in ILGS by reason of the reduced risk could not be said to be investing in a manner which was imprudent or unreasonable.

On behalf of the first and third defendants it was also submitted that there should not be a departure from the conventional approach to the multiplier based on an assumed return of 4 to 5% per annum because a plaintiff is under a duty to act reasonably and to mitigate his loss. This duty extended to prudent investment of his damages, and prudent investment required an investment in a mixed basket of equities and gilts. I have already given my reasons for not accepting the submission that it is imprudent for a gravely injured plaintiff to invest in ILGS to ensure the payment for future nursing care. I further consider that the concept of mitigation of damages does not apply to the investment of the damages after they have been awarded by the court. The duty to mitigate applies at an earlier stage in the process when the trial judge assesses what the damage suffered by the plaintiff has been and whether the plaintiff could reasonably have reduced the extent of his damage. But once the judge has assessed the damage his duty is to award full compensation. In the present cases there is nothing that the plaintiffs could do to reduce the extent of the nursing care that they will require in the future or to reduce the amount of the loss they will suffer from the extinction of their future earning capacity.

The defendants further relied on the point that the Court of Protection had not followed the policy of investing in ILGS and that its approach had been to invest in a portfolio comprising a substantial proportion of equities. But I consider that this point is of little weight because the investment of damages in the past by the Court of Protection has been made on the basis of the courts assuming a rate of 4 to 5% and what the Court of Protection may do in the future is uncertain. I also consider that there is little weight in the argument that ILGS may not be available for the full period during which a plaintiff must receive an income. I think it is most unlikely that ILGS will not continue to be issued. Accordingly I have reached the conclusion that under the present principles which govern the assessment of compensation and having regard to the availability of ILGS, the plaintiffs are entitled to compensation assessed by taking a discount rate based on the return on ILGS. The return on ILGS fluctuates but the schedules of the month end returns during the past three years show a net average return of about 3%. Therefore I consider that this rate should be adopted as the rate to arrive at the multiplier in the present cases in place of the conventional discount rate of 4·5% applied by the Court of Appeal.

Accordingly I would uphold the judgments of Dyson and Collins JJ in *Page v Sheerness Steel Co plc* and *Thomas v Brighton Health Authority* in taking a discount rate of 3%. In *Wells v Wells*, where it appears that Judge Wilcox took a discount rate of about 2·5%, I would alter the discount rate to 3%.

I further consider that in order to promote and facilitate settlements and to simplify the assessment of damages in actions which come on for trial the rate of 3% taken by this House in the present appeals should be applied in other cases notwithstanding fluctuations in the return on ILGS until the Lord Chancellor prescribes a different rate pursuant to his power under s 1 of the Damages Act 1996 or unless there is a very considerable change in economic circumstances. There is support for this course in the judgment of the High Court of Australia in *Todovoric v Waller* (1981) 150 CLR 402 at 423–424, where Gibbs CJ and Wilson J stated:

> 'In strictness perhaps this court should not declare the rate at which discounts should be effected, but should leave that to the discretion of the courts of trial, as was done in *Hawkins v Lindsley* (1974) 49 ALJR 5. However, it is most desirable that awards of damages should be predictable, so that settlements may be facilitated, and the task of the courts eased. Moreover, while general economic circumstances remain as they are, there is no compelling reason why one judge should select a discount rate different from that selected by another. In the interest of securing uniformity throughout Australia this court should therefore do what it has held that a Supreme Court of one state may not do, and that is to make an arbitrary ruling regarding interest rates of general application. We consider that in future the courts in Australia, in states where the question is not governed by statute, should, in assessing damages, arrive at the present value of a future loss by discounting at a fixed rate which will be applied in all cases and which will in itself reflect the effect of notional tax on notional income from the invested fund.'

I would make no alteration in the discount rate for higher rates of tax save that, as Lord Oliver of Aylmerton stated in *Hodgson v Trapp* [1988] 3 All ER 870 at 885, [1989] AC 807 at 835, it would be open to plaintiffs in very exceptional cases to contend that a higher multiplier should be taken.

The consequence of the present judgments of this House will be a very substantial rise in the level of awards to plaintiffs who by reason of the negligence of others sustain very grave injuries requiring nursing care in future years and causing a loss of future earning capacity, and there will be resultant increases in insurance premiums. But under the present principles of law governing the assessment of damages which provide that injured persons should receive full compensation plaintiffs are entitled to such increased awards. If the law is to be changed it can only be done by Parliament which, unlike the judges, is in a position to balance the many social, financial and economic factors which would have to be considered if such a change were contemplated.

In respect of the other individual points arising in the three cases I am in agreement with the speech of my noble and learned friend Lord Lloyd of Berwick, which I have had the advantage of reading in draft.

Appeals allowed.

Celia Fox
Barrister

3 The Ogden Tables (third edition)

Government Actuary's Department

Actuarial Tables

With explanatory notes
for use in

Personal Injury and Fatal Accident cases

Third edition

Her Majesty's Stationery Office

MEMBERS OF THE WORKING PARTY RESPONSIBLE FOR THE THIRD EDITION

Chairman: Sir Michael Ogden QC

Chris Daykin, CB, FIA	The Government Actuary
Ray Sams	Lord Chancellor's Department
Professor Burrows	The Law Commission
Harvey McGregor QC	Invited by the Chairman
John Crowley QC	Invited by the Chairman
Ashton West ACII, Chartered Insurer	Association of British Insurers
Alistair Kinley	Association of British Insurers
Dr Harry Reid, FIA	Association of British Insurers
Mrs Caroline Harmer, Barrister	Association of Personal Injuries Lawyers
Allan C Martin, FFA	Faculty of Actuaries and Institute of Actuaries
Mrs Ann Paton QC	Faculty of Advocates
Nicholas Mostyn QC	Family Law Bar Association
Tim Lawrence, FCA	Family Law Bar Association
Humphrey Morison, FCA	Family Law Bar Association
Tim Sexton, FIA	Family Law Bar Association
Martin Brufell, Solicitor	Forum of Insurance Lawyers
Graeme Garrett, Solicitor	Law Society of Scotland
Matthias Kelly, Barrister	Personal Injuries Bar Association
Andrew Dismore, MP	Association of Personal Injury Lawyers
Graham Codd	Association of Personal Injury Lawyers
John Home, BCL, Barrister (Secretary to the Working Party)	The General Council of the Bar

Government Actuary's Department

Actuarial Tables

With explanatory notes
for use in

Personal Injury and Fatal Accident cases

Prepared by an
Inter-disciplinary Working Party
of Actuaries, Lawyers, Accountants
and other interested parties

Third edition

LONDON: Her Majesty's Stationery Office

First published 1984

Second edition 1994

Third edition 1998

ISBN 0 11 702318 3

Printed in the United Kingdom for The Stationery Office Limited under the authority and superintendence of the Controller of Her Majesty's Stationery Office and the Queen's Printer of Acts of Parliament.
J51604 6/98 C20

Table of contents

* In this book.

Introduction to the third edition

This new edition of the tables has been prompted by the publication of English Life Tables No 15. The increased longevity shown in ELT 15 has resulted in changes to the tables published in the second edition.

It will also be seen that opportunity has been taken to make other significant changes and improvements, including the provision of tables which make appropriate prudent allowance for future improvements in mortality. where appropriate the tables have been extended to ages below 16 and above 70. Relevant tables have also been included for terms certain.

Once the Lord Chancellor has been able to consider the speeches in the House of Lords in *Wells v Wells* which is due to be heard in May, it is anticipated that Commencement Orders will be made bringing into force the Civil Evidence Act 1995 Section 10 and the Damages Act 1996 Section 1, which latter provision is likely to result in the Lord Chancellor fixing the rate of return. Consequently, this edition makes no reference in the main text to the choice of the rate of return, since the Court of Appeal in *Wells* decided that the appropriate rate is 4.5%. However, material relating thereto published in the Second Edition is to be found in Appendix B so that it will be available if the House of Lords takes a view different from that taken by the Court of Appeal.

After the Lord Chancellor has fixed the rate of return, a fourth edition of the tables will almost certainly be necessary to take account of that and what is said in the House of Lords in *Wells*. Happily, since pursuant to the Civil Evidence Act, the Government Actuary will become responsible for the tables, a fourth edition will be his responsibility, thereby releasing me from the task of being Chairman of the working party, which I was asked to undertake 15 years ago.

SIR MICHAEL OGDEN QC
May 1998

Introduction to the second edition

The principal reason for this edition is that it is now possible to give assistance about contingencies other than mortality. Tables A, A(60) and A(F)* together with explanatory notes, in which those tables are set out, show how these contingencies can be taken into account.

In addition, four further tables have been added so that figures for men and women whose retirement ages are 60 and 65 are now available.

The six original tables have been revised in the light of changes in life expectancy. All 10 tables are based on English Life Tables No 14.

It is intended to revise the tables when new Life Tables are published.

In Scotland in *O'Brien's Curator Bonis v British Steel plc* [1991] SLT 477 the Inner Rouse concluded that the tables can be used as a check on a multiplier arrived at by the conventional method. There has been no decision in the English Court of Appeal concerning use of the tables, however; they are now widely used by Judges at first instance. The Law Commission's Consultation Paper No 125 'Structured Settlements and Interim and Provisional Damages' states that, subject to the view of consultees, the Commission believes that the time has come to encourage the general use of the tables by legislation.

The Working Party is greatly indebted to Professor S Haberman and Mrs D S F Bloomfield who undertook much of the work which has enabled the Working Party to provide the new information contained in this edition.

SIR MICHAEL OGDEN
November 1993

* *In the third edition these tables have been relabelled as Tables A, B and C.*

Introduction to the first edition

Proposals have been made from time to time that actuarial tables might be produced to assist in assessing damages in cases of personal injuries and fatal accidents, for example, by the Law Commission (Law Com No 56, 1973) and by the former Solicitor-General during the passage of the Administration of Justice Act 1982. Both branches of the legal profession in Great Britain have recently co-operated with the Faculty of Actuaries and the Institute of Actuaries to produce the following tables and notes. The tables have been prepared by the Government Actuary's Department and the explanatory notes by actuaries and lawyers nominated by all their professional bodies in Great Britain. I am particularly grateful to the actuaries for having nominated representatives of the highest calibre including a former President of the Institute and the Government Actuary.

The Lord Chancellor, Lord Hailsham of St Marylebone. was informed in advance of the proposal that the actuarial and legal professions should co-operate in the production of such tables and agreed that it would be helpful if this avenue of co-operation between the professions could be explored. Of course, it must be understood that the tables have not been prepared under his direction nor published with his authority.

The purpose of the tables is to help the Courts in determining upon the appropriate figure for what lawyers describe as the 'multiplier'.

It must be emphasised that the tables do not take account of contingencies other than mortality. Consequently the Court will need to adjust the multiplier contained in the tables to take account of other factors.

Notwithstanding the need to adjust the multipliers contained in the tables. the size of some of the figures in the tables will undoubtedly come as a surprise to lawyers. However, the members of the Working Party unanimously concluded that the reasoning which leads to such figures could not be faulted. As will be seen, the existence of a new type of Government stock played a significant part in our reasoning.

The present position

The Courts seek, by the award of a lump sum, to put the wage earner or, if he has been killed, his dependant into the same financial position as if the accident had not happened. It is up to the Plaintiff to invest that lump sum as best he can to replace the income lost for which he is being compensated. The Courts have decided that, in the majority of cases, inflation is to be disregarded when assessing damages, one reason being that inflation is best left to be dealt with by prudent investment policy (see *Lim v Camden Health Authority*' [1980] AC 174 and cases cited therein). The Courts have taken the view that investment of the lump sum award in ordinary shares or a 'basket' of equities and gilts would enable the Plaintiff to have an income derived from dividends and sales of shares which would broadly match the income he had lost; inflation would increase the dividends and market prices at which he would gradually be able to realise his holdings over the years to which the loss relates. Such presumed matching is of necessity imprecise and there is an unavoidable risk of injustice to the Plaintiff or the Defendant.

Index-Linked Government Stock

Currently, the Courts are using multipliers which implicitly assume a discount rate of between 4% and 5% (*Lim v Camden*). This rate compares with the rate of about 5% currently obtainable on a spread of ordinary shares if no allowance is made for the effects of future inflation or for the relative future prosperity or adversity of the companies which issued those shares. However, the issue of Index-Linked Government Stock since 1981 has now made it possible to match the receipts from the investment of a lump sum almost precisely to the income loss for which the Plaintiff is being compensated. Such stocks are now an established part of the investment market. The nature of these stocks is such that the dividends rise in accordance with the rise in the Retail Price Index as does the payment on maturity.

A Plaintiff who has purchased ordinary shares or a basket of gilts and equities will receive interest and prices on sale which reflect market forces. In particular, market forces reflect views about anticipated inflation and, in the case of ordinary shares, views of the future prosperity of the particular company relative to other companies. As a result, particularly in the case of ordinary shares, the market price can alter considerably and very rapidly.

A Plaintiff who has bought Index-Linked Government Stock is in a very different position. The future payments under the stock reflect price inflation almost exactly and there is no question of the Government failing to make the stipulated payments. The market value of such stocks represents the value of the future stipulated payments of interest and capital (ignoring the effects of future inflation thereon) discounted at a rate usually lying in the bracket $2\frac{1}{2}\%$ to $3\frac{1}{2}\%$ per annum. It is within that bracket that the yield on index-linked stocks has generally lain since their introduction to the market. Therefore, it is possible to provide a Plaintiff with such index-linked stocks on which the sums received as interest and payments received on maturity and sale would almost exactly replace the income lost by the Plaintiff in respect of which he is being compensated over the period to which the loss relates.

It is because the effect of inflation, on capital and income alike, is taken into account in the case of Index-Linked Government Stocks that the yield upon such stocks is lower and their capital value more stable than in the case of non-index-linked-stocks. Whereas, in general, interest rates reflect expectations as to inflation based on past and existing inflation, and the fear of its continuance, the yield upon index-linked stocks is simply a measure of the real return which the market expects upon invested capital which is assumed to keep its value in real terms.

Obviously, if the Courts cease using multipliers which assume a discount rate of between 4% and 5% and use multipliers based upon the assumption that funds are to be invested in index-linked stocks discounted at a rate of between 2½% and 3½%, it is inevitable that the size of the multipliers will increase. The conversion of prospective income which has been lost to the Plaintiff into a capital sum of equivalent value would accordingly be by means of a multiplier which embodies a discount rate in the range 2½% to 3½% and also allows for the effects of mortality. That is in the first instance; the Courts will need to make such adjustments as are necessary, for example to reflect the possibility that receipt of the lost income was not certain (as a result of ill health, redundancy, early retirement etc.), or that the income might have increased otherwise than as a result of inflation (because of promotion etc.), or that the Plaintiff's chances of survival to draw the lost income are not properly represented by the mortality rates of which the multiplier takes account.

Our reasoning

The Working Party concluded that the following arguments could not be faulted. The Courts seek to put the wage earner or, if he has been killed, his dependant, into the same financial position as if the accident had not happened. Investment policy, however prudent, involves risks and it is not difficult to draw up a list of blue chip equities or reliable unit trusts which have performed poorly and, in some cases, disastrously. Index-Linked Government Stocks eliminate the risk. Whereas, in the past, a Plaintiff has had to speculate in the form of prudent investment by buying equities, or a 'basket' of equities and gilts or a selection of unit trusts, he need speculate no longer if he buys Index-Linked Government Stock. If the loss is, say, £5,000 per annum, he can be awarded damages which, if invested in such stocks, will provide him with almost exactly that sum in real terms.

It may be said that, in practice, the Plaintiff, having been awarded damages on the basis of assumed investment in Index-Linked Government Stocks, may invest in equities. However, the Working Party concluded that it is difficult to argue that any Plaintiff should be obliged to speculate if he does not wish to do so, when there exists an investment which enables him to avoid doing so. In any event, a Plaintiff. has been able to do the equivalent in the past in that he may not buy a prudent basket of equities or other investments. damages having been awarded on that basis, but may invest the entire sum in a single venture, for example a small shop. Alternatively, a Plaintiff may invest in a very speculative and imprudent investment or in something such as Krugerrands. For these reasons, the Working Party concluded that the fairest approach to the problem is to work on the basis of multipliers calculated upon the basis of presumed investment in Index-Linked Government Stock.

Since reaching this conclusion, the Working Party has read with great interest the speech of Lord Diplock in *Wright v British Railways Board* [1983] 2 All ER 698 on the subject of Index-Linked Government Stock.

The Tables†

The Tables take account of ordinary mortality risks. They are based upon the assumption that a capital sum will be awarded and that this sum will be exhausted at the end of the period during which the loss will occur.

The tables contain multipliers to be applied to figures of income after deduction of tax. If tax will be payable on the income derived from investing the award, the multiplier which is otherwise appropriate will need adjusting as described in the explanatory notes.

The tables take no account of risks other than mortality. For example, permanent ill health leading to loss of employment, whether due to accident or illness, is something to which any apparently healthy person is to some extent at risk, but which is not reflected in the tables. Of course the tables do not take account of factors such as loss of employment due to redundancy, early retirement, etc.

It will be seen that the tables cover rates between 1½% and 5%. This has been done in case the Courts do not accept the Working Party's view that the fairest solution is to use tables based on Index-Linked Government Stocks.

I am grateful for the assistance given by members of the stock-broking firm of Grieveson, Grant & Co.

MICHAEL OGDEN

† *What is said under this heading must now be read subject to what is included in the later editions.*

Explanatory notes

SECTION A: GENERAL

Purpose of tables

1. The tables have been prepared by the Government Actuary's Department. They provide an aid for those assessing the lump sum appropriate as compensation for a continuing future pecuniary loss or consequential expense in personal injury and fatal accident cases.

Application of tables

2. The tables set out multipliers. These multipliers enable the user to assess the present capital value of future annual loss (net of tax) or annual expense calculated on the basis of various assumptions which are explained below. Accordingly, to find the present capital value of a given annual loss or expense, it is necessary to select the appropriate table, find the appropriate multiplier and then multiply the amount of the annual loss or expense by that figure.

3. Tables 1 to 20 deal with annual loss or annual expense extending over three-different periods of time. In each case there are separate tables for men and women.

- In Tables 1, 2, 11 and 12 the loss or expense is assumed to begin immediately and to continue for the whole of the rest of the Plaintiff's life, allowing for the possibility of early death or prolonged life. ('The Plaintiff' here includes the deceased in fatal accident cases.)
- In Tables 3 to 6 and 13 to 16 the loss or expense is assumed to begin immediately but to continue only until the Plaintiff's retirement or earlier death. The age of retirement is assumed to be 65 in Tables 3 and 4 (and 13 and 14) and 60 in Tables 5 and 6 (and 15 and 16).
- In Tables 7 to 10 and 17 to 20 it is assumed that the annual loss or annual expense will not begin until the Plaintiff reaches retirement but will then continue for the whole of the rest of his or her life.

4. In Tables 7 and 17 (males) and Tables 8 and 18 (females) the age of retirement is assumed to be 65. In Tables 9 and 19 (males) and Tables 10 and 20 (females) the age of retirement is assumed to be 60. The tables make due allowance for the chance that the Plaintiff may not live to reach the age of retirement.

Mortality assumptions for Tables 1 to 10

5. As in previous editions of these tables, Tables 1 to 10 are based on the mortality rates experienced in England & Wales in a three-year period, in

this case the years 1990 to 1992, and published by the Government Actuary's Department as English Life Tables No 15 (ELT 15). Given this assumption about mortality, the accuracy of these tables, which were prepared by the Government Actuary's Department, has been accepted by all the actuaries on the Working Party, which included actuaries nominated by the Institute and the Faculty of Actuaries, the Association of British Insurers ('ABI') and the Family Law Bar Association. Consequently, the Courts can have confidence in the mathematical accuracy of these tables. Members of the Working Party nominated by the ABI have reservations about the application of the Tables and other matters and these are set out in Appendix C.

6. On the basis of some reported cases, it appears that tables for pecuniary loss for life, eg cost of care, may have been misunderstood. As stated hereafter in Paragraph 21, the tables take account of the possibilities that the Plaintiff will live for different periods, eg die soon or live to be very old. The mortality assumptions relate to the general population of England and Wales. Unless there is clear evidence in an individual case to support the view that the individual is atypical and will enjoy longer or shorter than average life no further increase or reduction is required for mortality alone.

Tables adjusted to take account of projected mortality (Tables 11 to 20)

7. The actuaries on the Working Party consider that failure to have regard to reasonable projected improvements in mortality rates will result in Plaintiffs receiving awards of damages which are lower than they should be. At Appendix A is an extract from ELT 15 which shows graphs indicating rates of mortality expressed in percentages of 1911 rates on a logarithmic scale. They demonstrate in a stark fashion the improvement in longevity which has taken place since 1911. The sole exception is a small increase recently in the mortality of males in their late twenties and early thirties due to AIDS and increasing numbers of suicides, the same effect being present, but to a lesser degree, for females. Even if this slight worsening of mortality at these ages were to continue, the effect on the tables of multipliers would not be significant. (For comments by the ABI see Appendix C.)

8. The graphs, and the figures on which they are based, point to the conclusion that, on the balance of probabilities, the mortality rates which will actually be experienced in future by those who are alive today will be lower than in ELT 15, and increasingly so the further into the future one goes. This, of course, would imply the need for higher multipliers. For the purposes of preparing the official national population projections, the Government Actuary makes a considered estimate of the extent of future improvements in mortality. Tables 11 to 20 show the multipliers which result from the application of these projected mortality rates. The actuaries on the Working Party (save for the dissenting views expressed at Appendix C) consider that these alternative tables may provide a more

appropriate estimate of the value of future income streams than Tables 1 to 10, which are based on historic mortality and almost certainly underestimate future longevity of the population as a whole. The Working Party therefore recommends the Courts to use Tables 11 to 20 rather than Tables 1 to 10.

Use of tables

9. To find the appropriate figure for the present value of a particular loss or expense the user must first choose that table which relates to the period of loss or expense for which the individual Plaintiff is to be compensated and to the sex of the Plaintiff.

10. If for some reason the facts in a particular case do not correspond with the assumptions on which one of the tables is based, (if, for instance it is known that the Plaintiff will have a different retiring age from that assumed in the tables) then the tables can only be used by making an appropriate allowance for this difference; for this purpose the assistance of an actuary should be sought.

Rate of return

11. The basis of the multipliers set out in the tables is that the lump sum will be invested and yield income (but that over the period in question the Plaintiff will gradually reduce the capital sum so that at the end of the period it is exhausted). Accordingly, an essential factor in arriving at the right figure is to choose the appropriate rate of return. The tables set out multipliers based on rates of return ranging from $1\frac{1}{2}\%$ to 5%, as in previous editions.

12. Currently, the rate of return to be applied is 4.5% (Wells v Wells [1997] 1 WLR 652). (NB this differs from the figures stated in *Hodgson v Trapp* [1989] AC 807, namely 4% to 5%, which allowed a degree of flexibility according to the prevailing economic circumstances). After a Commencement Order has been made in respect of the Damages Act 1996 Section 1, the rate or rates of return are likely to be specified by the Lord Chancellor after receiving advice from the Government Actuary and the Treasury. Should it become necessary, further tables will be issued.

13. Previous editions of these tables explained how the current yields on index-linked government bonds could be used as an indicator of the appropriate real rate of return for valuing future income streams. Since such considerations could apply again following the commencement of Section 1 of the Damages Act 1996, it has been thought desirable to retain tables for a range of possible rates of return, notwithstanding the Appeal Court judgment in *Wells v Wells*. A description of how to use market rates of return on index-linked gilts to determine the appropriate rate of return is given in Appendix B. In cases outwith the scope of these tables, the advice of an actuary should be sought.

Tax

14. In order to arrive at a true present capital value of the Plaintiff's future loss or expense it is necessary to consider whether he or she will have to pay a significant amount of tax on the investment return arising from his compensation. If he or she will pay little or no tax, no adjustment of the rate of return will be required. If he or she will have to pay a significant percentage of that income in tax, then the rate of return chosen to determine the present capital value of the loss or expense should be reduced accordingly. Attention is drawn to the decision of the House of Lords in *Hodgson v Trapp* [1989] AC 807 concerning the treatment of the incidence of higher rate tax on the income arising from a compensatory fund.

15. In cases where the impact of personal Income Tax and Capital Gains Tax is likely to be significant, more accurate calculation of the value net of tax of payments to the individual may be desirable. Such calculations can be carried out by using software of the type referred to in paragraph 45 or the advice of an actuary should be sought.

Different retirement ages

16. In paragraph 10 above, reference was made to the problem that will arise when the Plaintiff's retiring age is different from that assumed in the tables. Such a problem may arise in valuing a loss or expense beginning immediately but ending at retirement; or in valuing a loss or expense which will not begin until the Plaintiff reaches retirement but will then continue until death. In the former case, that is where the loss or expense to be valued covers the period up to retirement, the following procedure will be found to be satisfactory in most cases. Where the Plaintiff's actual retiring age would have been earlier than that assumed in the tables, he or she is treated as correspondingly older than his or her true age. Thus a woman of 42 who would have retired at 55 is treated as though she were 47 and retiring at 60. The appropriate multiplier is then obtained from the table (Table 6 or 16). A further correction should then be made, because the Plaintiff's chances of survival are greater at 42 than if she were in fact 47. There should therefore be added to the multiplier one quarter of one per cent for each year (here 5 years) by which the Plaintiff's personal retiring age is earlier than 60. In the case of a man the correction required is a half per cent for each such year. This difference is because, on average, women live longer than men.

17. When the Plaintiff would have expected to retire later than the age assumed in the table, the procedure is reversed. Thus a man of 42 who would have retired at 70 is treated as though he were 37 and retiring at 65. The appropriate multiplier is then obtained from the table (in this case Table 3 or 13) and the further correction required is made by reducing the multiplier by one half of one per cent for each year by which the retiring age of the Plaintiff exceeds the retiring age assumed in the table. In the case of a woman the reduction would, of course, be by one quarter per cent for each year.

18. When the loss or expense to be valued is that from the date of retirement to death, and the Plaintiff's date of retirement differs from that

assumed in the tables, a different approach is necessary. The first step is to assume that there is a present loss which will continue for the rest of the Plaintiff's life and from Table 1 or 2 (or 11 or 12) establish the value of that loss or expense over the whole period from the date of assessment until the Plaintiff's death. The second step is to establish the value of such loss or expense over the period from the date of assessment until the Plaintiff's expected date of retirement following the procedure explained in paragraphs 16 and 17 above. The third step is to subtract the second figure from the first. The balance remaining represents the present value of the Plaintiff's loss or expense between retirement and death.

Younger ages

19. Tables 1, 2, 11 and 12, which concern pecuniary loss for life, and Tables 7 to 10 and 17 to 20, which concern loss of pension from retirement age, have been extended down to age 0. In some circumstances the multiplier at age 0 is slightly lower than that at age 1; this arises because of the relatively high incidence of deaths immediately after birth.

20. Tables for multipliers for loss of earnings (Tables 3 to 6 and 13 to 16) have not been extended below age 16. In order to determine the multiplier for loss of earnings for someone who has not yet started work, it is first necessary to determine an assumed age at which the Plaintiff would have commenced work and to find the appropriate multiplier for that age from Tables 3 to 6 or 13 to 16, according to the assumed retirement age. This multiplier should then be multiplied by the deferment factor from Table 21 which corresponds to the appropriate rate of return and the period from the date of the trial to the date on which it is assumed that the Plaintiff would have started work. A similar approach can be used for determining a multiplier for pecuniary loss for life where the loss is assumed to commence a fixed period of years from the date of the trial. For simplicity the factors in Table 21 relate purely to the impact of the rate of return and ignore mortality. At ages below 30 this is a reasonable approximation (for example allowance for ELT 15 male mortality from age 5 to 25 would only reduce the multiplier by a further 1 per cent) but at higher ages it would normally be appropriate to allow explicitly for mortality and the advice of an actuary should be sought.

Contingencies

21. Tables 1 to 10 have been calculated to take into account the chances that the Plaintiff will live for different periods, including the possibility that he or she will die young or live to be very old, based on current levels of population mortality. Tables 11 to 20 make reasonable provision for the levels of mortality which members of the population of England and Wales may expect to experience in future. The tables do not take account of the other risks and vicissitudes of life, such as the possibility that the Plaintiff would for periods have ceased to earn due to ill-health or loss of employment. Nor do they take account of the fact that many people cease work for substantial periods to care for children or other dependants. Section B

suggests ways in which allowance may be made to the multipliers for loss of earnings to allow for certain risks other than mortality.

Impaired lives

22. In some cases medical evidence may be available which asserts that a Plaintiff's health impairments are equivalent to adding a certain number of years to the current age, or to treating the individual as having a specific age different from the actual age. In such cases, Tables 1, 2, 11 and 12 can be used with respect to the deemed higher age. For the other tables the adjustment is not so straightforward, as adjusting the age will also affect the period up to retirement age, but the procedures described in paragraphs 16 to 18 may be followed, or the advice of an actuary should be sought.

Fixed periods

23. In cases where pecuniary loss is to be valued for a fixed period, the multipliers in Table 22 may be used. These make no allowance for mortality or any other contingency but assume that regular frequent payments will continue throughout the period. These figures should in principle be adjusted to allow for less frequent periodicity of payment, especially if the payments in question are annually in advance or in arrears. An appropriate adjustment is to multiply by one plus half the rate of return for annual payments in advance (ie by 1.02 for a rate of return of 4%) and to divide the term certain multiplier by one plus half the rate of return for annual payments in arrears.

Variable loss or expense

24. The tables do not provide an immediate answer when the loss or expense to be valued is not assumed to be stable; where, for instance, the Plaintiff's lost earnings were on a sliding scale or he was expected to achieve promotion. It may be possible to use the tables to deal with such situations by increasing the basic figure of annual loss or expense; or by choosing a lower rate of interest and so a higher multiplier than would otherwise have been chosen. More complicated cases may be suited to the use of the software referred to in paragraph 45.

25. If doubt exists that the tables are appropriate to a particular case which appears to present significant difficulties of substance it would be prudent to take actuarial advice.

SECTION B: CONTINGENCIES OTHER THAN MORTALITY

26. As stated in paragraph 21, the tables for loss of earnings (Tables 3 to 6 and 13 to 16) take no account of risks other than mortality. This section shows how the multipliers in these tables may be reduced to take account of risks other than mortality. This is based on work commissioned by the

Institute of Actuaries and carried out by Professor S Haberman and Mrs D S F Bloomfield. (*Work time lost to sickness, unemployment and stoppages: measurement and application* (1990), Journal of the Institute of Actuaries 117, 533–595). Although there was some debate within the actuarial profession about the details of this work, and in particular about the scope for developing it further, the findings were broadly accepted and were adopted by the Government Actuary and the other actuaries who were members of the Working Party when the Second Edition of the Tables was published.

27. Reported cases suggest that the Courts have hesitated to accept these findings, which were based on scientific research. and continue to make reductions of as much as 20%, which appears to have been a figure adopted before any work on the subject had been carried out. Since the risk of mortality has already been taken into account in the Tables, the principal contingencies in respect of which a further reduction is to be made are illness and unemployment. Even with the effective disappearance of the 'job for life' there appears to be no scientific justification in the generality of cases for assuming significantly larger deductions than those given in this section. It should be noted that the authors of the 1990 paper (Professor Haberman and Mrs Bloomfield) wrote 'All the results discussed in this paper should be further qualified by the caveat that the underlying models ... assume that economic activity rates and labour force separation and accession rates do not vary in the future from the bases chosen. As mentioned already in the text, it is unlikely to be true that the future would be free from marked secular trends.' The paper relied on Labour Force Surveys for 1973, 1977, 1981 and 1985 and English Life Tables No 14 (1980–82). However, although it is now somewhat out of date, it is the best study presently available. It is hoped to commission some further research into the impact of contingencies other than mortality.

28. Specific factors in individual cases may necessitate larger reductions. By contrast, there will also be cases where the standard multipliers should be increased, to take into account positive factors of lifestyle, employment prospects and life expectancy.

29. The extent to which the multiplier needs to be reduced will reflect individual circumstances such as occupation and geographical region. In the short term, levels of economic activity and unemployment, including time lost through industrial action, are relevant. Reductions may be expected to be smaller for clerical workers than for manual workers, for those living in the South rather than the North, and for those in 'secure' jobs and in occupations less affected by redundancy or industrial action.

30. The suggestions which follow are intended only to provide a 'ready reckoner' as opposed to precise figures.

The basic deduction for contingencies other than mortality

31. Subject to the adjustments which may be made as described below, the multiplier which has been selected from the tables, ie in respect of risks of

mortality only, should be reduced by *multiplying* it by a figure selected from the table below, under the heading 'Medium'.

Table A Loss of earnings to pension age 65 (males)

Age at date of trial	*High*	*Medium*	*Low*
20	0.99	0.98	0.97
25	0.99	0.98	0.96
30	0.99	0.97	0.95
35	0.98	0.96	0.93
40	0.98	0.96	0.92
45	0.97	0.95	0.90
50	0.96	0.93	0.87
55	0.95	0.90	0.82
60	0.95	0.90	0.81

Levels of economic activity and employment

32. The medium set of reductions is appropriate if it is anticipated that economic activity is likely to correspond to that in the 1970s and 1980s (ignoring periods of high and low unemployment). The high set is appropriate if higher economic activity and lower unemployment rates are anticipated. The low set is appropriate if lower economic activity and higher unemployment rates are anticipated.

33. Whereas it is possible to reach conclusions about these factors in the short term the Courts are not prepared to speculate about such matters beyond the short term (*Auty v National Coal Board* [1985] 1 WLR 784). Consequently the headings 'High' and 'Low' may only be of limited value.

Lower pension ages (males)

34. The figures will be higher for a lower pension age. For example, if pension age is 60, the figures should be as shown in Table B.

Table B Loss of earnings to pension age 60 (males)

Age at date of trial	*High*	*Medium*	*Low*
20	0.99	0.99	0.98
25	0.99	0.99	0.97
30	0.99	0.98	0.97
35	0.99	0.98	0.96
40	0.98	0.97	0.94
45	0.98	0.96	0.93
50	0.97	0.94	0.92
55	0.96	0.93	0.88

Female lives

35. As a rough guide, for female lives between ages 35 and 55 with a pension age of 60, the figures should be as shown in Table C.

Table C Loss of earnings to pension age 60 (females)

Age at date of trial	*High*	*Medium*	*Low*
35	0.95	0.95	0.94
40	0.93	0.93	0.92
45	0.90	0.90	0.88
50	0.91	0.90	0.88
55	0.95	0.94	0.93

Variations by occupation

36. The risks of illness, injury and disability are less for persons in clerical or similar jobs, eg civil servants, the professions and financial services industries and greater for those in manual jobs, eg construction, mining, quarrying and ship-building. However what matters is the precise nature of the work undertaken by the person in question: for example, a secretary in the Headquarters office of a large construction company may be at no greater risk than a secretary in a solicitor's office.

37. In less risky occupations the figures in Tables A to C should be *increased* by a maximum of the order of 0.01 at age 25, 0.01 at age 40 and 0.03 at age 55.

38. In more risky occupations the figures in Tables A to C should be *reduced* by a maximum of the order of 0.01 at age 25, 0.02 at age 40 and 0.05 at age 55.

Variations by geographical region

39. For persons resident in the South East, East Anglia, South West and East Midlands, the figures in Tables A to C should be *increased* by a maximum of the order of 0.01 at age 25, 0.01 at age 40 and 0.03 at age 55.

40. For persons resident in the North, North West, Wales and Scotland, the figures in Tables A to C should be *reduced* by a maximum of the order of 0.01 at age 25, 0.02 at age 40 and 0.05 at age 55.

SECTION C: SUMMARY

41. To use the tables take the following steps:

(1) Choose the tables relating to the appropriate period of loss or expense.

(2) Choose the table, relating to that period, appropriate to the sex of the Plaintiff.
(3) Choose the appropriate rate of return, before allowing for the effect of tax on the income to be obtained from the lump sum.
(4) If appropriate, allow for a reduction in the rate of return to reflect the effect of tax on the income from the lump sum.
(5) Find the figure under the column in the table chosen given against the age at trial (or, in a fatal accident case, at the death) of the Plaintiff.
(6) Adjust the figure to take account of contingencies other than mortality, as specified in Section B above.
(7) Multiply the annual loss (net of tax) or expense by that figure.

42. In principle an allowance for an expected increase in the annual loss or expense (not due to inflation) can be made by choosing a lower rate of return or by increasing the figure of annual loss or expense. In cases where the Plaintiff's expected age of retirement differs from that assumed in the tables the more complicated procedure explained in paragraph 16 to 18 should be followed.

43. An example is given below:

EXAMPLE

The Plaintiff is female, aged 35. She lives in London and is an established civil servant who was working in an office at a salary of £25,000 net of tax. As a result of her injuries, she has lost her job. The task of estimating her loss of earnings to retirement age of 60 is to be undertaken as follows:

(1) Tables 6 and 16 assume a retirement age of 60 for females. If the projected mortality tables are accepted, then Table 16 is relevant.
(2) The appropriate rate of return is decided to be 4.5% (based on *Wells v Wells* [1997] 1 WLR 652).
(3) Table 16 shows that, on the basis of a 4.5% rate of return, the multiplier for a female aged 35 is 14.94.
(4) It is now necessary to take account of risks other than mortality. Let us assume that economic activity for the next few years, for the purpose of this exercise, is regarded as being 'high'. Table C would require 14.94 to be multiplied by 0.95.
(5) Further adjustment is necessary because the Plaintiff (a) is in a secure non-manual job. and (b) lives in the South East.

The adjustments should be made as follows:

Basic adjustment to allow for short-term high economic activity (Table C)	0.95
Adjustment to allow for occupation, say	+0.01
	0.96
Adjustment for geographical region, say	+0.01
	0.97

The original multiplier taken from Table 16, namely 14.94, must therefore be multiplied by 0.97, resulting in a revised multiplier for use of 14.49.

This example takes no account of the incidence of tax on investment return (see paragraph 14) above. It is assumed that this was taken into account when determining the 4.5% rate of return.

Final remarks

44. These tables are designed to assist the Courts to arrive at suitable multipliers in a range of possible situations. However, they do not cover all possibilities and in more complex situations advice should be sought from a Fellow of the Institute of Actuaries or a Fellow of the Faculty of Actuaries.

45. In the Family Division a software program (the Duxbury Method) is used for making similar calculations in complex cases. A similar facility would be useful for more complex personal injury and fatal accident cases and it is intended that such a programme will be made available shortly.

Christopher Daykin CB, MA, HA
Government Actuary

London
May 1998

Appendix A

Rates of mortality expressed as percentages of 1911 rates (logarithmic scale)

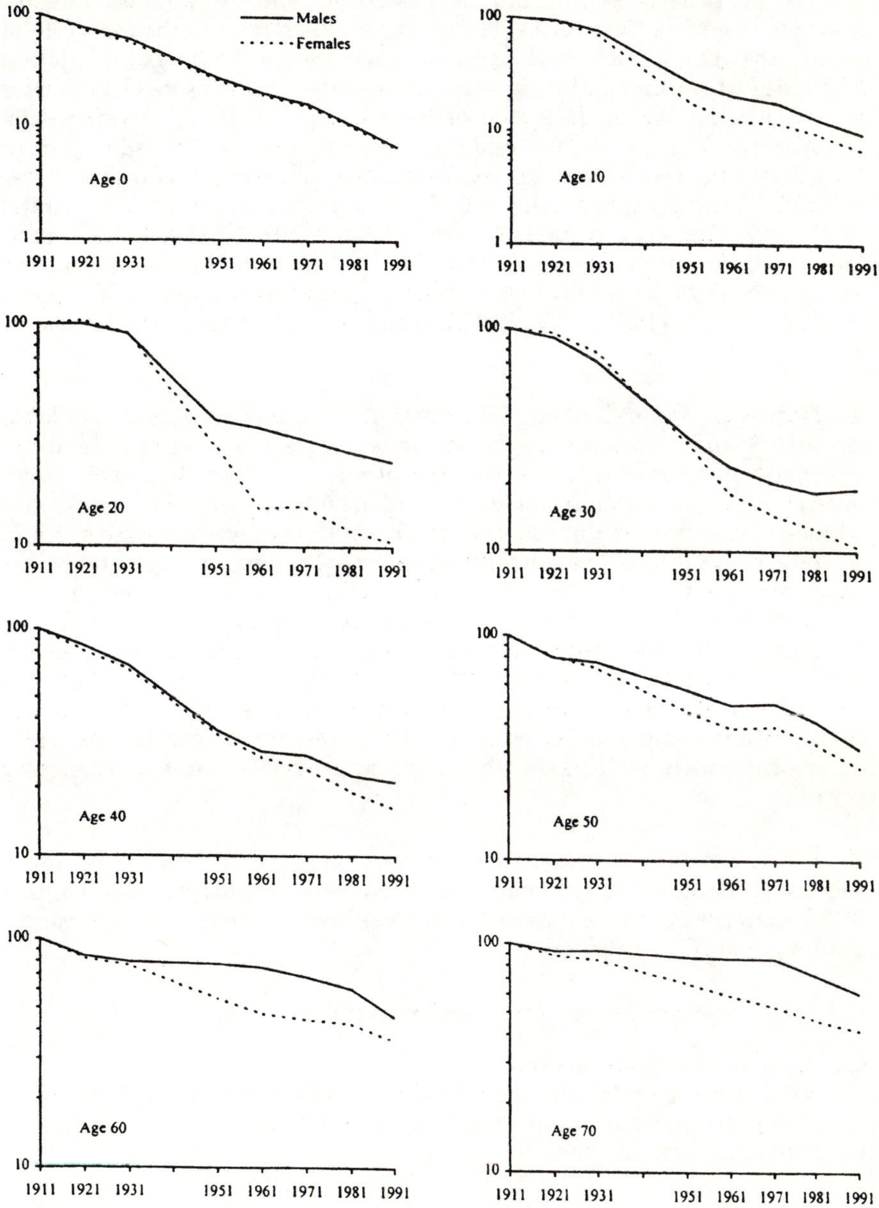

Appendix B

Selecting an appropriate real rate of return based on market considerations

1. The purpose of setting out figures based upon a range of rates of return is to enable the user to choose a rate which reflects the 'real rate of return' that can be obtained upon the capital sum. In times of inflation high rates of return can be obtained; these rates compensate the investor in part for the fall in the value of his capital and of the dividends he receives due to inflation. The real rate of return may be defined as part of the actual rate which excludes this element. It has been held that in times of stable currency, when there is little or no inflation, a return on capital of 4% or 5% has been usual (see *Lim v Camden* [19801 AC 174, cases cited there and *Hodgson v Trapp* [1989] AC 807). Reference has been made in paragraph 12 of the main text to the judgment of the Court of Appeal in *Wells v Wells* [1997] 1 WLR 652, which currently requires the use of $4\frac{1}{2}$%.

2. However, Index-Linked Government Stocks have been available since 1981 and it is accordingly no longer necessary to speculate about either future rates of inflation or the real rate of return obtainable on an investment. The redemption value and dividends of these stocks are adjusted from time to time so as to maintain the real value of the stock in the face of inflation. The current real rates of return on such stocks are published daily in the Financial Times and hitherto have fallen into the range of about $2\frac{1}{2}$% to $4\frac{1}{2}$% (gross, ie before the impact of taxation). It may be thought that the return on such Index-Linked Government Stocks is the most accurate reflection of the real rate of return available to Plaintiffs seeking the prudent investment of awards of damages. In any event, when using the tables it will be necessary to use the real rate of return which is deemed the most appropriate for the particular purpose.

3. To identify the real return on such stocks on a particular date, reference should be made to the section of the Financial Times for that day entitled 'FTSE Actuaries Govt. Securities UK Indices' (abbreviated to 'Fixed interest indices' in the Contents list).

4. The most appropriate figures will be found

(a) in the section 'Index-linked'
(b) within the sub-section on yields under the column for the day in question within the group of columns headed 'Inflation 5%'
(c) in the line 'Over 5 Years'

5. This figure is also published at quarterly intervals within the 'Data Page' in the Law Society's Gazette; real returns on index-linked securities are generally stable and major fluctuations between the intervals of publication in the Gazette are unusual.

6. The rate thus obtained by reference to the *Financial Times* or Law Society's Gazette makes no allowance for the incidence of tax on the income from a compensation award. Accordingly, the rate should be adjusted if necessary, as described in paragraphs 14 and 15 of Section A, in order to identify the correct column of the table to be used.

Appendix C

Comments by the Association of British Insurers (ABI)

Introduction

1. The Association of British Insurers (ABI) represents companies transacting some ninety-five per cent of insurance company business in the United Kingdom. The Forum of Insurance Lawyers (FOIL) fully supports the comments made in this appendix. Both ABI and FOIL are pleased to have participated for the first time in the Working Party which was responsible for the third edition of these tables and explanatory notes.

2. We believe that the central issue in the debate on the calculation of damages for future losses and expenses is ensuring that the Plaintiff, the recipient of the compensation, is able to meet his or her future needs and requirements for as long as they arise. There may be a number ways of calculating what the Plaintiff needs for the future. Using multipliers is one. Purchasing an annuity may be another. There is perhaps a danger that the use of any scientific approach in this area may bring a spurious accuracy to a calculation which, almost by definition, will prove wrong in the future.

3. Our contention is that none of the methods above addresses this key question. All that any of the currently used methods do is to calculate a sum of money which is given to the Plaintiff to do with as he or she wishes or sees fit. We nonetheless accept that a wider review of the means of addressing future financial provision for the victims of personal injury is outside the scope of this Working Party.

The Tables in the third edition

4. What the tables do is to give a multiplier for a particular individual in his or her particular circumstances which is based on the general mortality of the population at large. Insurers have no objection to the actuarial principles underlying the tables, because the figures which they include are derived from objective actuarial science applied to real mortality data from current English Life Tables.

5. The figures in the tables have been produced by the Government Actuary. We have no reason to dispute the mathematical accuracy or the rigour of the calculations used to derive any of the figures in any of the tables. What may be open to discussion is the suitability of using data drawn from a population of millions as a tool to predict what may be appropriate for an individual Plaintiff in his or her own particular environment.

6. The figures in Tables 1–10 could provide a useful starting point for assessment of an individual case, and will need adjustment to reflect accurately the individual circumstances of the person concerned. As the Chairman of this Working Party noted in the discussions prior to publication

of this edition: 'People show a marked disinclination to die in strict accordance with their life expectancy'

Projected Mortality Tables

7. Paragraphs 7 and 8 of the explanatory notes state that Tables 11–20 are concerned with projected improvements in mortality rates. It is noted that the Government Actuary makes a considered estimate of the future improvements in mortality for national population projections. We accept that the evidence of the twentieth century demonstrates that the mortality of the population as a whole has been improving. We understand that these improvements could provide a basis for projections for the national population as a whole. Nevertheless, we are aware of a number of factors which tend to question the continuation of such improvements.

8. We note that there is no objective evidence to which we have access of how the mortality patterns of a particular injury group are developing. We would strongly suggest that movements in the mortality of the group of victims of personal injury (of which an individual Plaintiff in his or her particular circumstances is a member) may not be properly represented by the projected improvement in mortality of the whole of the population of the United Kingdom.

9. For example, whilst the development of improved methods of resuscitation and treatment may result in fewer fatalities, those who survive as a consequence of these procedures may bring with them a heavier pattern of mortality which is at variance with national experience.

10. In our view the use of Tables 11–20 is not supportable for two reasons. First, because of uncertainty about the future movements in national mortality and second because of uncertainty about the movement of the mortality of victims of personal injury relative to it.

11. Our conclusion on mortality is that whilst we accept with some reservations the updating of the tables of multipliers represented by Tables 1–10, we see no valid argument for further modifying the mortality basis to include speculative assessments of future changes. For these reasons, insurers are unable to recommend the use of Tables 11–20 to the Courts.

Explanatory Notes—Section B: Contingencies other than mortality

12. Paragraphs 26–40 attempt to deal with the deductions to be made for contingencies other than mortality, especially the risk of unemployment. A 'ready reckoner' to assess the deduction to be made from the multiplier is proposed at paragraphs 31–40.

13. A different approach is generally adopted in the Courts when assessing the deduction to be made for these contingencies. The practice is to consider all the evidence relating to how the individual is affected in his or her own

particular circumstances, and then to decide on an appropriate adjustment which reflects these circumstances.

14. The paper from which Section B is derived is now over eight years old and was based on data which is at least thirteen years old. Some of the data analysed in the paper is now twenty-five years old. It is our considered view that the use of such limited and out of date information which does not accurately reflect economic conditions at the time of trial or settlement is wholly anomalous.

15. Paragraph 27 mentions that further research is being considered. ABI is keen to facilitate and contribute to such research and, at the time of writing, is in discussion with the Government Actuary's Department on this subject.

Rates of return

16. It is not for this Working Party to advocate the use of any particular rate of return. Under the Damages Act 1996, this is a matter for the Lord Chancellor (if he is so minded) who is likely to make his decision after the House of Lords has given its judgment in *Wells v Wells*. Until *Wells* is decided and until the Lord Chancellor has considered exercising his power under the Damages Act, we would therefore caution against adoption of the argument in support of Index-Linked Government Stock; proposed in the 'Introduction to the First Edition' which is found in this (third) edition at pages 12–14* and further discussed in paragraphs 2–5 of Appendix B at page 31†.

17. FOIL suggests that in changing economic conditions there may be a case for including rates of return beyond the 1–5 per cent range, which earlier editions of these tables adopted and which is used in the current edition.

Association of British Insurers
6 April 1998

* Pages 62–65 in this book.
† Page 78 in this book.

Table 1 Multipliers for pecuniary loss for life (males)

Age at date of trial	*Multiplier calculated with allowance for population mortality and rate of return of*								*Age at date of trial*
	1.5%	*2.0%*	*2.5%*	*3.0%*	*3.5%*	*4.0%*	*4.5%*	*5.0%*	
0	43.97	38.02	33.25	29.38	26.22	23.60	21.41	19.57	0
1	43.98	38.08	33.34	29.49	26.34	23.72	21.53	19.68	1
2	43.66	37.86	33.18	29.38	26.26	23.67	21.49	19.66	2
3	43.32	37.62	33.01	29.26	26.17	23.60	21.45	19.62	3
4	42.98	37.37	32.84	29.13	26.08	23.53	21.40	19.58	4
5	42.63	37.12	32.65	29.00	25.98	23.46	21.34	19.54	5
6	42.27	36.86	32.47	28.86	25.88	23.39	21.28	19.50	6
7	41.90	36.59	32.27	28.72	25.77	23.31	21.22	19.45	7
8	41.53	36.32	32.07	28.57	25.66	23.22	21.16	19.41	8
9	41.16	36.05	31.87	28.42	25.55	23.14	21.10	19.35	9
10	40.77	35.76	31.66	28.26	25.43	23.05	21.03	19.30	10
11	40.38	35.48	31.44	28.10	25.31	22.95	20.95	19.24	11
12	39.99	35.18	31.22	27.93	25.18	22.85	20.88	19.19	12
13	39.59	34.88	30.99	27.76	25.05	22.75	20.80	19.12	13
14	39.19	34.58	30.76	27.58	24.91	22.65	20.72	19.06	14
15	38.78	34.27	30.53	27.41	24.77	22.54	20.63	18.99	15
16	38.37	33.96	30.29	27.22	24.63	22.43	20.55	18.93	16
17	37.96	33.65	30.05	27.04	24.49	22.32	20.46	18.86	17
18	37.55	33.33	29.82	26.86	24.35	22.21	20.38	18.79	18
19	37.13	33.02	29.57	26.67	24.21	22.10	20.29	18.72	19
20	36.71	32.70	29.33	26.48	24.06	21.98	20.20	18.65	20
21	36.29	32.37	29.07	26.28	23.90	21.86	20.10	18.57	21
22	35.86	32.03	28.81	26.08	23.74	21.74	20.00	18.49	22
23	35.42	31.69	28.55	25.87	23.58	21.60	19.90	18.41	23
24	34.97	31.35	28.27	25.65	23.41	21.47	19.79	18.32	24
25	34.52	30.99	27.99	25.43	23.23	21.33	19.67	18.23	25

26	34.06	30.63	27.70	25.20	23.04	21.18	19.55	18.13	26
27	33.59	30.26	27.41	24.96	22.85	21.02	19.43	18.03	27
28	33.12	29.88	27.10	24.72	22.66	20.86	19.30	17.92	28
29	32.64	29.49	26.79	24.47	22.45	20.70	19.16	17.81	29
30	32.15	29.10	26.47	24.21	22.24	20.52	19.02	17.69	30
31	31.65	28.70	26.15	23.94	22.02	20.34	18.87	17.57	31
32	31.15	28.29	25.81	23.67	21.80	20.16	18.71	17.44	32
33	30.64	27.87	25.47	23.38	21.56	19.96	18.55	17.30	33
34	30.12	27.44	25.12	23.09	21.32	19.76	18.38	17.16	34
35	29.60	27.01	24.76	22.80	21.07	19.55	18.21	17.01	35
36	29.07	26.57	24.40	22.49	20.82	19.34	18.03	16.86	36
37	28.54	26.13	24.03	22.18	20.56	19.12	17.84	16.70	37
38	28.00	25.68	23.65	21.86	20.29	18.89	17.64	16.53	38
39	27.45	25.22	23.26	21.54	20.01	18.65	17.44	16.36	39
40	26.90	24.76	22.87	21.20	19.73	18.41	17.23	16.18	40
41	26.34	24.28	22.47	20.86	19.43	18.16	17.02	15.99	41
42	25.78	23.80	22.06	20.51	19.13	17.90	16.79	15.80	42
43	25.21	23.32	21.64	20.15	18.82	17.63	16.56	15.60	43
44	24.63	22.83	21.22	19.79	18.51	17.36	16.32	15.39	44
45	24.05	22.33	20.79	19.41	18.18	17.07	16.07	15.17	45
46	23.47	21.82	20.35	19.03	17.85	16.78	15.82	14.94	46
47	22.89	21.31	19.91	18.65	17.51	16.48	15.55	14.71	47
48	22.30	20.80	19.46	18.25	17.16	16.18	15.28	14.47	48
49	21.71	20.28	19.01	17.85	16.81	15.87	15.01	14.22	49
50	21.11	19.76	18.55	17.45	16.45	15.55	14.72	13.97	50
51	20.52	19.24	18.09	17.04	16.09	15.22	14.43	13.71	51
52	19.93	18.72	17.62	16.62	15.72	14.89	14.14	13.44	52
53	19.33	18.19	17.15	16.20	15.34	14.55	13.83	13.17	53
54	18.74	17.66	16.68	15.78	14.96	14.21	13.52	12.89	54
55	18.15	17.13	16.20	15.35	14.57	13.86	13.21	12.60	55

Table 1 Multipliers for pecuniary loss for life (males) *continued*

Age at date of trial	*Multiplier calculated with allowance for population mortality and rate of return of*								*Age at date of trial*
	1.5%	*2.0%*	*2.5%*	*3.0%*	*3.5%*	*4.0%*	*4.5%*	*5.0%*	
56	17.55	16.60	15.72	14.92	14.18	13.51	12.88	12.31	56
57	16.97	16.07	15.24	14.49	13.79	13.15	12.56	12.01	57
58	16.38	15.54	14.76	14.05	13.39	12.79	12.23	11.71	58
59	15.80	15.01	14.28	13.61	13.00	12.42	11.89	11.40	59
60	15.22	14.49	13.81	13.18	12.60	12.06	11.56	11.09	60
61	14.66	13.97	13.33	12.74	12.20	11.69	11.22	10.78	61
62	14.10	13.45	12.86	12.31	11.80	11.32	10.88	10.46	62
63	13.55	12.95	12.40	11.88	11.40	10.95	10.54	10.15	63
64	13.01	12.45	11.94	11.46	11.01	10.59	10.20	9.83	64
65	12.48	11.97	11.49	11.04	10.62	10.23	9.86	9.52	65
66	11.96	11.49	11.04	10.63	10.24	9.87	9.53	9.21	66
67	11.46	11.02	10.61	10.22	9.86	9.52	9.20	8.90	67
68	10.97	10.56	10.18	9.82	9.49	9.17	8.87	8.59	68
69	10.49	10.11	9.76	9.43	9.12	8.82	8.55	8.28	69
70	10.02	9.67	9.35	9.04	8.75	8.48	8.22	7.98	70
71	9.55	9.24	8.94	8.66	8.39	8.14	7.90	7.68	71
72	9.10	8.81	8.54	8.28	8.04	7.80	7.58	7.37	72
73	8.67	8.40	8.15	7.91	7.69	7.47	7.27	7.08	73
74	8.25	8.00	7.77	7.56	7.35	7.15	6.97	6.79	74
75	7.84	7.62	7.41	7.21	7.02	6.84	6.67	6.50	75
76	7.44	7.24	7.05	6.87	6.69	6.53	6.37	6.22	76
77	7.05	6.87	6.70	6.53	6.37	6.22	6.08	5.94	77
78	6.69	6.52	6.36	6.21	6.07	5.93	5.80	5.67	78
79	6.33	6.18	6.04	5.90	5.77	5.65	5.53	5.41	79
80	5.99	5.86	5.73	5.61	5.49	5.37	5.26	5.16	80

81	5.67	5.55	5.43	5.32	5.21	5.11	5.01	4.91	81
82	5.36	5.25	5.14	5.04	4.94	4.85	4.76	4.67	82
83	5.06	4.96	4.86	4.77	4.68	4.60	4.52	4.44	83
84	4.77	4.68	4.60	4.52	4.44	4.36	4.28	4.21	84
85	4.50	4.42	4.35	4.27	4.20	4.13	4.06	4.00	85
86	4.25	4.17	4.10	4.04	3.97	3.91	3.85	3.79	86
87	4.01	3.94	3.88	3.82	3.76	3.70	3.65	3.59	87
88	3.78	3.72	3.67	3.61	3.56	3.51	3.46	3.41	88
89	3.57	3.52	3.47	3.42	3.37	3.32	3.28	3.24	89
90	3.36	3.31	3.27	3.23	3.18	3.14	3.10	3.06	90
91	3.15	3.11	3.07	3.03	3.00	2.96	2.92	2.89	91
92	2.95	2.92	2.88	2.85	2.81	2.78	2.75	2.72	92
93	2.77	2.74	2.70	2.67	2.64	2.61	2.59	2.56	93
94	2.60	2.57	2.54	2.52	2.49	2.46	2.44	2.41	94
95	2.45	2.42	2.40	2.37	2.35	2.33	2.30	2.28	95
96	2.31	2.29	2.26	2.24	2.22	2.20	2.18	2.16	96
97	2.18	2.16	2.14	2.12	2.10	2.08	2.06	2.04	97
98	2.06	2.04	2.02	2.00	1.98	1.97	1.95	1.93	98
99	1.94	1.92	1.91	1.89	1.87	1.86	1.84	1.83	99
100	1.83	1.81	1.80	1.78	1.77	1.76	1.74	1.73	100

Table 2 Multipliers for pecuniary loss for life (females)

Age at date of trial	*Multiplier calculated with allowance for population mortality and rate of return of*								*Age at date of trial*
	1.5%	*2.0%*	*2.5%*	*3.0%*	*3.5%*	*4.0%*	*4.5%*	*5.0%*	
0	45.85	39.35	34.21	30.08	26.73	23.99	21.70	19.79	0
1	45.82	39.38	34.27	30.16	26.83	24.08	21.80	19.88	1
2	45.53	39.18	34.14	30.07	26.76	24.04	21.77	19.86	2
3	45.21	38.97	33.99	29.97	26.69	23.99	21.73	19.84	3
4	44.90	38.75	33.83	29.86	26.61	23.93	21.69	19.81	4
5	44.57	38.52	33.67	29.75	26.53	23.87	21.65	19.78	5
6	44.24	38.28	33.51	29.63	26.45	23.81	21.61	19.75	6
7	43.90	38.05	33.34	29.51	26.36	23.75	21.56	19.71	7
8	43.56	37.80	33.16	29.38	26.27	23.68	21.51	19.68	8
9	43.21	37.55	32.98	29.25	26.17	23.61	21.46	19.64	9
10	42.86	37.30	32.80	29.12	26.08	23.54	21.41	19.60	10
11	42.50	37.04	32.61	28.98	25.97	23.47	21.35	19.56	11
12	42.13	36.78	32.42	28.84	25.87	23.39	21.29	19.51	12
13	41.76	36.51	32.22	28.69	25.76	23.31	21.23	19.46	13
14	41.39	36.23	32.02	28.54	25.65	23.22	21.17	19.42	14
15	41.01	35.95	31.81	28.39	25.54	23.14	21.10	19.37	15
16	40.63	35.67	31.60	28.23	25.42	23.05	21.03	19.31	16
17	40.24	35.38	31.39	28.07	25.30	22.95	20.96	19.26	17
18	39.85	35.09	31.17	27.91	25.17	22.86	20.89	19.20	18
19	39.45	34.80	30.95	27.74	25.04	22.76	20.82	19.15	19
20	39.05	34.49	30.72	27.57	24.91	22.66	20.74	19.08	20
21	38.64	34.18	30.48	27.39	24.77	22.55	20.65	19.02	21
22	38.22	33.87	30.24	27.20	24.63	22.44	20.57	18.95	22
23	37.80	33.55	30.00	27.01	24.48	22.33	20.48	18.88	23
24	37.37	33.22	29.74	26.82	24.33	22.21	20.38	18.81	24
25	36.94	32.88	29.49	26.61	24.17	22.09	20.29	18.73	25

26	36.50	32.54	29.22	26.41	24.01	21.96	20.18	18.65	26
27	36.05	32.20	28.95	26.19	23.84	21.82	20.08	18.56	27
28	35.59	31.84	28.67	25.97	23.67	21.68	19.97	18.47	28
29	35.13	31.48	28.39	25.75	23.49	21.54	19.85	18.38	29
30	34.67	31.11	28.09	25.52	23.30	21.39	19.73	18.28	30
31	34.20	30.74	27.80	25.28	23.11	21.23	19.60	18.18	31
32	33.72	30.36	27.49	25.03	22.91	21.07	19.47	18.07	32
33	33.23	29.97	27.18	24.78	22.71	20.91	19.34	17.96	33
34	32.74	29.58	26.86	24.53	22.50	20.74	19.20	17.84	34
35	32.25	29.18	26.54	24.26	22.28	20.56	19.05	17.72	35
36	31.75	28.77	26.21	23.99	22.06	20.38	18.90	17.59	36
37	31.24	28.36	25.87	23.71	21.83	20.19	18.74	17.46	37
38	30.73	27.94	25.53	23.43	21.60	19.99	18.58	17.32	38
39	30.21	27.51	25.18	23.14	21.36	19.79	18.41	17.18	39
40	29.68	27.08	24.82	22.84	21.11	19.58	18.23	17.03	40
41	29.15	26.64	24.45	22.54	20.85	19.37	18.05	16.88	41
42	28.61	26.19	24.08	22.22	20.59	19.14	17.86	16.72	42
43	28.07	25.74	23.70	21.91	20.32	18.92	17.67	16.55	43
44	27.53	25.28	23.31	21.58	20.04	18.68	17.46	16.38	44
45	26.98	24.82	22.92	21.25	19.76	18.44	17.25	16.20	45
46	26.42	24.35	22.52	20.91	19.47	18.19	17.04	16.01	46
47	25.86	23.88	22.12	20.56	19.17	17.93	16.82	15.82	47
48	25.30	23.40	21.71	20.21	18.87	17.67	16.59	15.62	48
49	24.73	22.91	21.29	19.85	18.56	17.40	16.36	15.41	49
50	24.16	22.42	20.87	19.48	18.24	17.12	16.11	15.20	50
51	23.59	21.92	20.44	19.11	17.91	16.84	15.86	14.98	51
52	23.01	21.42	20.00	18.73	17.58	16.55	15.61	14.76	52
53	22.43	20.92	19.56	18.34	17.24	16.25	15.35	14.52	53
54	21.84	20.41	19.12	17.95	16.90	15.94	15.07	14.28	54
55	21.26	19.89	18.66	17.55	16.54	15.63	14.80	14.03	55

Table 2 Multipliers for pecuniary loss for life (females) *continued*

Age at date of trial	*Multiplier calculated with allowance for population mortality and rate of return of* 1.5%	2.0%	2.5%	3.0%	3.5%	4.0%	4.5%	5.0%	*Age at date of trial*
56	20.67	19.38	18.21	17.15	16.19	15.31	14.51	13.78	56
57	20.08	18.86	17.75	16.74	15.82	14.98	14.22	13.52	57
58	19.49	18.33	17.28	16.33	15.45	14.65	13.92	13.25	58
59	18.91	17.81	16.82	15.91	15.08	14.32	13.62	12.98	59
60	18.32	17.29	16.35	15.49	14.70	13.98	13.31	12.70	60
61	17.74	16.77	15.88	15.07	14.32	13.63	13.00	12.42	61
62	17.16	16.25	15.41	14.64	13.94	13.29	12.69	12.13	62
63	16.58	15.73	14.94	14.22	13.55	12.93	12.36	11.84	63
64	16.01	15.21	14.47	13.79	13.16	12.58	12.04	11.54	64
65	15.45	14.70	14.00	13.37	12.77	12.22	11.71	11.24	65
66	14.89	14.19	13.54	12.94	12.38	11.87	11.38	10.94	66
67	14.33	13.68	13.07	12.51	11.99	11.50	11.05	10.63	67
68	13.77	13.17	12.61	12.08	11.59	11.14	10.71	10.32	68
69	13.23	12.66	12.14	11.65	11.20	10.77	10.37	10.00	69
70	12.68	12.16	11.68	11.23	10.80	10.40	10.03	9.68	70
71	12.14	11.66	11.21	10.79	10.40	10.03	9.68	9.36	71
72	11.61	11.17	10.75	10.36	10.00	9.65	9.33	9.03	72
73	11.09	10.68	10.30	9.94	9.60	9.28	8.98	8.70	73
74	10.58	10.21	9.86	9.53	9.21	8.92	8.64	8.38	74
75	10.08	9.74	9.42	9.11	8.83	8.56	8.30	8.06	75
76	9.58	9.27	8.98	8.70	8.44	8.19	7.95	7.73	76
77	9.09	8.81	8.54	8.29	8.05	7.82	7.60	7.40	77
78	8.62	8.36	8.12	7.89	7.67	7.46	7.26	7.07	78
79	8.16	7.93	7.71	7.50	7.30	7.11	6.93	6.75	79
80	7.72	7.51	7.31	7.12	6.94	6.76	6.60	6.44	80

81	7.29	7.10	6.92	6.75	6.58	6.43	6.28	6.13	81
82	6.88	6.70	6.54	6.39	6.24	6.10	5.96	5.83	82
83	6.47	6.32	6.18	6.04	5.90	5.77	5.65	5.53	83
84	6.09	5.95	5.82	5.69	5.57	5.46	5.35	5.24	84
85	5.71	5.59	5.48	5.36	5.26	5.15	5.05	4.96	85
86	5.36	5.25	5.15	5.05	4.95	4.86	4.77	4.68	86
87	5.04	4.94	4.85	4.76	4.67	4.59	4.51	4.43	87
88	4.72	4.64	4.56	4.48	4.40	4.32	4.25	4.18	88
89	4.42	4.34	4.27	4.20	4 13	4.06	4.00	3.94	89
90	4.14	4.07	4.00	3.94	3.88	3.82	3.76	3.71	90
91	3.87	3.81	3.75	3.70	3.64	3.59	3.54	3.49	91
92	3.63	3.57	3.52	3.47	3.42	3.37	3.33	3.28	92
93	3.40	3.35	3.31	3.26	3.22	3.18	3.13	3.09	93
94	3.19	3.15	3.11	3.07	3.03	2.99	2.95	2.92	94
95	2.99	2.95	2.92	2.88	2.85	2.81	2.78	2.75	95
96	2.82	2.78	2.75	2.72	2.69	2.66	2.63	2.60	96
97	2.66	2.63	2.60	2.57	2.54	2.52	2.49	2.47	97
98	2.50	2.48	2.45	2.43	2.40	2.38	2.35	2.33	98
99	2.35	2.32	2.30	2.28	2.26	2.23	2.21	2.19	99
100	2.20	2.18	2.16	2.14	2.12	2.10	2.08	2.06	100

Table 3 Multipliers for loss of earnings to pension age 65 (males)

Age at date of trial	*Multiplier calculated with allowance for population mortality and rate of return of*								*Age at date of trial*
	1.5%	*2.0%*	*2.5%*	*3.0%*	*3.5%*	*4.0%*	*4.5%*	*5.0%*	
16	33.54	30.32	27.54	25.14	23.05	21.23	19.63	18.23	16
17	33.05	29.93	27.23	24.89	22.86	21.07	19.51	18.12	17
18	32.56	29.54	26.92	24.65	22.66	20.91	19.38	18.02	18
19	32.07	29.15	26.61	24.39	22.45	20.75	19.24	17.91	19
20	31.57	28.75	26.28	24.13	22.24	20.57	19.10	17.80	20
21	31.07	28.34	25.95	23.86	22.02	20.39	18.96	17.68	21
22	30.55	27.92	25.61	23.58	21.79	20.21	18.80	17.55	22
23	30.03	27.49	25.26	23.29	21.56	20.01	18.64	17.42	23
24	29.50	27.05	24.90	23.00	21.31	19.81	18.48	17.28	24
25	28.96	26.61	24.53	22.69	21.06	19.60	18.30	17.14	25
26	28.41	26.15	24.15	22.38	20.80	19.39	18.12	16.98	26
27	27.85	25.69	23.77	22.05	20.53	19.16	17.93	16.82	27
28	27.29	25.22	23.37	21.72	20.24	18.92	17.73	16.65	28
29	26.71	24.73	22.96	21.38	19.95	18.67	17.52	16.48	29
30	26.13	24.24	22.54	21.02	19.65	18.42	17.30	16.29	30
31	25.54	23.73	22.11	20.66	19.34	18.15	17.07	16.10	31
32	24.94	23.22	21.68	20.28	19.02	17.87	16.84	15.89	32
33	24.33	22.70	21.23	19.89	18.69	17.59	16.59	15.68	33
34	23.71	22.17	20.77	19.50	18.34	17.29	16.33	15.45	34
35	23.08	21.62	20.29	19.09	17.98	16.98	16.06	15.22	35
36	22.45	21.07	19.81	18.67	17.62	16.66	15.78	14.97	36
37	21.81	20.51	19.32	18.24	17.24	16.33	15.49	14.71	37
38	21.16	19.94	18.82	17.79	16.85	15.98	15.18	14.44	38
39	20.50	19.35	18.30	17.34	16.45	15.63	14.87	14.16	39
40	19.83	18.76	17.78	16.87	16.03	15.26	14.54	13.87	40

41	19.15	18.16	17.24	16.39	15.60	14.87	14.19	13.56	41
42	18.47	17.55	16.69	15.90	15.16	14.48	13.84	13.24	42
43	17.78	16.92	16.13	15.39	14.71	14.06	13.47	12.91	43
44	17.07	16.29	15.56	14.87	14.24	13.64	13.08	12.56	44
45	16.36	15.64	14.97	14.34	13.75	13.20	12.68	12.19	45
46	15.64	14.99	14.37	13.79	13.25	12.74	12.26	11.81	46
47	14.92	14.32	13.76	13.23	12.74	12.27	11.83	11.41	47
48	14.18	13.64	13.14	12.66	12.21	11.78	11.37	10.99	48
49	13.44	12.96	12.50	12.07	11.66	11.27	10.91	10.56	49
50	12.69	12.26	11.85	11.47	11.10	10.75	10.42	10.10	50
51	11.93	11.55	11.19	10.85	10.52	10.21	9.92	9.63	51
52	11.16	10.83	10.52	10.22	9.93	9.65	9.39	9.14	52
53	10.38	10.10	9.83	9.56	9.31	9.07	8.84	8.62	53
54	9.60	9.35	9.12	8.90	8.68	8.48	8.28	8.08	54
55	8.80	8.60	8.40	8.21	8.03	7.85	7.68	7.52	55
56	7.99	7.82	7.66	7.51	7.36	7.21	7.07	6.93	56
57	7.17	7.04	6.91	6.78	6.66	6.54	6.43	6.31	57
58	6.34	6.23	6.13	6.04	5.94	5.85	5.76	5.67	58
59	5.49	5.42	5.34	5.27	5.19	5.12	5.05	4.99	59
60	4.63	4.58	4.52	4.47	4.42	4.37	4.32	4.27	60
61	3.75	3.72	3.68	3.65	3.61	3.58	3.55	3.51	61
62	2.85	2.83	2.81	2.79	2.77	2.75	2.73	2.72	62
63	1.93	1.92	1.91	1.90	1.89	1.89	1.88	1.87	63
64	0.98	0.98	0.98	0.97	0.97	0.97	0.97	0.97	64

Table 4 Multipliers for loss of earnings to pension age 65 (females)

Age at date of trial	*Multiplier calculated with allowance for population mortality and rate of return of*								*Age at date of trial*
	1.5%	*2.0%*	*2.5%*	*3.0%*	*3.5%*	*4.0%*	*4.5%*	*5.0%*	
16	34.08	30.78	27.93	25.47	23.34	21.47	19.84	18.41	16
17	33.59	30.39	27.62	25.23	23.14	21.32	19.72	18.31	17
18	33.10	30.00	27.31	24.98	22.94	21.16	19.59	18.21	18
19	32.60	29.60	26.99	24.72	22.73	20.99	19.46	18.10	19
20	32.09	29.19	26.66	24.45	22.52	20.82	19.31	17.98	20
21	31.57	28.77	26.32	24.18	22.30	20.64	19.17	17.86	21
22	31.05	28.34	25.98	23.90	22.07	20.45	19.01	17.74	22
23	30.52	27.91	25.62	23.61	21.83	20.25	18.85	17.61	23
24	29.98	27.47	25.26	23.31	21.58	20.05	18.69	17.47	24
25	29.43	27.02	24.89	23.00	21.33	19.84	18.51	17.32	25
26	28.87	26.56	24.51	22.69	21.07	19.62	18.33	17.17	26
27	28.31	26.09	24.11	22.36	20.79	19.39	18.14	17.01	27
28	27.74	25.61	23.71	22.02	20.51	19.16	17.94	16.84	28
29	27.16	25.12	23.30	21.68	20.22	18 91	17.73	16.66	29
30	26.57	24.62	22.88	21.32	19.92	18 65	17.51	16.48	30
31	25.97	24.12	22.45	20.96	19.61	18.39	17.29	16.29	31
32	25.36	23.60	22.01	20.58	19.28	18.11	17.05	16.08	32
33	24.75	23.07	21.56	20.19	18.95	17.83	16.80	15.87	33
34	24.13	22.54	21.10	19.79	18.61	17.53	16.55	15.65	34
35	23.50	21.99	20.63	19.39	18.26	17.22	16.28	15.42	35
36	22.86	21.44	20.14	18.97	17.89	16.90	16.00	15.17	36
37	22.21	20.87	19.65	18.53	17.51	16.57	15.71	14.92	37
38	21.55	20.30	19.15	18.09	17.12	16.23	15.41	14.65	38
39	20.89	19.71	18.63	17.63	16.72	15.87	15.09	14.37	39
40	20.22	19.11	18.10	17.17	16.30	15.50	14.77	14.08	40

41	19.53	18.51	17.56	16.68	15.87	15.12	14.42	13.78	41
42	18.84	17.89	17.01	16.19	15.43	14.72	14.07	13.46	42
43	18.14	17.26	16.44	15.68	14.97	14.31	13.70	13.12	43
44	17.43	16.62	15.86	15.16	14.50	13.89	13.31	12.77	44
45	16.71	15.97	15.27	14.62	14.01	13.44	12.91	12.41	45
46	15.98	15.31	14.67	14.07	13.51	12.99	12.49	12.02	46
47	15.25	14.63	14.05	13.51	12.99	12.51	12.05	11.62	47
48	14.50	13.95	13.42	12.93	12.46	12.02	11.60	11.21	48
49	13.75	13.25	12.78	12.33	11.91	11.51	11.13	10.77	49
50	12.98	12.54	12.12	11.72	11.34	10.98	10.64	10.31	50
51	12.20	11.81	11.44	11.09	10.75	10.43	10.12	9.83	51
52	11.42	11.08	10.75	10.44	10.15	9.86	9.59	9.33	52
53	10.62	10.33	10.05	9.78	9.52	9.27	9.03	8.81	53
54	9.81	9.56	9.32	9.09	8.87	8.66	8.45	8.25	54
55	8.99	8.79	8.58	8.39	8.20	8.02	7.85	7.68	55
56	8.16	7.99	7.83	7.66	7.51	7.36	7.21	7.07	56
57	7.32	7.18	7.05	6.92	6.79	6.67	6.55	6.44	57
58	6.46	6.36	6.25	6.15	6.05	5.96	5.86	5.77	58
59	5.59	5.51	5.44	5.36	5.29	5.21	5.14	5.07	59
60	4.71	4.65	4.60	4.54	4.49	4.44	4.39	4.34	60
61	3.81	3.77	3.73	3.70	3.66	3.63	3.60	3.56	61
62	2.89	2.87	2.85	2.83	2.81	2.79	2.77	2.75	62
63	1.95	1.94	1.93	1.92	1.91	1.90	1.89	1.88	63
64	0.99	0.98	0.98	0.98	0.98	0.97	0.97	0.97	64

Table 5 Multipliers for loss of earnings to pension age 60 (males)

Age at date of trial	*Multiplier calculated with allowance for population mortality and rate of return of*								*Age at date of trial*
	1.5%	*2.0%*	*2.5%*	*3.0%*	*3.5%*	*4.0%*	*4.5%*	*5.0%*	
16	31.43	28.64	26.20	24.07	22.20	20.55	19.09	17.79	16
17	30.91	28.22	25.86	23.79	21.97	20.36	18.93	17.66	17
18	30.39	27.79	25.51	23.51	21.74	20.17	18.78	17.54	18
19	29.86	27.36	25.16	23.22	21.50	19.98	18.62	17.40	19
20	29.33	26.92	24.80	22.92	21.26	19.77	18.45	17.26	20
21	28.78	26.47	24.43	22.61	21.00	19.56	18.27	17.12	21
22	28.23	26.01	24.05	22.30	20.74	19.34	18.09	16.96	22
23	27.67	25.55	23.66	21.97	20.46	19.11	17.90	16.80	23
24	27.11	25.07	23.26	21.64	20.18	18.87	17.69	16.63	24
25	26.53	24.59	22.85	21.29	19.89	18.62	17.48	16.45	25
26	25.94	24.09	22.43	20.93	19.58	18.37	17.26	16.26	26
27	25.34	23.58	21.99	20.56	19.27	18.10	17.03	16.07	27
28	24.74	23.06	21.55	20.18	18.94	17.82	16.79	15.86	28
29	24.12	22.53	21.09	19.79	18.60	17.52	16.54	15.64	29
30	23.50	21.99	20.63	19.39	18.25	17.22	16.28	15.41	30
31	22.87	21.44	20.15	18.97	17.89	16.91	16.00	15.17	31
32	22.22	20.88	19.66	18.54	17 52	16.58	15.72	14.92	32
33	21.57	20.31	19.16	18.10	17.13	16.24	15.42	14.66	33
34	20.91	19.73	18.64	17.65	16.73	15.88	15.10	14.38	34
35	20.24	19.13	18.12	17.18	16.32	15.52	14.78	14.09	35
36	19.55	18.53	17.58	16.70	15.89	15.14	14.44	13.79	36
37	18.87	17.91	17.03	16.21	15.45	14.74	14.08	13.47	37
38	18.17	17.28	16.47	15.70	14.99	14.33	13.71	13.14	38
39	17.46	16.65	15.89	15.18	14.52	13.91	13.33	12.79	39
40	16.74	16.00	15.30	14.65	14.04	13.46	12.93	12.42	40

41	16.01	15.33	14.70	14.10	13.53	13.01	12.51	12.04	41
42	15.27	14.66	14.08	13.53	13.02	12.53	12.07	11.64	42
43	14.53	13.97	13.44	12.95	12.48	12.04	11.62	11.22	43
44	13.77	13.27	12.80	12.35	11.93	11.53	11.15	10.78	44
45	13.00	12.56	12.14	11.74	11.36	10.99	10.65	10.32	45
46	12.22	11.83	11.46	11.10	10.77	10.44	10.14	9.84	46
47	11.43	11.09	10.77	10.45	10.16	9.87	9.60	9.34	47
48	10.63	10.34	10.06	9.79	9.53	9.28	9.04	8.81	48
49	9.82	9.57	9.33	9.10	8.88	8.67	8.46	8.26	49
50	9.00	8.79	8.59	8.40	8.21	8.03	7.85	7.68	50
51	8.17	8.00	7.83	7.67	7.52	7.37	7.22	7.08	51
52	7.33	7.19	7.05	6.93	6.80	6.68	6.56	6.44	52
53	6.47	6.36	6.26	6.16	6.06	5.96	5.87	5.78	53
54	5.60	5.52	5.44	5.36	5.29	5.22	5.15	5.08	54
55	4.71	4.65	4.60	4.55	4.49	4.44	4.39	4.34	55
56	3.81	3.77	3.74	3.70	3.67	3.63	3.60	3.57	56
57	2.89	2.87	2.85	2.83	2.81	2.79	2.77	2.75	57
58	1.95	1.94	1.93	1.92	1.91	1.90	1.89	1.88	58
59	0.99	0.98	0.98	0.98	0.98	0.97	0.97	0.97	59

Table 6 Multipliers for loss of earnings to pension age 60 (females)

Age at date of trial	*Multiplier calculated with allowance for population mortality and rate of return of*								*Age at date of trial*
	1.5%	*2.0%*	*2.5%*	*3.0%*	*3.5%*	*4.0%*	*4.5%*	*5.0%*	
16	31.81	28.97	26.50	24.33	22.42	20.74	19.26	17.94	16
17	31.29	28.55	26.15	24.05	22.19	20.56	19.11	17.82	17
18	30.76	28.12	25.80	23.76	21.96	20.37	18.95	17.69	18
19	30.23	27.68	25.44	23.47	21.72	20.17	18.79	17.55	19
20	29.68	27.23	25.07	23.16	21.47	19.96	18.62	17.41	20
21	29.13	26.78	24.70	22.85	21.21	19.75	18.44	17.26	21
22	28.57	26.31	24.31	22.53	20.94	19.52	18.25	17.11	22
23	28.00	25.84	23.91	22.20	20.66	19.29	18.06	16.94	23
24	27.42	25.35	23.51	21.86	20.38	19.05	17.85	16.77	24
25	26.83	24.86	23.09	21.50	20.08	18.80	17.64	16.59	25
26	26.24	24.35	22.66	21.14	19.77	18.53	17.42	16.40	26
27	25.63	23.84	22.22	20.77	19.45	18.26	17.18	16.20	27
28	25.02	23.31	21.77	20.38	19.12	17.98	16.94	15.99	28
29	24.40	22.78	21.31	19.99	18.78	17.69	16.69	15.77	29
30	23.77	22.23	20.84	19.58	18.43	17.38	16.42	15.55	30
31	23.12	21.68	20.36	19.16	18.07	17.06	16.15	15.30	31
32	22.47	21.11	19.87	18.73	17.69	16.73	15.86	15.05	32
33	21.82	20.53	19.36	18.29	17.30	16.39	15.56	14.79	33
34	21.15	19.95	18.84	17.83	16.90	16.04	15.24	14.51	34
35	20.47	19.35	18.32	17.36	16.48	15.67	14.92	14.22	35
36	19.78	18.74	17.77	16.88	16.05	15.29	14.58	13.92	36
37	19.09	18.12	17.22	16.38	15.61	14.89	14.22	13.60	37
38	18.38	17.48	16.65	15.87	15.15	14.48	13.85	13.27	38
39	17.67	16.84	16.07	15.35	14.68	14.09	13.47	12.92	39
40	16.94	16.18	15.47	14.81	14.19	13.61	13.06	12.55	40

41	16.21	15.51	14.86	14.26	13.68	13.15	12.64	12.17	41
42	15.46	14.83	14.24	13.69	13.16	12.67	12.20	11.76	42
43	14.70	14.14	13.60	13.10	12.62	12.17	11.75	11.34	43
44	13.94	13.43	12.95	12.49	12.06	11.66	11.27	10.90	44
45	13.16	12.71	12.28	11.87	11.49	11.12	10.77	10.44	45
46	12.37	11.98	11.60	11.24	10.89	10.56	10.25	9.95	46
47	11.58	11.23	10.90	10.58	10.28	9.99	9.71	9.45	47
48	10.77	10.47	10.18	9.91	9.64	9.39	9.15	8.91	48
49	9.95	9.69	9.45	9.21	8.99	8.77	8.56	8.36	49
50	9.11	8.90	8.69	8.50	8.31	8.12	7.94	7.77	50
51	8.27	8.09	7.92	7.76	7.60	7.45	7.30	7.16	51
52	7.41	7.27	7.14	7.00	6.88	6.75	6.63	6.51	52
53	6.54	6.43	6.33	6.22	6.12	6.03	5.93	5.84	53
54	5.65	5.57	5.49	5.42	5.34	5.27	5.20	5.13	54
55	4.75	4.70	4.64	4.59	4.53	4.48	4.43	4.38	55
56	3.84	3.80	3.77	3.73	3.69	3.66	3.63	3.59	56
57	2.91	2.89	2.86	2.84	2.82	2.80	2.78	2.77	57
58	1.96	1.95	1.94	1.93	1.92	1.91	1.90	1.89	58
59	0.99	0.99	0.98	0.98	0.98	0.98	0.97	0.97	59

Table 7 Multipliers for loss of pension commencing age 65 (males)

Age at date of trial	*Multiplier calculated with allowance for population mortality and rate of return of*								*Age at date of trial*
	1.5%	*2.0%*	*2.5%*	*3.0%*	*3.5%*	*4.0%*	*4.5%*	*5.0%*	
0	3.76	2.62	1.83	1.28	0.90	0.63	0.45	0.32	0
1	3.85	2.69	1.89	1.33	0.94	0.66	0.47	0.34	1
2	3.91	2.75	1.94	1.37	0.97	0.69	0.49	0.35	2
3	3.97	2.81	1.99	1.41	1.01	0.72	0.52	0.37	3
4	4.03	2.86	2.04	1.46	1.04	0.75	0.54	0.39	4
5	4.09	2.92	2.09	1.50	1.08	0.78	0.56	0.41	5
6	4.15	2.98	2.14	1.55	1.12	0.81	0.59	0.43	6
7	4.22	3.04	2.20	1.59	1.16	0.84	0.62	0.45	7
8	4.28	3.10	2.25	1.64	1.20	0.88	0.64	0.47	8
9	4.34	3.16	2.31	1.69	1.24	0.91	0.67	0.50	9
10	4.41	3.23	2.37	1.74	1.28	0.95	0.70	0.52	10
11	4.48	3.29	2.43	1.79	1 33	0.99	0.73	0.55	11
12	4.55	3.36	2.49	1.85	1.38	1.03	0.77	0.57	12
13	4.61	3.43	2.55	1.90	1.42	1.07	0.80	0.60	13
14	4.68	3.50	2.62	1.96	1.47	1.11	0.84	0.63	14
15	4.76	3.57	2.68	2.02	1 53	1.15	0.88	0.67	15
16	4.83	3.64	2.75	2.08	1.58	1.20	0.92	0.70	16
17	4.90	3.71	2.82	2.15	1.64	1.25	0.96	0.73	17
18	4.98	3.79	2.89	2.21	1.69	1 30	1.00	0.77	18
19	5.06	3.87	2.97	2.28	1.76	1.35	1.05	0.81	19
20	5.14	3.95	3.04	2.35	1.82	1.41	1.10	0.85	20
21	5.22	4.03	3.12	2.42	1.88	1.47	1.15	0.90	21
22	5.31	4.12	3.20	2.50	1.95	1.53	1.20	0.94	22
23	5.39	4.20	3.29	2.57	2.02	1.59	1.25	0.99	23
24	5.48	4.29	3.37	2.65	2.09	1.66	1.31	1.04	24
25	5.56	4.38	3.46	2.74	2.17	1.72	1.37	1.09	25
26	5.65	4.47	3.55	2.82	2.25	1.79	1.43	1.15	26
27	5.74	4.57	3.64	2.91	2.33	1.87	1.50	1.21	27
28	5.83	4.66	3.73	3.00	2.41	1.94	1.97	1.27	28
29	5.92	4.76	3.83	3.09	2.50	2.02	1.64	1.33	29
30	6.02	4.86	3.93	3.19	2.59	2.11	1.72	1.40	30

31	6.11	4.96	4.03	3.28	2.68	2.19	1.79	1.47	31
32	6.21	5.06	4.14	3.39	2.78	2.28	1.88	1.55	32
33	6.31	5.17	4.24	3.49	2.88	2.37	1.96	1.63	33
34	6.41	5.28	4.35	3.60	2.98	2.47	2.05	1.71	34
35	6.52	5.39	4.47	3.71	3.09	2.57	2.15	1.80	35
36	6.62	5.50	4.59	3.83	3.20	2.68	2.25	1.89	36
37	6.73	5.62	4.71	3.95	3.32	2.79	2.35	1.99	37
38	6.84	5.74	4.83	4.07	3.44	2.91	2.46	2.09	38
39	6.95	5.87	4.96	4.20	3.56	3.03	2.58	2.20	39
40	7.07	5.99	5.09	4.33	3.69	3.15	2.70	2.31	40
41	7.19	6.12	5.23	4.47	3.83	3.28	2.82	2.43	41
42	7.31	6.26	5.37	4.61	3.97	3.42	2.96	2.56	42
43	7.43	6.40	5.51	4.76	4.12	3.57	3.09	2.69	43
44	7.56	6.54	5.66	4.91	4.27	3.72	3.24	2.83	44
45	7.69	6.68	5.82	5.07	4.43	3.88	3.39	2.98	45
46	7.83	6.84	5.98	5.24	4.60	4.04	3.56	3.14	46
47	7.97	6.99	6.15	5.41	4.77	4.22	3.73	3.30	47
48	8.12	7.16	6.32	5.59	4.96	4.40	3.91	3.48	48
49	8.27	7.33	6.50	5.78	5.15	4.59	4.10	3.67	49
50	8.43	7.51	6.70	5.98	5.35	4.80	4.30	3.87	50
51	8.59	7.69	6.89	6.19	5.57	5.01	4.52	4.08	51
52	8.77	7.89	7.10	6.41	5.79	5.24	4.74	4.30	52
53	8.95	8.09	7.32	6.64	6.03	5.48	4.99	4.55	53
54	9.14	8.31	7.56	6.88	6.28	5.74	5.25	4.80	54
55	9.35	8.53	7.80	7.14	6.55	6.01	5.52	5.08	55
56	9.56	8.77	8.06	7.41	6.83	6.30	5.82	5.38	56
57	9.79	9.03	8.33	7.70	7.13	6.61	6.13	5.70	57
58	10.04	9.30	8.63	8.02	7.45	6.94	6.47	6.04	58
59	10.31	9.59	8.94	8.35	7.80	7.30	6.84	6.41	59
60	10.59	9.91	9.28	8.71	8.18	7.69	7.24	6.82	60
61	10.90	10.25	9.65	9.10	8.58	8.11	7.67	7.26	61
62	11.24	10.62	10.05	9.52	9.02	8.57	8.14	7.75	62
63	11.61	11.03	10.48	9.98	9.51	9.07	8.66	8.28	63
64	12.02	11.47	10.96	10.48	10.04	9.62	9.23	8.87	64
65	12.48	11.97	11.49	11.04	10.62	10.23	9.86	9.52	65

Table 8 Multipliers for loss of pension commencing age 65 (females)

Age at date of trial	*Multiplier calculated with allowance for population mortality and rate of return of*								*Age at date of trial*
	1.5%	*2.0%*	*2.5%*	*3.0%*	*3.5%*	*4.0%*	*4.5%*	*5.0%*	
0	5.11	3.53	2.45	1.70	1.19	0.83	0.58	0.41	0
1	5.22	3.63	2.53	1.77	1.24	0.87	0.61	0.43	1
2	5.30	3.70	2.59	1.82	1.28	0.91	0.64	0.46	2
3	5.38	3.78	2.66	1.88	1.33	0.94	0.67	0.48	3
4	5.47	3.85	2.72	1.93	1.37	0.98	0.70	0.50	4
5	5.55	3.93	2.79	1.99	1.42	1.02	0.73	0.53	5
6	5.63	4.01	2.86	2.05	1 47	1.06	0.77	0.55	6
7	5.72	4.09	2.94	2.11	1.52	1.10	0.80	0.58	7
8	5.80	4.17	3.01	2.18	1.58	1.15	0.84	0.61	8
9	5.89	4.26	3.09	2.24	1.63	1.19	0.87	0.64	9
10	5.98	4.34	3.16	2.31	1.69	1.24	0.91	0.67	10
11	6.07	4.43	3.24	2.38	1.75	1.29	0.96	0.71	11
12	6.16	4.52	3.32	2.45	1.81	1.34	1.00	0.74	12
13	6.26	4.61	3.41	2.52	1.88	1.40	1.04	0.78	13
14	6.35	4.70	3.49	2.60	1.94	1.45	1.09	0.82	14
15	6.45	4.80	3.58	2.68	2.01	1.51	1.14	0.86	15
16	6.55	4.90	3.67	2.76	2.08	1.57	1.19	0.90	16
17	6.65	5.00	3.76	2.84	2.15	1.64	1.25	0.95	17
18	6.75	5.10	3.86	2.93	2.23	1.70	1.30	1.00	18
19	6.85	5.20	3.96	3.02	2.31	1 77	1.36	1.05	19
20	6.96	5.31	4.06	3.11	2.39	1.84	1.42	1.10	20
21	7.06	5.41	4.16	3.20	2.48	1.92	1.49	1.16	21
22	7.17	5.52	4.27	3.30	2.56	1.99	1.55	1.21	22
23	7.28	5.64	4.37	3.40	2.65	2.07	1.62	1.28	23
24	7.39	5.75	4.48	3.51	2.75	2.16	1.70	1.34	24
25	7.51	5.87	4.60	3.61	2.84	2.24	1.78	1.41	25
26	7.62	5.99	4.71	3.72	2.94	2.34	1.86	1.48	26
27	7.74	6.11	4.83	3.83	3.05	2.43	1.94	1.55	27
28	7.86	6.23	4.96	3.95	3.16	2.53	2.03	1.63	28
29	7.98	6.36	5.08	4.07	3.27	2.63	2.12	1.71	29
30	8.10	6.49	5.21	4.19	3.38	2.74	2.22	1.80	30

31	8.23	6.62	5.34	4.32	3.50	2.85	2.32	1.89	31
32	8.35	6.76	5.48	4.45	3.63	2.96	2.42	1.99	32
33	8.48	6.90	5.62	4.59	3.76	3.08	2.53	2.09	33
34	8.62	7.04	5.76	4.73	3.89	3.21	2.65	2.19	34
35	8.75	7.18	5.91	4.88	4.03	3.34	2.77	2.30	35
36	8.89	7.33	6.06	5.03	4.17	3.47	2.90	2.42	36
37	9.03	7.49	6.22	5.18	4.32	3.61	3.03	2.54	37
38	9.17	7.64	6.38	5.34	4.48	3 76	3.17	2.67	38
39	9.32	7.80	6.55	5.51	4.64	3.92	3.31	2.81	39
40	9.47	7.97	6.72	5.68	4.81	4.08	3.47	2.95	40
41	9.62	8.13	6.89	5.85	4.98	4.24	3.63	3.10	41
42	9.77	8.31	7.07	6.03	5.16	4.42	3.79	3.26	42
43	9.93	8.48	7.26	6.22	5.35	4.60	3.97	3.43	43
44	10.10	8.66	7.45	6.42	5.54	4.79	4.15	3.60	44
45	10.26	8.85	7.65	6.62	5.75	4.99	4.35	3.79	45
46	10.44	9.04	7.85	6.83	5.96	5.20	4.55	3.99	46
47	10.61	9.24	8.07	7.05	6.18	5.42	4.76	4.20	47
48	10.80	9.45	8.29	7.28	6.41	5.65	4.99	4.41	48
49	10.99	9.66	8.51	7.52	6.65	5.89	5.23	4.65	49
50	11.18	9.88	8.75	7.76	6.90	6.14	5.48	4.89	50
51	11.38	10.11	9.00	8.02	7.16	6.41	5.74	5.15	51
52	11.59	10.34	9.25	8.29	7.44	6.68	6.02	5.43	52
53	11.81	10.59	9.52	8.57	7.72	6.98	6.31	5.72	53
54	12.03	10.84	9.79	8.86	8.03	7.28	6.62	6.03	54
55	12.26	11.11	10.08	9.16	8.34	7.61	6.95	6.36	55
56	12.51	11.38	10.38	9.48	8.68	7.95	7.30	6.71	56
57	12.76	11.67	10.70	9.82	9.03	8.31	7.67	7.08	57
58	13.03	11.98	11.03	10.17	9.40	8.70	8.06	7.48	58
59	13.31	12.30	11.38	10.55	9.79	9.10	8.48	7.90	59
60	13.61	12.64	11.75	10.95	10.21	9.54	8.92	8.36	60
61	13.93	13.00	12.15	11.37	10.66	10.00	9.40	8.85	61
62	14.27	13.38	12.57	11.82	11.13	10.50	9.92	9.38	62
63	14.64	13.79	13.01	12.30	11.64	11.03	10.47	9.95	63
64	15.03	14.23	13.49	12.81	12.18	11.60	11.07	10.57	64
65	15.45	14.70	14.00	13.37	12.77	12.22	11.71	11.24	65

Table 9 Multipliers for loss of pension commencing age 60 (males)

Age at date of trial	*Multiplier calculated with allowance for population mortality and rate of return of*								*Age at date of trial*
	1.5%	*2.0%*	*2.5%*	*3.0%*	*3.5%*	*4.0%*	*4.5%*	*5.0%*	
0	5.40	3.83	2.72	1.94	1.39	0.99	0.71	0.51	0
1	5.53	3.94	2.81	2.01	1.45	1.04	0.75	0.55	1
2	5.62	4.02	2.88	2.08	1.50	1.08	0.79	0.57	2
3	5.70	4.10	2.96	2.14	1.55	1.13	0.82	0.60	3
4	5.79	4.18	3.03	2.20	1.61	1.17	0.86	0.63	4
5	5.88	4.27	3.11	2.27	1.66	1.22	0.90	0.66	5
6	5.97	4.35	3.19	2.34	1.72	1.27	0.94	0.70	6
7	6.06	4.44	3.27	2.41	1.78	1.32	0.98	0.73	7
8	6.15	4.53	3.35	2.48	1.84	1.37	1.03	0.77	8
9	6.24	4.62	3.43	2.56	1.91	1.43	1.07	0.81	9
10	6.34	4.72	3.52	2.63	1.98	1.49	1.12	0.85	10
11	6.43	4.81	3.61	2.71	2.05	1.55	1.17	0.89	11
12	6.53	4.91	3.70	2.80	2.12	1.61	1.22	0.93	12
13	6.63	5.01	3.79	2.88	2.19	1.67	1.28	0.98	13
14	6.73	5.11	3.89	2.97	2.27	1.74	1.34	1.03	14
15	6.84	5.21	3.99	3.06	2.35	1.81	1.40	1.08	15
16	6.94	5.32	4.09	3.15	2.43	1.88	1.46	1.14	16
17	7.05	5.43	4.19	3.25	2.52	1.96	1.53	1.20	17
18	7.16	5.54	4.30	3.35	2.61	2.04	1.60	1.26	18
19	7.27	5.66	4.41	3.45	2.70	2.12	1.67	1.32	19
20	7.39	5.78	4.53	3.56	2.80	2.21	1.75	1.39	20
21	7.51	5.90	4.64	3.67	2.90	2.30	1.83	1.46	21
22	7.63	6.02	4.76	3.78	3.01	2.40	1.91	1.53	22
23	7.75	6.15	4.89	3.90	3.11	2.49	2.00	1.61	23
24	7.87	6.27	5.01	4.02	3.23	2.60	2.09	1.69	24
25	7.99	6.41	5.14	4.14	3.34	2.70	2.19	1.78	25
26	8.12	6.54	5.28	4.27	3.46	2.81	2.29	1.87	26
27	8.25	6.68	5.41	4.40	3.59	2.93	2.39	1.96	27
28	8.38	6.81	5.55	4.54	3.71	3.05	2.50	2.06	28
29	8.51	6.96	5.70	4.68	3.85	3.17	2.62	2.17	29
30	8.65	7.10	5.85	4.82	3.99	3.30	2.74	2.28	30

31	8.79	7.25	6.00	4.97	4.13	3.44	2.87	2.39	31
32	8.93	7.40	6.15	5.12	4.28	3.58	3.00	2.52	32
33	9.07	7.56	6.31	5.28	4.43	3.72	3.14	2.65	33
34	9.22	7.72	6.48	5.45	4.59	3.88	3.28	2.78	34
35	9.36	7.88	6.65	5.62	4.76	4.04	3.43	2.92	35
36	9.52	8.05	6.82	5.79	4.93	4.20	3.59	3.07	36
37	9.67	8.22	7.00	5.97	5.11	4.38	3.76	3.23	37
38	9.83	8.39	7.18	6.16	5.29	4.56	3.93	3.40	38
39	9.99	8.57	7.37	6.36	5.49	4.75	4.11	3.57	39
40	10.16	8.76	7.57	6.56	5.69	4.94	4.31	3.76	40
41	10.33	8.95	7.77	6.76	5.90	5.15	4.51	3.95	41
42	10.50	9.15	7.98	6.98	6.12	5.37	4.72	4.16	42
43	10.68	9.35	8.20	7.20	6.34	5.59	4.94	4.37	43
44	10.87	9.56	8.42	7.44	6.58	5.83	5.17	4.60	44
45	11.05	9.77	8.65	7.68	6.83	6.08	5.42	4.84	45
46	11.25	9.99	8.89	7.93	7.08	6.34	5.68	5.10	46
47	11.45	10.22	9.14	8.19	7.35	6.61	5.95	5.37	47
48	11.66	10.46	9.40	8.47	7.64	6.90	6.24	5.66	48
49	11.88	10.71	9.67	8.75	7.93	7.20	6.55	5.96	49
50	12.11	10.97	9.96	9.05	8.24	7.52	6.87	6.29	50
51	12.35	11.24	10.25	9.37	8.57	7.86	7.21	6.63	51
52	12.60	11.53	10.56	9.70	8.92	8.21	7.58	7.00	52
53	12.86	11.83	10.89	10.05	9.28	8.59	7.96	7.39	53
54	13.14	12.14	11.24	10.42	9.67	8.99	8.38	7.81	54
55	13.43	12.47	11.60	10.81	10.08	9.42	8.82	8.26	55
56	13.75	12.82	11.99	11.22	10.52	9.88	9.29	8.74	56
57	14.08	13.20	12.40	11.66	10.98	10.36	9.79	9.26	57
58	14.43	13.60	12.83	12.13	11.48	10.89	10.33	9.82	58
59	14.81	14.03	13.30	12.63	12.02	11.45	10.92	10.43	59
60	15.22	14.49	13.81	13.18	12.60	12.06	11.56	11.09	60

Table 10 Multipliers for loss of pension commencing age 60 (females)

Age at date of trial	*Multiplier calculated with allowance for population mortality and rate of return of*								*Age at date of trial*
	1.5%	*2.0%*	*2.5%*	*3.0%*	*3.5%*	*4.0%*	*4.5%*	*5.0%*	
0	6.88	4.83	3.41	2.41	1.71	1.22	0.87	0.62	0
1	7.03	4.96	3.52	2.50	1.78	1.28	0.92	0.66	1
2	7.14	5.06	3.61	2.58	1.85	1.33	0.96	0.69	2
3	7.25	5.17	3.70	2.65	1.91	1.38	1.00	0.73	3
4	7.36	5.27	3.79	2.73	1.98	1.44	1.05	0.76	4
5	7.47	5.38	3.89	2.82	2.05	1.49	1.09	0.80	5
6	7.58	5.49	3.98	2.90	2.12	1.55	1.14	0.84	6
7	7.70	5.60	4.08	2.99	2.20	1.62	1.19	0.88	7
8	7.81	5.71	4.19	3.08	2.27	1.68	1.25	0.93	8
9	7.93	5.82	4.29	3.17	2.35	1.75	1.30	0.98	9
10	8.05	5.94	4.40	3.27	2.43	1.82	1.36	1.02	10
11	8.17	6.06	4.51	3.37	2.52	1.89	1.42	1.08	11
12	8.30	6.18	4.62	3.47	2.61	1.97	1.49	1.13	12
13	8.42	6.31	4.74	3.57	2.70	2.05	1.56	1.19	13
14	8.55	6.44	4.86	3.68	2.80	2.13	1.63	1.25	14
15	8.68	6.57	4.98	3.79	2.89	2.22	1.70	1.31	15
16	8.81	6.70	5.11	3.91	3.00	2.30	1.78	1.37	16
17	8.95	6.83	5.24	4.02	3.10	2.40	1.86	1.44	17
18	9.08	6.97	5.37	4.15	3.21	2.49	1.94	1.52	18
19	9.22	7.11	5.50	4.27	3.32	2.59	2.03	1.59	19
20	9.36	7.26	5.64	4.40	3.44	2.70	2.12	1.67	20
21	9.51	7.41	5.79	4.53	3.56	2.81	2.22	1.76	21
22	9.65	7.56	5.93	4.67	3.69	2.92	2.32	1.84	22
23	9.80	7.71	6.08	4.81	3.82	3.04	2.42	1.94	23
24	9.95	7.87	6.24	4.96	3.99	3.16	2.53	2.04	24
25	10.10	8.03	6.40	5.11	4.09	3.29	2.65	2.14	25
26	10.26	8.19	6.56	5.27	4.24	3.42	2.77	2.25	26
27	10.41	8.36	6.72	5.43	4.39	3.56	2.89	2.36	27
28	10.57	8.53	6.90	5.59	4.54	3.70	3.03	2.48	28
29	10.74	8.70	7.07	5.76	4.71	3.85	3.16	2.60	29
30	10.90	8.88	7.25	5.94	4.87	4.01	3.31	2.73	30

31	11.07	9.06	7.43	6.12	5.04	4.17	3.46	2.87	31
32	11.24	9.25	7.62	6.30	5.22	4.34	3.61	3.02	32
33	11.42	9.44	7.82	6.50	5.41	4.52	3.78	3.17	33
34	11.60	9.63	8.02	6.69	5.60	4.70	3.95	3.33	34
35	11.78	9.83	8.22	6.90	5.80	4.89	4.13	3.50	35
36	11.96	10.03	8.44	7.11	6.01	5.09	4.32	3.67	36
37	12.15	10.24	8.65	7.33	6.22	5.30	4.52	3.86	37
38	12.34	10.45	8.88	7.56	6.45	5.51	4.72	4.06	38
39	12.54	10.67	9.11	7.79	6.68	5.74	4.94	4.26	39
40	12.74	10.90	9.34	8.03	6.92	5.97	5.17	4.48	40
41	12.94	11.13	9.59	8.28	7.17	6.22	5.41	4.71	41
42	13.15	11.36	9.84	8.54	7.43	6.48	5.66	4.95	42
43	13.37	11.60	10.10	8.81	7.70	6.74	5.92	5.21	43
44	13.59	11.85	10.36	9.08	7.98	7.02	6.19	5.48	44
45	13.81	12.11	10.64	9.37	8.27	7.32	6.48	5.76	45
46	14.05	12.37	10.93	9.67	8.58	7.62	6.79	6.06	46
47	14.28	12.65	11.22	9.98	8.89	7.94	7.11	6.37	47
48	14.53	12.93	11.53	10.30	9.23	8.28	7.44	6.71	48
49	14.78	13.22	11.84	10.64	9.57	8.63	7.80	7.06	49
50	15.05	13.52	12.17	10.98	9.93	9.00	8.17	7.43	50
51	15.32	13.83	12.51	11.35	10.31	9.39	8.56	7.82	51
52	15.60	14.15	12.87	11.73	10.71	9.79	8.98	8.24	52
53	15.89	14.49	13.24	12.12	11.12	10.22	9.41	8.69	53
54	16.19	14.83	13.62	12.53	11.56	10.67	9.88	9.16	54
55	16.50	15.20	14.02	12.97	12.01	11.15	10.37	9.66	55
56	16.83	15.57	14.44	13.42	12.49	11.65	10.88	10.19	56
57	17.17	15.97	14.88	13.89	13.00	12.18	11.43	10.75	57
58	17.54	16.39	15.34	14.40	13.53	12.74	12.02	11.36	58
59	17.92	16.83	15.83	14.93	14.10	13.34	12.64	12.00	59
60	18.32	17.29	16.35	15.49	14.70	13.98	13.31	12.70	60

Table 11 Multipliers for pecuniary loss for life (males)

Age at date of trial	*Multiplier calculated with allowance for projected mortality from the 1996-based population projections and rate of return of* 1.5%	2.0%	2.5%	3.0%	3.5%	4.0%	4.5%	5.0%	Age at date of trial
0	45.80	39.31	34.17	30.05	26.70	23.96	21.68	19.77	0
1	45.73	39.31	34.20	30.10	26.77	24.04	21.76	19.85	1
2	45.43	39.09	34.06	30.00	26.70	23.99	21.73	19.83	2
3	45.11	38.87	33.90	29.89	26.62	23.93	21.69	19.80	3
4	44.78	38.64	33.74	29.78	26.54	23.87	21.64	19.76	4
5	44.45	38.41	33.57	29.66	26.46	23.81	21.60	19.73	5
6	44.11	38.17	33.40	29.54	26.37	23.74	21.55	19.69	6
7	43.76	37.92	33.22	29.41	26.27	23.67	21.50	19.65	7
8	43.41	37.67	33.04	29.28	26 18	23.60	21.44	19.61	8
9	43.05	37.41	32.86	29.14	26.08	23.53	21.38	19.57	9
10	42.69	37.15	32.67	29.00	25.97	23.45	21.33	19.53	10
11	42.32	36.88	32.47	28.85	25.86	23.37	21.26	19.48	11
12	41.94	36.61	32.27	28.70	25.75	23.28	21.20	19.43	12
13	41.57	36.33	32.06	28.55	25.64	23.20	21.13	19.38	13
14	41.18	36.05	31.85	28.40	25.52	23.11	21.06	19.32	14
15	40.79	35.76	31.64	28.24	25.40	23.01	20.99	19.27	15
16	40.40	35.47	31.42	28.07	25.27	22.92	20.92	19.21	16
17	40.01	35.18	31.20	27.91	25.15	22.82	20.84	19.15	17
18	39.62	34.89	30.98	27.74	25.02	22.72	20.77	19.09	18
19	39.22	34.59	30.76	27.57	24.90	22.63	20.70	19.04	19
20	38.83	34.30	30.54	27.40	24.77	22.53	20.62	18.98	20
21	38.42	33.99	30.31	27.23	24.63	22.45	20.54	18.91	21
22	38.02	33.68	30.08	27.05	24.49	22.32	20.46	18.85	22
23	37.60	33.37	29.83	26.87	24.35	22.21	20.37	18.78	23
24	37.18	33.04	29.59	26.67	24.20	22.09	20.28	18.71	24
25	36.75	32.71	29.33	26.48	24.05	21.97	20.18	18.63	25

26	36.31	32.38	29.07	26.27	23.89	21.85	20.08	18.55	26
27	35.87	32.04	28.80	26.06	23.72	21.72	19.98	18.47	27
28	35.42	31.69	28.53	25.85	23.55	21.58	19.87	18.38	28
29	34.97	31.33	28.25	25.63	23.38	21.44	19.76	18.29	29
30	34.50	30.96	27.96	25.40	23.19	21.29	19.64	18.20	30
31	34.02	30.59	27.66	25.16	23.00	21.14	19.51	18.10	31
32	33.54	30.20	27.36	24.91	22.81	20.98	19.38	17.99	32
33	33.05	29.81	27.04	24.66	22.60	20.81	19.25	17.88	33
34	32.56	29.42	26.72	24.40	22.39	20.64	19.11	17.76	34
35	32.05	29.01	26.39	24.13	22.17	20.46	18.96	17.64	35
36	31.54	28.59	26.05	23.85	21.94	20.27	18.80	17.51	36
37	31.01	28.16	25.70	23.57	21.70	20.07	18.64	17.37	37
38	30.48	27.73	25.34	23.27	21.46	19.87	18.47	17.23	38
39	29.94	27.29	24.98	22.97	21.21	19.66	18.29	17.08	39
40	29.40	26.84	24.61	22.66	20.95	19.44	18.11	16.92	40
41	28.85	26.38	24.23	22.34	20.68	19.22	17.92	16.76	41
42	28.29	25.92	23.84	22.02	20.41	18.98	17.72	16.59	42
43	27.73	25.44	23.44	21.68	20.13	18.74	17.52	16.42	43
44	27.15	24.96	23.04	21.34	19.83	18.49	17.30	16.23	44
45	26.57	24.47	22.62	20.98	19.53	18.23	17.08	16.04	45
46	25.98	23.96	22.19	20.61	19.21	17.96	16.84	15.84	46
47	25.37	23.45	21.75	20.23	18.89	17.68	16.60	15.62	47
48	24.76	22.93	21.30	19.85	18.55	17.39	16.34	15.40	48
49	24.14	22.39	20.84	19.45	18.20	17.08	16.08	15.16	49
50	23.52	21.86	20.37	19.04	17.85	16.78	15.80	14.93	50
51	22.90	21.32	19.90	18.63	17.49	16.46	15.53	14.68	51
52	22.28	20.78	19.43	18.22	17.12	16.14	15.24	14.43	52
53	21.65	20.23	18.95	17.79	16.75	15.80	14.95	14.16	53
54	21.02	19.67	18.46	17.36	16.37	15.46	14.64	13.89	54
55	20.38	19.11	17.96	16.92	15.98	15.12	14.33	13.62	55

Table 11 Multipliers for pecuniary loss for life (males) *continued*

Age at date of trial	*Multiplier calculated with allowance for projected mortality from the 1996-based population projections and rate of return of* 1.5%	2.0%	2.5%	3.0%	3.5%	4.0%	4.5%	5.0%	*Age at date of trial*
56	19.75	18.55	17.47	16.48	15.58	14.77	14.02	13.33	56
57	19.12	17.99	16.97	16.04	15.19	14.41	13.70	13.04	57
58	18.50	17.44	16.47	15.59	14.78	14.05	13.37	12.74	58
59	17.87	16.87	15.97	15.14	14.38	13.68	13.03	12.44	59
60	17.24	16.31	15.46	14.68	13.96	13.30	12.69	12.13	60
61	16.61	15.74	14.94	14.21	13.54	12.92	12.34	11.81	61
62	15.98	15.17	14.43	13.74	13.11	12.52	11.98	11.48	62
63	15.35	14.60	13.90	13.26	12.67	12.12	11.62	11.14	63
64	14.72	14.02	13.38	12.78	12.23	11.72	11.24	10.80	64
65	14.09	13.45	12.85	12.30	11.78	11.31	10.86	10.45	65
66	13.46	12.87	12.32	11.81	11.33	10.89	10.48	10.09	66
67	12.85	12.30	11.80	11.32	10.88	10.47	10.09	9.73	67
68	12.24	11.74	11.28	10.84	10.44	10.06	9.70	9.36	68
69	11.64	11.19	10.76	10.36	9.99	9.64	9.31	9.00	69
70	11.06	10.65	10.26	9.89	9.55	9.23	8.92	8.64	70
71	10.51	10.13	9.77	9.44	9.12	8.83	8.55	8.29	71
72	9.97	9.63	9.30	9.00	8.71	8.44	8.18	7.94	72
73	9.45	9.14	8.84	8.56	8.30	8.05	7.82	7.59	73
74	8.95	8.67	8.40	8.15	7.91	7.68	7.46	7.26	74
75	8.46	8.21	7.97	7.74	7.52	7.31	7.11	6.93	75
76	8.00	7.77	7.55	7.34	7.14	6.95	6.77	6.60	76
77	7.56	7.35	7.15	6.96	6.78	6.61	6.45	6.29	77
78	7.14	6.95	6.77	6.60	6.13	6.28	6.13	5.99	78
79	6.73	6.56	6.40	6.25	6.10	5.96	5.82	5.70	79
80	6.35	6.20	6.06	5.92	5.78	5.65	5.53	5.41	80

81	6.00	5.86	5.73	5.60	5.48	5.36	5.25	5.14	81
82	5.66	5.54	5.42	5.30	5.19	5.09	4.99	4.89	82
83	5.35	5.24	5.13	5.03	4.93	4.83	4.74	4.65	83
84	5.07	4.97	4.87	4.78	4.69	4.60	4.52	4.43	84
85	4.81	4.72	4.63	4.54	4.46	4.38	4.30	4.23	85
86	4.56	4.48	4.40	4.32	4.24	4.17	4.10	4.04	86
87	4.32	4.24	4.17	4.10	4.03	3.96	3.90	3.84	87
88	4.07	4.01	3.94	3.88	3.82	3.76	3.70	3.64	88
89	3.84	3.78	3.72	3.66	3.61	3.56	3.50	3.45	89
90	3.62	3.56	3.51	3.46	3.41	3.36	3.32	3.27	90
91	3.40	3.35	3.31	3.26	3.22	3.17	3.13	3.09	91
92	3.19	3.14	3.10	3.06	3.02	2.99	2.95	2.91	92
93	2.99	2.96	2.92	2.88	2.85	2.81	2.78	2.75	93
94	2.82	2.78	2.75	2.72	2.69	2.66	2.63	2.60	94
95	2.65	2.62	2.59	2.56	2.53	2.50	2.48	2.45	95
96	2.48	2.45	2.43	2.40	2.38	2.35	2.33	2.31	96
97	2.32	2.29	2.27	2.25	2.23	2.21	2.19	2.16	97
98	2.15	2.13	2.11	2.10	2.08	2.06	2.04	2.02	98
99	1.99	1.98	1.96	1.94	1.93	1.91	1.90	1.88	99
100	1.83	1.82	1.81	1.79	1.78	1.76	1.75	1.74	100

Table 12 Multipliers for pecuniary loss for life (females)

Age at date of trial	*Multiplier calculated with allowance for projected mortality from the 1996-based population projections and rate of return of*								*Age at date of trial*
	1.5%	*2.0%*	*2.5%*	*3.0%*	*3.5%*	*4.0%*	*4.5%*	*5.0%*	
0	47.34	40.38	34.93	30.59	27.10	24.25	21.90	19.94	0
1	47.25	40.36	34.95	30.64	27.16	24.31	21.97	20.01	1
2	46.97	40.18	34.82	30.55	27.10	24.28	21.94	19.99	2
3	46.67	39.97	34.69	30.46	27.04	24.23	21.91	19.97	3
4	46.37	39.77	34.54	30.36	26.97	24.18	21.88	19.94	4
5	46.06	39.55	34.40	30.26	26.89	24.13	21.84	19.92	5
6	45.74	39.34	34.24	30.15	26.82	24.08	21.80	19.89	6
7	45.42	39.11	34.09	30.04	26.74	24.02	21.76	19.86	7
8	45.09	38.88	33.93	29.93	26.66	23.97	21.72	19.83	8
9	44.76	38.65	33.76	29.81	26.58	23.91	21.68	19.80	9
10	44.42	38.41	33.59	29.69	26.49	23.84	21.63	19.76	10
11	44.08	38.17	33.42	29.56	26.40	23.78	21.58	19.72	11
12	43.73	37.92	33.24	29.44	26.31	23.71	21.53	19.69	12
13	43.38	37.67	33.06	29.30	26.21	23.64	21.48	19.65	13
14	43.02	37.41	32.87	29.17	26.11	23.56	21.42	19.60	14
15	42.65	37.15	32.68	29.03	26.01	23.48	21.36	19.56	15
16	42.29	36.88	32.49	28.89	25.90	23.41	21.30	19.52	16
17	41.91	36.61	32.29	28.74	25.79	23.32	21.24	19.47	17
18	41.54	36.34	32.09	28.59	25.68	23.24	21.18	19.42	18
19	41.15	36.05	31.88	28.43	25.56	23.15	21.11	19.37	19
20	40.77	35.77	31.67	28.28	25.44	23.06	21.04	19.32	20
21	40.37	35.48	31.45	28.11	25.32	22.97	20.97	19.26	21
22	39.97	35.18	31.23	27.94	25.19	22.87	20.90	19.20	22
23	39.57	34.88	31.00	27.77	25.06	22.77	20.82	19.14	23
24	39.16	34.57	30.77	27.59	24.93	22.67	20.74	19.08	24
25	38.74	34.25	30.53	27.41	24.79	22.56	20.65	19.01	25

26	38.32	33.93	30.28	27.22	24.64	22.44	20.56	18.94	26
27	37.89	33.61	30.03	27.03	24.49	22.33	20.47	18.87	27
28	37.46	33.27	29.78	26.83	24.34	22.21	20.38	18.79	28
29	37.01	32.93	29.51	26.63	24.18	22.08	20.28	18.71	29
30	36.57	32.59	29.24	26.42	24.01	21.95	20.17	18.63	30
31	36.11	32.23	28.97	26.20	23.84	21.81	20.06	18.54	31
32	35.65	31.87	28.68	25.98	23.66	21.67	19.95	18.45	32
33	35.18	31.50	28.39	25.75	23.48	21.52	19.83	18.35	33
34	34.70	31.13	28.10	25.51	23.29	21.37	19.71	18.25	34
35	34.22	30.74	27.79	25.26	23.09	21.21	19.58	18.15	35
36	33.73	30.35	27.48	25.01	22.89	21.05	19.44	18.04	36
37	33.23	29.96	27.16	24.75	22.68	20.88	19.30	17.92	37
38	32.72	29.55	26.83	24.49	22.46	20.70	19.16	17.80	38
39	32.21	29.14	26.50	24.22	22.24	20.51	19.00	17.67	39
40	31.69	28.72	26.16	23.94	22.01	20.33	18.85	17.54	40
41	31.17	28.29	25.81	23.65	21.77	20.13	18.68	17.41	41
42	30.64	27.86	25.45	23.36	21.53	19.93	18.51	17.26	42
43	30.10	27.42	25.09	23.06	21.28	19.72	18.34	17.12	43
44	29.56	26.97	24.71	22.75	21.02	19.50	18.16	16.96	44
45	29.00	26.51	24.33	22.43	20.75	19.28	17.97	16.80	45
46	28.44	26.04	23.94	22.10	20.48	19.04	17.77	16.63	46
47	27.88	25.57	23.55	21.77	20.20	18.80	17.56	16.46	47
48	27.30	25.09	23.14	21.42	19.90	18.55	17.35	16.27	48
49	26.72	24.60	22.73	21.07	19.60	18.30	17.13	16.08	49
50	26.14	24.10	22.30	20.71	19.30	18.03	16.90	15.88	50
51	25.54	23.60	21.87	20.34	18.98	17.76	16.60	15.68	51
52	24.95	23.09	21.44	19.97	18.69	17.48	16.42	15.47	52
53	24.36	22.58	21.00	19.59	18.33	17.20	16.17	15.25	53
54	23.78	22.09	20.58	19.22	18.01	16.92	15.93	15.04	54
55	23.21	21.59	20.15	18.85	17.69	16.64	15.68	14.82	55

Table 12 Multipliers for pecuniary loss for life (females) *continued*

Age at date of trial	*Multiplier calculated with allowance for projected mortality from the 1996-based population projections and rate of return of* 1.5%	2.0%	2.5%	3.0%	3.5%	4.0%	4.5%	5.0%	*Age at date of trial*
56	22.63	21.10	19.72	18.47	17.36	16.35	15.43	14.60	56
57	22.05	20.59	19.27	18.09	17.02	16.05	15.16	14.36	57
58	21.46	20.07	18.82	17.69	16.66	15.74	14.89	14.12	58
59	20.85	19.54	18.35	17.27	16 30	15.41	14.60	13.86	59
60	20.22	18.98	17.86	16.84	15.91	15.07	14.29	13.58	60
61	19.57	18.40	17.35	16.38	15.50	14.70	13.97	13.29	61
62	18.90	17.81	16.81	15.91	15.08	14.32	13.62	12.98	62
63	18.21	17.19	16.26	15.41	14.63	13.92	13.26	12.65	63
64	17.52	16.57	15.70	14.90	14.17	13.50	12.88	12.31	64
65	16.81	15.94	15.13	14.39	13.70	13.07	12.49	11.95	65
66	16.11	15.30	14.55	13.86	13.23	12.64	12.09	11.59	66
67	15.42	14.67	13.98	13.34	12.75	12.20	11.69	11.22	67
68	14.75	14.05	13.42	12.82	12.27	11.76	11.29	10.85	68
69	14.08	13.45	12.86	12.31	11.80	11.33	10.89	11.47	69
70	13.44	12.85	12.31	11.81	11.34	10.90	10.49	10.11	70
71	12.8	12.28	11.79	11.32	10.89	10.48	10.10	9.74	71
72	12.2	11.74	11.28	10.85	10.45	10.08	9.72	9.39	72
73	11.7	11.21	10.79	10.40	10.03	9.68	9.35	9.05	73
74	11.1	10.69	10.31	9.94	9.60	9.28	8.98	8.70	74
75	10.6	10.18	9.83	9.50	9.19	8.89	8.61	8.35	75
76	10.0	9.68	9.36	9.06	8.77	8.50	8.25	8.00	76
77	9.5	9.19	8.90	8.62	8.36	8.11	7.88	7.66	77
78	9.0	8.70	8.44	8.19	7.95	7.73	7.51	7.31	78
79	8.5	8.22	7.99	7.76	7.55	7.34	7.15	6.96	79
80	8.0	7.76	7.55	7.34	7.15	6.96	6.79	6.62	80

81	7.5	7.32	7.12	6.94	6.76	6.60	6.44	6.28	81
82	7.1	6.89	6.72	6.55	6.39	6.24	6.10	5.96	82
83	6.7	6.49	6.33	6.19	6.04	5.91	5.78	5.65	83
84	6.3	6.12	5.98	5.85	5.72	5.59	5.47	5.36	84
85	5.9	5.78	5.65	5.53	5.42	5.30	5.20	5.09	85
86	5.6	5.46	5.35	5.24	5.13	5.03	4.93	4.84	86
87	5.3	5.16	5.06	4.96	4.86	4.77	4.68	4.60	87
88	5.0	4.88	4.79	4.70	4.61	4.53	4.45	4.37	88
89	4.7	4.62	4.53	4.45	4.37	4.30	4.22	4.15	89
90	4.5	4.37	4.30	4.22	4.15	4.08	4.02	3.95	90
91	4.2	4.13	4.07	4.00	3.93	3.87	3.81	3.75	91
92	4.0	3.90	3.84	3.78	3.72	3.67	3.61	3.56	92
93	3.7	3.68	3.62	3.57	3.52	3.47	3.42	3.37	93
94	3.5	3.46	3.41	3.36	3.32	3.27	3.23	3.18	94
95	3.3	3.25	3.21	3.16	3.12	3.08	3.04	3.00	95
96	3.1	3.05	3.01	2.97	2.93	2.90	2.86	2.83	96
97	2.9	2.87	2.83	2.80	2.77	2.73	2.70	2.67	97
98	2.7	2.70	2.67	2.64	2.61	2.58	2.55	2.53	98
99	2.6	2.53	2.51	2.48	2.45	2.43	2.40	2.38	99
100	2.4	2.37	2.34	2.32	2.29	2.27	2.25	2.23	100

Table 13 Multipliers for loss of earnings to pension age 65 (males)

Age at date of trial	*Multiplier calculated with allowance for projected mortality from the 1996-based population projections and rate of return of*								*Age at date of trial*
	1.5%	*2.0%*	*2.5%*	*3.0%*	*3.5%*	*4.0%*	*4.5%*	*5.0%*	
16	33.83	30.56	27.74	25.30	23.19	21.34	19.72	18.30	16
17	33.34	30.17	27.43	25.05	22.99	21.18	19.59	18.20	17
18	32.85	29.78	27.12	24.80	22.79	21.02	19.47	18.09	18
19	32.36	29.38	26.80	24.55	22.58	20.85	19.33	17.99	19
20	31.86	28.98	26.48	24.29	22.37	20.68	19.19	17.87	20
21	31.35	28.57	26.15	24.02	22.15	20.51	19.05	17.76	21
22	30.84	28.16	25.81	23.75	21.93	20.32	18.90	17.63	22
23	30.32	27.73	25.46	23.46	21.70	20.13	18.74	17.50	23
24	29.78	27.29	25.10	23.17	21.46	19.93	18.58	17.37	24
25	29.25	26.85	24.74	22.87	21.21	19.73	18.41	17.23	25
26	28.70	26.40	24.36	22.56	20.95	19.51	18.23	17.08	26
27	28.15	25.94	23.98	22.24	20.68	19.29	18.04	16.92	27
28	27.58	25.47	23.59	21.91	20.41	19.06	17.85	16.76	28
29	27.01	24.99	23.18	21.57	20.12	18.82	17.64	16.59	29
30	26.43	24.50	22.77	21.22	19.82	18.57	17.43	16.40	30
31	25.84	24.00	22.34	20.86	19.52	18.30	17.21	16.21	31
32	25.24	23.49	21.91	20.49	19.20	18.03	16.98	16.01	32
33	24.63	22.97	21.46	20.10	18.87	17.75	16.73	15.80	33
34	24.02	22.44	21.01	19.71	18.53	17.46	16.48	15.59	34
35	23.39	21.90	20.54	19.30	18.18	17.15	16.21	15.36	35
36	22.76	21.34	20.06	18.89	17.81	16.83	15.94	15.11	36
37	22.11	20.78	19.56	18.45	17.44	16.50	15.65	14.86	37
38	21.45	20.20	19.06	18.01	17.05	16.16	15.34	14.59	38
39	20.79	19.62	18.54	17.55	16.64	15.80	15.03	14.31	39
40	20.12	19.02	18.02	17.09	16.23	15.44	14.70	14.02	40

41	19.44	18.42	17.48	16.61	15.80	15.05	14.36	13.72	41
42	18.75	17.80	16.93	16.12	15.36	14.66	14.01	13.40	42
43	18.05	17.18	16.37	15.61	14.91	14.25	13.64	13.07	43
44	17.34	16.54	15.79	15.09	14.44	13.82	13.25	12.72	44
45	16.63	15.89	15.20	14.55	13.95	13.38	12.85	12.35	45
46	15.90	15.22	14.59	14.00	13.44	12.92	12.43	11.97	46
47	15.15	14.54	13.97	13.43	12.92	12.44	11.99	11.56	47
48	14.40	13.85	13.33	12.84	12.38	11.94	11.53	11.14	48
49	13.64	13.15	12.69	12.24	11.83	11.43	11.05	10.70	49
50	12.88	12.44	12.02	11.63	11.25	10.90	10.56	10.24	50
51	12.10	11.72	11.35	11.00	10.67	10.35	10.04	9.76	51
52	11.32	10.98	10.60	10.35	10.06	9.78	9.51	9.25	52
53	10.52	10.23	9.96	9.69	9.44	9.19	8.96	8.73	53
54	9.72	9.48	9.24	9.01	8.79	8.58	8.38	8.18	54
55	8.91	8.70	8.50	8.31	8.13	7.95	7.78	7.61	55
56	8.09	7.92	7.75	7.59	7.44	7.29	7.15	7.01	56
57	7.25	7.12	6.99	6.86	6.73	6.61	6.50	6.38	57
58	6.41	6.30	6.20	6.10	6.00	5.91	5.81	5.72	58
59	5.55	5.47	5.39	5.32	5.24	5.17	5.10	5.03	59
60	4.67	4.62	4.56	4.51	4.46	4.41	4.36	4.31	60
61	3.78	3.75	3.71	3.67	3.64	3.61	3.57	3.54	61
62	2.87	2.85	2.83	2.81	2.79	2.77	2.75	2.73	62
63	1.94	1.93	1.92	1.91	1.90	1.89	1.89	1.88	63
64	0.98	0.98	0.98	0.98	0.97	0.97	0.97	0.97	64

Table 14 Multipliers for loss of earnings to pension age 65 (females)

Age at date of trial	*Multiplier calculated with allowance for projected mortality from the 1996-based population projections and rate of return of*								*Age at date of trial*
	1.5%	*2.0%*	*2.5%*	*3.0%*	*3.5%*	*4.0%*	*4.5%*	*5.0%*	
16	34.22	30.89	28.03	25.55	23.40	21.53	19.89	18.45	16
17	33.73	30.50	27.72	25.31	23.21	21.37	19.76	18.35	17
18	33.23	30.11	27.40	25.05	23.01	21.21	19.63	18.24	18
19	32.73	29.70	27.08	24.79	22.80	21.04	19.50	18.13	19
20	32.22	29.29	26.75	24.53	22.58	20.87	19.36	18.02	20
21	31.70	28.87	26.41	24.25	22.36	20.69	19.21	17.90	21
22	31.17	28.45	26.06	23.97	22.13	20.50	19.06	17.77	22
23	30.64	28.01	25.71	23.68	21.89	20.30	18.90	17.64	23
24	30.10	27.57	25.34	23.38	21.64	20.10	18.73	17.50	24
25	29.55	27.12	24.97	23.07	21.39	19.89	18.55	17.36	25
26	28.99	26.66	24.59	22.76	21.13	19.67	18.37	17.21	26
27	28.43	26.19	24.20	22.43	20.86	19.45	18.18	17.05	27
28	27.86	25.71	23.80	22.10	20.58	19.21	17.99	16.88	28
29	27.28	25.22	23.39	21.75	20.29	18.97	17.78	16.71	29
30	26.69	24.73	22.97	21.40	19.99	18.71	17.56	16.52	30
31	26.09	24.22	22.54	21.03	19.68	18.45	17.34	16.33	31
32	25.48	23.70	22.10	20.66	19.35	18.17	17.10	16.13	32
33	24.87	23.18	21.65	20.27	19.02	17.89	16.86	15.92	33
34	24.24	22.64	21.19	19.87	18.68	17.59	16.60	15.70	34
35	23.61	22.09	20.72	19.47	18.33	17.29	16.33	15.47	35
36	22.97	21.54	20.23	19.04	17.96	16.97	16.06	15.22	36
37	22.32	20.97	19.74	18.61	17.98	16.64	15.77	14.97	37
38	21.66	20.39	19.23	18.17	17.19	16.29	15.46	14.70	38
39	20.99	19.81	18.71	17.71	16.79	15.94	15.15	14.42	39
40	20.32	19.21	18.19	17.24	16.37	15.57	14.82	14.13	40

41	19.63	18.60	17.64	16.76	15.94	15.18	14.48	13.83	41
42	18.94	17.98	17.09	16.27	15.50	14.79	14.13	13.51	42
43	18.24	17.35	16.53	15.76	15.04	14.38	13.76	13.18	43
44	17.53	16.71	15.95	15.24	14.57	13.95	13.37	12.83	44
45	16.81	16.06	15.35	14.70	14.08	13.51	12.97	12.46	45
46	16.08	15.39	14.75	14.15	13.58	13.05	12.55	12.08	46
47	15.33	14.71	14.13	13.58	13.06	12.57	12.11	11.68	47
48	14.58	14.02	13.49	13.00	12.52	12.08	11.66	11.26	48
49	13.82	13.32	12.85	12.40	11.97	11.57	11.18	10.82	49
50	13.05	12.61	12.18	11.78	11.40	11.03	10.69	10.36	50
51	12.27	11.88	11.50	11.15	10.81	10.48	10.17	9.88	51
52	11.48	11.14	10.81	10.49	10.20	9.91	9.64	9.37	52
53	10.68	10.38	10.10	9.83	9.57	9.32	9.08	8.85	53
54	9.87	9.62	9.38	9.14	8.92	8.70	8.50	8.30	54
55	9.05	8.84	8.63	8.44	8.25	8.07	7.89	7.72	55
56	8.21	8.04	7.87	7.71	7.55	7.40	7.26	7.11	56
57	7.37	7.23	7.09	6.96	6.84	6.71	6.59	6.48	57
58	6.50	6.40	6.29	6.19	6.09	5.99	5.90	5.81	58
59	5.63	5.55	5.47	5.39	5.32	5.24	5.17	5.10	59
60	4.73	4.68	4.62	4.57	4.51	4.46	4.41	4.36	60
61	3.82	3.79	3.75	3.72	3.68	3.65	3.61	3.58	61
62	2.90	2.88	2.86	2.84	2.82	2.80	2.78	2.76	62
63	1.95	1.94	1.93	1.92	1.92	1.91	1.90	1.89	63
64	0.99	0.99	0.98	0.98	0.98	0.98	0.97	0.97	64

Table 15 Multipliers for loss of earnings to pension age 60 (males)

Age at date of trial	*Multiplier calculated with allowance for projected mortality from the 1996-based population projections and rate of return of* 1.5%	2.0%	2.5%	3.0%	3.5%	4.0%	4.5%	5.0%	*Age at date of trial*
16	31.58	28.77	26.31	24.16	22.28	20.61	19.14	17.84	16
17	31.06	28.34	25.97	23.88	22.05	20.42	18.99	17.71	17
18	30.53	27.91	25.62	23.60	21.81	20.23	18.83	17.58	18
19	30.00	27.48	25.26	23.30	21.57	20.04	18.67	17.45	19
20	29.47	27.04	24.90	23.01	21.33	19.83	18.50	17.31	20
21	28.92	26.59	24.53	22.70	21.07	19.62	18.32	17.16	21
22	28.37	26.13	24.15	22.38	20.81	19.40	18.14	17.01	22
23	27.81	25.67	23.76	22.06	20.54	19.17	17.95	16.85	23
24	27.24	25.19	23.36	21.72	20.25	18.94	17.75	16.68	24
25	26.66	24.70	22.95	21.38	19.96	18.69	17.54	16.50	25
26	26.08	24.21	22.53	21.02	19.66	18.43	17.32	16.31	26
27	25.48	23.70	22.10	20.65	19.35	18.17	17.09	16.12	27
28	24.88	23.19	21.66	20.28	19.02	17.89	16.86	15.92	28
29	24.27	22.66	21.21	19.89	18.69	17.60	16.61	15.70	29
30	23.64	22.12	20.74	19.49	18.34	17.30	16.35	15.48	30
31	23.01	21.57	20.26	19.07	17.98	16.99	16.08	15.24	31
32	22.37	21.01	19.78	18.65	17.61	16.66	15.79	14.99	32
33	21.72	20.44	19.28	18.21	17.23	16.32	15.49	14.73	33
34	21.06	19.86	18.77	17.76	16.83	15.97	15.18	14.46	34
35	20.38	19.27	18.24	17.29	16.42	15.61	14.86	14.17	35
36	19.70	18.66	17.70	16.81	15.99	15.23	14.52	13.86	36
37	19.01	18.04	17.15	16.32	15.55	14.83	14.17	13.55	37
38	18.30	17.41	16.58	15.81	15.09	14.42	13.80	13.21	38
39	17.59	16.77	16.00	15.29	14.62	14.00	13.41	12.87	39
40	16.87	16.12	15.41	14.75	14.13	13.55	13.01	12.50	40

41	16.14	15.45	14.81	14.20	13.63	13.10	12.59	12.12	41
42	15.40	14.77	14.19	13.63	13.11	12.62	12.16	11.72	42
43	14.65	14.08	13.55	13.05	12.58	12.13	11.70	11.30	43
44	13.89	13.38	12.90	12.45	12.02	11.62	11.23	10.86	44
45	13.11	12.66	12.24	11.83	11.45	11.08	10.73	10.40	45
46	12.33	11.93	11.55	11.19	10.85	10.53	10.22	9.92	46
47	11.53	11.18	10.85	10.54	10.24	9.95	9.67	9.41	47
48	10.72	10.42	10.13	9.86	9.60	9.35	9.11	8.88	48
49	9.90	9.64	9.40	9.17	8.94	8.73	8.52	8.32	49
50	9.07	8.85	8.65	8.45	8.26	8.08	7.90	7.73	50
51	8.22	8.05	7.88	7.72	7.56	7.41	7.26	7.12	51
52	7.37	7.23	7.10	6.97	6.84	6.72	6.60	6.48	52
53	6.50	6.40	6.29	6.19	6.09	5.99	5.90	5.81	53
54	5.62	5.54	5.47	5.39	5.32	5.24	5.17	5.10	54
55	4.73	4.67	4.62	4.57	4.51	4.46	4.41	4.36	55
56	3.82	3.79	3.75	3.71	3.08	3.65	3.61	3.58	56
57	2.90	2.88	2.85	2.83	2.81	2.79	2.78	2.76	57
58	1.95	1.94	1.93	1.92	1.92	1.91	1.90	1.89	58
59	0.99	0.99	0.98	0.98	0.98	0.98	0.97	0.97	59

Table 16 Multipliers for loss of earnings to pension age 60 (females)

Age at date of trial	*Multiplier calculated with allowance for projected mortality from the 1996-based population projections and rate of return of*								*Age at date of trial*
	1.5%	*2.0%*	*2.5%*	*3.0%*	*3.5%*	*4.0%*	*4.5%*	*5.0%*	
16	31.88	29.03	26.55	24.37	22.46	20.77	19.28	17.96	16
17	31.36	28.61	26.20	24.09	22.23	20.59	19.13	17.84	17
18	30.83	28.17	25.85	23.80	21.99	20.40	18.98	17.71	18
19	30.29	27.73	25.49	23.50	21.75	20.19	18.81	17.57	19
20	29.74	27.28	25.11	23.20	21.50	19.99	18.64	17.43	20
21	29.18	26.82	24.73	22.88	21.24	19.77	18.46	17.28	21
22	28.62	26.35	24.35	22.56	20.97	19.55	18.27	17.12	22
23	28.05	25.88	23.95	22.23	20.69	19.31	18.07	16.96	23
24	27.47	25.39	23.54	21.88	20.40	19.07	17.87	16.79	24
25	26.88	24.90	23.12	21.53	20.10	18.82	17.66	16.61	25
26	26.28	24.39	22.69	21.17	19.80	18.56	17.43	16.42	26
27	25.68	23.88	22.26	20.80	19.48	18.28	17.20	16.22	27
28	25.06	23.35	21.81	20.41	19.15	18.00	16.96	16.01	28
29	24.44	22.82	21.35	20.02	18.81	17.71	16.71	15.79	29
30	23.81	22.27	20.88	19.61	18.46	17.41	16.44	15.56	30
31	23.17	21.72	20.40	19.19	18.09	17.09	16.17	15.32	31
32	22.52	21.15	19.90	18.76	17.72	16.76	15.88	15.07	32
33	21.86	20.57	19.40	18.32	17.33	16.42	15.58	14.81	33
34	21.19	19.98	18.88	17.86	16.93	16.06	15.27	14.53	34
35	20.51	19.38	18.35	17.39	16.51	15.69	14.94	14.24	35
36	19.82	18.77	17.80	16.91	16.08	15.31	14.60	13.94	36
37	19.12	18.15	17.25	16.41	15.64	14.91	14.24	13.62	37
38	18.42	17.52	16.68	15.90	15.18	14.50	13.87	13.28	38
30	17.70	16.87	16.10	15.38	14.70	14.07	13.48	12.93	39
40	16.97	16.21	15.50	14.84	14.21	13.63	13.08	12.57	40

41	16.24	15.54	14.89	14.28	13.71	13.17	12.66	12.18	41
42	15.49	14.86	14.27	13.71	13.18	12.69	12.22	11.78	42
43	14.73	14.17	13.63	13.12	12.64	12.19	11.77	11.36	43
44	13.97	13.46	12.98	12.52	12.09	11.68	11.29	10.92	44
45	13.19	12.74	12.31	11.90	11.51	11.14	10.79	10.46	45
46	12.40	12.00	11.62	11.26	10.91	10.59	10.27	9.97	46
47	11.60	11.25	10.92	10.60	10.30	10.01	9.73	9.46	47
48	10.79	10.49	10.20	9.93	9.66	9.41	9.16	8.93	48
49	9.97	9.71	9.46	9.23	9.00	8.78	8.57	8.37	49
50	9.13	8.92	8.71	8.51	8.32	8.14	7.96	7.79	50
51	8.28	8.11	7.94	7.77	7.62	7.46	7.31	7.17	51
52	7.42	7.28	7.15	7.01	6.89	6.76	6.64	6.52	52
53	6.55	6.44	6.34	6.23	6.13	6.03	5.94	5.85	53
54	5.66	5.58	5.50	5.43	5.35	5.28	5.21	5.13	54
55	4.76	4.71	4.65	4.59	4.54	4.49	4.44	4.39	55
56	3.84	3.81	3.77	3.74	3.70	3.67	3.63	3.60	56
57	2.91	2.89	2.87	2.85	2.83	2.81	2.79	2.77	57
58	1.96	1.95	1.94	1.93	1.92	1.91	1.90	1.90	58
59	0.99	0.99	0.98	0.98	0.98	0.98	0.98	0.97	59

Table 17 Multipliers for loss of pension commencing age 65 (males)

Age at date of trial	*Multiplier calculated with allowance for projected mortality from the 1996-based population projections and rate of return of*								*Age at date of trial*
	1.5%	*2.0%*	*2.5%*	*3.0%*	*3.5%*	*4.0%*	*4.5%*	*5.0%*	
0	5.17	3.58	2.48	1.72	1.20	0.84	0.59	0.42	0
1	5.28	3.67	2.55	1.79	1.25	0.88	0.62	0.44	1
2	5.36	3.74	2.62	1.84	1.30	0.91	0.65	0.46	2
3	5.44	3.81	2.68	1.89	1.34	0.95	0.68	0.48	3
4	5.52	3.89	2.75	1.95	1.39	0.99	0.71	0.51	4
5	5.60	3.97	2.82	2.01	1.44	1.03	0.74	0.53	5
6	5.68	4.05	2.89	2.07	1.48	1.07	0.77	0.56	6
7	5.77	4.13	2.96	2.13	1.54	1.11	0.81	0.59	7
8	5.85	4.21	3.03	2.19	1.59	1.16	0.84	0.62	8
9	5.94	4.29	3.11	2.26	1.64	1.20	0.88	0.65	9
10	6.02	4.37	3.18	2.32	1.70	1.25	0.92	0.68	10
11	6.11	4.46	3.26	2.39	1.76	1.30	0.96	0.71	11
12	6.20	4.55	3.34	2.46	1.82	1.35	1.00	0.75	12
13	6.29	4.63	3.42	2.54	1.88	1.40	1.05	0.78	13
14	6.38	4.73	3.51	2.61	1.95	1.46	1.09	0.82	14
15	6.48	4.82	3.59	2.69	2.02	1.52	1.14	0.86	15
16	6.57	4.91	3.68	2.77	2.09	1.58	1.19	0.91	16
17	6.67	5.01	3.77	2.85	2.16	1.64	1.25	0.95	17
18	6.77	5.11	3.87	2.94	2.23	1.70	1.30	1.00	18
19	6.87	5.21	3.96	3.02	2.31	1.77	1.36	1.05	19
20	6.97	5.31	4.06	3.11	2.39	1.84	1.42	1.10	20
21	7.07	5.42	4.17	3.21	2.48	1.92	1.49	1.16	21
22	7.18	5.53	4.27	3.30	2.56	1.99	1.56	1.22	22
23	7.29	5.64	4.38	3.40	2.65	2.07	1.63	1.28	23
24	7.39	5.75	4.48	3.50	2 75	2.16	1.70	1.34	24
25	7.50	5.86	4.60	3.61	2.84	2.24	1.77	1.41	25
26	7.61	5.98	4.71	3.72	2.94	2.33	1.85	1.48	26
27	7.73	6.10	4.83	3.83	3.04	2.43	1.94	1.55	27
28	7.84	6.22	4.94	3.94	3.15	2.52	2.02	1.63	28
29	7.95	6.34	5.07	4.06	3.26	2.62	2.11	1.71	29
30	8.07	6.46	5.19	4.18	3.37	2.73	2.21	1.79	30

31	8.18	6.59	5.32	4.30	3.49	2.83	2.31	1.88	31
32	8.30	6.72	5.45	4.43	3.61	2.94	2.41	1.97	32
33	8.42	6.85	5.58	4.56	3.73	3.06	2.52	2.07	33
34	8.54	6.98	5.72	4.69	3.86	3.18	2.63	2.17	34
35	8.66	7.11	5.85	4.83	3.99	3.31	2.74	2.28	35
36	8.78	7.25	5.99	4.97	4.13	3.44	2.87	2.39	36
37	8.90	7.39	6.14	5.11	4.27	3.57	2.99	2.51	37
38	9.03	7.53	6.29	5.26	4.41	3.71	3 12	2.64	38
39	9.15	7.67	6.44	5.41	4.56	3.85	3.26	2.77	39
40	9.28	7.81	6.59	5.57	4.72	4.01	3.41	2.90	40
41	9.41	7.96	6.75	5.73	4.88	4.16	3.56	3.04	41
42	9.54	8.11	6.91	5.90	5.05	4.33	3.71	3.19	42
43	9.67	8.27	7.08	6.07	5.22	4.49	3.88	3.35	43
44	9.81	8.42	7.25	6.25	5.40	4.67	4.05	3.52	44
45	9.94	8.58	7.42	6.43	5.58	4.85	4.23	3.69	45
46	10.08	8.74	7.60	6.61	5.77	5.04	4.41	3.87	46
47	10.22	8.91	7.78	6.80	5.96	5.24	4.61	4.06	47
48	10.36	9.07	7.96	7.00	6.17	5.44	4.81	4.26	48
49	10.50	9.24	8.15	7.20	6.38	5.65	5.02	4.47	49
50	10.65	9.42	8.35	7.42	6.60	5.88	5.25	4.69	50
51	10.80	9.60	8.56	7.64	6.83	6.11	5.48	4.92	51
52	10.96	9.79	8.77	7.86	7.07	6.36	5.73	5.17	52
53	11.12	9.99	8.99	8.10	7.31	6.61	5.99	5.43	53
54	11.29	10.20	9.22	8.35	7.58	6.88	6.27	5.71	54
55	11.47	10.41	9.46	8.61	7.85	7.17	6.56	6.01	55
56	11.67	10.64	9.71	8.89	8.14	7.47	6.87	6.32	56
57	11.87	10.88	9.98	9.18	8.45	7.80	7.20	6.66	57
58	12.09	11.13	10.27	9.49	8.78	8.14	7.55	7.02	58
59	12.32	11.41	10.57	9.82	9.13	8.50	7.93	7.41	59
60	12.57	11.69	10.90	10.17	9.50	8.89	8.34	7.82	60
61	12.83	12.00	11.23	10.54	9.90	9.31	8.77	8.27	61
62	13.11	12.32	11.60	10.93	10.32	9.75	9.23	8.75	62
63	13.41	12.67	11.98	11.35	10.77	10.23	9.73	9.27	63
64	13.73	13.04	12.40	11.81	11.26	10.75	10.27	9.83	64
65	14.09	13.45	12.85	12.30	11.78	11.31	10.86	10.45	65

Table 18 Multipliers for loss of pension commencing age 65 (females)

Age at date of trial	Multiplier calculated with allowance for projected mortality from the 1996-based population projections and rate of return of 1.5%	2.0%	2.5%	3.0%	3.5%	4.0%	4.5%	5.0%	Age at date of trial
0	6.35	4.36	3.00	2.08	1.44	1.00	0.70	0.49	0
1	6.47	4.47	3.09	2.15	1.50	1.05	0.73	0.52	1
2	6.57	4.56	3.17	2.21	1.55	1.09	0.77	0.54	2
3	6.67	4.65	3.25	2.28	1.60	1.13	0.80	0.57	3
4	6.77	4.74	3.33	2.35	1.66	1.18	0.84	0.60	4
5	6.87	4.83	3.41	2.42	1.72	1.22	0.87	0.63	5
6	6.97	4.93	3.50	2.49	1.78	1.27	0.91	0.66	6
7	7.07	5.03	3.58	2.56	1.84	1.32	0.95	0.69	7
8	7.18	5.13	3.67	2.64	1.90	1.38	1.00	0.73	8
9	7.28	5.23	3.76	2.72	1.97	1.43	1.04	0.76	9
10	7.39	5.33	3.86	2.80	2.04	1.49	1.09	0.80	10
11	7.50	5.43	3.95	2.88	2.11	1.55	1.14	0.84	11
12	7.61	5.54	4.05	2.97	2.18	1.61	1.19	0.88	12
13	7.72	5.65	4.15	3.05	2.26	1.67	1.24	0.92	13
14	7.83	5.76	4.25	3.14	2.33	1.74	1.30	0.97	14
15	7.95	5.87	4.35	3.24	2.41	1.81	1.35	1.02	15
16	8.07	5.99	4.46	3.33	2.50	1.88	1.41	1.07	16
17	8.18	6.11	4.57	3.43	2.58	1.95	1.48	1.12	17
18	8.30	6.23	4.69	3.53	2.67	2.03	1.54	1.18	18
19	8.43	6.35	4.80	3.64	2.77	2.11	1.61	1.24	19
20	8.55	6.48	4.92	3.75	2.86	2.19	1.69	1.30	20
21	8.67	6.60	5.04	3.86	2.96	2.28	1.76	1.36	21
22	8.80	6.73	5.16	3.97	3.07	2.37	1.84	1.43	22
23	8.93	6.86	5.29	4.09	3.17	2.47	1.92	1.50	23
24	9.06	7.00	5.42	4.21	3.28	2.56	2.01	1.58	24
25	9.19	7.14	5.56	4.34	3.40	2.66	2.10	1.65	25
26	9.33	7.28	5.69	4.47	3.51	2.77	2.19	1.74	26
27	9.46	7.42	5.83	4.60	3.63	2.88	2.29	1.82	27
28	9.60	7.56	5.98	4.73	3.76	2.99	2.39	1.91	28
29	9.74	7.71	6.12	4.87	3.89	3.11	2.50	2.01	29
30	9.88	7.86	6.27	5.02	4.02	3.24	2.61	2.11	30

31	10.02	8.01	6.43	5.17	4.16	3.36	2.72	2.21	31
32	10.17	8.17	6.58	5.32	4.31	3.50	2.85	2.32	32
33	10.31	8.33	6.74	5.47	4.45	3.63	2.97	2.44	33
34	10.46	8.49	6.91	5.63	4.61	3.78	3.10	2.56	34
35	10.61	8.65	7.07	5.80	4.77	3.93	3.24	2.68	35
36	10.76	8.82	7.25	5.97	4.93	4.08	3.38	2.81	36
37	10.91	8.99	7.42	6.14	5.10	4.24	3.53	2.95	37
38	11.06	9.16	7.60	6.32	5.27	4.41	3.69	3.10	38
39	11.22	9.33	7.78	6.51	5.45	4.58	3.85	3.25	39
40	11.38	9.51	7.97	6.70	5.64	4.76	4.02	3.41	40
41	11.54	9.69	8.16	6.89	5.83	4.95	4.20	3.58	41
42	11.70	9.88	8.36	7.09	6.03	5.14	4.39	3.76	42
43	11.86	10.06	8.56	7.30	6.24	5.34	4.58	3.94	43
44	12.03	10.26	8.77	7.51	6.45	5.55	4.79	4.14	44
45	12.20	10.45	8.98	7.73	6.67	5.77	5.00	4.34	45
46	12.37	10.65	9.20	7.96	6.90	5.99	5.22	4.55	46
47	12.54	10.86	9.42	8.19	7.14	6.23	5.45	4.78	47
48	12.72	11.06	9.65	8.43	7.38	6.48	5.69	5.02	48
49	12.90	11.28	9.88	8.68	7.63	6.73	5.95	5.26	49
50	13.08	11.50	10.12	8.93	7.90	7.00	6.21	5.53	50
51	13.27	11.72	10.37	9.20	8.17	7.28	6.49	5.80	51
52	13.47	11.95	10.63	9.47	8.46	7.57	6.78	6.09	52
53	13.68	12.20	10.90	9.77	8.76	7.88	7.10	6.40	53
54	13.92	12.47	11.20	10.08	9.09	8.21	7.44	6.74	54
55	14.16	12.76	11.52	10.42	9.44	8.57	7.79	7.10	55
56	14.42	13.05	11.84	10.76	9.80	8.94	8.17	7.48	56
57	14.68	13.36	12.18	11.13	10.18	9.33	8.57	7.89	57
58	14.95	13.67	12.53	11.50	10.57	9.74	8.99	8.31	58
59	15.22	13.99	12.88	11.88	10.98	10.17	9.43	8.76	59
60	15.49	14.30	13.24	12.27	11.40	10.60	9.88	9.22	60
61	15.75	14.62	13.59	12.67	11.82	11.05	10.35	9.71	61
62	16.00	14.93	13.96	13.07	12.26	11.52	10.84	10.22	62
63	16.26	15.25	14.33	13.49	12.72	12.01	11.36	10.76	63
64	16.53	15.58	14.72	13.92	13.20	12.52	11.91	11.33	64
65	16.81	15.94	15.13	14.39	13.70	13.07	12.49	11.95	65

Table 19 Multipliers for loss of pension commencing age 60 (males)

Age at date of trial	*Multiplier calculated with allowance for projected mortality from the 1996-based population projections and rate of return of*								*Age at date of trial*
	1.5%	*2.0%*	*2.5%*	*3.0%*	*3.5%*	*4.0%*	*4.5%*	*5.0%*	
0	6.94	4.88	3.44	2.43	1.73	1.23	0.88	0.63	0
1	7.08	5.00	3.54	2.52	1.80	1.28	0.92	0.66	1
2	7.19	5.10	3.63	2.59	1.86	1.34	0.96	0.70	2
3	7.30	5.20	3.72	2.67	1.92	1.39	1.01	0.73	3
4	7.41	5.31	3.81	2.75	1.99	1.44	1.05	0.77	4
5	7.52	5.41	3.91	2.83	2.06	1.50	1.10	0.81	5
6	7.63	5.52	4.01	2.92	2.13	1.56	1.15	0.85	6
7	7.74	5.63	4.10	3.00	2.20	1.62	1.20	0.89	7
8	7.85	5.74	4.21	3.09	2.28	1.69	1.25	0.93	8
9	7.97	5.85	4.31	3.18	2.36	1.75	1.31	0.98	9
10	8.08	5.97	4.42	3.28	2.44	1.82	1.37	1.03	10
11	8.20	6.08	4.52	3.38	2.53	1.90	1.43	1.08	11
12	8.32	6.20	4.64	3.48	2.61	1.97	1.49	1.13	12
13	8.44	6.32	4.75	3.58	2.71	2.05	1.56	1.19	13
14	8.57	6.45	4.87	3.69	2.80	2.13	1.63	1.25	14
15	8.69	6.57	4.99	3.80	2.90	2.22	1.70	1.31	15
16	8.82	6.70	5.11	3.91	3.00	2.30	1.78	1.37	16
17	8.95	6.84	5.24	4.02	3.10	2.40	1.86	1.44	17
18	9.08	6.97	5.37	4.14	3.21	2.49	1.94	1.51	18
19	9.22	7.11	5.50	4.27	3.32	2.59	2.03	1.59	19
20	9.36	7.26	5.64	4.40	3.44	2.70	2.12	1.67	20
21	9.50	7.40	5.78	4.53	3.56	2.80	2.21	1.75	21
22	9.65	7.55	5.93	4.67	3.68	2.92	2.31	1.84	22
23	9.79	7.70	6.08	4.81	3.81	3.03	2.42	1.93	23
24	9.94	7.86	6.23	4.95	3.99	3.16	2.53	2.03	24
25	10.08	8.01	6.38	5.10	4.09	3.28	2.64	2.13	25

26	10.24	8.17	6.54	5.25	4.23	3.41	2.76	2.24	26
27	10.39	8.33	6.71	5.41	4.38	3.55	2.89	2.35	27
28	10.54	8.50	6.87	5.57	4.53	3.69	3.02	2.47	28
29	10.70	8.67	7.04	5.74	4.69	3.84	3.15	2.59	29
30	10.86	8.84	7.22	5.91	4.85	3.99	3.29	2.72	30
31	11.01	9.01	7.40	6.09	5.02	4.15	3.44	2.86	31
32	11.18	9.19	7.58	6.27	5.19	4.32	3.59	3.00	32
33	11.34	9.37	7.77	6.45	5.37	4.49	3.75	3.15	33
34	11.50	9.55	7.96	6.64	5.56	4.67	3.92	3.31	34
35	11.67	9.74	8.15	6.84	5.75	4.85	4.10	3.47	35
36	11.84	9.93	8.35	7.04	5.95	5.04	4.28	3.64	36
37	12.01	10.12	8.56	7.25	6.16	5.24	4.47	3.82	37
38	12.18	10.32	8.76	7.46	6.37	5.45	4.67	4.01	38
39	12.35	10.52	8.98	7.68	6.59	5.66	4.88	4.21	39
40	12.53	10.72	9.20	7.91	6.82	5.89	5.10	4.42	40
41	12.71	10.93	9.42	8.14	7.05	6.12	5.32	4.64	41
42	12.89	11.14	9.65	8.38	7.30	6.36	5.56	4.87	42
43	13.08	11.36	9.89	8.63	7.55	6.62	5.81	5.11	43
44	13.27	11.58	10.13	8.89	7.81	6.88	6.07	5.37	44
45	13.46	11.81	10.38	9.15	8.08	7.15	6.34	5.64	45
46	13.65	12.03	10.64	9.42	8.36	7.44	6.63	5.92	46
47	13.84	12.27	10.89	9.70	8.65	7.73	6.92	6.21	47
48	14.04	12.51	11.16	9.98	8.95	8.04	7.23	6.52	48
49	14.25	12.75	11.44	10.28	9.26	8.36	7.56	6.85	49
50	14.46	13.01	11.72	10.59	9.59	8.70	7.90	7.19	50
51	14.68	13.27	12.02	10.91	9.93	9.05	8.26	7.56	51
52	14.91	13.54	12.33	11.25	10.29	9.42	8.64	7.95	52
53	15.14	13.83	12.65	11.60	10.66	9.81	9.05	8.36	53
54	15.39	14.13	12.99	11.97	11.05	10.22	9.47	8.79	54
55	15.65	14.44	13.34	12.36	11.47	10.66	9.92	9.26	55
56	15.93	14.77	13.72	12.77	11.91	11.12	10.41	9.75	56
57	16.23	15.12	14.12	13.20	12.37	11.61	10.92	10.28	57
58	16.54	15.49	14.54	13.67	12.87	12.14	11.47	10.86	58
59	16.88	15.89	14.98	14.16	13.40	12.70	12.06	11.47	59
60	17.24	16.31	15.46	14.68	13.96	13.30	12.69	12.13	60

Table 20 Multipliers for loss of pension commencing age 60 (females)

Age at date of trial	Multiplier calculated with allowance for projected mortality from the 1996-based population projections and rate of return of 1.5%	2.0%	2.5%	3.0%	3.5%	4.0%	4.5%	5.0%	Age at date of trial
0	8.19	5.71	4.00	2.81	1.98	1.40	1.00	0.71	0
1	8.34	5.85	4.12	2.91	2.06	1.47	1.05	0.75	1
2	8.47	5.97	4.22	2.99	2.13	1.52	1.09	0.79	2
3	8.60	6.09	4.32	3.08	2.21	1.59	1.14	0.83	3
4	8.73	6.21	4.43	3.18	2.28	1.65	1.19	0.87	4
5	8.85	6.33	4.54	3.27	2.36	1.71	1.25	0.91	5
6	8.99	6.46	4.65	3.37	2.45	1.78	1.30	0.96	6
7	9.12	6.58	4.77	3.47	2.53	1.85	1.36	1.00	7
8	9.25	6.71	4.89	3.57	2.62	1.93	1.42	1.05	8
9	9.39	6.85	5.01	3.68	2.71	2.00	1.49	1.11	9
10	9.53	6.98	5.13	3.79	2.80	2.08	1.55	1.16	10
11	9.67	7.12	5.26	3.90	2.90	2.17	1.62	1.22	11
12	9.81	7.26	5.39	4.02	3.00	2.25	1.69	1.28	12
13	9.96	7.40	5.52	4.14	3.11	2.34	1.77	1.34	13
14	10.10	7.55	5.66	4.26	3.21	2.43	1.85	1.41	14
15	10.25	7.70	5.80	4.39	3.33	2.53	1.93	1.48	15
16	10.40	7.85	5.94	4.52	3.44	2.63	2.02	1.55	16
17	10.55	8.00	6.09	4.65	3.56	2.74	2.11	1.63	17
18	10.71	8.16	6.24	4.79	3.69	2.85	2.20	1.71	18
19	10.87	8.32	6.40	4.93	3.81	2.96	2.30	1.80	19
20	11.03	8.49	6.55	5.08	3.95	3.08	2.41	1.89	20
21	11.19	8.65	6.72	5.23	4.08	3.20	2.51	1.98	21
22	11.35	8.83	6.88	5.38	4.23	3.33	2.63	2.08	22
23	11.52	9.00	7.05	5.54	4.37	3.46	2.74	2.18	23
24	11.69	9.18	7.23	5.71	4.52	3.60	2.87	2.29	24
25	11.86	9.36	7.41	5.88	4.68	3.74	2.99	2.40	25

26	12.04	9.54	7.59	6.05	4.84	3.89	3.13	2.52	26
27	12.21	9.73	7.78	6.23	5.01	4.04	3.27	2.65	27
28	12.39	9.92	7.97	6.42	5.19	4.20	3.41	2.78	28
29	12.57	10.12	8.16	6.61	5.37	4.37	3.57	2.92	29
30	12.76	10.31	8.37	6.81	5.55	4.54	3.73	3.07	30
31	12.94	10.52	8.57	7.01	5.74	4.72	3.89	3.22	31
32	13.13	10.72	8.78	7.21	5.94	4.91	4.07	3.38	32
33	13.32	10.93	9.00	7.43	6.15	5.10	4.25	3.55	33
34	13.51	11.14	9.22	7.65	6.36	5.31	4.44	3.72	34
35	13.71	11.36	9.44	7.87	6.58	5.52	4.64	3.91	35
36	13.91	11.58	9.67	8.10	6.81	5.73	4.84	4.10	36
37	14.11	11.81	9.91	8.34	7.04	5.96	5.06	4.30	37
38	14.31	12.03	10.15	8.59	7.29	6.20	5.28	4.52	38
39	14.51	12.27	10.40	8.84	7.54	6.44	5.52	4.74	39
40	14.72	12.51	10.66	9.10	7.80	6.70	5.77	4.98	40
41	14.93	12.75	10.92	9.37	8.07	6.96	6.02	5.22	41
42	15.15	13.00	11.18	9.65	8.35	7.24	6.29	5.48	42
43	15.37	13.25	11.46	9.93	8.64	7.52	6.57	5.76	43
44	15.59	13.51	11.74	10.23	8.93	7.82	6.87	6.04	44
45	15.81	13.77	12.03	10.53	9.24	8.13	7.18	6.34	45
46	16.04	14.04	12.32	10.84	9.57	8.46	7.50	6.66	46
47	16.28	14.32	12.63	11.17	9.90	8.80	7.83	6.99	47
48	16.51	14.60	12.94	11.50	10.24	9.15	8.19	7.34	48
49	16.76	14.89	13.26	11.84	10.60	9.51	8.56	7.71	49
50	17.01	15.18	13.59	12.20	10.98	9.90	8.94	8.10	50
51	17.26	15.49	13.94	12.57	11.36	10.30	9.35	8.51	51
52	17.52	15.80	14.29	12.95	11.77	10.72	9.78	8.94	52
53	17.81	16.14	14.67	13.36	12.20	11.16	10.24	9.40	53
54	18.12	16.51	15.07	13.80	12.66	11.64	10.73	9.90	54
55	18.45	16.89	15.50	14.26	13.15	12.15	11.25	10.43	55
56	18.79	17.29	15.94	14.74	13.66	12.68	11.80	11.00	56
57	19.14	17.70	16.40	15.24	14.19	13.24	12.38	11.59	57
58	19.50	18.12	16.88	15.76	14.74	13.82	12.99	12.22	58
59	19.86	18.55	17.36	16.29	15.32	14.43	13.62	12.89	59
60	20.22	18.98	17.86	16.84	15.91	15.07	14.29	13.58	60

Table 21 Discounting factors for term certain

Term	1.5%	2.0%	2.5%	3.0%	3.5%	4.0%	4.5%	5.0%	Term
	Factor to discount value of multiplier for a period of deferment								
1	0.9852	0.9804	0.9756	0.9709	0.9662	0.9615	0.9569	0.9524	1
2	0.9707	0.9612	0.9518	0.9426	0.9335	0.9246	0.9157	0.9070	2
3	0.9563	0.9423	0.9286	0.9151	0.9019	0.8890	0.8763	0.8638	3
4	0.9422	0.9238	0.9060	0.8885	0.8714	0.8548	0.8386	0.8227	4
5	0.9283	0.9057	0.8839	0.8626	0.8420	0.8219	0.8025	0.7835	5
6	0.9145	0.8880	0.8623	0.8375	0.8135	0.7903	0.7679	0.7462	6
7	0.9010	0.8706	0.8413	0.8131	0.7860	0.7599	0.7348	0.7107	7
8	0.8877	0.8535	0.8207	0.7894	0.7594	0.7307	0.7032	0.6768	8
9	0.8746	0.8368	0.8007	0.7664	0.7337	0.7026	0.6729	0.6446	9
10	0.8617	0.8203	0.7812	0.7441	0.7089	0.6756	0.6439	0.6139	10
11	0.8489	0.8043	0.7621	0.7224	0.6849	0.6496	0.6162	0.5847	11
12	0.8364	0.7885	0.7436	0.7014	0.6618	0.6246	0.5897	0.5568	12
13	0.8240	0.7730	0.7254	0.6810	0.6394	0.6006	0.5643	0.5303	13
14	0.8118	0.7579	0.7077	0.6611	0.6178	0.5775	0.5400	0.5051	14
15	0.7999	0.7430	0.6905	0.6419	0.5969	0.5553	0.5167	0.4810	15
16	0.7880	0.7284	0.6736	0.6232	0.5767	0.5339	0.4945	0.4581	16
17	0.7764	0.7142	0.6572	0.6050	0.5572	0.5134	0.4732	0.4363	17
18	0.7649	0.7002	0.6412	0.5874	0.5384	0.4936	0.4528	0.4155	18
19	0.7536	0.6864	0.6255	0.5703	0.5202	0.4746	0.4333	0.3957	19
20	0.7425	0.6730	0.6103	0.5537	0.5026	0.4564	0.4146	0.3769	20
21	0.7315	0.6598	0.5954	0.5375	0.4856	0.4388	0.3968	0.3589	21
22	0.7207	0.6468	0.5809	0.5219	0.4692	0.4220	0.3797	0.3418	22
23	0.7100	0.6342	0.5667	0.5067	0.4533	0.4057	0.3634	0.3256	23
24	0.6995	0.6217	0.5529	0.4919	0.4380	0.3901	0.3477	0.3101	24
25	0.6892	0.6095	0.5394	0.4776	0.4231	0.3751	0.3327	0.2953	25
26	0.6790	0.5976	0.5262	0.4637	0.4088	0.3607	0.3184	0.2812	26
27	0.6690	0.5859	0.5134	0.4502	0.3950	0.3468	0.3047	0.2678	27
28	0.6591	0.5744	0.5009	0.4371	0.3817	0.3335	0.2916	0.2551	28
29	0.6494	0.5631	0.4887	0.4243	0.3687	0.3207	0.2790	0.2429	29
30	0.6398	0.5521	0.4767	0.4120	0.3563	0.3083	0.2670	0.2314	30

Table 22 Multipliers for pecuniary loss for term certain

	Multiplier for regular frequent payments fcr a term certain at rate of return of								
Term	*1.5%*	*2.0%*	*2.5%*	*3.0%*	*3.5%*	*4.0%*	*4.5%*	*5.0%*	*Term*
1	0.99	0.99	0.99	0.99	0.98	0.98	0.98	0.98	1
2	1.97	1.96	1.95	1.94	1.93	1.92	1.91	1.91	2
3	2.93	2.91	2.89	2.87	2.85	2.83	2.81	2.79	3
4	3.88	3.85	3.81	3.77	3.74	3.70	3.67	3.63	4
5	4.82	4.76	4.70	4.65	4.59	4.54	4.49	4.44	5
6	5.74	5.66	5.58	5.50	5.42	5.35	5.27	5.20	6
7	6.65	6.54	6.43	6.32	6.22	6.12	6.02	5.93	7
8	7.54	7.40	7.26	7.12	6.99	6.87	6.74	6.62	8
9	8.42	8.24	8.07	7.90	7.74	7.58	7.43	7.28	9
10	9.29	9.07	8.86	8.66	8.46	8.27	8.09	7.91	10
11	10.15	9.88	9.63	9.39	9.16	8.93	8.72	8.51	11
12	10.99	10.68	10.39	10.10	9.83	9.57	9.32	9.08	12
13	11.82	11.46	11.12	10.79	10.48	10.18	9.90	9.63	13
14	12.64	12.23	11.84	11.46	11.11	10.77	10.45	10.14	14
15	13.44	12.98	12.54	12.12	11.72	11.34	10.98	10.64	15
16	14.24	13.71	13.22	12.75	12.30	11.88	11.48	11.11	16
17	15.02	14.43	13.88	13.36	12.87	12.41	11.97	11.55	17
18	15.79	15.14	14.53	13.96	13.42	12.91	12.43	11.98	18
19	16.55	15.83	15.17	14.54	13.95	13.39	12.87	12.38	19
20	17.30	16.51	15.78	15.10	14.46	13.86	13.30	12.77	20
21	18.03	17.18	16.39	15.65	14.95	14.31	13.70	13.14	21
22	18.76	17.83	16.97	16.17	15.43	14.74	14.09	13.49	22
23	19.48	18.47	17.55	16.69	15.89	15.15	14.46	13.82	23
24	20.18	19.10	18.11	17.19	16.34	15.55	14.82	14.14	24
25	20.87	19.72	18.65	17.67	16.77	15.93	15.16	14.44	25
26	21.56	20.32	19.19	18.14	17.18	16.30	15.48	14.73	26
27	22.23	20.91	19.71	18.60	17.59	16.65	15.80	15.01	27
28	22.90	21.49	20.21	19.04	17.97	16.99	16.09	15.27	28
29	23.55	22.06	20.71	19.47	18.35	17.32	16.38	15.52	29
30	24.20	22.62	21.19	19.89	18.71	17.64	16.65	15.75	30

Table 22 Multipliers for pecuniary loss for term certain *continued*

	Multiplier for regular frequent payments for a term certain at rate of return of								
Term	*1.5%*	*2.0%*	*2.5%*	*3.0%*	*3.5%*	*4.0%*	*4.5%*	*5.0%*	*Term*
31	24.83	23.17	21.66	20.30	19.06	17.94	16.91	15.98	31
32	25.46	23.70	22.12	20.69	19.40	18.23	17.16	16.19	32
33	26.07	24.23	22.57	21.08	19.73	18.51	17.40	16.40	33
34	26.68	24.74	23.01	21.45	20.04	18.78	17.63	16.59	34
35	27.28	25.25	23.43	21.81	20.35	19.04	17.85	16.78	35
36	27.87	25.74	23.85	22.16	20.64	19.28	18.06	16.96	36
37	28.45	26.23	24.26	22.50	20.93	19.52	18.26	17.13	37
38	29.02	26.70	24.65	22.83	21.20	19.75	18.45	17.29	38
39	29.58	27.17	25.04	23.15	21.47	19.97	18.64	17.44	39
40	30.14	27.63	25.42	23.46	21.73	20.19	18.81	17.58	40

Actuarial formulae and basis

The functions tabulated are:

Tables 1, 2, 11 and 12	$\bar{a}_x$
Tables 3, 4, 13 and 14	$\bar{a}_{x:\overline{65-x}|}$
Tables 5, 6, 15 and 16	$\bar{a}_{x:\overline{60-x}|}$
Tables 7, 8, 17 and 18	$_{(65-x)|}\bar{a}_{65}$
Tables 9, 10, 19 and 20	$_{(60-x)|}\bar{a}_{60}$
Table 21:	$1 / (1+i)^n$
Table 22:	$\bar{a}_{\overline{n}|}$

Mortality: English Life Tables No 15 (Tables 1 to 10)
Mortality assumptions for 1996-based official population projections for England and Wales (Tables 11 to 20)

Loadings: None

Rate of return: As stated in the Tables

4 The CPID Tables

GUIDE TO THE TABLES

General points

The CPID Tables are based on precisely the same software program as the third edition of the Ogden Tables. Where the two sets of tables cover exactly the same ground, they return exactly the same answers. The CPID Tables simply extend the Ogden Tables by providing more detailed ranges of multipliers.

The terminology used in the CPID age related multiplier tables is as follows:

(1) The heading states the age at trial: eg 'Males aged 30' gives the multipliers for a man aged 30 at the date of hearing.
(2) 'Life multiplier', to be found just beneath this, gives the multiplier for the whole of the remaining lifespan of a person of that age and gender, assuming normal life expectancy.
(3) 'Retirement age' means the age at which the plaintiff would have retired.
(4) 'Earnings multiplier' is the multiplier for the loss of earnings up to retirement age.
(5) The subdivisions 'Earnings 16 multiplier' etc. used in the pages for those aged 1 to 15 signify the multiplier for the loss of earnings from the age at which the plaintiff would have commenced paid work (eg 16) up to retirement age.
(6) 'Pensions multiplier' is the multiplier for the loss of pension income from retirement age.

Like the Ogden Tables, the CPID Tables provide multipliers to two decimal places. Occasionally this gives rise to an apparent anomaly. In theory, the earnings multiplier plus the pensions multiplier should exactly equal the life multiplier. Sometimes in the CPID (and the Ogden) Tables they seem to miss it by 0.01. This does not connote error; it is simply the result of only showing multipliers to two decimal places. 15.363 + 3.274 = 18.637; confined to two decimal places, the constituents appear as 15.36 and 3.27 and the total as 18.64. It hardly matters. Readers can be reassured that the totals are correct, and so are each of the subtotals.

The CPID tables may be used to produce split multipliers where the ages on which the split is based fall between 50 and 75. For example, suppose that a seriously injured man is aged 30 at trial and that:

(1) his loss of earnings is £x pa to the age of 50;
(2) his loss of earnings is thereafter £y pa until his posited retirement age of 63; and
(3) his loss of pension, and extra expenses, then continue for the remainder of his unaffected life span.

The recommended solution is to look up the 3% pa column in the page headed 'Males aged 30', which shows that

(1) the earnings multiplier to age 50 is 14.91, so 14.91 is the multiplier for the first part of the split period;
(2) the earnings multiplier to age 63 is 20.41, so the multiplier for the second page of the split period is 5.50 (20.41–14.91);
(3) the life multiplier is 24.21, so the multiplier for the third part of the split period is 3.80 (24.21–20.41).

It may be noted that the above example demonstrates the apparent 0.01 decimal place anomaly described above, in that the pensions multiplier for retirement at age 63 is shown as 3.79.

A program is being developed for the disk of *Computing Personal Injury Damages* which will yield as many split multipliers, and between as many combinations of different dates, as may be required.

Like the Ogden Tables, the CPID Tables deal with round years. The earnings and pensions multipliers shown for a woman aged 40 due to retire at age 60 are those applicable as at her 40th and 60th birthdays. If she is in fact 40½ at trial, it is appropriate to take a multiplier halfway between those shown on the 'Female aged 40' and 'Female aged 41' pages. The disk of *Computing Personal Injury Damages* goes beyond this by providing multipliers for exact dates: eg a woman born on 25 February 1958 whose case is heard on 11 October 1998 and who if fit would have retired on 31 December 2020.

Individual tables

The first set is headed 'Age multipliers', providing separate tables for males and females for each year of life between 1 and 100. These tables may be subdivided into three categories.

(1) Ages 1–15, for which alternative multipliers are given according to whether the Plaintiff would have started paid employment at the age of 16, 18, 21 or 24. For example, for a 10 year old boy who would if fit have commenced work at the age of 21 and have retired at the age of 62, the life multiplier (stated at the top) is 28.26, the earnings multiplier from age 21 to age 62 (discounted for the fact that the loss will not start for 11 years and for the risks of mortality) is 16.63, and the pensions multiplier from age 62 (similarly discounted) is 2.25.

(2) Ages 16–75, which show, for any age within this bracket, the life multiplier (stated at the top) and the earnings multiplier and pensions multiplier for each retirement age between 50 and 75. Therefore, for a 36 year old man the life multiplier is 22.49, and if he planned to retire at the age of 58, the earnings multiplier is 15.78 and the pensions multiplier is 6.71.

(3) Ages 76–100, which assume that the plaintiff has retired by then. Consequently the life multiplier and the pensions multiplier is the same: eg 5.70 for an 84 year old woman.

The multipliers in the age multiplier tables allow for the risk of mortality. No discount should be given on the life multipliers, since they incorporate this. A discount may be required on the earnings multipliers and pensions multipliers, however, to take account of other contingencies such as sickness, redundancy and early retirement. The amount of this discount is a matter of individual judgment (and if necessary judicial decision) on the facts of each case.

The second set is headed 'Fixed term multipliers'. These do not incorporate any allowance for the risk of mortality. They are for use in cases of agreed life expectancy or where for any other reason the exact term of the loss is fixed. No discount is appropriate. Therefore, for example, the fixed term multiplier for a period of 12 years is 10.10. As with Ogden Table 22, it is assumed that the loss or expenses are spread evenly throughout the year.

The third set is called 'Consolidated compound interest. These tables show the present discounted value of a sum payable in the future. Suppose that if fit the plaintiff would have received a £50,000 retirement lump sum in 30 years' time. The present value of this on a 3% pa discount basis is £50,000 × 0.411987 = £20,599.35. No further discount is required.

Age multipliers

Males aged 1

Retirement age	2.5% pa Life multiplier—33.34 *E.M. 16*	*E.M. 18*	*E.M. 21*	*E.M. 24*	*P.M.*	*E.M. 16*	*E.M. 18*
50	15.59	14.25	12.37	10.62	5.24	13.52	12.28
51	15.87	14.53	12.64	10.90	4.96	13.74	12.50
52	16.14	14.80	12.91	11.17	4.69	13.95	12.71
53	16.41	15.06	13.18	11.43	4.43	14.16	12.92
54	16.66	15.32	13.43	11.68	4.17	14.35	13.11
55	16.91	15.56	13.68	11.93	3.93	14.54	13.30
56	17.14	15.80	13.92	12.17	3.69	14.73	13.48
57	17.38	16.03	14.15	12.40	3.46	14.90	13.66
58	17.60	16.26	14.37	12.62	3.23	15.07	13.83
59	17.81	16.47	14.58	12.84	3.02	15.23	13.99
60	18.02	16.68	14.79	13.04	2.81	15.39	14.15
61	18.22	16.88	14.99	13.24	2.61	15.54	14.30
62	18.41	17.07	15.18	13.43	2.42	15.68	14.44
63	18.60	17.26	15.37	13.62	2.24	15.82	14.58
64	18.77	17.43	15.54	13.80	2.06	15.95	14.71
65	18.94	17.60	15.71	13.96	1.89	16.07	14.83
66	19.10	17.76	15.87	14.12	1.73	16.19	14.95
67	19.26	17.91	16.03	14.28	1.58	16.30	15.06
68	19.40	18.06	16.17	14.42	1.43	16.41	15.17
69	19.54	18.20	16.31	14.56	1.30	16.50	15.26
70	19.67	18.32	16.44	14.69	1.17	16.60	15.36
71	19.79	18.45	16.56	14.81	1.05	16.68	15.44
72	19.90	18.56	16.67	14.92	0.93	16.76	15.52
73	20.01	18.66	16.78	15.03	0.83	16.84	15.60
74	20.10	18.76	16.87	15.13	0.73	16.91	15.67
75	20.19	18.85	16.96	15.22	0.64	16.97	15.73

3% pa Life multiplier—29.49			3.5% pa Life multiplier—26.34				
E.M. 21	*E.M. 24*	*P.M.*	*E.M. 16*	*E.M. 18*	*E.M. 21*	*E.M. 24*	*P.M.*
10.56	8.98	3.88	11.76	10.61	9.03	7.61	2.89
10.77	9.20	3.66	11.93	10.78	9.20	7.78	2.72
10.99	9.41	3.45	12.10	10.95	9.37	7.95	2.55
11.19	9.61	3.25	12.25	11.11	9.53	8.11	2.39
11.39	9.81	3.05	12.41	11.26	9.68	8.26	2.24
11.58	10.00	2.86	12.55	11.41	9.83	8.41	2.09
11.76	10.18	2.68	12.69	11.55	9.97	8.55	1.95
11.94	10.36	2.50	12.83	11.68	10.10	8.68	1.82
12.10	10.53	2.33	12.96	11.81	10.23	8.81	1.69
12.27	10.69	2.17	13.08	11.93	10.35	8.93	1.56
12.42	10.85	2.01	13.20	12.05	10.47	9.05	1.45
12.57	11.00	1.86	13.31	12.16	10.58	9.16	1.33
12.72	11.14	1.72	13.42	12.27	10.69	9.27	1.23
12.85	11.28	1.58	13.52	12.37	10.79	9.37	1.13
12.98	11.41	1.45	13.61	12.47	10.89	9.47	1.03
13.11	11.53	1.33	13.71	12.56	10.98	9.56	0.94
13.22	11.65	1.21	13.79	12.64	11.07	9.65	0.85
13.34	11.76	1.10	13.87	12.72	11.15	9.73	0.77
13.44	11.86	1.00	13.95	12.80	11.22	9.80	0.70
13.54	11.96	0.90	14.02	12.87	11.29	9.87	0.63
13.63	12.06	0.81	14.09	12.94	11.36	9.94	0.56
13.72	12.14	0.72	14.15	13.00	11.42	10.00	0.50
13.80	12.22	0.64	14.20	13.06	11.48	10.06	0.44
13.87	12.30	0.57	14.26	13.11	11.53	10.11	0.39
13.94	12.37	0.50	14.31	13.16	11.58	10.16	0.34
14.00	12.43	0.43	14.35	13.20	11.62	10.20	0.30

Males aged 2

Retirement age	2.5% pa Life multiplier—33.18						
	E.M. 16	*E.M. 18*	*E.M. 21*	*E.M. 24*	*P.M.*	*E.M. 16*	*E.M. 18*
50	15.99	14.62	12.68	10.89	5.37	13.94	12.66
51	16.28	14.90	12.97	11.17	5.09	14.16	12.88
52	16.56	15.18	13.25	11.45	4.81	14.38	13.10
53	16.83	15.45	13.51	11.72	4.54	14.59	13.31
54	17.09	15.71	13.77	11.98	4.28	14.79	13.51
55	17.34	15.96	14.03	12.23	4.03	14.99	13.71
56	17.58	16.21	14.27	12.48	3.78	15.18	13.90
57	17.82	16.44	14.51	12.72	3.55	15.36	14.08
58	18.05	16.67	14.74	12.94	3.32	15.53	14.25
59	18.27	16.89	14.96	13.16	3.10	15.70	14.42
60	18.48	17.11	15.17	13.38	2.88	15.86	14.58
61	18.69	17.31	15.38	13.58	2.68	16.02	14.74
62	18.88	17.51	15.57	13.78	2.48	16.16	14.88
63	19.07	17.70	15.76	13.97	2.29	16.30	15.03
64	19.25	17.88	15.94	14.15	2.11	16.44	15.16
65	19.43	18.05	16.12	14.32	1.94	16.57	15.29
66	19.59	18.22	16.28	14.49	1.77	16.69	15.41
67	19.75	18.37	16.44	14.64	1.62	16.80	15.52
68	19.90	18.52	16.59	14.79	1.47	16.91	15.63
69	20.04	18.66	16.73	14.93	1.33	17.01	15.73
70	20.17	18.79	16.86	15.06	1.20	17.11	15.83
71	20.29	18.92	16.98	15.19	1.07	17.19	15.92
72	20.41	19.03	17.10	15.30	0.96	17.28	16.00
73	20.52	19.14	17.21	15.41	0.85	17.35	16.08
74	20.62	19.24	17.31	15.51	0.75	17.42	16.15
75	20.71	19.34	17.40	15.61	0.66	17.49	16.21

3% pa Life multiplier—29.38			**3.5% pa Life multiplier—26.26**				
E.M. 21	*E.M. 24*	*P.M.*	*E.M. 16*	*E.M. 18*	*E.M. 21*	*E.M. 24*	*P.M.*
10.88	9.26	4.00	12.18	10.99	9.35	7.88	2.99
11.10	9.48	3.78	12.35	11.17	9.53	8.06	2.81
11.32	9.70	3.56	12.53	11.34	9.70	8.23	2.64
11.53	9.91	3.35	12.69	11.50	9.87	8.40	2.48
11.74	10.11	3.14	12.85	11.66	10.03	8.56	2.32
11.93	10.31	2.95	13.00	11.81	10.18	8.71	2.17
12.12	10.50	2.76	13.15	11.96	10.32	8.85	2.02
12.30	10.68	2.58	13.29	12.10	10.46	8.99	1.88
12.48	10.85	2.40	13.42	12.23	10.60	9.13	1.75
12.64	11.02	2.24	13.55	12.36	10.72	9.25	1.62
12.80	11.18	2.08	13.67	12.48	10.85	9.38	1.50
12.96	11.34	1.92	13.78	12.60	10.96	9.49	1.38
13.11	11.48	1.77	13.90	12.71	11.07	9.60	1.27
13.25	11.62	1.63	14.00	12.81	11.18	9.71	1.17
13.38	11.76	1.50	14.10	12.91	11.28	9.81	1.07
13.51	11.88	1.37	14.19	13.00	11.37	9.90	0.97
13.63	12.01	1.25	14.28	13.09	11.46	9.99	0.88
13.74	12.12	1.14	14.37	13.18	11.54	10.07	0.80
13.85	12.23	1.03	14.45	13.26	11.62	10.15	0.72
13.95	12.33	0.93	14.52	13.33	11.70	10.23	0.65
14.05	12.42	0.83	14.59	13.40	11.76	10.29	0.58
14.14	12.51	0.74	14.65	13.46	11.83	10.36	0.52
14.22	12.60	0.66	14.71	13.52	11.89	10.42	0.46
14.30	12.67	0.58	14.77	13.58	11.94	10.47	0.40
14.37	12.74	0.51	14.82	13.63	11.99	10.52	0.35
14.43	12.81	0.45	14.86	13.67	12.04	10.57	0.31

Males aged 3

Retirement age	2.5% pa Life multiplier—33.01						
	E.M. 16	*E.M. 18*	*E.M. 21*	*E.M. 24*	*P.M.*	*E.M. 16*	*E.M. 18*
50	16.40	14.99	13.00	11.17	5.51	14.36	13.04
51	16.69	15.28	13.30	11.46	5.22	14.59	13.27
52	16.98	15.57	13.58	11.74	4.93	14.82	13.50
53	17.25	15.84	13.86	12.02	4.66	15.03	13.72
54	17.52	16.11	14.12	12.29	4.39	15.24	13.92
55	17.78	16.37	14.38	12.54	4.13	15.44	14.13
56	18.03	16.62	14.63	12.80	3.88	15.64	14.32
57	18.27	16.86	14.88	13.04	3.64	15.83	14.51
58	18.51	17.10	15.11	13.27	3.40	16.01	14.69
59	18.73	17.32	15.34	13.50	3.18	16.18	14.86
60	18.95	17.54	15.56	13.72	2.96	16.34	15.03
61	19.16	17.75	15.77	13.93	2.75	16.50	15.18
62	19.36	17.95	15.97	14.13	2.55	16.65	15.34
63	19.56	18.15	16.16	14.32	2.35	16.80	15.48
64	19.74	18.33	16.35	14.51	2.17	16.94	15.62
65	19.92	18.51	16.52	14.69	1.99	17.07	15.75
66	20.09	18.68	16.69	14.85	1.82	17.19	15.88
67	20.25	18.84	16.85	15.02	1.66	17.31	15.99
68	20.40	18.99	17.01	15.17	1.51	17.42	16.11
69	20.55	19.14	17.15	15.31	1.36	17.53	16.21
70	20.68	19.27	17.29	15.45	1.23	17.63	16.31
71	20.81	19.40	17.41	15.57	1.10	17.72	16.40
72	20.93	19.52	17.53	15.69	0.98	17.80	16.48
73	21.04	19.63	17.64	15.80	0.87	17.88	16.56
74	21.14	19.73	17.75	15.91	0.77	17.95	16.64
75	21.24	19.83	17.84	16.00	0.67	18.02	16.70

3% pa Life multiplier—29.26			3.5% pa Life multiplier—26.17				
E.M. 21	*E.M. 24*	*P.M.*	*E.M. 16*	*E.M. 18*	*E.M. 21*	*E.M. 24*	*P.M.*
11.21	9.54	4.12	12.61	11.38	9.68	8.16	3.10
11.44	9.77	3.89	12.79	11.56	9.87	8.35	2.91
11.67	9.99	3.67	12.97	11.74	10.05	8.52	2.73
11.88	10.21	3.45	13.14	11.91	10.22	8.69	2.56
12.09	10.42	3.24	13.30	12.07	10.38	8.86	2.40
12.29	10.62	3.04	13.46	12.23	10.54	9.02	2.24
12.49	10.82	2.84	13.61	12.38	10.69	9.17	2.09
12.67	11.00	2.66	13.76	12.52	10.83	9.31	1.95
12.85	11.18	2.48	13.89	12.66	10.97	9.45	1.81
13.03	11.35	2.30	14.03	12.79	11.10	9.58	1.68
13.19	11.52	2.14	14.15	12.92	11.23	9.71	1.55
13.35	11.68	1.98	14.27	13.04	11.35	9.83	1.43
13.50	11.83	1.83	14.39	13.16	11.46	9.94	1.32
13.65	11.98	1.68	14.50	13.26	11.57	10.05	1.21
13.79	12.11	1.54	14.60	13.37	11.68	10.15	1.10
13.92	12.25	1.41	14.70	13.47	11.77	10.25	1.01
14.04	12.37	1.29	14.79	13.56	11.87	10.34	0.92
14.16	12.49	1.17	14.88	13.64	11.95	10.43	0.83
14.27	12.60	1.06	14.96	13.73	12.03	10.51	0.75
14.38	12.70	0.96	15.03	13.80	12.11	10.59	0.67
14.48	12.80	0.86	15.10	13.87	12.18	10.66	0.60
14.57	12.89	0.77	15.17	13.94	12.25	10.72	0.53
14.65	12.98	0.68	15.23	14.00	12.31	10.79	0.47
14.73	13.06	0.60	15.29	14.06	12.36	10.84	0.42
14.80	13.13	0.53	15.34	14.11	12.42	10.89	0.36
14.87	13.20	0.46	15.39	14.16	12.46	10.94	0.32

Males aged 4

Retirement age	2.5% pa Life multiplier—32.84						
	E.M. 16	*E.M. 18*	*E.M. 21*	*E.M. 24*	*P.M.*	*E.M. 16*	*E.M. 18*
50	16.82	15.37	13.33	11.45	5.65	14.79	13.44
51	17.12	15.67	13.63	11.75	5.35	15.03	13.68
52	17.41	15.96	13.93	12.04	5.06	15.27	13.91
53	17.69	16.24	14.21	12.32	4.77	15.49	14.13
54	17.96	16.52	14.48	12.60	4.50	15.70	14.35
55	18.23	16.78	14.75	12.86	4.23	15.91	14.55
56	18.49	17.04	15.00	13.12	3.98	16.11	14.75
57	18.74	17.29	15.25	13.37	3.73	16.30	14.95
58	18.98	17.53	15.49	13.61	3.49	16.49	15.13
59	19.21	17.76	15.73	13.84	3.26	16.67	15.31
60	19.43	17.99	15.95	14.06	3.03	16.84	15.48
61	19.65	18.20	16.17	14.28	2.82	17.00	15.64
62	19.85	18.41	16.37	14.49	2.61	17.16	15.80
63	20.05	18.61	16.57	14.69	2.41	17.31	15.95
64	20.24	18.80	16.76	14.88	2.22	17.45	16.09
65	20.43	18.98	16.94	15.06	2.04	17.59	16.23
66	20.60	19.15	17.12	15.23	1.87	17.71	16.36
67	20.76	19.32	17.28	15.40	1.70	17.84	16.48
68	20.92	19.47	17.44	15.55	1.54	17.95	16.59
69	21.07	19.62	17.58	15.70	1.40	18.06	16.70
70	21.21	19.76	17.72	15.84	1.26	18.16	16.80
71	21.34	19.89	17.85	15.97	1.13	18.25	16.90
72	21.46	20.01	17.98	16.09	1.01	18.34	16.98
73	21.57	20.13	18.09	16.20	0.89	18.42	17.07
74	21.68	20.23	18.19	16.31	0.79	18.50	17.14
75	21.77	20.33	18.29	16.41	0.69	18.57	17.21

3% pa Life multiplier—29.13			3.5% pa Life multiplier—26.08				
E.M. 21	*E.M. 24*	*P.M.*	*E.M. 16*	*E.M. 18*	*E.M. 21*	*E.M. 24*	*P.M.*
11.55	9.83	4.25	13.05	11.78	10.03	8.45	3.21
11.79	10.07	4.01	13.24	11.97	10.22	8.64	3.01
12.02	10.30	3.78	13.43	12.15	10.40	8.83	2.83
12.24	10.52	3.55	13.60	12.33	10.58	9.00	2.65
12.46	10.74	3.34	13.77	12.50	10.75	9.17	2.48
12.67	10.94	3.13	13.94	12.66	10.91	9.33	2.32
12.87	11.14	2.93	14.09	12.82	11.07	9.49	2.17
13.06	11.34	2.74	14.24	12.97	11.22	9.64	2.02
13.24	11.52	2.55	14.38	13.11	11.36	9.78	1.87
13.42	11.70	2.37	14.52	13.25	11.50	9.92	1.74
13.59	11.87	2.20	14.65	13.38	11.63	10.05	1.61
13.76	12.03	2.04	14.78	13.50	11.75	10.17	1.48
13.91	12.19	1.88	14.90	13.62	11.87	10.29	1.36
14.06	12.34	1.73	15.01	13.73	11.98	10.41	1.25
14.21	12.48	1.59	15.11	13.84	12.09	10.51	1.14
14.34	12.62	1.46	15.22	13.94	12.19	10.61	1.04
14.47	12.75	1.33	15.31	14.04	12.28	10.71	0.95
14.59	12.87	1.21	15.40	14.13	12.37	10.80	0.86
14.71	12.98	1.09	15.48	14.21	12.46	10.88	0.77
14.81	13.09	0.98	15.56	14.29	12.54	10.96	0.69
14.91	13.19	0.88	15.64	14.36	12.61	11.03	0.62
15.01	13.28	0.79	15.71	14.43	12.68	11.10	0.55
15.10	13.37	0.70	15.77	14.49	12.74	11.17	0.49
15.18	13.45	0.62	15.83	14.55	12.80	11.22	0.43
15.25	13.53	0.54	15.88	14.61	12.85	11.28	0.38
15.32	13.60	0.48	15.93	14.66	12.90	11.33	0.33

Males aged 5

Retirement age	2.5% pa Life multiplier—32.65						
	E.M. 16	*E.M. 18*	*E.M. 21*	*E.M. 24*	*P.M.*	*E.M. 16*	*E.M. 18*
50	17.24	15.76	13.67	11.74	5.79	15.24	13.84
51	17.55	16.07	13.98	12.05	5.48	15.49	14.09
52	17.85	16.36	14.28	12.34	5.18	15.73	14.33
53	18.14	16.65	14.57	12.63	4.89	15.96	14.56
54	18.42	16.93	14.85	12.91	4.61	16.18	14.78
55	18.69	17.21	15.12	13.19	4.34	16.39	14.99
56	18.95	17.47	15.38	13.45	4.08	16.60	15.20
57	19.21	17.73	15.64	13.71	3.82	16.80	15.40
58	19.46	17.97	15.89	13.95	3.58	16.99	15.59
59	19.69	18.21	16.12	14.19	3.34	17.17	15.77
60	19.92	18.44	16.35	14.42	3.11	17.35	15.95
61	20.14	18.66	16.57	14.64	2.89	17.52	16.12
62	20.36	18.87	16.79	14.85	2.68	17.68	16.28
63	20.56	19.08	16.99	15.06	2.47	17.83	16.43
64	20.75	19.27	17.18	15.25	2.28	17.98	16.58
65	20.94	19.46	17.37	15.44	2.09	18.12	16.72
66	21.12	19.64	17.55	15.62	1.91	18.25	16.85
67	21.29	19.80	17.72	15.78	1.74	18.38	16.98
68	21.45	19.96	17.88	15.94	1.58	18.49	17.10
69	21.60	20.12	18.03	16.10	1.43	18.61	17.21
70	21.74	20.26	18.17	16.24	1.29	18.71	17.31
71	21.87	20.39	18.30	16.37	1.16	18.81	17.41
72	22.00	20.52	18.43	16.50	1.03	18.90	17.50
73	22.12	20.63	18.55	16.61	0.91	18.98	17.58
74	22.22	20.74	18.65	16.72	0.81	19.06	17.66
75	22.32	20.84	18.75	16.82	0.71	19.13	17.73

3% pa Life multiplier—29.00			**3.5% pa Life multiplier—25.98**				
E.M. 21	*E.M. 24*	*P.M.*	*E.M. 16*	*E.M. 18*	*E.M. 21*	*E.M. 24*	*P.M.*
11.90	10.12	4.38	13.51	12.19	10.38	8.75	3.32
12.15	10.37	4.13	13.71	12.39	10.58	8.95	3.12
12.38	10.61	3.89	13.90	12.58	10.77	9.14	2.93
12.61	10.84	3.66	14.08	12.76	10.95	9.32	2.75
12.84	11.06	3.44	14.26	12.94	11.13	9.49	2.57
13.05	11.27	3.23	14.43	13.11	11.29	9.66	2.40
13.26	11.48	3.02	14.59	13.27	11.46	9.82	2.24
13.45	11.68	2.82	14.74	13.42	11.61	9.98	2.09
13.65	11.87	2.63	14.89	13.57	11.76	10.13	1.94
13.83	12.05	2.45	15.03	13.71	11.90	10.27	1.80
14.00	12.23	2.27	15.17	13.85	12.04	10.40	1.66
14.17	12.40	2.10	15.30	13.98	12.16	10.53	1.53
14.33	12.56	1.94	15.42	14.10	12.29	10.66	1.41
14.49	12.71	1.79	15.54	14.22	12.40	10.77	1.29
14.64	12.86	1.64	15.65	14.33	12.51	10.88	1.18
14.77	13.00	1.50	15.75	14.43	12.62	10.99	1.08
14.91	13.13	1.37	15.85	14.53	12.72	11.09	0.98
15.03	13.26	1.24	15.94	14.62	12.81	11.18	0.89
15.15	13.37	1.12	16.03	14.71	12.90	11.27	0.80
15.26	13.49	1.01	16.11	14.79	12.98	11.35	0.72
15.37	13.59	0.91	16.19	14.87	13.06	11.42	0.64
15.46	13.69	0.81	16.26	14.94	13.13	11.49	0.57
15.55	13.78	0.72	16.32	15.01	13.19	11.56	0.51
15.64	13.86	0.64	16.39	15.07	13.25	11.62	0.45
15.71	13.94	0.56	16.44	15.12	13.31	11.68	0.39
15.79	14.01	0.49	16.49	15.17	13.36	11.73	0.34

Males aged 6

Retirement age	2.5% pa Life multiplier—32.47						
	E.M. 16	*E.M. 18*	*E.M. 21*	*E.M. 24*	*P.M.*	*E.M. 16*	*E.M. 18*
50	17.68	16.16	14.02	12.03	5.94	15.70	14.26
51	17.99	16.47	14.33	12.35	5.62	15.96	14.52
52	18.30	16.78	14.64	12.66	5.32	16.20	14.76
53	18.59	17.07	14.93	12.95	5.02	16.44	15.00
54	18.88	17.36	15.22	13.24	4.73	16.67	15.23
55	19.16	17.64	15.50	13.52	4.45	16.89	15.45
56	19.43	17.91	15.77	13.79	4.18	17.10	15.66
57	19.69	18.17	16.03	14.05	3.92	17.31	15.86
58	19.95	18.43	16.29	14.30	3.67	17.50	16.06
59	20.19	18.67	16.53	14.55	3.42	17.69	16.25
60	20.43	18.91	16.77	14.78	3.19	17.87	16.43
61	20.65	19.13	16.99	15.01	2.96	18.05	16.61
62	20.87	19.35	17.21	15.23	2.74	18.21	16.77
63	21.08	19.56	17.42	15.44	2.53	18.37	16.93
64	21.28	19.76	17.62	15.64	2.33	18.52	17.08
65	21.47	19.95	17.81	15.83	2.14	18.67	17.23
66	21.65	20.13	17.99	16.01	1.96	18.80	17.36
67	21.82	20.30	18.16	16.18	1.79	18.93	17.49
68	21.99	20.47	18.33	16.35	1.62	19.05	17.61
69	22.14	20.62	18.48	16.50	1.47	19.17	17.73
70	22.29	20.77	18.63	16.65	1.32	19.27	17.83
71	22.43	20.91	18.77	16.78	1.19	19.37	17.93
72	22.55	21.03	18.89	16.91	1.06	19.47	18.03
73	22.67	21.15	19.01	17.03	0.94	19.55	18.11
74	22.78	21.26	19.12	17.14	0.83	19.63	18.19
75	22.89	21.37	19.23	17.25	0.73	19.71	18.27

3% pa Life multiplier—28.86			**3.5% pa Life multiplier—25.88**				
E.M. 21	*E.M. 24*	*P.M.*	*E.M. 16*	*E.M. 18*	*E.M. 21*	*E.M. 24*	*P.M.*
12.26	10.43	4.51	13.99	12.62	10.75	9.06	3.44
12.51	10.68	4.25	14.19	12.83	10.95	9.26	3.23
12.76	10.93	4.01	14.39	13.02	11.15	9.46	3.03
12.99	11.17	3.77	14.58	13.21	11.34	9.65	2.84
13.22	11.39	3.54	14.76	13.40	11.52	9.83	2.66
13.44	11.61	3.32	14.94	13.57	11.69	10.00	2.49
13.66	11.83	3.11	15.10	13.74	11.86	10.17	2.32
13.86	12.03	2.91	15.26	13.90	12.02	10.33	2.16
14.06	12.23	2.71	15.42	14.05	12.17	10.48	2.01
14.25	12.42	2.52	15.56	14.20	12.32	10.63	1.86
14.43	12.60	2.34	15.70	14.34	12.46	10.77	1.72
14.60	12.77	2.17	15.84	14.47	12.59	10.90	1.59
14.77	12.94	2.00	15.96	14.60	12.72	11.03	1.46
14.93	13.10	1.84	16.08	14.72	12.84	11.15	1.34
15.08	13.25	1.69	16.20	14.83	12.95	11.27	1.23
15.22	13.39	1.55	16.31	14.94	13.06	11.37	1.12
15.36	13.53	1.41	16.41	15.04	13.17	11.48	1.02
15.49	13.66	1.28	16.51	15.14	13.26	11.57	0.92
15.61	13.78	1.16	16.60	15.23	13.35	11.66	0.83
15.72	13.89	1.04	16.68	15.31	13.44	11.75	0.74
15.83	14.00	0.94	16.76	15.39	13.52	11.83	0.67
15.93	14.10	0.84	16.83	15.47	13.59	11.90	0.59
16.02	14.19	0.74	16.90	15.53	13.66	11.97	0.52
16.11	14.28	0.66	16.96	15.60	13.72	12.03	0.46
16.19	14.36	0.58	17.02	15.65	13.78	12.09	0.40
16.26	14.43	0.50	17.07	15.71	13.83	12.14	0.35

Males aged 7

Retirement age	2.5% pa Life multiplier—32.27						
	E.M. 16	*E.M. 18*	*E.M. 21*	*E.M. 24*	*P.M.*	*E.M. 16*	*E.M. 18*
50	18.12	16.56	14.37	12.34	6.09	16.18	14.69
51	18.44	16.89	14.69	12.66	5.76	16.44	14.95
52	18.76	17.20	15.01	12.97	5.45	16.69	15.21
53	19.06	17.50	15.31	13.28	5.14	16.94	15.45
54	19.36	17.80	15.61	13.57	4.85	17.17	15.69
55	19.64	18.09	15.89	13.86	4.56	17.40	15.91
56	19.92	18.36	16.17	14.14	4.29	17.62	16.13
57	20.19	18.63	16.44	14.41	4.02	17.83	16.34
58	20.45	18.89	16.70	14.66	3.76	18.03	16.55
59	20.70	19.14	16.95	14.91	3.51	18.23	16.74
60	20.94	19.38	17.19	15.16	3.27	18.41	16.93
61	21.17	19.61	17.42	15.39	3.04	18.59	17.11
62	21.40	19.84	17.64	15.61	2.81	18.76	17.28
63	21.61	20.05	17.86	15.83	2.60	18.93	17.44
64	21.81	20.26	18.06	16.03	2.39	19.08	17.60
65	22.01	20.45	18.26	16.23	2.20	19.23	17.75
66	22.20	20.64	18.44	16.41	2.01	19.37	17.89
67	22.37	20.82	18.62	16.59	1.83	19.50	18.02
68	22.54	20.98	18.79	16.76	1.66	19.63	18.14
69	22.70	21.14	18.95	16.92	1.51	19.75	18.26
70	22.85	21.29	19.10	17.07	1.36	19.86	18.37
71	22.99	21.43	19.24	17.21	1.22	19.96	18.48
72	23.12	21.56	19.37	17.34	1.08	20.06	18.57
73	23.25	21.69	19.49	17.46	0.96	20.15	18.66
74	23.36	21.80	19.61	17.58	0.85	20.23	18.74
75	23.46	21.91	19.71	17.68	0.74	20.30	18.82

3% pa Life multiplier—28.72			3.5% pa Life multiplier—25.77				
E.M. 21	*E.M. 24*	*P.M.*	*E.M. 16*	*E.M. 18*	*E.M. 21*	*E.M. 24*	*P.M.*
12.63	10.74	4.64	14.48	13.07	11.12	9.38	3.56
12.89	11.01	4.38	14.69	13.28	11.34	9.59	3.34
13.14	11.26	4.13	14.90	13.48	11.54	9.79	3.14
13.39	11.50	3.89	15.09	13.68	11.74	9.99	2.94
13.62	11.74	3.65	15.28	13.87	11.92	10.18	2.76
13.85	11.97	3.42	15.46	14.05	12.10	10.36	2.58
14.07	12.18	3.20	15.63	14.22	12.28	10.53	2.40
14.28	12.40	2.99	15.80	14.39	12.44	10.69	2.24
14.48	12.60	2.79	15.96	14.54	12.60	10.85	2.08
14.68	12.79	2.60	16.11	14.70	12.75	11.00	1.93
14.86	12.98	2.41	16.26	14.84	12.90	11.15	1.78
15.04	13.16	2.23	16.39	14.98	13.04	11.29	1.64
15.21	13.33	2.06	16.53	15.11	13.17	11.42	1.51
15.38	13.49	1.90	16.65	15.24	13.29	11.54	1.39
15.53	13.65	1.74	16.77	15.35	13.41	11.66	1.27
15.68	13.80	1.59	16.88	15.47	13.52	11.77	1.16
15.82	13.94	1.45	16.99	15.57	13.63	11.88	1.05
15.95	14.07	1.32	17.09	15.67	13.73	11.98	0.95
16.08	14.20	1.19	17.18	15.77	13.82	12.07	0.86
16.20	14.31	1.08	17.27	15.85	13.91	12.16	0.77
16.31	14.42	0.97	17.35	15.93	13.99	12.24	0.69
16.41	14.53	0.86	17.42	16.01	14.07	12.32	0.61
16.51	14.62	0.77	17.50	16.08	14.14	12.39	0.54
16.60	14.71	0.68	17.56	16.15	14.20	12.45	0.48
16.68	14.79	0.60	17.62	16.21	14.26	12.51	0.42
16.75	14.87	0.52	17.67	16.26	14.32	12.57	0.36

Males aged 8

Retirement age	2.5% pa Life multiplier—32.07 E.M. 16	E.M. 18	E.M. 21	E.M. 24	P.M.	E.M. 16	E.M. 18
50	18.58	16.98	14.73	12.65	6.24	16.67	15.14
51	18.91	17.31	15.06	12.98	5.91	16.94	15.41
52	19.23	17.63	15.38	13.30	5.59	17.20	15.67
53	19.54	17.95	15.70	13.61	5.27	17.45	15.92
54	19.85	18.25	16.00	13.92	4.97	17.69	16.16
55	20.14	18.54	16.29	14.21	4.68	17.92	16.39
56	20.42	18.83	16.58	14.49	4.39	18.15	16.62
57	20.70	19.10	16.85	14.77	4.12	18.37	16.84
58	20.96	19.37	17.12	15.03	3.85	18.58	17.05
59	21.22	19.62	17.37	15.29	3.60	18.78	17.25
60	21.47	19.87	17.62	15.54	3.35	18.97	17.44
61	21.71	20.11	17.86	15.78	3.11	19.15	17.62
62	21.93	20.34	18.09	16.00	2.88	19.33	17.80
63	22.15	20.56	18.31	16.22	2.66	19.50	17.97
64	22.36	20.77	18.52	16.43	2.45	19.66	18.13
65	22.56	20.97	18.72	16.64	2.25	19.81	18.28
66	22.76	21.16	18.91	16.83	2.06	19.96	18.43
67	22.94	21.34	19.09	17.01	1.88	20.09	18.56
68	23.11	21.51	19.26	17.18	1.71	20.22	18.69
69	23.27	21.68	19.43	17.34	1.54	20.34	18.81
70	23.43	21.83	19.58	17.50	1.39	20.46	18.93
71	23.57	21.97	19.72	17.64	1.25	20.56	19.03
72	23.71	22.11	19.86	17.78	1.11	20.66	19.13
73	23.83	22.23	19.98	17.90	0.99	20.75	19.22
74	23.95	22.35	20.10	18.02	0.87	20.84	19.31
75	24.06	22.46	20.21	18.13	0.76	20.92	19.39

3% pa Life multiplier—28.57			**3.5% pa Life multiplier—25.66**				
E.M. 21	*E.M. 24*	*P.M.*	*E.M. 16*	*E.M. 18*	*E.M. 21*	*E.M. 24*	*P.M.*
13.01	11.07	4.78	14.99	13.53	11.52	9.71	3.68
13.28	11.34	4.52	15.21	13.75	11.73	9.92	3.46
13.54	11.60	4.25	15.42	13.96	11.95	10.14	3.25
13.79	11.85	4.00	15.62	14.16	12.15	10.34	3.05
14.03	12.09	3.76	15.82	14.35	12.34	10.53	2.85
14.27	12.33	3.53	16.01	14.54	12.53	10.72	2.67
14.49	12.55	3.30	16.19	14.72	12.71	10.90	2.49
14.71	12.77	3.08	16.36	14.89	12.88	11.07	2.32
14.92	12.98	2.88	16.52	15.06	13.05	11.24	2.15
15.12	13.18	2.67	16.68	15.21	13.20	11.39	1.99
15.31	13.37	2.48	16.83	15.36	13.35	11.54	1.84
15.50	13.56	2.30	16.97	15.51	13.50	11.69	1.70
15.67	13.73	2.12	17.11	15.64	13.63	11.82	1.57
15.84	13.90	1.95	17.24	15.77	13.76	11.95	1.44
16.00	14.06	1.79	17.36	15.89	13.88	12.07	1.31
16.15	14.21	1.64	17.48	16.01	14.00	12.19	1.20
16.30	14.36	1.50	17.58	16.12	14.11	12.30	1.09
16.44	14.49	1.36	17.69	16.22	14.21	12.40	0.98
16.57	14.62	1.23	17.78	16.32	14.31	12.50	0.89
16.69	14.75	1.11	17.88	16.41	14.40	12.59	0.80
16.80	14.86	0.99	17.96	16.50	14.48	12.67	0.71
16.91	14.97	0.89	18.04	16.57	14.56	12.75	0.63
17.01	15.06	0.79	18.11	16.65	14.63	12.82	0.56
17.10	15.16	0.70	18.18	16.71	14.70	12.89	0.49
17.18	15.24	0.61	18.24	16.78	14.76	12.95	0.43
17.26	15.32	0.54	18.30	16.83	14.82	13.01	0.38

Males aged 9

Retirement age	2.5% pa Life multiplier—31.87						
	E.M. 16	*E.M. 18*	*E.M. 21*	*E.M. 24*	*P.M.*	*E.M. 16*	*E.M. 18*
50	19.05	17.41	15.10	12.97	6.40	17.17	15.59
51	19.39	17.75	15.44	13.31	6.06	17.45	15.87
52	19.72	18.08	15.77	13.64	5.73	17.72	16.14
53	20.04	18.40	16.09	13.96	5.41	17.97	16.40
54	20.35	18.71	16.40	14.27	5.10	18.22	16.65
55	20.65	19.01	16.70	14.57	4.80	18.47	16.89
56	20.94	19.30	16.99	14.86	4.50	18.70	17.12
57	21.22	19.58	17.28	15.14	4.22	18.92	17.35
58	21.49	19.85	17.55	15.41	3.95	19.14	17.56
59	21.75	20.12	17.81	15.68	3.69	19.34	17.77
60	22.01	20.37	18.06	15.93	3.43	19.54	17.97
61	22.25	20.61	18.31	16.17	3.19	19.73	18.16
62	22.49	20.85	18.54	16.41	2.96	19.91	18.34
63	22.71	21.07	18.77	16.63	2.73	20.09	18.51
64	22.93	21.29	18.98	16.85	2.51	20.25	18.68
65	23.13	21.50	19.19	17.05	2.31	20.41	18.83
66	23.33	21.69	19.39	17.25	2.11	20.56	18.98
67	23.52	21.88	19.57	17.44	1.93	20.70	19.12
68	23.69	22.05	19.75	17.61	1.75	20.83	19.26
69	23.86	22.22	19.92	17.78	1.58	20.96	19.38
70	24.02	22.38	20.07	17.94	1.43	21.07	19.50
71	24.16	22.53	20.22	18.09	1.28	21.18	19.61
72	24.30	22.66	20.36	18.22	1.14	21.29	19.71
73	24.43	22.79	20.49	18.35	1.01	21.38	19.80
74	24.55	22.91	20.61	18.47	0.89	21.47	19.89
75	24.66	23.02	20.72	18.58	0.78	21.55	19.97

3% pa Life multiplier—28.42			**3.5% pa Life multiplier—25.55**				
E.M. 21	*E.M. 24*	*P.M.*	*E.M. 16*	*E.M. 18*	*E.M. 21*	*E.M. 24*	*P.M.*
13.40	11.40	4.93	15.52	14.00	11.92	10.05	3.81
13.68	11.68	4.65	15.75	14.23	12.15	10.27	3.58
13.95	11.95	4.38	15.96	14.45	12.37	10.49	3.37
14.21	12.21	4.12	16.17	14.66	12.58	10.70	3.16
14.46	12.46	3.87	16.38	14.86	12.78	10.90	2.95
14.70	12.70	3.63	16.57	15.05	12.97	11.10	2.76
14.93	12.93	3.40	16.75	15.24	13.16	11.28	2.58
15.15	13.15	3.18	16.93	15.42	13.33	11.46	2.40
15.37	13.37	2.96	17.10	15.59	13.50	11.63	2.23
15.58	13.58	2.76	17.27	15.75	13.67	11.79	2.06
15.77	13.77	2.56	17.42	15.90	13.82	11.95	1.91
15.96	13.96	2.37	17.57	16.05	13.97	12.10	1.76
16.15	14.15	2.19	17.71	16.19	14.11	12.24	1.62
16.32	14.32	2.01	17.84	16.33	14.24	12.37	1.49
16.49	14.49	1.85	17.97	16.45	14.37	12.50	1.36
16.64	14.64	1.69	18.09	16.57	14.49	12.62	1.24
16.79	14.79	1.54	18.20	16.69	14.61	12.73	1.13
16.93	14.93	1.40	18.31	16.79	14.71	12.84	1.02
17.07	15.07	1.27	18.41	16.89	14.81	12.94	0.92
17.19	15.19	1.14	18.50	16.99	14.91	13.03	0.83
17.31	15.31	1.02	18.59	17.08	14.99	13.12	0.74
17.42	15.42	0.92	18.67	17.16	15.07	13.20	0.66
17.52	15.52	0.81	18.75	17.23	15.15	13.28	0.58
17.61	15.61	0.72	18.82	17.30	15.22	13.35	0.51
17.70	15.70	0.63	18.88	17.37	15.28	13.41	0.45
17.78	15.78	0.55	18.94	17.42	15.34	13.47	0.39

Males aged 10

Retirement age	2.5% pa Life multiplier—31.66						
	E.M. 16	E.M. 18	E.M. 21	E.M. 24	P.M.	E.M. 16	E.M. 18
50	19.53	17.85	15.48	13.29	6.56	17.69	16.06
51	19.87	18.19	15.83	13.64	6.21	17.97	16.35
52	20.21	18.53	16.17	13.98	5.87	18.25	16.63
53	20.54	18.86	16.50	14.31	5.54	18.52	16.89
54	20.86	19.18	16.82	14.63	5.22	18.77	17.15
55	21.17	19.49	17.12	14.93	4.92	19.02	17.40
56	21.47	19.79	17.42	15.23	4.62	19.26	17.64
57	21.75	20.07	17.71	15.52	4.33	19.49	17.87
58	22.03	20.35	17.99	15.80	4.05	19.71	18.09
59	22.30	20.62	18.26	16.07	3.78	19.93	18.30
60	22.56	20.88	18.52	16.33	3.52	20.13	18.51
61	22.81	21.13	18.77	16.58	3.27	20.33	18.70
62	23.05	21.37	19.01	16.82	3.03	20.51	18.89
63	23.28	21.60	19.24	17.05	2.80	20.69	19.07
64	23.50	21.83	19.46	17.27	2.58	20.86	19.24
65	23.72	22.04	19.67	17.48	2.37	21.02	19.40
66	23.92	22.24	19.87	17.68	2.17	21.18	19.56
67	24.11	22.43	20.07	17.88	1.97	21.32	19.70
68	24.29	22.61	20.25	18.06	1.79	21.46	19.84
69	24.46	22.78	20.42	18.23	1.62	21.59	19.97
70	24.62	22.94	20.58	18.39	1.46	21.71	20.09
71	24.77	23.09	20.73	18.54	1.31	21.82	20.20
72	24.92	23.24	20.87	18.68	1.17	21.93	20.30
73	25.05	23.37	21.00	18.81	1.04	22.03	20.40
74	25.17	23.49	21.13	18.94	0.91	22.12	20.49
75	25.28	23.60	21.24	19.05	0.80	22.20	20.57

3% pa Life multiplier—28.26			3.5% pa Life multiplier—25.43				
E.M. 21	*E.M. 24*	*P.M.*	*E.M. 16*	*E.M. 18*	*E.M. 21*	*E.M. 24*	*P.M.*
13.81	11.75	5.08	16.07	14.50	12.34	10.40	3.95
14.09	12.03	4.79	16.30	14.73	12.58	10.64	3.71
14.37	12.31	4.52	16.53	14.96	12.80	10.86	3.48
14.64	12.58	4.25	16.74	15.17	13.02	11.08	3.27
14.89	12.83	3.99	16.95	15.38	13.23	11.29	3.06
15.14	13.08	3.74	17.15	15.58	13.43	11.49	2.86
15.38	13.32	3.50	17.34	15.78	13.62	11.68	2.67
15.61	13.55	3.27	17.53	15.96	13.80	11.86	2.48
15.83	13.77	3.05	17.70	16.14	13.98	12.04	2.31
16.05	13.99	2.84	17.87	16.30	14.15	12.21	2.14
16.25	14.19	2.63	18.03	16.46	14.31	12.37	1.98
16.45	14.39	2.44	18.19	16.62	14.46	12.52	1.82
16.63	14.57	2.25	18.33	16.76	14.61	12.67	1.68
16.81	14.75	2.07	18.47	16.90	14.75	12.81	1.54
16.98	14.92	1.90	18.60	17.03	14.88	12.94	1.41
17.14	15.08	1.74	18.73	17.16	15.00	13.06	1.28
17.30	15.24	1.59	18.84	17.28	15.12	13.18	1.17
17.44	15.38	1.44	18.95	17.39	15.23	13.29	1.06
17.58	15.52	1.31	19.06	17.49	15.33	13.39	0.95
17.71	15.65	1.18	19.16	17.59	15.43	13.49	0.85
17.83	15.77	1.06	19.25	17.68	15.52	13.58	0.76
17.94	15.88	0.94	19.33	17.76	15.60	13.67	0.68
18.05	15.99	0.84	19.41	17.84	15.68	13.74	0.60
18.15	16.08	0.74	19.48	17.91	15.75	13.82	0.53
18.23	16.17	0.65	19.55	17.98	15.82	13.88	0.46
18.32	16.26	0.57	19.61	18.04	15.88	13.94	0.40

Males aged 11

Retirement age	2.5% pa Life multiplier—31.44						
	E.M. 16	*E.M. 18*	*E.M. 21*	*E.M. 24*	*P.M.*	*E.M. 16*	*E.M. 18*
50	20.02	18.30	15.87	13.63	6.72	18.22	16.55
51	20.37	18.65	16.23	13.98	6.37	18.52	16.84
52	20.72	19.00	16.58	14.33	6.02	18.80	17.13
53	21.06	19.34	16.91	14.67	5.68	19.08	17.40
54	21.38	19.66	17.24	14.99	5.36	19.34	17.67
55	21.70	19.98	17.55	15.31	5.04	19.60	17.93
56	22.01	20.28	17.86	15.62	4.73	19.84	18.17
57	22.30	20.58	18.16	15.91	4.44	20.08	18.41
58	22.59	20.87	18.44	16.20	4.15	20.31	18.64
59	22.86	21.14	18.72	16.48	3.88	20.53	18.86
60	23.13	21.41	18.99	16.74	3.61	20.74	19.07
61	23.39	21.67	19.24	17.00	3.35	20.94	19.27
62	23.63	21.91	19.49	17.24	3.11	21.13	19.46
63	23.87	22.15	19.73	17.48	2.87	21.32	19.65
64	24.10	22.38	19.95	17.71	2.64	21.49	19.82
65	24.31	22.59	20.17	17.92	2.43	21.66	19.99
66	24.52	22.80	20.37	18.13	2.22	21.82	20.15
67	24.72	22.99	20.57	18.33	2.02	21.97	20.30
68	24.90	23.18	20.76	18.51	1.84	22.11	20.44
69	25.08	23.36	20.93	18.69	1.66	22.24	20.57
70	25.24	23.52	21.10	18.85	1.50	22.37	20.69
71	25.40	23.68	21.25	19.01	1.34	22.48	20.81
72	25.54	23.82	21.40	19.15	1.20	22.59	20.92
73	25.68	23.96	21.53	19.29	1.06	22.69	21.02
74	25.80	24.08	21.66	19.41	0.94	22.78	21.11
75	25.92	24.20	21.77	19.53	0.82	22.87	21.20

3% pa Life multiplier—28.10			3.5% pa Life multiplier—25.31				
E.M. 21	*E.M. 24*	*P.M.*	*E.M. 16*	*E.M. 18*	*E.M. 21*	*E.M. 24*	*P.M.*
14.22	12.10	5.23	16.63	15.01	12.77	10.77	4.08
14.52	12.40	4.94	16.87	15.25	13.02	11.01	3.84
14.80	12.68	4.65	17.11	15.48	13.25	11.24	3.61
15.08	12.96	4.38	17.33	15.71	13.48	11.47	3.38
15.34	13.22	4.11	17.55	15.92	13.69	11.68	3.17
15.60	13.48	3.86	17.76	16.13	13.90	11.89	2.96
15.85	13.72	3.61	17.95	16.33	14.10	12.09	2.76
16.08	13.96	3.37	18.15	16.52	14.29	12.28	2.57
16.31	14.19	3.14	18.33	16.70	14.47	12.46	2.39
16.53	14.41	2.92	18.50	16.88	14.65	12.64	2.21
16.74	14.62	2.71	18.67	17.04	14.81	12.80	2.05
16.94	14.82	2.51	18.83	17.20	14.97	12.96	1.89
17.14	15.01	2.32	18.98	17.35	15.12	13.11	1.74
17.32	15.20	2.14	19.12	17.50	15.26	13.26	1.59
17.50	15.37	1.96	19.26	17.63	15.40	13.39	1.46
17.66	15.54	1.79	19.39	17.76	15.53	13.52	1.33
17.82	15.70	1.64	19.51	17.88	15.65	13.64	1.21
17.97	15.85	1.49	19.62	18.00	15.77	13.76	1.09
18.11	15.99	1.34	19.73	18.10	15.87	13.86	0.99
18.24	16.12	1.21	19.83	18.20	15.97	13.97	0.88
18.37	16.25	1.09	19.92	18.30	16.07	14.06	0.79
18.48	16.36	0.97	20.01	18.39	16.15	14.15	0.70
18.59	16.47	0.86	20.09	18.47	16.23	14.23	0.62
18.69	16.57	0.76	20.17	18.54	16.31	14.30	0.55
18.79	16.66	0.67	20.23	18.61	16.38	14.37	0.48
18.87	16.75	0.59	20.30	18.67	16.44	14.43	0.42

Males aged 12

Retirement age	2.5% pa Life multiplier—31.22						
	E.M. 16	*E.M. 18*	*E.M. 21*	*E.M. 24*	*P.M.*	*E.M. 16*	*E.M. 18*
50	20.52	18.76	16.27	13.97	6.89	18.77	17.05
51	20.89	19.12	16.64	14.34	6.53	19.08	17.35
52	21.24	19.48	16.99	14.69	6.17	19.37	17.65
53	21.59	19.82	17.34	15.04	5.83	19.65	17.93
54	21.92	20.16	17.67	15.37	5.49	19.93	18.20
55	22.25	20.48	18.00	15.70	5.17	20.19	18.47
56	22.56	20.80	18.31	16.01	4.85	20.44	18.72
57	22.86	21.10	18.61	16.31	4.55	20.69	18.96
58	23.16	21.39	18.91	16.61	4.26	20.92	19.20
59	23.44	21.68	19.19	16.89	3.97	21.15	19.43
60	23.71	21.95	19.46	17.16	3.70	21.36	19.64
61	23.98	22.21	19.73	17.43	3.44	21.57	19.85
62	24.23	22.46	19.98	17.68	3.18	21.77	20.05
63	24.47	22.71	20.22	17.92	2.94	21.96	20.24
64	24.70	22.94	20.45	18.15	2.71	22.14	20.42
65	24.93	23.16	20.68	18.38	2.49	22.31	20.59
66	25.14	23.37	20.89	18.59	2.28	22.48	20.75
67	25.34	23.57	21.09	18.79	2.08	22.63	20.91
68	25.53	23.76	21.28	18.98	1.89	22.78	21.05
69	25.71	23.94	21.46	19.16	1.71	22.91	21.19
70	25.88	24.11	21.63	19.33	1.54	23.04	21.32
71	26.04	24.27	21.79	19.49	1.38	23.16	21.44
72	26.19	24.42	21.94	19.64	1.23	23.27	21.55
73	26.32	24.56	22.08	19.77	1.09	23.38	21.65
74	26.45	24.69	22.20	19.90	0.96	23.47	21.75
75	26.57	24.81	22.32	20.02	0.84	23.56	21.84

3% pa Life multiplier—27.93			3.5% pa Life multiplier—25.18				
E.M. 21	*E.M. 24*	*P.M.*	*E.M. 16*	*E.M. 18*	*E.M. 21*	*E.M. 24*	*P.M.*
14.65	12.47	5.39	17.22	15.53	13.22	11.15	4.23
14.96	12.77	5.09	17.47	15.79	13.48	11.40	3.98
15.25	13.06	4.79	17.71	16.03	13.72	11.64	3.73
15.53	13.35	4.51	17.94	16.26	13.95	11.87	3.50
15.81	13.62	4.24	18.17	16.48	14.17	12.10	3.28
16.07	13.88	3.97	18.38	16.70	14.39	12.31	3.06
16.32	14.14	3.72	18.59	16.91	14.59	12.52	2.86
16.57	14.38	3.47	18.78	17.10	14.79	12.71	2.66
16.80	14.62	3.24	18.97	17.29	14.98	12.90	2.47
17.03	14.84	3.01	19.15	17.47	15.16	13.08	2.29
17.25	15.06	2.80	19.32	17.64	15.33	13.25	2.12
17.45	15.27	2.59	19.49	17.81	15.50	13.42	1.95
17.65	15.47	2.39	19.65	17.96	15.65	13.57	1.80
17.84	15.66	2.20	19.79	18.11	15.80	13.72	1.65
18.02	15.84	2.02	19.93	18.25	15.94	13.86	1.51
18.20	16.01	1.85	20.07	18.39	16.08	14.00	1.38
18.36	16.17	1.68	20.19	18.51	16.20	14.12	1.25
18.51	16.33	1.53	20.31	18.63	16.32	14.24	1.13
18.66	16.47	1.39	20.42	18.74	16.43	14.35	1.02
18.79	16.61	1.25	20.53	18.85	16.54	14.46	0.92
18.92	16.74	1.12	20.62	18.94	16.63	14.55	0.82
19.04	16.86	1.00	20.71	19.03	16.72	14.64	0.73
19.15	16.97	0.89	20.80	19.12	16.81	14.73	0.65
19.26	17.07	0.79	20.87	19.19	16.88	14.80	0.57
19.35	17.17	0.69	20.95	19.26	16.95	14.88	0.50
19.44	17.25	0.60	21.01	19.33	17.02	14.94	0.43

Males aged 13

Retirement age	2.5% pa Life multiplier—30.99						
	E.M. 16	*E.M. 18*	*E.M. 21*	*E.M. 24*	*P.M.*	*E.M. 16*	*E.M. 18*
50	21.04	19.23	16.68	14.32	7.07	19.34	17.56
51	21.41	19.60	17.06	14.70	6.69	19.65	17.88
52	21.78	19.97	17.42	15.06	6.33	19.95	18.18
53	22.13	20.32	17.78	15.42	5.97	20.25	18.47
54	22.47	20.67	18.12	15.76	5.63	20.53	18.75
55	22.81	21.00	18.45	16.09	5.30	20.80	19.02
56	23.13	21.32	18.77	16.41	4.98	21.06	19.29
57	23.44	21.63	19.08	16.72	4.66	21.31	19.54
58	23.74	21.93	19.38	17.03	4.36	21.55	19.78
59	24.03	22.22	19.67	17.32	4.07	21.79	20.01
60	24.31	22.50	19.95	17.60	3.79	22.01	20.24
61	24.58	22.77	20.22	17.87	3.52	22.22	20.45
62	24.84	23.03	20.48	18.12	3.26	22.43	20.65
63	25.09	23.28	20.73	18.37	3.02	22.62	20.85
64	25.33	23.52	20.97	18.61	2.78	22.81	21.04
65	25.55	23.74	21.20	18.84	2.55	22.99	21.21
66	25.77	23.96	21.41	19.06	2.33	23.16	21.38
67	25.98	24.17	21.62	19.26	2.13	23.31	21.54
68	26.17	24.36	21.82	19.46	1.93	23.46	21.69
69	26.36	24.55	22.00	19.64	1.75	23.60	21.83
70	26.53	24.72	22.17	19.81	1.57	23.74	21.96
71	26.69	24.88	22.34	19.98	1.41	23.86	22.09
72	26.85	25.04	22.49	20.13	1.26	23.97	22.20
73	26.99	25.18	22.63	20.27	1.12	24.08	22.31
74	27.12	25.31	22.76	20.40	0.98	24.18	22.40
75	27.24	25.43	22.89	20.53	0.86	24.27	22.49

3% pa Life multiplier—27.76			**3.5% pa Life multiplier—25.05**				
E.M. 21	*E.M. 24*	*P.M.*	*E.M. 16*	*E.M. 18*	*E.M. 21*	*E.M. 24*	*P.M.*
15.10	12.84	5.55	17.82	16.08	13.69	11.54	4.38
15.41	13.16	5.24	18.08	16.34	13.95	11.80	4.12
15.71	13.46	4.94	18.33	16.59	14.20	12.05	3.86
16.00	13.75	4.65	18.57	16.83	14.44	12.29	3.62
16.28	14.03	4.36	18.81	17.07	14.67	12.52	3.39
16.56	14.30	4.09	19.03	17.29	14.90	12.74	3.17
16.82	14.56	3.83	19.24	17.50	15.11	12.96	2.96
17.07	14.82	3.58	19.44	17.70	15.31	13.16	2.75
17.31	15.06	3.34	19.64	17.90	15.51	13.36	2.56
17.54	15.29	3.10	19.83	18.09	15.69	13.54	2.37
17.77	15.52	2.88	20.01	18.26	15.87	13.72	2.19
17.98	15.73	2.67	20.17	18.43	16.04	13.89	2.02
18.19	15.93	2.46	20.34	18.60	16.20	14.05	1.86
18.38	16.13	2.27	20.49	18.75	16.36	14.21	1.71
18.57	16.32	2.08	20.64	18.90	16.50	14.35	1.56
18.74	16.49	1.90	20.77	19.03	16.64	14.49	1.42
18.91	16.66	1.74	20.90	19.16	16.77	14.62	1.29
19.07	16.82	1.58	21.03	19.29	16.89	14.74	1.17
19.22	16.97	1.43	21.14	19.40	17.01	14.86	1.06
19.36	17.11	1.29	21.25	19.51	17.12	14.97	0.95
19.49	17.24	1.15	21.35	19.61	17.22	15.07	0.85
19.62	17.36	1.03	21.44	19.70	17.31	15.16	0.75
19.73	17.48	0.92	21.53	19.79	17.40	15.25	0.67
19.84	17.59	0.81	21.61	19.87	17.48	15.33	0.59
19.94	17.68	0.71	21.68	19.94	17.55	15.40	0.51
20.03	17.77	0.62	21.75	20.01	17.62	15.47	0.45

Males aged 14

Retirement age	2.5% pa Life multiplier—30.76						
	E.M. 16	*E.M. 18*	*E.M. 21*	*E.M. 24*	*P.M.*	*E.M. 16*	*E.M. 18*
50	21.57	19.71	17.10	14.68	7.24	19.92	18.09
51	21.95	20.10	17.49	15.07	6.86	20.25	18.42
52	22.33	20.47	17.86	15.44	6.49	20.56	18.73
53	22.69	20.84	18.22	15.81	6.12	20.86	19.03
54	23.04	21.19	18.58	16.16	5.77	21.15	19.32
55	23.38	21.53	18.92	16.50	5.43	21.43	19.60
56	23.71	21.86	19.25	16.83	5.10	21.70	19.87
57	24.03	22.18	19.57	17.15	4.78	21.96	20.13
58	24.34	22.48	19.87	17.46	4.47	22.21	20.38
59	24.64	22.78	20.17	17.75	4.18	22.45	20.62
60	24.92	23.07	20.46	18.04	3.89	22.68	20.85
61	25.20	23.35	20.73	18.32	3.61	22.90	21.07
62	25.47	23.61	21.00	18.58	3.35	23.11	21.28
63	25.72	23.87	21.26	18.84	3.09	23.31	21.48
64	25.97	24.11	21.50	19.08	2.85	23.50	21.67
65	26.20	24.34	21.73	19.31	2.62	23.68	21.85
66	26.42	24.57	21.95	19.54	2.39	23.86	22.03
67	26.63	24.78	22.17	19.75	2.18	24.02	22.19
68	26.83	24.98	22.37	19.95	1.98	24.17	22.34
69	27.02	25.17	22.56	20.14	1.79	24.32	22.49
70	27.20	25.34	22.73	20.31	1.61	24.45	22.63
71	27.37	25.51	22.90	20.48	1.45	24.58	22.75
72	27.52	25.67	23.06	20.64	1.29	24.70	22.87
73	27.67	25.81	23.20	20.78	1.14	24.81	22.98
74	27.80	25.95	23.34	20.92	1.01	24.91	23.08
75	27.93	26.07	23.46	21.04	0.88	25.00	23.18

3% pa Life multiplier—27.58			**3.5% pa Life multiplier—24.91**				
E.M. 21	*E.M. 24*	*P.M.*	*E.M. 16*	*E.M. 18*	*E.M. 21*	*E.M. 24*	*P.M.*
15.55	13.23	5.72	18.45	16.65	14.17	11.94	4.53
15.87	13.55	5.40	18.72	16.92	14.44	12.21	4.26
16.19	13.87	5.09	18.98	17.18	14.70	12.47	4.00
16.49	14.17	4.79	19.23	17.43	14.95	12.72	3.75
16.78	14.46	4.50	19.47	17.67	15.19	12.96	3.51
17.06	14.74	4.22	19.70	17.90	15.42	13.19	3.28
17.33	15.01	3.95	19.92	18.12	15.64	13.41	3.06
17.59	15.26	3.69	20.13	18.33	15.85	13.62	2.85
17.84	15.51	3.44	20.33	18.53	16.05	13.83	2.65
18.08	15.75	3.20	20.53	18.72	16.25	14.02	2.45
18.31	15.98	2.97	20.71	18.91	16.43	14.20	2.27
18.53	16.20	2.75	20.89	19.08	16.61	14.38	2.09
18.74	16.42	2.54	21.05	19.25	16.78	14.55	1.93
18.94	16.62	2.34	21.21	19.41	16.93	14.71	1.77
19.13	16.81	2.14	21.36	19.56	17.09	14.86	1.62
19.31	16.99	1.96	21.51	19.70	17.23	15.00	1.47
19.48	17.16	1.79	21.64	19.84	17.36	15.14	1.34
19.65	17.33	1.62	21.77	19.97	17.49	15.26	1.21
19.80	17.48	1.47	21.89	20.09	17.61	15.38	1.09
19.95	17.63	1.33	22.00	20.20	17.72	15.49	0.98
20.08	17.76	1.19	22.10	20.30	17.82	15.60	0.88
20.21	17.89	1.06	22.20	20.40	17.92	15.69	0.78
20.33	18.01	0.94	22.29	20.49	18.01	15.78	0.69
20.44	18.12	0.83	22.37	20.57	18.09	15.87	0.61
20.54	18.22	0.73	22.45	20.65	18.17	15.94	0.53
20.63	18.31	0.64	22.52	20.71	18.24	16.01	0.46

Males aged 15

Retirement age	2.5% pa Life multiplier—30.53 E.M. 16	E.M. 18	E.M. 21	E.M. 24	P.M.	E.M. 16	E.M. 18
50	22.11	20.21	17.54	15.06	7.43	20.53	18.64
51	22.51	20.61	17.93	15.45	7.03	20.86	18.98
52	22.89	20.99	18.31	15.83	6.65	21.18	19.30
53	23.26	21.36	18.69	16.21	6.28	21.49	19.61
54	23.62	21.72	19.05	16.57	5.92	21.79	19.90
55	23.97	22.07	19.39	16.92	5.57	22.08	20.19
56	24.31	22.41	19.73	17.25	5.23	22.35	20.47
57	24.64	22.74	20.06	17.58	4.90	22.62	20.74
58	24.96	23.05	20.38	17.90	4.59	22.88	21.00
59	25.26	23.36	20.68	18.20	4.28	23.13	21.24
60	25.56	23.65	20.98	18.50	3.99	23.36	21.48
61	25.84	23.94	21.26	18.78	3.70	23.59	21.71
62	26.11	24.21	21.53	19.05	3.43	23.81	21.92
63	26.37	24.47	21.79	19.31	3.17	24.01	22.13
64	26.62	24.72	22.04	19.56	2.92	24.21	22.33
65	26.86	24.96	22.28	19.80	2.68	24.40	22.52
66	27.09	25.19	22.51	20.03	2.45	24.58	22.69
67	27.31	25.40	22.73	20.25	2.24	24.75	22.86
68	27.51	25.61	22.93	20.45	2.03	24.91	23.02
69	27.70	25.80	23.13	20.65	1.84	25.06	23.17
70	27.89	25.99	23.31	20.83	1.66	25.20	23.31
71	28.06	26.16	23.48	21.00	1.48	25.33	23.44
72	28.22	26.32	23.64	21.16	1.32	25.45	23.56
73	28.37	26.47	23.79	21.31	1.17	25.56	23.68
74	28.51	26.61	23.93	21.45	1.04	25.67	23.78
75	28.64	26.73	24.06	21.58	0.91	25.76	23.88

3% pa Life multiplier—27.41			3.5% pa Life multiplier—24.77				
E.M. 21	*E.M. 24*	*P.M.*	*E.M. 16*	*E.M. 18*	*E.M. 21*	*E.M. 24*	*P.M.*
16.02	13.63	5.89	19.10	17.24	14.67	12.37	4.69
16.36	13.96	5.56	19.38	17.51	14.95	12.65	4.41
16.68	14.29	5.24	19.65	17.78	15.22	12.91	4.14
16.99	14.60	4.93	19.91	18.04	15.48	13.17	3.88
17.29	14.89	4.63	20.16	18.29	15.73	13.42	3.64
17.57	15.18	4.34	20.39	18.53	15.96	13.66	3.40
17.85	15.46	4.07	20.62	18.76	16.19	13.89	3.17
18.12	15.73	3.80	20.84	18.98	16.41	14.11	2.95
18.38	15.98	3.54	21.05	19.18	16.62	14.31	2.74
18.62	16.23	3.29	21.25	19.38	16.82	14.52	2.54
18.86	16.47	3.06	21.44	19.58	17.01	14.71	2.35
19.09	16.70	2.83	21.62	19.76	17.19	14.89	2.17
19.30	16.91	2.61	21.80	19.93	17.37	15.06	1.99
19.51	17.12	2.41	21.96	20.10	17.53	15.23	1.83
19.71	17.32	2.21	22.12	20.25	17.69	15.38	1.67
19.90	17.51	2.02	22.27	20.40	17.84	15.53	1.53
20.08	17.68	1.84	22.41	20.54	17.98	15.67	1.39
20.24	17.85	1.67	22.54	20.67	18.11	15.80	1.25
20.40	18.01	1.51	22.66	20.79	18.23	15.92	1.13
20.55	18.16	1.37	22.78	20.91	18.35	16.04	1.02
20.69	18.30	1.23	22.88	21.02	18.45	16.15	0.91
20.82	18.43	1.09	22.98	21.12	18.55	16.25	0.81
20.94	18.55	0.97	23.08	21.21	18.65	16.34	0.72
21.06	18.67	0.86	23.16	21.30	18.73	16.43	0.63
21.16	18.77	0.76	23.24	21.37	18.81	16.50	0.55
21.26	18.87	0.66	23.31	21.45	18.88	16.58	0.48

Males aged 16

Retirement age	2.5% pa Life multiplier—30.29		3% pa Life multiplier—27.22		3.5% pa Life multiplier—24.63	
	Earnings multiplier	*Pensions multiplier*	*Earnings multiplier*	*Pensions multiplier*	*Earnings multiplier*	*Pensions multiplier*
50	22.68	7.62	21.15	6.07	19.78	4.86
51	23.08	7.21	21.49	5.73	20.07	4.57
52	23.47	6.82	21.82	5.40	20.35	4.29
53	23.86	6.44	22.14	5.08	20.61	4.02
54	24.23	6.07	22.45	4.77	20.87	3.76
55	24.58	5.71	22.75	4.48	21.12	3.52
56	24.93	5.36	23.03	4.19	21.35	3.28
57	25.27	5.03	23.31	3.91	21.58	3.06
58	25.59	4.70	23.57	3.65	21.80	2.84
59	25.90	4.39	23.83	3.39	22.00	2.63
60	26.20	4.09	24.07	3.15	22.20	2.43
61	26.50	3.80	24.31	2.92	22.39	2.24
62	26.77	3.52	24.53	2.69	22.57	2.07
63	27.04	3.25	24.74	2.48	22.74	1.89
64	27.30	2.99	24.95	2.28	22.90	1.73
65	27.54	2.75	25.14	2.08	23.05	1.58
66	27.78	2.52	25.33	1.90	23.20	1.44
67	28.00	2.29	25.50	1.72	23.33	1.30
68	28.21	2.08	25.66	1.56	23.46	1.17
69	28.41	1.88	25.82	1.41	23.58	1.05
70	28.60	1.70	25.96	1.26	23.69	0.94
71	28.77	1.52	26.10	1.13	23.80	0.84
72	28.94	1.36	26.22	1.00	23.89	0.74
73	29.09	1.20	26.34	0.89	23.98	0.65
74	29.23	1.06	26.45	0.78	24.06	0.57
75	29.36	0.93	26.54	0.68	24.14	0.50

Males aged 17

Retirement age	2.5% pa Life multiplier—30.05		3% pa Life multiplier—27.04		3.5% pa Life multiplier—24.49	
	Earnings multiplier	*Pensions multiplier*	*Earnings multiplier*	*Pensions multiplier*	*Earnings multiplier*	*Pensions multiplier*
50	22.24	7.81	20.78	6.26	19.46	5.03
51	22.66	7.40	21.13	5.91	19.76	4.73
52	23.06	6.99	21.48	5.56	20.05	4.44
53	23.45	6.60	21.80	5.24	20.33	4.16
54	23.83	6.22	22.12	4.92	20.59	3.90
55	24.20	5.86	22.43	4.61	20.85	3.64
56	24.55	5.50	22.72	4.32	21.09	3.40
57	24.90	5.16	23.01	4.03	21.33	3.16
58	25.23	4.82	23.28	3.76	21.55	2.94
59	25.55	4.50	23.54	3.50	21.77	2.72
60	25.86	4.19	23.79	3.25	21.97	2.52
61	26.16	3.90	24.03	3.01	22.17	2.32
62	26.45	3.61	24.27	2.77	22.35	2.14
63	26.72	3.33	24.49	2.55	22.53	1.96
64	26.98	3.07	24.70	2.34	22.70	1.79
65	27.23	2.82	24.89	2.15	22.86	1.64
66	27.47	2.58	25.08	1.96	23.01	1.49
67	27.70	2.35	25.26	1.78	23.15	1.35
68	27.92	2.14	25.43	1.61	23.28	1.21
69	28.12	1.93	25.59	1.45	23.40	1.09
70	28.31	1.74	25.74	1.30	23.52	0.97
71	28.49	1.56	25.88	1.16	23.62	0.87
72	28.66	1.39	26.01	1.03	23.72	0.77
73	28.82	1.23	26.13	0.91	23.82	0.68
74	28.97	1.09	26.24	0.80	23.90	0.59
75	29.10	0.95	26.34	0.70	23.98	0.51

Males aged 18

Retirement age	2.5% pa Life multiplier—29.82 *Earnings multiplier*	*Pensions multiplier*	3% pa Life multiplier—26.86 *Earnings multiplier*	*Pensions multiplier*	3.5% pa Life multiplier—24.35 *Earnings multiplier*	*Pensions multiplier*
50	21.80	8.01	20.41	6.45	19.14	5.21
51	22.23	7.59	20.77	6.09	19.45	4.90
52	22.64	7.17	21.12	5.74	19.75	4.60
53	23.04	6.77	21.46	5.40	20.04	4.31
54	23.43	6.38	21.79	5.07	20.31	4.04
55	23.81	6.01	22.10	4.75	20.58	3.77
56	24.17	5.64	22.41	4.45	20.83	3.52
57	24.53	5.29	22.70	4.16	21.07	3.28
58	24.87	4.95	22.98	3.88	21.31	3.04
59	25.20	4.62	23.25	3.61	21.53	2.82
60	25.51	4.30	23.51	3.35	21.74	2.61
61	25.82	4.00	23.76	3.10	21.94	2.41
62	26.11	3.70	24.00	2.86	22.14	2.22
63	26.40	3.42	24.22	2.63	22.32	2.03
64	26.67	3.15	24.44	2.42	22.49	1.86
65	26.92	2.89	24.65	2.21	22.66	1.69
66	27.17	2.65	24.84	2.02	22.81	1.54
67	27.40	2.41	25.03	1.83	22.96	1.39
68	27.62	2.19	25.20	1.66	23.09	1.26
69	27.83	1.98	25.36	1.49	23.22	1.13
70	28.03	1.79	25.52	1.34	23.34	1.01
71	28.22	1.60	25.66	1.20	23.45	0.90
72	28.39	1.43	25.79	1.06	23.56	0.80
73	28.55	1.27	25.92	0.94	23.65	0.70
74	28.70	1.12	26.03	0.83	23.74	0.61
75	28.84	0.98	26.14	0.72	23.82	0.53

Males aged 19

Retirement age	2.5% pa Life multiplier—29.57		3% pa Life multiplier—26.67		3.5% pa Life multiplier—24.21	
	Earnings multiplier	*Pensions multiplier*	*Earnings multiplier*	*Pensions multiplier*	*Earnings multiplier*	*Pensions multiplier*
50	21.35	8.22	20.02	6.65	18.81	5.40
51	21.79	7.78	20.40	6.28	19.13	5.07
52	22.22	7.36	20.76	5.91	19.44	4.77
53	22.63	6.95	21.11	5.56	19.74	4.47
54	23.03	6.55	21.44	5.23	20.02	4.18
55	23.41	6.16	21.77	4.90	20.30	3.91
56	23.79	5.79	22.08	4.59	20.56	3.65
57	24.15	5.43	22.38	4.29	20.81	3.39
58	24.50	5.08	22.68	4.00	21.05	3.15
59	24.84	4.74	22.95	3.72	21.28	2.92
60	25.16	4.41	23.22	3.45	21.50	2.70
61	25.48	4.10	23.48	3.19	21.71	2.49
62	25.78	3.80	23.72	2.95	21.91	2.29
63	26.07	3.51	23.96	2.71	22.10	2.11
64	26.34	3.23	24.18	2.49	22.28	1.93
65	26.61	2.97	24.39	2.28	22.45	1.76
66	26.86	2.72	24.59	2.08	22.61	1.59
67	27.10	2.48	24.78	1.89	22.76	1.44
68	27.33	2.25	24.96	1.71	22.90	1.30
69	27.54	2.03	25.13	1.54	23.04	1.17
70	27.74	1.83	25.29	1.38	23.16	1.05
71	27.93	1.64	25.44	1.23	23.28	0.93
72	28.11	1.46	25.57	1.10	23.38	0.82
73	28.28	1.30	25.70	0.97	23.48	0.73
74	28.43	1.15	25.82	0.85	23.57	0.63
75	28.57	1.00	25.93	0.74	23.65	0.55

Males aged 20

Retirement age	2.5% pa Life multiplier—29.33 Earnings multiplier	2.5% pa Pensions multiplier	3% pa Life multiplier—26.48 Earnings multiplier	3% pa Pensions multiplier	3.5% pa Life multiplier—24.06 Earnings multiplier	3.5% pa Pensions multiplier
50	20.89	8.43	19.62	6.86	18.47	5.59
51	21.34	7.98	20.01	6.47	18.80	5.26
52	21.78	7.55	20.38	6.10	19.12	4.94
53	22.20	7.13	20.74	5.74	19.43	4.63
54	22.61	6.72	21.09	5.39	19.72	4.33
55	23.00	6.32	21.43	5.05	20.01	4.05
56	23.39	5.94	21.75	4.73	20.28	3.78
57	23.76	5.57	22.06	4.42	20.54	3.52
58	24.12	5.21	22.36	4.12	20.79	3.27
59	24.47	4.86	22.65	3.83	21.03	3.03
60	24.80	4.53	22.92	3.56	21.26	2.80
61	25.12	4.21	23.19	3.29	21.47	2.58
62	25.43	3.90	23.44	3.04	21.68	2.38
63	25.73	3.60	23.68	2.80	21.88	2.18
64	26.01	3.32	23.91	2.57	22.06	1.99
65	26.28	3.04	24.13	2.35	22.24	1.82
66	26.54	2.79	24.34	2.14	22.40	1.65
67	26.79	2.54	24.53	1.95	22.56	1.50
68	27.02	2.31	24.72	1.76	22.71	1.35
69	27.24	2.09	24.89	1.59	22.85	1.21
70	27.45	1.88	25.05	1.42	22.97	1.08
71	27.64	1.68	25.21	1.27	23.09	0.96
72	27.82	1.50	25.35	1.13	23.20	0.85
73	27.99	1.33	25.48	1.00	23.31	0.75
74	28.15	1.18	25.60	0.88	23.40	0.66
75	28.30	1.03	25.71	0.77	23.48	0.57

Males aged 21

Retirement age	2.5% pa Life multiplier—29.07		3% pa Life multiplier—26.28		3.5% pa Life multiplier—23.90	
	Earnings multiplier	*Pensions multiplier*	*Earnings multiplier*	*Pensions multiplier*	*Earnings multiplier*	*Pensions multiplier*
50	20.42	8.65	19.21	7.07	18.11	5.79
51	20.88	8.19	19.61	6.67	18.46	5.45
52	21.33	7.74	20.00	6.28	18.79	5.11
53	21.76	7.31	20.37	5.91	19.11	4.79
54	22.18	6.89	20.73	5.55	19.41	4.49
55	22.59	6.49	21.07	5.21	19.71	4.19
56	22.98	6.09	21.41	4.88	19.99	3.91
57	23.36	5.71	21.73	4.55	20.26	3.64
58	23.73	5.34	22.03	4.25	20.52	3.38
59	24.09	4.99	22.33	3.95	20.76	3.14
60	24.43	4.64	22.61	3.67	21.00	2.90
61	24.76	4.31	22.89	3.39	21.23	2.68
62	25.08	4.00	23.15	3.13	21.44	2.46
63	25.38	3.69	23.40	2.88	21.64	2.26
64	25.67	3.40	23.63	2.65	21.84	2.07
65	25.95	3.12	23.86	2.42	22.02	1.88
66	26.21	2.86	24.07	2.21	22.19	1.71
67	26.47	2.61	24.27	2.01	22.35	1.55
68	26.71	2.37	24.46	1.82	22.50	1.40
69	26.93	2.14	24.64	1.64	22.65	1.25
70	27.14	1.93	24.81	1.47	22.78	1.12
71	27.34	1.73	24.97	1.31	22.90	1.00
72	27.53	1.54	25.11	1.17	23.02	0.88
73	27.71	1.37	25.25	1.03	23.12	0.78
74	27.87	1.21	25.38	0.91	23.22	0.68
75	28.02	1.06	25.49	0.79	23.31	0.59

Males aged 22

Retirement age	2.5% pa Life multiplier—28.81		3% pa Life multiplier—26.08		3.5% pa Life multiplier—23.74	
	Earnings multiplier	*Pensions multiplier*	*Earnings multiplier*	*Pensions multiplier*	*Earnings multiplier*	*Pensions multiplier*
50	19.94	8.87	18.79	7.29	17.74	6.00
51	20.41	8.40	19.20	6.87	18.10	5.64
52	20.87	7.95	19.60	6.48	18.45	5.30
53	21.31	7.50	19.98	6.10	18.78	4.97
54	21.74	7.07	20.35	5.73	19.09	4.65
55	22.16	6.65	20.71	5.37	19.40	4.34
56	22.56	6.25	21.05	5.03	19.69	4.05
57	22.95	5.86	21.38	4.70	19.97	3.77
58	23.33	5.48	21.70	4.38	20.24	3.51
59	23.70	5.12	22.00	4.07	20.49	3.25
60	24.05	4.76	22.30	3.78	20.74	3.01
61	24.39	4.43	22.58	3.50	20.97	2.77
62	24.71	4.10	22.85	3.23	21.19	2.55
63	25.02	3.79	23.10	2.97	21.40	2.34
64	25.32	3.49	23.35	2.73	21.60	2.14
65	25.61	3.20	23.58	2.50	21.79	1.95
66	25.88	2.93	23.80	2.28	21.97	1.77
67	26.14	2.67	24.01	2.07	22.14	1.60
68	26.38	2.43	24.20	1.87	22.29	1.45
69	26.62	2.20	24.39	1.69	22.44	1.30
70	26.83	1.98	24.56	1.51	22.58	1.16
71	27.04	1.77	24.72	1.35	22.71	1.03
72	27.23	1.58	24.88	1.20	22.83	0.92
73	27.41	1.40	25.01	1.06	22.94	0.81
74	27.58	1.24	25.14	0.93	23.04	0.71
75	27.73	1.08	25.26	0.82	23.13	0.61

Males aged 23

Retirement age	**2.5% pa Life multiplier—28.55** *Earnings multiplier*	*Pensions multiplier*	**3% pa Life multiplier—25.87** *Earnings multiplier*	*Pensions multiplier*	**3.5% pa Life multiplier—23.58** *Earnings multiplier*	*Pensions multiplier*
50	19.44	9.10	18.36	7.51	17.36	6.21
51	19.92	8.62	18.78	7.09	17.73	5.84
52	20.39	8.15	19.19	6.68	18.09	5.49
53	20.85	7.70	19.58	6.28	18.43	5.14
54	21.29	7.25	19.97	5.90	18.76	4.82
55	21.72	6.83	20.33	5.54	19.08	4.50
56	22.13	6.41	20.69	5.18	19.38	4.20
57	22.54	6.01	21.03	4.84	19.67	3.91
58	22.92	5.62	21.35	4.51	19.95	3.63
59	23.30	5.25	21.67	4.20	20.21	3.37
60	23.66	4.89	21.97	3.90	20.46	3.11
61	24.01	4.54	22.26	3.61	20.70	2.87
62	24.34	4.21	22.54	3.33	20.93	2.64
63	24.66	3.89	22.80	3.07	21.15	2.42
64	24.97	3.58	23.05	2.81	21.36	2.22
65	25.26	3.29	23.29	2.57	21.56	2.02
66	25.54	3.01	23.52	2.35	21.74	1.84
67	25.80	2.74	23.74	2.13	21.91	1.66
68	26.06	2.49	23.94	1.93	22.08	1.50
69	26.29	2.25	24.13	1.74	22.23	1.35
70	26.52	2.03	24.31	1.56	22.37	1.20
71	26.73	1.82	24.47	1.39	22.51	1.07
72	26.92	1.62	24.63	1.24	22.63	0.95
73	27.11	1.44	24.77	1.10	22.74	0.84
74	27.28	1.27	24.91	0.96	22.85	0.73
75	27.43	1.11	25.03	0.84	22.94	0.64

Males aged 24

Retirement age	2.5% pa Life multiplier—28.27 Earnings multiplier	2.5% pa Pensions multiplier	3% pa Life multiplier—25.65 Earnings multiplier	3% pa Pensions multiplier	3.5% pa Life multiplier—23.41 Earnings multiplier	3.5% pa Pensions multiplier
50	18.93	9.34	17.91	7.74	16.97	6.44
51	19.43	8.84	18.35	7.31	17.35	6.05
52	19.91	8.36	18.77	6.88	17.72	5.68
53	20.38	7.89	19.17	6.48	18.08	5.33
54	20.83	7.44	19.57	6.09	18.42	4.99
55	21.27	7.00	19.95	5.71	18.74	4.66
56	21.70	6.58	20.31	5.34	19.06	4.35
57	22.11	6.17	20.66	4.99	19.36	4.05
58	22.50	5.77	21.00	4.65	19.64	3.76
59	22.89	5.38	21.32	4.33	19.92	3.49
60	23.26	5.01	21.64	4.02	20.18	3.23
61	23.61	4.66	21.93	3.72	20.43	2.98
62	23.96	4.32	22.22	3.43	20.67	2.74
63	24.29	3.99	22.49	3.16	20.89	2.51
64	24.60	3.67	22.75	2.90	21.11	2.30
65	24.90	3.37	23.00	2.65	21.31	2.09
66	25.19	3.09	23.23	2.42	21.50	1.90
67	25.46	2.81	23.45	2.20	21.68	1.72
68	25.72	2.55	23.66	1.99	21.85	1.55
69	25.96	2.31	23.86	1.79	22.01	1.39
70	26.19	2.08	24.04	1.61	22.16	1.25
71	26.41	1.87	24.21	1.44	22.30	1.11
72	26.61	1.66	24.37	1.28	22.42	0.98
73	26.80	1.48	24.52	1.13	22.54	0.87
74	26.97	1.30	24.66	0.99	22.65	0.76
75	27.13	1.14	24.79	0.87	22.75	0.66

Males aged 25

	2.5% pa Life multiplier—27.99		**3% pa Life multiplier—25.43**		**3.5% pa Life multiplier—23.23**	
Retirement age	*Earnings multiplier*	*Pensions multiplier*	*Earnings multiplier*	*Pensions multiplier*	*Earnings multiplier*	*Pensions multiplier*
50	18.41	9.58	17.45	7.98	16.56	6.67
51	18.92	9.07	17.90	7.53	16.96	6.27
52	19.41	8.58	18.33	7.10	17.34	5.89
53	19.89	8.10	18.75	6.68	17.71	5.52
54	20.36	7.63	19.16	6.27	18.06	5.17
55	20.81	7.18	19.55	5.88	18.40	4.83
56	21.24	6.75	19.92	5.51	18.72	4.51
57	21.67	6.33	20.29	5.14	19.03	4.19
58	22.07	5.92	20.63	4.80	19.33	3.90
59	22.47	5.52	20.97	4.46	19.62	3.61
60	22.85	5.14	21.29	4.14	19.89	3.34
61	23.21	4.78	21.60	3.83	20.15	3.08
62	23.56	4.43	21.89	3.54	20.39	2.84
63	23.90	4.09	22.17	3.26	20.63	2.60
64	24.22	3.77	22.44	2.99	20.85	2.38
65	24.53	3.46	22.69	2.74	21.06	2.17
66	24.83	3.16	22.93	2.49	21.26	1.97
67	25.11	2.89	23.16	2.27	21.44	1.78
68	25.37	2.62	23.38	2.05	21.62	1.61
69	25.62	2.37	23.58	1.85	21.78	1.44
70	25.86	2.14	23.77	1.66	21.94	1.29
71	26.08	1.91	23.95	1.48	22.08	1.15
72	26.28	1.71	24.11	1.32	22.21	1.02
73	26.48	1.51	24.27	1.16	22.33	0.90
74	26.66	1.34	24.41	1.02	22.44	0.78
75	26.82	1.17	24.54	0.89	22.55	0.68

Males aged 26

Retirement age	2.5% pa Life multiplier—27.70 Earnings multiplier	Pensions multiplier	3% pa Life multiplier—25.20 Earnings multiplier	Pensions multiplier	3.5% pa Life multiplier—23.04 Earnings multiplier	Pensions multiplier
50	17.87	9.83	16.97	8.23	16.14	6.91
51	18.40	9.31	17.44	7.76	16.55	6.50
52	18.90	8.80	17.88	7.32	16.94	6.10
53	19.39	8.31	18.32	6.88	17.33	5.72
54	19.87	7.83	18.73	6.47	17.69	5.35
55	20.33	7.37	19.14	6.06	18.04	5.00
56	20.78	6.92	19.52	5.68	18.38	4.67
57	21.21	6.49	19.90	5.30	18.70	4.35
58	21.63	6.07	20.26	4.94	19.01	4.04
59	22.04	5.67	20.60	4.60	19.30	3.74
60	22.43	5.28	20.93	4.27	19.58	3.46
61	22.80	4.90	21.25	3.95	19.85	3.19
62	23.16	4.54	21.55	3.65	20.11	2.94
63	23.51	4.20	21.84	3.36	20.35	2.69
64	23.84	3.86	22.12	3.08	20.58	2.46
65	24.15	3.55	22.38	2.82	20.80	2.25
66	24.46	3.25	22.63	2.57	21.00	2.04
67	24.74	2.96	22.86	2.34	21.20	1.85
68	25.01	2.69	23.09	2.11	21.38	1.67
69	25.27	2.43	23.29	1.91	21.55	1.50
70	25.51	2.19	23.49	1.71	21.71	1.34
71	25.74	1.96	23.67	1.53	21.85	1.19
72	25.95	1.75	23.84	1.36	21.99	1.05
73	26.15	1.55	24.00	1.20	22.12	0.93
74	26.33	1.37	24.15	1.05	22.23	0.81
75	26.50	1.20	24.28	0.92	22.34	0.71

Males aged 27

Retirement age	2.5% pa Life multiplier—27.41		3% pa Life multiplier—24.96		3.5% pa Life multiplier—22.85	
	Earnings multiplier	*Pensions multiplier*	*Earnings multiplier*	*Pensions multiplier*	*Earnings multiplier*	*Pensions multiplier*
50	17.32	10.08	16.48	8.48	15.70	7.15
51	17.86	9.55	16.96	8.00	16.12	6.73
52	18.38	9.03	17.42	7.54	16.53	6.32
53	18.88	8.52	17.87	7.10	16.93	5.92
54	19.37	8.03	18.30	6.67	17.31	5.55
55	19.85	7.56	18.71	6.25	17.67	5.18
56	20.31	7.10	19.11	5.85	18.02	4.83
57	20.75	6.66	19.50	5.47	18.35	4.50
58	21.18	6.23	19.87	5.10	18.67	4.18
59	21.59	5.81	20.22	4.74	18.98	3.88
60	21.99	5.41	20.56	4.40	19.27	3.59
61	22.38	5.03	20.89	4.07	19.55	3.31
62	22.75	4.66	21.20	3.76	19.81	3.04
63	23.10	4.30	21.50	3.46	20.06	2.79
64	23.44	3.96	21.78	3.18	20.30	2.55
65	23.77	3.64	22.05	2.91	20.53	2.33
66	24.08	3.33	22.31	2.65	20.74	2.11
67	24.37	3.04	22.55	2.41	20.94	1.91
68	24.65	2.76	22.78	2.18	21.13	1.73
69	24.91	2.50	23.00	1.96	21.30	1.55
70	25.16	2.25	23.20	1.76	21.47	1.39
71	25.39	2.01	23.39	1.57	21.62	1.23
72	25.61	1.80	23.56	1.40	21.76	1.09
73	25.81	1.59	23.73	1.24	21.89	0.96
74	26.00	1.41	23.88	1.09	22.01	0.84
75	26.18	1.23	24.01	0.95	22.12	0.73

Males aged 28

Retirement age	2.5% pa Life multiplier—27.10 *Earnings multiplier*	 *Pensions multiplier*	3% pa Life multiplier—24.72 *Earnings multiplier*	 *Pensions multiplier*	3.5% pa Life multiplier—22.66 *Earnings multiplier*	 *Pensions multiplier*
50	16.76	10.35	15.97	8.74	15.24	7.41
51	17.31	9.80	16.47	8.25	15.69	6.97
52	17.84	9.26	16.94	7.78	16.11	6.55
53	18.36	8.74	17.40	7.32	16.52	6.14
54	18.86	8.24	17.85	6.87	16.91	5.74
55	19.35	7.76	18.27	6.44	17.29	5.37
56	19.82	7.28	18.68	6.03	17.65	5.01
57	20.27	6.83	19.08	5.64	17.99	4.66
58	20.71	6.39	19.46	5.25	18.32	4.33
59	21.14	5.96	19.83	4.89	18.64	4.02
60	21.55	5.55	20.18	4.54	18.94	3.71
61	21.94	5.16	20.52	4.20	19.23	3.43
62	22.32	4.78	20.84	3.88	19.50	3.15
63	22.69	4.42	21.15	3.57	19.76	2.89
64	23.04	4.07	21.44	3.28	20.01	2.64
65	23.37	3.73	21.72	3.00	20.24	2.41
66	23.69	3.42	21.98	2.73	20.46	2.19
67	23.99	3.12	22.23	2.48	20.67	1.98
68	24.27	2.83	22.47	2.25	20.87	1.79
69	24.54	2.56	22.69	2.03	21.05	1.61
70	24.80	2.31	22.90	1.82	21.22	1.44
71	25.04	2.07	23.09	1.62	21.38	1.28
72	25.26	1.84	23.28	1.44	21.52	1.13
73	25.47	1.63	23.44	1.27	21.66	1.00
74	25.66	1.44	23.60	1.12	21.78	0.87
75	25.84	1.26	23.74	0.98	21.90	0.76

Males aged 29

Retirement age	2.5% pa Life multiplier—26.79 Earnings multiplier	2.5% pa Pensions multiplier	3% pa Life multiplier—24.47 Earnings multiplier	3% pa Pensions multiplier	3.5% pa Life multiplier—22.45 Earnings multiplier	3.5% pa Pensions multiplier
50	16.18	10.61	15.45	9.01	14.77	7.68
51	16.74	10.05	15.96	8.51	15.23	7.22
52	17.29	9.50	16.45	8.02	15.67	6.78
53	17.82	8.97	16.92	7.54	16.09	6.36
54	18.34	8.46	17.38	7.08	16.50	5.95
55	18.84	7.96	17.82	6.64	16.89	5.56
56	19.32	7.47	18.25	6.22	17.26	5.19
57	19.79	7.01	18.66	5.81	17.62	4.83
58	20.24	6.55	19.05	5.42	17.96	4.49
59	20.67	6.12	19.43	5.04	18.29	4.16
60	21.09	5.70	19.79	4.68	18.60	3.85
61	21.50	5.29	20.14	4.33	18.90	3.55
62	21.89	4.90	20.47	4.00	19.19	3.26
63	22.26	4.53	20.79	3.68	19.46	3.00
64	22.62	4.17	21.09	3.38	19.71	2.74
65	22.96	3.83	21.38	3.09	19.95	2.50
66	23.29	3.51	21.65	2.82	20.18	2.27
67	23.60	3.20	21.91	2.56	20.40	2.05
68	23.89	2.90	22.15	2.32	20.60	1.85
69	24.17	2.63	22.38	2.09	20.79	1.66
70	24.43	2.36	22.59	1.87	20.96	1.49
71	24.67	2.12	22.79	1.67	21.13	1.32
72	24.90	1.89	22.98	1.49	21.28	1.17
73	25.11	1.68	23.15	1.31	21.42	1.03
74	25.31	1.48	23.31	1.15	21.55	0.90
75	25.50	1.30	23.46	1.01	21.66	0.79

Males aged 30

Retirement age	2.5% pa Life multiplier—26.47 *Earnings multiplier*	*Pensions multiplier*	3% pa Life multiplier—24.21 *Earnings multiplier*	*Pensions multiplier*	3.5% pa Life multiplier—22.24 *Earnings multiplier*	*Pensions multiplier*
50	15.58	10.89	14.91	9.29	14.29	7.95
51	16.16	10.31	15.44	8.77	14.76	7.48
52	16.73	9.75	15.94	8.26	15.22	7.02
53	17.27	9.20	16.43	7.78	15.65	6.59
54	17.80	8.67	16.90	7.30	16.07	6.16
55	18.31	8.16	17.36	6.85	16.48	5.76
56	18.81	7.67	17.80	6.41	16.87	5.37
57	19.29	7.19	18.22	5.99	17.24	5.00
58	19.75	6.72	18.62	5.58	17.59	4.65
59	20.20	6.28	19.01	5.19	17.93	4.31
60	20.63	5.85	19.39	4.82	18.25	3.99
61	21.04	5.43	19.74	4.46	18.56	3.68
62	21.44	5.03	20.09	4.12	18.86	3.38
63	21.83	4.65	20.41	3.79	19.14	3.10
64	22.19	4.28	20.73	3.48	19.40	2.84
65	22.54	3.93	21.02	3.19	19.65	2.59
66	22.88	3.60	21.30	2.90	19.89	2.35
67	23.19	3.28	21.57	2.64	20.11	2.13
68	23.50	2.98	21.82	2.39	20.32	1.92
69	23.78	2.69	22.05	2.15	20.52	1.72
70	24.05	2.43	22.28	1.93	20.70	1.54
71	24.30	2.17	22.48	1.73	20.87	1.37
72	24.53	1.94	22.67	1.53	21.03	1.21
73	24.75	1.72	22.85	1.35	21.17	1.07
74	24.96	1.52	23.02	1.19	21.30	0.94
75	25.14	1.33	23.17	1.04	21.43	0.81

Males aged 31

Retirement age	2.5% pa Life multiplier—26.15		3% pa Life multiplier—23.94		3.5% pa Life multiplier—22.02	
	Earnings multiplier	*Pensions multiplier*	*Earnings multiplier*	*Pensions multiplier*	*Earnings multiplier*	*Pensions multiplier*
50	14.98	11.17	14.36	9.58	13.78	8.24
51	15.57	10.58	14.90	9.04	14.27	7.75
52	16.15	10.00	15.42	8.52	14.74	7.28
53	16.70	9.44	15.92	8.02	15.20	6.82
54	17.25	8.90	16.41	7.53	15.63	6.39
55	17.77	8.37	16.88	7.06	16.05	5.97
56	18.28	7.87	17.33	6.61	16.45	5.57
57	18.77	7.37	17.77	6.18	16.84	5.18
58	19.25	6.90	18.18	5.76	17.21	4.82
59	19.71	6.44	18.58	5.36	17.56	4.46
60	20.15	6.00	18.97	4.97	17.89	4.13
61	20.58	5.57	19.34	4.60	18.21	3.81
62	20.99	5.16	19.69	4.25	18.52	3.50
63	21.38	4.77	20.03	3.91	18.81	3.21
64	21.76	4.39	20.35	3.59	19.08	2.94
65	22.11	4.03	20.66	3.28	19.34	2.68
66	22.46	3.69	20.95	2.99	19.59	2.44
67	22.78	3.36	21.22	2.72	19.82	2.20
68	23.09	3.06	21.48	2.46	20.03	1.99
69	23.38	2.76	21.72	2.22	20.24	1.79
70	23.66	2.49	21.95	1.99	20.42	1.60
71	23.92	2.23	22.16	1.78	20.60	1.42
72	24.16	1.99	22.36	1.58	20.76	1.26
73	24.38	1.77	22.54	1.40	20.91	1.11
74	24.59	1.56	22.71	1.23	21.05	0.97
75	24.78	1.36	22.87	1.07	21.18	0.84

Males aged 32

Retirement age	2.5% pa Life multiplier—25.81 Earnings multiplier	Pensions multiplier	3% pa Life multiplier—23.67 Earnings multiplier	Pensions multiplier	3.5% pa Life multiplier—21.80 Earnings multiplier	Pensions multiplier
50	14.35	11.46	13.79	9.88	13.26	8.54
51	14.96	10.85	14.35	9.32	13.77	8.03
52	15.55	10.26	14.88	8.78	14.26	7.54
53	16.13	9.69	15.40	8.26	14.73	7.07
54	16.68	9.13	15.90	7.76	15.18	6.62
55	17.22	8.59	16.39	7.28	15.61	6.18
56	17.74	8.07	16.85	6.81	16.03	5.77
57	18.25	7.57	17.30	6.37	16.43	5.37
58	18.74	7.08	17.73	5.94	16.81	4.99
59	19.21	6.61	18.15	5.52	17.17	4.62
60	19.66	6.15	18.54	5.12	17.52	4.28
61	20.10	5.72	18.92	4.74	17.85	3.95
62	20.52	5.30	19.29	4.38	18.17	3.63
63	20.92	4.89	19.63	4.03	18.47	3.33
64	21.31	4.51	19.97	3.70	18.75	3.05
65	21.68	4.14	20.28	3.39	19.02	2.78
66	22.03	3.79	20.58	3.09	19.27	2.52
67	22.36	3.45	20.86	2.80	19.51	2.28
68	22.68	3.13	21.13	2.54	19.74	2.06
69	22.98	2.84	21.38	2.29	19.95	1.85
70	23.26	2.55	21.61	2.05	20.14	1.65
71	23.52	2.29	21.83	1.83	20.32	1.47
72	23.77	2.04	22.04	1.63	20.49	1.30
73	24.00	1.81	22.23	1.44	20.65	1.15
74	24.22	1.60	22.40	1.27	20.79	1.00
75	24.41	1.40	22.56	1.11	20.92	0.87

Males aged 33

Retirement age	2.5% pa Life multiplier—25.47 *Earnings multiplier*	*Pensions multiplier*	3% pa Life multiplier—23.38 *Earnings multiplier*	*Pensions multiplier*	3.5% pa Life multiplier—21.56 *Earnings multiplier*	*Pensions multiplier*
50	13.71	11.76	13.20	10.18	12.72	8.84
51	14.34	11.13	13.78	9.61	13.25	8.32
52	14.94	10.53	14.33	9.06	13.75	7.81
53	15.53	9.94	14.86	8.52	14.24	7.32
54	16.10	9.37	15.38	8.00	14.71	6.85
55	16.66	8.82	15.88	7.51	15.16	6.41
56	17.19	8.28	16.36	7.03	15.59	5.98
57	17.71	7.76	16.82	6.56	16.00	5.56
58	18.21	7.26	17.27	6.12	16.39	5.17
59	18.69	6.78	17.69	5.69	16.77	4.79
60	19.16	6.31	18.10	5.28	17.13	4.43
61	19.61	5.86	18.49	4.89	17.47	4.09
62	20.04	5.43	18.87	4.52	17.80	3.76
63	20.45	5.02	19.23	4.16	18.11	3.45
64	20.85	4.62	19.57	3.82	18.41	3.16
65	21.23	4.24	19.89	3.49	18.69	2.88
66	21.59	3.88	20.20	3.18	18.95	2.61
67	21.93	3.54	20.49	2.89	19.20	2.37
68	22.25	3.22	20.77	2.62	19.43	2.13
69	22.56	2.91	21.03	2.36	19.65	1.92
70	22.85	2.62	21.27	2.12	19.85	1.71
71	23.12	2.35	21.49	1.89	20.04	1.52
72	23.38	2.09	21.70	1.68	20.21	1.35
73	23.61	1.86	21.90	1.48	20.37	1.19
74	23.83	1.64	22.08	1.30	20.52	1.04
75	24.03	1.44	22.25	1.14	20.66	0.91

Males aged 34

Retirement age	2.5% pa Life multiplier—25.12 *Earnings multiplier*	*Pensions multiplier*	3% pa Life multiplier—23.09 *Earnings multiplier*	*Pensions multiplier*	3.5% pa Life multiplier—21.32 *Earnings multiplier*	*Pensions multiplier*
50	13.06	12.06	12.60	10.50	12.16	9.16
51	13.70	11.42	13.19	9.91	12.71	8.62
52	14.32	10.80	13.76	9.34	13.23	8.09
53	14.92	10.20	14.31	8.78	13.74	7.59
54	15.51	9.61	14.84	8.25	14.22	7.10
55	16.08	9.04	15.36	7.74	14.68	6.64
56	16.63	8.50	15.85	7.24	15.13	6.19
57	17.16	7.96	16.33	6.77	15.56	5.76
58	17.67	7.45	16.79	6.31	15.97	5.35
59	18.17	6.95	17.23	5.87	16.36	4.96
60	18.64	6.48	17.65	5.45	16.73	4.59
61	19.10	6.02	18.05	5.04	17.09	4.23
62	19.55	5.57	18.44	4.66	17.42	3.90
63	19.97	5.15	18.81	4.29	17.75	3.57
64	20.38	4.74	19.16	3.93	18.05	3.27
65	20.77	4.35	19.50	3.60	18.34	2.98
66	21.14	3.98	19.81	3.28	18.61	2.71
67	21.49	3.63	20.11	2.98	18.87	2.45
68	21.82	3.30	20.40	2.70	19.11	2.21
69	22.14	2.98	20.66	2.43	19.34	1.99
70	22.43	2.69	20.91	2.18	19.55	1.77
71	22.71	2.41	21.15	1.95	19.74	1.58
72	22.97	2.15	21.36	1.73	19.92	1.40
73	23.21	1.91	21.56	1.53	20.09	1.23
74	23.44	1.68	21.75	1.35	20.24	1.08
75	23.65	1.47	21.92	1.17	20.38	0.94

Males aged 35

	2.5% pa Life multiplier—24.76		**3% pa Life multiplier—22.80**		**3.5% pa Life multiplier—21.07**	
Retirement age	*Earnings multiplier*	*Pensions multiplier*	*Earnings multiplier*	*Pensions multiplier*	*Earnings multiplier*	*Pensions multiplier*
50	12.38	12.38	11.97	10.83	11.58	9.49
51	13.04	11.72	12.58	10.22	12.15	8.93
52	13.68	11.08	13.17	9.63	12.69	8.38
53	14.30	10.46	13.74	9.06	13.21	7.86
54	14.90	9.86	14.29	8.51	13.72	7.36
55	15.48	9.28	14.82	7.98	14.20	6.88
56	16.05	8.72	15.33	7.47	14.66	6.41
57	16.59	8.17	15.82	6.98	15.10	5.97
58	17.12	7.64	16.29	6.51	15.52	5.55
59	17.63	7.14	16.75	6.05	15.93	5.14
60	18.12	6.65	17.18	5.62	16.32	4.76
61	18.59	6.17	17.60	5.20	16.69	4.39
62	19.04	5.72	18.00	4.80	17.04	4.04
63	19.48	5.28	18.38	4.42	17.37	3.70
64	19.90	4.87	18.74	4.06	17.69	3.39
65	20.29	4.47	19.09	3.71	17.98	3.09
66	20.67	4.09	19.41	3.38	18.27	2.81
67	21.04	3.73	19.72	3.07	18.53	2.54
68	21.38	3.39	20.02	2.78	18.78	2.29
69	21.70	3.06	20.29	2.51	19.02	2.06
70	22.00	2.76	20.55	2.25	19.23	1.84
71	22.29	2.47	20.79	2.01	19.44	1.64
72	22.56	2.21	21.01	1.79	19.62	1.45
73	22.81	1.96	21.22	1.58	19.80	1.28
74	23.04	1.73	21.41	1.39	19.96	1.12
75	23.25	1.51	21.59	1.21	20.10	0.97

Males aged 36

Retirement age	2.5% pa Life multiplier—24.40		3% pa Life multiplier—22.49		3.5% pa Life multiplier—20.82	
	Earnings multiplier	*Pensions multiplier*	*Earnings multiplier*	*Pensions multiplier*	*Earnings multiplier*	*Pensions multiplier*
50	11.70	12.70	11.33	11.16	10.98	9.84
51	12.37	12.03	11.96	10.53	11.57	9.25
52	13.03	11.37	12.57	9.93	12.13	8.69
53	13.66	10.74	13.15	9.34	12.67	8.14
54	14.28	10.12	13.72	8.77	13.19	7.62
55	14.87	9.52	14.27	8.23	13.69	7.13
56	15.45	8.95	14.79	7.70	14.17	6.65
57	16.01	8.39	15.30	7.20	14.63	6.19
58	16.55	7.85	15.78	6.71	15.07	5.75
59	17.08	7.32	16.25	6.24	15.49	5.33
60	17.58	6.82	16.70	5.79	15.89	4.93
61	18.06	6.34	17.13	5.36	16.27	4.55
62	18.53	5.87	17.54	4.95	16.63	4.18
63	18.98	5.42	17.94	4.56	16.98	3.84
64	19.40	4.99	18.31	4.18	17.31	3.51
65	19.81	4.59	18.67	3.83	17.62	3.20
66	20.20	4.20	19.00	3.49	17.91	2.91
67	20.57	3.83	19.32	3.17	18.19	2.63
68	20.92	3.47	19.62	2.87	18.44	2.37
69	21.26	3.14	19.91	2.59	18.69	2.13
70	21.57	2.83	20.17	2.32	18.91	1.91
71	21.86	2.54	20.42	2.07	19.12	1.70
72	22.14	2.26	20.65	1.84	19.32	1.50
73	22.39	2.01	20.87	1.63	19.50	1.32
74	22.63	1.77	21.06	1.43	19.66	1.16
75	22.85	1.55	21.24	1.25	19.81	1.01

Males aged 37

Retirement age	2.5% pa Life multiplier—24.03		3% pa Life multiplier—22.18		3.5% pa Life multiplier—20.56	
	Earnings multiplier	*Pensions multiplier*	*Earnings multiplier*	*Pensions multiplier*	*Earnings multiplier*	*Pensions multiplier*
50	10.99	13.04	10.67	11.51	10.36	10.19
51	11.68	12.35	11.32	10.86	10.97	9.59
52	12.35	11.67	11.94	10.24	11.55	9.00
53	13.01	11.02	12.55	9.63	12.12	8.44
54	13.64	10.39	13.13	9.05	12.65	7.90
55	14.25	9.77	13.70	8.49	13.17	7.38
56	14.85	9.18	14.24	7.94	13.67	6.89
57	15.42	8.61	14.76	7.42	14.14	6.41
58	15.98	8.05	15.26	6.92	14.60	5.96
59	16.51	7.52	15.75	6.44	15.03	5.52
60	17.03	7.00	16.21	5.97	15.45	5.11
61	17.53	6.50	16.65	5.53	15.84	4.71
62	18.00	6.02	17.08	5.11	16.22	4.33
63	18.46	5.56	17.48	4.70	16.58	3.98
64	18.90	5.13	17.87	4.31	16.92	3.64
65	19.32	4.71	18.24	3.95	17.24	3.32
66	19.72	4.31	18.58	3.60	17.54	3.01
67	20.10	3.93	18.91	3.27	17.83	2.73
68	20.46	3.57	19.22	2.96	18.10	2.46
69	20.80	3.23	19.52	2.67	18.35	2.21
70	21.12	2.91	19.79	2.39	18.58	1.97
71	21.42	2.60	20.04	2.14	18.80	1.76
72	21.71	2.32	20.28	1.90	19.00	1.56
73	21.97	2.06	20.50	1.68	19.19	1.37
74	22.21	1.82	20.71	1.48	19.36	1.20
75	22.43	1.59	20.89	1.29	19.51	1.04

Males aged 38

Retirement age	2.5% pa Life multiplier—23.65		3% pa Life multiplier—21.86		3.5% pa Life multiplier—20.29	
	Earnings multiplier	*Pensions multiplier*	*Earnings multiplier*	*Pensions multiplier*	*Earnings multiplier*	*Pensions multiplier*
50	10.27	13.38	9.99	11.87	9.72	10.56
51	10.98	12.67	10.66	11.21	10.35	9.93
52	11.67	11.98	11.30	10.56	10.96	9.33
53	12.34	11.31	11.93	9.94	11.54	8.75
54	12.99	10.66	12.53	9.33	12.10	8.19
55	13.62	10.03	13.11	8.75	12.63	7.65
56	14.23	9.42	13.67	8.19	13.15	7.14
57	14.82	8.83	14.21	7.65	13.64	6.65
58	15.38	8.26	14.73	7.14	14.11	6.17
59	15.93	7.71	15.23	6.64	14.56	5.72
60	16.47	7.18	15.70	6.16	14.99	5.29
61	16.98	6.67	16.16	5.70	15.40	4.88
62	17.47	6.18	16.60	5.27	15.79	4.49
63	17.94	5.71	17.02	4.85	16.16	4.12
64	18.39	5.26	17.41	4.45	16.52	3.77
65	18.82	4.83	17.79	4.07	16.85	3.44
66	19.23	4.42	18.15	3.71	17.16	3.12
67	19.62	4.03	18.49	3.37	17.46	2.83
68	19.99	3.66	18.81	3.05	17.74	2.55
69	20.34	3.31	19.11	2.75	18.00	2.29
70	20.67	2.98	19.40	2.47	18.24	2.05
71	20.98	2.67	19.66	2.20	18.47	1.82
72	21.27	2.38	19.90	1.96	18.67	1.61
73	21.53	2.11	20.13	1.73	18.87	1.42
74	21.78	1.86	20.34	1.52	19.04	1.24
75	22.01	1.63	20.53	1.33	19.21	1.08

Males aged 39

	2.5% pa Life multiplier—23.26		**3% pa Life multiplier—21.54**		**3.5% pa Life multiplier—20.01**	
Retirement age	*Earnings multiplier*	*Pensions multiplier*	*Earnings multiplier*	*Pensions multiplier*	*Earnings multiplier*	*Pensions multiplier*
50	9.53	13.74	9.29	12.25	9.06	10.95
51	10.26	13.01	9.98	11.56	9.71	10.30
52	10.96	12.30	10.64	10.89	10.34	9.67
53	11.65	11.61	11.29	10.25	10.94	9.07
54	12.32	10.94	11.91	9.63	11.52	8.49
55	12.96	10.30	12.51	9.03	12.08	7.93
56	13.59	9.67	13.09	8.45	12.61	7.40
57	14.20	9.07	13.64	7.90	13.12	6.89
58	14.78	8.48	14.18	7.36	13.61	6.40
59	15.34	7.92	14.69	6.85	14.08	5.93
60	15.89	7.37	15.18	6.36	14.52	5.49
61	16.41	6.85	15.65	5.88	14.95	5.06
62	16.92	6.35	16.11	5.43	15.35	4.66
63	17.40	5.86	16.54	5.00	15.74	4.27
64	17.86	5.40	16.95	4.59	16.10	3.91
65	18.30	4.96	17.34	4.20	16.45	3.56
66	18.73	4.54	17.71	3.83	16.77	3.24
67	19.13	4.14	18.06	3.48	17.08	2.93
68	19.51	3.76	18.39	3.15	17.37	2.64
69	19.86	3.40	18.70	2.84	17.64	2.37
70	20.20	3.06	18.99	2.55	17.89	2.12
71	20.52	2.74	19.26	2.27	18.12	1.89
72	20.82	2.45	19.52	2.02	18.34	1.67
73	21.09	2.17	19.75	1.79	18.54	1.47
74	21.35	1.91	19.97	1.57	18.72	1.29
75	21.59	1.68	20.17	1.37	18.89	1.12

Males aged 40

Retirement age	2.5% pa Life multiplier—22.87 Earnings multiplier	Pensions multiplier	3% pa Life multiplier—21.20 Earnings multiplier	Pensions multiplier	3.5% pa Life multiplier—19.73 Earnings multiplier	Pensions multiplier
50	8.77	14.10	8.57	12.64	8.37	11.35
51	9.52	13.35	9.28	11.93	9.05	10.68
52	10.24	12.63	9.97	11.24	9.70	10.02
53	10.95	11.92	10.63	10.57	10.33	9.40
54	11.63	11.24	11.27	9.93	10.93	8.80
55	12.30	10.57	11.89	9.31	11.50	8.22
56	12.94	9.93	12.48	8.72	12.05	7.67
57	13.56	9.31	13.06	8.15	12.58	7.14
58	14.16	8.71	13.61	7.59	13.09	6.63
59	14.74	8.13	14.14	7.06	13.57	6.15
60	15.30	7.57	14.65	6.56	14.04	5.69
61	15.84	7.03	15.13	6.07	14.48	5.25
62	16.35	6.52	15.60	5.60	14.90	4.83
63	16.85	6.02	16.04	5.16	15.30	4.43
64	17.33	5.54	16.47	4.74	15.67	4.05
65	17.78	5.09	16.87	4.33	16.03	3.69
66	18.21	4.66	17.25	3.95	16.37	3.36
67	18.62	4.25	17.61	3.59	16.69	3.04
68	19.01	3.86	17.96	3.25	16.99	2.74
69	19.38	3.49	18.28	2.93	17.27	2.46
70	19.73	3.14	18.58	2.63	17.53	2.20
71	20.05	2.82	18.86	2.35	17.77	1.96
72	20.36	2.51	19.12	2.08	17.99	1.73
73	20.64	2.23	19.36	1.84	18.20	1.53
74	20.90	1.97	19.58	1.62	18.39	1.34
75	21.15	1.72	19.79	1.41	18.56	1.16

Males aged 41

	2.5% pa Life multiplier—22.47		**3% pa Life multiplier—20.86**		**3.5% pa Life multiplier—19.43**	
Retirement age	*Earnings multiplier*	*Pensions multiplier*	*Earnings multiplier*	*Pensions multiplier*	*Earnings multiplier*	*Pensions multiplier*
50	7.99	14.48	7.82	13.04	7.66	11.77
51	8.76	13.71	8.56	12.30	8.36	11.07
52	9.50	12.96	9.27	11.59	9.04	10.39
53	10.23	12.24	9.95	10.91	9.69	9.75
54	10.93	11.54	10.61	10.25	10.31	9.12
55	11.61	10.86	11.25	9.61	10.91	8.53
56	12.27	10.20	11.87	9.00	11.48	7.95
57	12.91	9.56	12.46	8.40	12.03	7.40
58	13.53	8.94	13.03	7.84	12.55	6.88
59	14.12	8.35	13.57	7.29	13.06	6.38
60	14.70	7.77	14.10	6.76	13.53	5.90
61	15.25	7.22	14.60	6.26	13.99	5.44
62	15.78	6.69	15.08	5.78	14.43	5.01
63	16.29	6.18	15.54	5.32	14.84	4.59
64	16.78	5.69	15.98	4.89	15.23	4.20
65	17.24	5.23	16.39	4.47	15.60	3.83
66	17.69	4.78	16.79	4.08	15.95	3.48
67	18.11	4.36	17.16	3.70	16.28	3.15
68	18.51	3.96	17.51	3.35	16.59	2.84
69	18.89	3.58	17.84	3.02	16.88	2.55
70	19.24	3.23	18.15	2.71	17.15	2.28
71	19.58	2.89	18.44	2.42	17.40	2.03
72	19.89	2.58	18.71	2.15	17.64	1.80
73	20.18	2.29	18.96	1.90	17.85	1.58
74	20.45	2.02	19.19	1.67	18.05	1.38
75	20.70	1.77	19.40	1.46	18.23	1.20

Males aged 42

Retirement age	2.5% pa Life multiplier—22.06 Earnings multiplier	2.5% pa Pensions multiplier	3% pa Life multiplier—20.51 Earnings multiplier	3% pa Pensions multiplier	3.5% pa Life multiplier—19.13 Earnings multiplier	3.5% pa Pensions multiplier
50	7.19	14.87	7.06	13.46	6.93	12.20
51	7.98	14.08	7.81	12.70	7.65	11.48
52	8.75	13.31	8.55	11.96	8.35	10.78
53	9.49	12.57	9.25	11.26	9.03	10.11
54	10.21	11.85	9.94	10.57	9.67	9.46
55	10.91	11.15	10.59	9.92	10.29	8.84
56	11.59	10.47	11.23	9.28	10.89	8.25
57	12.24	9.82	11.84	8.67	11.45	7.68
58	12.88	9.18	12.43	8.09	12.00	7.13
59	13.49	8.57	12.99	7.52	12.52	6.61
60	14.08	7.98	13.53	6.98	13.02	6.12
61	14.64	7.42	14.05	6.46	13.49	5.64
62	15.19	6.87	14.55	5.97	13.94	5.19
63	15.71	6.35	15.02	5.49	14.37	4.76
64	16.21	5.85	15.47	5.04	14.78	4.35
65	16.69	5.37	15.90	4.61	15.16	3.97
66	17.15	4.91	16.31	4.21	15.52	3.61
67	17.58	4.48	16.69	3.82	15.87	3.27
68	17.99	4.07	17.05	3.46	16.19	2.94
69	18.38	3.68	17.39	3.12	16.49	2.64
70	18.75	3.31	17.71	2.80	16.77	2.36
71	19.09	2.97	18.01	2.50	17.03	2.10
72	19.41	2.65	18.29	2.22	17.27	1.86
73	19.71	2.35	18.55	1.96	17.49	1.64
74	19.99	2.07	18.79	1.72	17.70	1.44
75	20.24	1.82	19.01	1.51	17.88	1.25

Males aged 43

Retirement age	2.5% pa Life multiplier—21.64 Earnings multiplier	2.5% pa Pensions multiplier	3% pa Life multiplier—20.15 Earnings multiplier	3% pa Pensions multiplier	3.5% pa Life multiplier—18.82 Earnings multiplier	3.5% pa Pensions multiplier
50	6.37	15.27	6.27	13.89	6.17	12.66
51	7.18	14.46	7.05	13.10	6.92	11.90
52	7.97	13.67	7.80	12.35	7.65	11.18
53	8.73	12.91	8.53	11.62	8.34	10.48
54	9.48	12.17	9.24	10.91	9.01	9.81
55	10.19	11.45	9.92	10.24	9.65	9.17
56	10.89	10.75	10.57	9.58	10.27	8.55
57	11.56	10.08	11.20	8.95	10.86	7.96
58	12.21	9.43	11.81	8.34	11.43	7.40
59	12.84	8.80	12.39	7.76	11.97	6.86
60	13.44	8.20	12.95	7.20	12.48	6.34
61	14.03	7.62	13.48	6.67	12.97	5.85
62	14.59	7.06	14.00	6.16	13.44	5.38
63	15.12	6.52	14.48	5.67	13.88	4.94
64	15.64	6.00	14.95	5.20	14.31	4.52
65	16.13	5.51	15.39	4.76	14.71	4.12
66	16.60	5.04	15.81	4.34	15.08	3.74
67	17.04	4.60	16.21	3.94	15.44	3.39
68	17.47	4.18	16.58	3.57	15.77	3.05
69	17.86	3.78	16.94	3.22	16.08	2.74
70	18.24	3.40	17.27	2.89	16.37	2.45
71	18.59	3.05	17.58	2.58	16.64	2.18
72	18.92	2.72	17.86	2.29	16.89	1.93
73	19.23	2.41	18.13	2.02	17.12	1.70
74	19.52	2.13	18.37	1.78	17.33	1.49
75	19.78	1.87	18.60	1.55	17.53	1.30

Males aged 44

Retirement age	2.5% pa Life multiplier—21.22 *Earnings multiplier*	*Pensions multiplier*	3% pa Life multiplier—19.79 *Earnings multiplier*	*Pensions multiplier*	3.5% pa Life multiplier—18.51 *Earnings multiplier*	*Pensions multiplier*
50	5.53	15.69	5.45	14.33	5.38	13.13
51	6.36	14.86	6.26	13.53	6.16	12.35
52	7.17	14.05	7.04	12.75	6.91	11.59
53	7.96	13.26	7.79	11.99	7.63	10.87
54	8.72	12.50	8.52	11.27	8.33	10.18
55	9.46	11.76	9.22	10.57	9.00	9.51
56	10.17	11.05	9.90	9.89	9.63	8.87
57	10.86	10.36	10.55	9.24	10.25	8.26
58	11.53	9.69	11.17	8.61	10.83	7.67
59	12.18	9.04	11.77	8.01	11.39	7.11
60	12.80	8.42	12.35	7.44	11.93	6.58
61	13.40	7.82	12.90	6.88	12.44	6.07
62	13.97	7.25	13.43	6.36	12.92	5.58
63	14.52	6.70	13.94	5.85	13.38	5.12
64	15.05	6.17	14.42	5.37	13.82	4.68
65	15.56	5.66	14.87	4.91	14.24	4.27
66	16.04	5.18	15.31	4.48	14.63	3.88
67	16.50	4.72	15.72	4.07	14.99	3.51
68	16.93	4.29	16.10	3.68	15.34	3.17
69	17.34	3.88	16.47	3.32	15.66	2.84
70	17.72	3.50	16.81	2.98	15.96	2.54
71	18.09	3.13	17.13	2.66	16.24	2.26
72	18.43	2.79	17.42	2.36	16.50	2.00
73	18.74	2.48	17.70	2.09	16.74	1.76
74	19.03	2.19	17.95	1.84	16.96	1.54
75	19.30	1.92	18.18	1.60	17.16	1.34

Males aged 45

Retirement age	2.5% pa Life multiplier—20.79		3% pa Life multiplier—19.41		3.5% pa Life multiplier—18.18	
	Earnings multiplier	*Pensions multiplier*	*Earnings multiplier*	*Pensions multiplier*	*Earnings multiplier*	*Pensions multiplier*
50	4.67	16.12	4.61	14.80	4.56	13.62
51	5.53	15.26	5.45	13.97	5.37	12.81
52	6.36	14.43	6.25	13.16	6.15	12.03
53	7.16	13.63	7.03	12.38	6.90	11.28
54	7.95	12.84	7.78	11.63	7.62	10.56
55	8.70	12.09	8.51	10.91	8.31	9.87
56	9.44	11.35	9.20	10.21	8.98	9.20
57	10.15	10.64	9.87	9.54	9.61	8.57
58	10.83	9.95	10.52	8.89	10.22	7.96
59	11.50	9.29	11.14	8.27	10.80	7.38
60	12.14	8.65	11.74	7.68	11.36	6.83
61	12.75	8.04	12.31	7.11	11.88	6.30
62	13.34	7.45	12.85	6.56	12.39	5.79
63	13.91	6.88	13.37	6.04	12.87	5.31
64	14.45	6.34	13.87	5.55	13.32	4.86
65	14.97	5.82	14.34	5.07	13.75	4.43
66	15.46	5.32	14.79	4.63	14.16	4.03
67	15.93	4.85	15.21	4.20	14.54	3.64
68	16.38	4.41	15.61	3.80	14.89	3.29
69	16.80	3.99	15.99	3.43	15.23	2.95
70	17.20	3.59	16.34	3.08	15.54	2.64
71	17.57	3.22	16.67	2.75	15.83	2.35
72	17.92	2.87	16.97	2.44	16.10	2.08
73	18.24	2.55	17.26	2.16	16.35	1.83
74	18.54	2.25	17.52	1.90	16.58	1.60
75	18.82	1.97	17.76	1.66	16.79	1.39

Males aged 46

Retirement age	2.5% pa Life multiplier—20.35 Earnings multiplier	Pensions multiplier	3% pa Life multiplier—19.03 Earnings multiplier	Pensions multiplier	3.5% pa Life multiplier—17.85 Earnings multiplier	Pensions multiplier
50	3.78	16.57	3.75	15.29	3.71	14.14
51	4.66	15.69	4.61	14.42	4.56	13.29
52	5.52	14.83	5.44	13.59	5.37	12.48
53	6.35	14.00	6.25	12.79	6.14	11.70
54	7.15	13.20	7.02	12.01	6.89	10.96
55	7.93	12.42	7.77	11.27	7.61	10.24
56	8.69	11.67	8.49	10.55	8.30	9.55
57	9.42	10.94	9.18	9.85	8.96	8.89
58	10.12	10.23	9.85	9.19	9.59	8.26
59	10.80	9.55	10.49	8.54	10.19	7.66
60	11.46	8.89	11.10	7.93	10.77	7.08
61	12.09	8.26	11.69	7.34	11.31	6.53
62	12.70	7.65	12.26	6.78	11.84	6.01
63	13.28	7.07	12.79	6.24	12.33	5.51
64	13.84	6.51	13.31	5.73	12.81	5.04
65	14.37	5.98	13.79	5.24	13.25	4.60
66	14.88	5.47	14.26	4.78	13.67	4.18
67	15.36	4.99	14.69	4.34	14.07	3.78
68	15.82	4.53	15.11	3.93	14.44	3.41
69	16.25	4.10	15.49	3.54	14.79	3.06
70	16.66	3.69	15.86	3.18	15.11	2.74
71	17.04	3.31	16.20	2.84	15.41	2.44
72	17.40	2.95	16.51	2.52	15.69	2.16
73	17.73	2.62	16.80	2.23	15.95	1.90
74	18.04	2.31	17.08	1.96	16.19	1.66
75	18.33	2.02	17.32	1.71	16.40	1.45

Males aged 47

Retirement age	2.5% pa Life multiplier—19.91 Earnings multiplier	2.5% pa Pensions multiplier	3% pa Life multiplier—18.65 Earnings multiplier	3% pa Pensions multiplier	3.5% pa Life multiplier—17.51 Earnings multiplier	3.5% pa Pensions multiplier
50	2.88	17.03	2.86	15.79	2.84	14.67
51	3.78	16.13	3.75	14.90	3.71	13.80
52	4.66	15.25	4.61	14.04	4.55	12.96
53	5.51	14.40	5.44	13.21	5.36	12.15
54	6.34	13.57	6.24	12.41	6.14	11.37
55	7.14	12.77	7.01	11.64	6.88	10.63
56	7.92	11.99	7.75	10.89	7.59	9.92
57	8.67	11.24	8.47	10.18	8.28	9.23
58	9.39	10.52	9.16	9.49	8.93	8.58
59	10.09	9.82	9.82	8.83	9.56	7.95
60	10.77	9.14	10.45	8.19	10.16	7.35
61	11.42	8.49	11.06	7.58	10.73	6.78
62	12.04	7.87	11.64	7.00	11.27	6.24
63	12.64	7.27	12.20	6.45	11.78	5.72
64	13.21	6.70	12.73	5.92	12.27	5.24
65	13.76	6.15	13.23	5.41	12.74	4.77
66	14.28	5.63	13.71	4.94	13.17	4.34
67	14.78	5.13	14.16	4.48	13.58	3.93
68	15.25	4.66	14.59	4.06	13.97	3.54
69	15.69	4.21	14.99	3.66	14.33	3.18
70	16.11	3.80	15.36	3.28	14.67	2.84
71	16.51	3.40	15.71	2.93	14.98	2.53
72	16.87	3.03	16.04	2.60	15.27	2.24
73	17.22	2.69	16.34	2.30	15.54	1.97
74	17.54	2.37	16.62	2.02	15.78	1.73
75	17.83	2.08	16.88	1.77	16.01	1.50

Males aged 48

Retirement age	2.5% pa Life multiplier—19.46		3% pa Life multiplier—18.25		3.5% pa Life multiplier—17.16	
	Earnings multiplier	*Pensions multiplier*	*Earnings multiplier*	*Pensions multiplier*	*Earnings multiplier*	*Pensions multiplier*
50	1.94	17.52	1.93	16.32	1.93	15.24
51	2.87	16.59	2.85	15.40	2.83	14.33
52	3.78	15.68	3.74	14.51	3.71	13.46
53	4.65	14.81	4.60	13.65	4.55	12.62
54	5.50	13.96	5.43	12.83	5.35	11.81
55	6.33	13.13	6.23	12.03	6.13	11.04
56	7.13	12.33	6.99	11.26	6.87	10.30
57	7.90	11.56	7.74	10.52	7.58	9.59
58	8.64	10.82	8.45	9.81	8.26	8.91
59	9.36	10.10	9.13	9.12	8.91	8.26
60	10.06	9.40	9.79	8.47	9.53	7.64
61	10.73	8.73	10.42	7.84	10.12	7.04
62	11.37	8.09	11.02	7.24	10.68	6.48
63	11.98	7.48	11.59	6.66	11.22	5.94
64	12.57	6.89	12.14	6.11	11.73	5.44
65	13.14	6.32	12.66	5.59	12.21	4.96
66	13.67	5.79	13.15	5.10	12.66	4.50
67	14.19	5.27	13.62	4.63	13.09	4.08
68	14.67	4.79	14.06	4.19	13.49	3.68
69	15.13	4.33	14.47	3.78	13.86	3.30
70	15.56	3.90	14.86	3.39	14.21	2.95
71	15.96	3.50	15.22	3.03	14.54	2.63
72	16.34	3.12	15.56	2.69	14.84	2.33
73	16.69	2.77	15.87	2.38	15.12	2.05
74	17.02	2.44	16.16	2.09	15.37	1.79
75	17.32	2.14	16.43	1.83	15.60	1.56

Males aged 49

	2.5% pa Life multiplier—19.01		**3% pa Life multiplier—17.85**		**3.5% pa Life multiplier—16.81**	
Retirement age	*Earnings multiplier*	*Pensions multiplier*	*Earnings multiplier*	*Pensions multiplier*	*Earnings multiplier*	*Pensions multiplier*
50	0.99	18.02	0.98	16.87	0.98	15.83
51	1.94	17.06	1.93	15.92	1.92	14.89
52	2.87	16.13	2.85	15.00	2.83	13.98
53	3.77	15.23	3.74	14.12	3.70	13.11
54	4.65	14.36	4.59	13.26	4.54	12.27
55	5.50	13.51	5.42	12.43	5.34	11.47
56	6.32	12.69	6.21	11.64	6.11	10.70
57	7.11	11.90	6.98	10.87	6.85	9.96
58	7.88	11.13	7.72	10.14	7.56	9.25
59	8.62	10.39	8.42	9.43	8.23	8.58
60	9.33	9.67	9.10	8.75	8.88	7.93
61	10.02	8.99	9.75	8.10	9.49	7.32
62	10.68	8.33	10.37	7.48	10.08	6.73
63	11.31	7.69	10.97	6.89	10.64	6.18
64	11.92	7.08	11.53	6.32	11.16	5.65
65	12.50	6.50	12.07	5.78	11.66	5.15
66	13.05	5.95	12.58	5.27	12.13	4.68
67	13.58	5.43	13.06	4.79	12.58	4.24
68	14.08	4.93	13.52	4.34	12.99	3.82
69	14.55	4.46	13.95	3.91	13.38	3.43
70	14.99	4.02	14.35	3.51	13.74	3.07
71	15.41	3.60	14.72	3.13	14.08	2.73
72	15.80	3.21	15.07	2.78	14.40	2.42
73	16.16	2.85	15.39	2.46	14.68	2.13
74	16.50	2.51	15.69	2.16	14.95	1.86
75	16.81	2.20	15.97	1.89	15.19	1.62

Males aged 50

Retirement age	2.5% pa Life multiplier—18.55		3% pa Life multiplier—17.45		3.5% pa Life multiplier—16.45	
	Earnings multiplier	*Pensions multiplier*	*Earnings multiplier*	*Pensions multiplier*	*Earnings multiplier*	*Pensions multiplier*
50	—	18.55	—	17.45	—	16.45
51	0.99	17.56	0.98	16.47	0.98	15.47
52	1.94	16.61	1.93	15.52	1.92	14.53
53	2.87	15.68	2.85	14.60	2.83	13.62
54	3.77	14.78	3.73	13.71	3.70	12.75
55	4.64	13.91	4.59	12.86	4.53	11.92
56	5.49	13.06	5.41	12.04	5.34	11.12
57	6.30	12.24	6.20	11.25	6.10	10.35
58	7.09	11.45	6.96	10.49	6.84	9.62
59	7.86	10.69	7.69	9.75	7.54	8.91
60	8.59	9.96	8.40	9.05	8.21	8.24
61	9.30	9.25	9.07	8.38	8.85	7.60
62	9.98	8.57	9.71	7.74	9.46	7.00
63	10.63	7.92	10.33	7.12	10.03	6.42
64	11.26	7.29	10.91	6.54	10.58	5.87
65	11.85	6.70	11.47	5.98	11.10	5.35
66	12.42	6.13	11.99	5.45	11.59	4.86
67	12.96	5.59	12.49	4.96	12.05	4.40
68	13.48	5.07	12.96	4.48	12.48	3.97
69	13.96	4.59	13.41	4.04	12.89	3.56
70	14.42	4.13	13.82	3.63	13.27	3.19
71	14.84	3.70	14.21	3.24	13.62	2.84
72	15.24	3.30	14.57	2.88	13.94	2.51
73	15.62	2.93	14.91	2.54	14.24	2.21
74	15.96	2.58	15.21	2.24	14.52	1.94
75	16.28	2.27	15.50	1.95	14.77	1.68

Males aged 51

Retirement age	2.5% pa Life multiplier—18.09 Earnings multiplier	Pensions multiplier	3% pa Life multiplier—17.04 Earnings multiplier	Pensions multiplier	3.5% pa Life multiplier—16.09 Earnings multiplier	Pensions multiplier
50	—	—	—	—	—	—
51	—	18.09	—	17.04	—	16.09
52	0.99	17.10	0.98	16.06	0.98	15.11
53	1.94	16.14	1.93	15.11	1.92	14.17
54	2.87	15.22	2.85	14.19	2.83	13.26
55	3.77	14.32	3.73	13.31	3.70	12.39
56	4.64	13.45	4.58	12.46	4.53	11.56
57	5.48	12.61	5.40	11.64	5.33	10.76
58	6.29	11.80	6.19	10.85	6.09	10.00
59	7.08	11.01	6.95	10.09	6.82	9.27
60	7.83	10.25	7.67	9.37	7.52	8.57
61	8.56	9.53	8.37	8.67	8.18	7.91
62	9.26	8.82	9.03	8.01	8.81	7.28
63	9.93	8.15	9.67	7.37	9.41	6.67
64	10.58	7.51	10.27	6.77	9.98	6.10
65	11.19	6.89	10.85	6.19	10.52	5.57
66	11.78	6.31	11.40	5.64	11.03	5.06
67	12.33	5.75	11.91	5.13	11.51	4.58
68	12.86	5.22	12.40	4.64	11.96	4.13
69	13.36	4.73	12.86	4.18	12.38	3.71
70	13.83	4.26	13.29	3.75	12.77	3.31
71	14.27	3.82	13.69	3.35	13.14	2.95
72	14.68	3.40	14.06	2.98	13.48	2.61
73	15.07	3.02	14.41	2.63	13.79	2.30
74	15.42	2.66	14.73	2.31	14.08	2.01
75	15.75	2.33	15.02	2.02	14.34	1.75

Males aged 52

Retirement age	2.5% pa Life multiplier—17.62 Earnings multiplier	Pensions multiplier	3% pa Life multiplier—16.62 Earnings multiplier	Pensions multiplier	3.5% pa Life multiplier—15.72 Earnings multiplier	Pensions multiplier
50	—	—	—	—	—	—
51	—	—	—	—	—	—
52	—	17.62	—	16.62	—	15.72
53	0.98	16.63	0.98	15.64	0.98	14.74
54	1.94	15.68	1.93	14.69	1.92	13.80
55	2.87	14.75	2.85	13.78	2.82	12.89
56	3.76	13.86	3.73	12.90	3.69	12.03
57	4.63	12.99	4.57	12.05	4.52	11.20
58	5.47	12.15	5.39	11.23	5.32	10.40
59	6.28	11.34	6.17	10.45	6.07	9.64
60	7.05	10.56	6.93	9.70	6.80	8.92
61	7.81	9.81	7.65	8.98	7.49	8.23
62	8.53	9.09	8.33	8.29	8.15	7.57
63	9.22	8.40	8.99	7.63	8.77	6.94
64	9.88	7.74	9.62	7.00	9.37	6.35
65	10.52	7.10	10.22	6.41	9.93	5.79
66	11.12	6.50	10.78	5.84	10.46	5.26
67	11.69	5.93	11.32	5.31	10.96	4.76
68	12.24	5.38	11.82	4.80	11.42	4.29
69	12.75	4.87	12.29	4.33	11.86	3.86
70	13.23	4.39	12.74	3.89	12.27	3.45
71	13.69	3.93	13.15	3.47	12.65	3.07
72	14.11	3.51	13.54	3.08	13.00	2.72
73	14.51	3.11	13.90	2.73	13.33	2.39
74	14.88	2.74	14.23	2.40	13.62	2.09
75	15.22	2.40	14.53	2.09	13.90	1.82

Males aged 53

	2.5% pa Life multiplier—17.15		**3% pa Life multiplier—16.20**		**3.5% pa Life multiplier—15.34**	
Retirement age	*Earnings multiplier*	*Pensions multiplier*	*Earnings multiplier*	*Pensions multiplier*	*Earnings multiplier*	*Pensions multiplier*
50	—	—	—	—	—	—
51	—	—	—	—	—	—
52	—	—	—	—	—	—
53	—	17.15	—	16.20	—	15.34
54	0.98	16.17	0.98	15.22	0.98	14.36
55	1.94	15.21	1.93	14.27	1.92	13.42
56	2.86	14.29	2.84	13.36	2.82	12.52
57	3.76	13.39	3.72	12.48	3.69	11.66
58	4.62	12.53	4.57	11.64	4.51	10.83
59	5.45	11.70	5.38	10.83	5.30	10.04
60	6.26	10.89	6.16	10.05	6.06	9.28
61	7.03	10.12	6.90	9.30	6.78	8.56
62	7.78	9.37	7.62	8.59	7.46	7.88
63	8.49	8.66	8.30	7.91	8.11	7.23
64	9.17	7.98	8.95	7.26	8.73	6.61
65	9.83	7.32	9.56	6.64	9.31	6.03
66	10.45	6.70	10.15	6.05	9.87	5.48
67	11.04	6.11	10.70	5.50	10.38	4.96
68	11.60	5.55	11.23	4.98	10.87	4.47
69	12.13	5.02	11.72	4.49	11.33	4.01
70	12.63	4.52	12.18	4.03	11.75	3.59
71	13.10	4.05	12.61	3.60	12.15	3.19
72	13.54	3.61	13.01	3.20	12.51	2.83
73	13.94	3.21	13.38	2.82	12.85	2.49
74	14.32	2.83	13.72	2.48	13.16	2.18
75	14.67	2.48	14.04	2.17	13.45	1.90

Males aged 54

Retirement age	2.5% pa Life multiplier—16.68 *Earnings multiplier*	*Pensions multiplier*	3% pa Life multiplier—15.78 *Earnings multiplier*	*Pensions multiplier*	3.5% pa Life multiplier—14.96 *Earnings multiplier*	*Pensions multiplier*
50	—	—	—	—	—	—
51	—	—	—	—	—	—
52	—	—	—	—	—	—
53	—	—	—	—	—	—
54	—	16.68	—	15.78	—	14.96
55	0.98	15.69	0.98	14.80	0.98	13.98
56	1.94	14.74	1.93	13.85	1.92	13.04
57	2.86	13.82	2.84	12.94	2.82	12.14
58	3.75	12.93	3.71	12.07	3.68	11.28
59	4.61	12.07	4.56	11.22	4.50	10.46
60	5.44	11.24	5.36	10.42	5.29	9.67
61	6.24	10.44	6.14	9.64	6.04	8.92
62	7.01	9.67	6.88	8.90	6.75	8.21
63	7.74	8.93	7.58	8.20	7.43	7.53
64	8.45	8.23	8.26	7.52	8.07	6.89
65	9.12	7.56	8.90	6.88	8.68	6.28
66	9.76	6.91	9.50	6.28	9.26	5.70
67	10.37	6.30	10.08	5.70	9.80	5.16
68	10.95	5.73	10.62	5.16	10.30	4.66
69	11.50	5.18	11.13	4.65	10.78	4.18
70	12.01	4.66	11.61	4.17	11.22	3.74
71	12.50	4.18	12.05	3.73	11.63	3.33
72	12.95	3.73	12.47	3.31	12.01	2.95
73	13.37	3.31	12.85	2.93	12.37	2.59
74	13.76	2.92	13.21	2.57	12.69	2.27
75	14.12	2.56	13.53	2.25	12.99	1.98

Males aged 55

	2.5% pa Life multiplier—16.20		**3% pa Life multiplier—15.35**		**3.5% pa Life multiplier—14.57**	
Retirement age	*Earnings multiplier*	*Pensions multiplier*	*Earnings multiplier*	*Pensions multiplier*	*Earnings multiplier*	*Pensions multiplier*
50	—	—	—	—	—	—
51	—	—	—	—	—	—
52	—	—	—	—	—	—
53	—	—	—	—	—	—
54	—	—	—	—	—	—
55	—	16.20	—	15.35	—	14.57
56	0.98	15.22	0.98	14.37	0.98	13.60
57	1.94	14.26	1.93	13.43	1.92	12.66
58	2.86	13.34	2.84	12.52	2.82	11.76
59	3.74	12.46	3.71	11.64	3.67	10.90
60	4.60	11.60	4.55	10.81	4.49	10.08
61	5.42	10.78	5.35	10.00	5.27	9.30
62	6.22	9.98	6.12	9.24	6.02	8.56
63	6.98	9.22	6.85	8.50	6.73	7.85
64	7.70	8.50	7.55	7.80	7.40	7.18
65	8.40	7.80	8.21	7.14	8.03	6.55
66	9.06	7.14	8.84	6.51	8.63	5.95
67	9.69	6.51	9.44	5.91	9.19	5.38
68	10.29	5.91	10.00	5.35	9.72	4.85
69	10.85	5.35	10.53	4.82	10.22	4.36
70	11.39	4.81	11.02	4.33	10.68	3.90
71	11.88	4.32	11.48	3.87	11.11	3.47
72	12.35	3.85	11.92	3.44	11.50	3.07
73	12.79	3.41	12.31	3.04	11.87	2.70
74	13.19	3.01	12.68	2.67	12.21	2.37
75	13.56	2.64	13.02	2.33	12.52	2.06

Males aged 56

Retirement age	2.5% pa Life multiplier—15.72 Earnings multiplier	2.5% pa Pensions multiplier	3% pa Life multiplier—14.92 Earnings multiplier	3% pa Pensions multiplier	3.5% pa Life multiplier—14.18 Earnings multiplier	3.5% pa Pensions multiplier
50	—	—	—	—	—	—
51	—	—	—	—	—	—
52	—	—	—	—	—	—
53	—	—	—	—	—	—
54	—	—	—	—	—	—
55	—	—	—	—	—	—
56	—	15.72	—	14.92	—	14.18
57	0.98	14.74	0.98	13.94	0.98	13.21
58	1.93	13.79	1.92	13.00	1.92	12.27
59	2.85	12.87	2.83	12.09	2.81	11.37
60	3.74	11.99	3.70	11.22	3.67	10.52
61	4.59	11.13	4.53	10.39	4.48	9.70
62	5.41	10.32	5.33	9.59	5.26	8.93
63	6.19	9.53	6.09	8.83	5.99	8.19
64	6.94	8.78	6.82	8.10	6.69	7.49
65	7.66	8.06	7.51	7.41	7.36	6.83
66	8.35	7.37	8.16	6.76	7.98	6.20
67	9.00	6.72	8.78	6.14	8.57	5.62
68	9.61	6.11	9.36	5.56	9.12	5.06
69	10.20	5.52	9.91	5.01	9.64	4.55
70	10.75	4.97	10.42	4.50	10.12	4.07
71	11.26	4.46	10.91	4.01	10.57	3.62
72	11.74	3.98	11.35	3.57	10.98	3.20
73	12.19	3.53	11.77	3.15	11.36	2.82
74	12.61	3.11	12.15	2.77	11.71	2.47
75	12.99	2.73	12.50	2.42	12.04	2.15

Males aged 57

	2.5% pa Life multiplier—15.24		**3% pa Life multiplier—14.49**		**3.5% pa Life multiplier—13.79**	
Retirement age	*Earnings multiplier*	*Pensions multiplier*	*Earnings multiplier*	*Pensions multiplier*	*Earnings multiplier*	*Pensions multiplier*
50	—	—	—	—	—	—
51	—	—	—	—	—	—
52	—	—	—	—	—	—
53	—	—	—	—	—	—
54	—	—	—	—	—	—
55	—	—	—	—	—	—
56	—	—	—	—	—	—
57	—	15.24	—	14.49	—	13.79
58	0.98	14.26	0.98	13.51	0.98	12.81
59	1.93	13.31	1.92	12.56	1.91	11.88
60	2.85	12.40	2.83	11.66	2.81	10.98
61	3.73	11.51	3.69	10.79	3.66	10.13
62	4.57	10.67	4.52	9.97	4.47	9.32
63	5.39	9.86	5.31	9.17	5.24	8.55
64	6.16	9.08	6.07	8.42	5.97	7.82
65	6.91	8.33	6.78	7.70	6.66	7.13
66	7.62	7.63	7.46	7.03	7.31	6.48
67	8.29	6.95	8.10	6.38	7.93	5.87
68	8.93	6.32	8.71	5.78	8.50	5.29
69	9.53	5.71	9.28	5.21	9.04	4.75
70	10.10	5.15	9.81	4.67	9.54	4.25
71	10.63	4.61	10.31	4.17	10.01	3.78
72	11.13	4.11	10.78	3.71	10.44	3.35
73	11.59	3.65	11.21	3.28	10.84	2.95
74	12.02	3.22	11.61	2.88	11.21	2.58
75	12.42	2.82	11.97	2.51	11.55	2.24

Males aged 58

Retirement age	2.5% pa Life multiplier—14.76 Earnings multiplier	2.5% pa Life multiplier—14.76 Pensions multiplier	3% pa Life multiplier—14.05 Earnings multiplier	3% pa Life multiplier—14.05 Pensions multiplier	3.5% pa Life multiplier—13.39 Earnings multiplier	3.5% pa Life multiplier—13.39 Pensions multiplier
50	—	—	—	—	—	—
51	—	—	—	—	—	—
52	—	—	—	—	—	—
53	—	—	—	—	—	—
54	—	—	—	—	—	—
55	—	—	—	—	—	—
56	—	—	—	—	—	—
57	—	—	—	—	—	—
58	—	14.76	—	14.05	—	13.39
59	0.98	13.78	0.98	13.07	0.98	12.42
60	1.93	12.83	1.92	12.13	1.91	11.48
61	2.84	11.92	2.82	11.23	2.80	10.59
62	3.72	11.04	3.68	10.37	3.65	9.75
63	4.56	10.20	4.51	9.54	4.45	8.94
64	5.36	9.40	5.29	8.76	5.22	8.18
65	6.13	8.63	6.04	8.02	5.94	7.45
66	6.87	7.90	6.74	7.31	6.62	6.77
67	7.56	7.20	7.41	6.64	7.26	6.13
68	8.22	6.54	8.04	6.01	7.87	5.53
69	8.85	5.91	8.63	5.42	8.43	4.97
70	9.44	5.33	9.19	4.86	8.95	4.44
71	9.99	4.77	9.71	4.34	9.44	3.95
72	10.50	4.26	10.19	3.86	9.90	3.50
73	10.99	3.78	10.64	3.41	10.31	3.08
74	11.43	3.33	11.06	3.00	10.70	2.70
75	11.84	2.92	11.43	2.62	11.05	2.35

Males aged 59

Retirement age	2.5% pa Life multiplier—14.28		3% pa Life multiplier—13.61		3.5% pa Life multiplier—13.00	
	Earnings multiplier	*Pensions multiplier*	*Earnings multiplier*	*Pensions multiplier*	*Earnings multiplier*	*Pensions multiplier*
50	—	—	—	—	—	—
51	—	—	—	—	—	—
52	—	—	—	—	—	—
53	—	—	—	—	—	—
54	—	—	—	—	—	—
55	—	—	—	—	—	—
56	—	—	—	—	—	—
57	—	—	—	—	—	—
58	—	—	—	—	—	—
59	—	14.28	—	13.61	—	13.00
60	0.98	13.30	0.98	12.63	0.98	12.02
61	1.93	12.36	1.92	11.70	1.91	11.09
62	2.84	11.45	2.82	10.80	2.80	10.20
63	3.71	10.58	3.67	9.94	3.64	9.36
64	4.54	9.74	4.49	9.13	4.44	8.56
65	5.34	8.94	5.27	8.35	5.19	7.80
66	6.10	8.18	6.00	7.61	5.91	7.09
67	6.82	7.46	6.70	6.92	6.58	6.42
68	7.51	6.78	7.35	6.26	7.21	5.79
69	8.15	6.13	7.97	5.64	7.80	5.20
70	8.76	5.52	8.55	5.06	8.35	4.65
71	9.33	4.95	9.09	4.52	8.86	4.14
72	9.87	4.41	9.60	4.02	9.33	3.66
73	10.37	3.92	10.06	3.55	9.77	3.22
74	10.83	3.45	10.49	3.12	10.17	2.82
75	11.26	3.03	10.89	2.72	10.54	2.46

Males aged 60

Retirement age	2.5% pa Life multiplier—13.81		3% pa Life multiplier—13.18		3.5% pa Life multiplier—12.60	
	Earnings multiplier	*Pensions multiplier*	*Earnings multiplier*	*Pensions multiplier*	*Earnings multiplier*	*Pensions multiplier*
50	—	—	—	—	—	—
51	—	—	—	—	—	—
52	—	—	—	—	—	—
53	—	—	—	—	—	—
54	—	—	—	—	—	—
55	—	—	—	—	—	—
56	—	—	—	—	—	—
57	—	—	—	—	—	—
58	—	—	—	—	—	—
59	—	—	—	—	—	—
60	—	13.81	—	13.18	—	12.60
61	0.98	12.83	0.98	12.20	0.98	11.62
62	1.92	11.88	1.91	11.26	1.91	10.69
63	2.83	10.98	2.81	10.37	2.79	9.81
64	3.70	10.11	3.66	9.52	3.63	8.97
65	4.52	9.28	4.47	8.71	4.42	8.18
66	5.31	8.49	5.24	7.94	5.17	7.43
67	6.06	7.74	5.96	7.21	5.87	6.73
68	6.77	7.03	6.65	6.53	6.53	6.07
69	7.44	6.36	7.29	5.88	7.15	5.45
70	8.08	5.73	7.90	5.28	7.73	4.87
71	8.67	5.14	8.46	4.72	8.26	4.33
72	9.23	4.58	8.99	4.19	8.76	3.84
73	9.74	4.06	9.47	3.70	9.22	3.38
74	10.22	3.58	9.92	3.25	9.64	2.96
75	10.66	3.14	10.34	2.84	10.02	2.57

Males aged 61

	2.5% pa Life multiplier—13.33		**3% pa Life multiplier—12.74**		**3.5% pa Life multiplier—12.20**	
Retirement age	*Earnings multiplier*	*Pensions multiplier*	*Earnings multiplier*	*Pensions multiplier*	*Earnings multiplier*	*Pensions multiplier*
50	—	—	—	—	—	—
51	—	—	—	—	—	—
52	—	—	—	—	—	—
53	—	—	—	—	—	—
54	—	—	—	—	—	—
55	—	—	—	—	—	—
56	—	—	—	—	—	—
57	—	—	—	—	—	—
58	—	—	—	—	—	—
59	—	—	—	—	—	—
60	—	—	—	—	—	—
61	—	13.33	—	12.74	—	12.20
62	0.98	12.35	0.98	11.76	0.98	11.22
63	1.92	11.41	1.91	10.83	1.90	10.29
64	2.82	10.51	2.80	9.94	2.78	9.41
65	3.68	9.65	3.65	9.10	3.61	8.58
66	4.50	8.83	4.45	8.29	4.40	7.80
67	5.28	8.05	5.21	7.53	5.14	7.06
68	6.02	7.31	5.92	6.82	5.83	6.37
69	6.72	6.61	6.60	6.15	6.48	5.72
70	7.37	5.96	7.23	5.52	7.08	5.11
71	7.99	5.34	7.82	4.93	7.65	4.55
72	8.57	4.76	8.37	4.38	8.17	4.03
73	9.11	4.22	8.87	3.87	8.65	3.55
74	9.61	3.73	9.34	3.40	9.09	3.10
75	10.07	3.27	9.77	2.97	9.50	2.70

Males aged 62

Retirement age	2.5% pa Life multiplier—12.86 Earnings multiplier	2.5% pa Pensions multiplier	3% pa Life multiplier—12.31 Earnings multiplier	3% pa Pensions multiplier	3.5% pa Life multiplier—11.80 Earnings multiplier	3.5% pa Pensions multiplier
50	—	—	—	—	—	—
51	—	—	—	—	—	—
52	—	—	—	—	—	—
53	—	—	—	—	—	—
54	—	—	—	—	—	—
55	—	—	—	—	—	—
56	—	—	—	—	—	—
57	—	—	—	—	—	—
58	—	—	—	—	—	—
59	—	—	—	—	—	—
60	—	—	—	—	—	—
61	—	—	—	—	—	—
62	—	12.86	—	12.31	—	11.80
63	0.98	11.88	0.98	11.33	0.97	10.82
64	1.92	10.94	1.91	10.40	1.90	9.90
65	2.81	10.05	2.79	9.52	2.77	9.02
66	3.67	9.19	3.63	8.68	3.60	8.20
67	4.48	8.38	4.43	7.88	4.38	7.42
68	5.25	7.61	5.17	7.13	5.10	6.69
69	5.97	6.89	5.88	6.43	5.79	6.01
70	6.66	6.20	6.54	5.77	6.42	5.37
71	7.30	5.56	7.16	5.15	7.01	4.78
72	7.90	4.96	7.73	4.58	7.56	4.23
73	8.46	4.40	8.26	4.05	8.07	3.73
74	8.98	3.88	8.75	3.56	8.53	3.26
75	9.46	3.40	9.20	3.11	8.96	2.84

Males aged 63

	2.5% pa Life multiplier—12.40		3% pa Life multiplier—11.88		3.5% pa Life multiplier—11.40	
Retirement age	*Earnings multiplier*	*Pensions multiplier*	*Earnings multiplier*	*Pensions multiplier*	*Earnings multiplier*	*Pensions multiplier*
50	—	—	—	—	—	—
51	—	—	—	—	—	—
52	—	—	—	—	—	—
53	—	—	—	—	—	—
54	—	—	—	—	—	—
55	—	—	—	—	—	—
56	—	—	—	—	—	—
57	—	—	—	—	—	—
58	—	—	—	—	—	—
59	—	—	—	—	—	—
60	—	—	—	—	—	—
61	—	—	—	—	—	—
62	—	—	—	—	—	—
63	—	12.40	—	11.88	—	11.40
64	0.98	11.42	0.98	10.90	0.97	10.43
65	1.91	10.48	1.90	9.98	1.89	9.51
66	2.80	9.59	2.78	9.10	2.76	8.64
67	3.65	8.75	3.62	8.26	3.58	7.82
68	4.45	7.94	4.40	7.48	4.35	7.05
69	5.21	7.18	5.14	6.74	5.07	6.33
70	5.92	6.47	5.83	6.05	5.74	5.66
71	6.59	5.80	6.48	5.40	6.36	5.04
72	7.22	5.17	7.08	4.80	6.94	4.46
73	7.81	4.59	7.64	4.24	7.47	3.93
74	8.35	4.05	8.15	3.73	7.96	3.44
75	8.85	3.55	8.62	3.26	8.41	2.99

Males aged 64

Retirement age	2.5% pa Life multiplier—11.94 Earnings multiplier	2.5% pa Pensions multiplier	3% pa Life multiplier—11.46 Earnings multiplier	3% pa Pensions multiplier	3.5% pa Life multiplier—11.01 Earnings multiplier	3.5% pa Pensions multiplier
50	—	—	—	—	—	—
51	—	—	—	—	—	—
52	—	—	—	—	—	—
53	—	—	—	—	—	—
54	—	—	—	—	—	—
55	—	—	—	—	—	—
56	—	—	—	—	—	—
57	—	—	—	—	—	—
58	—	—	—	—	—	—
59	—	—	—	—	—	—
60	—	—	—	—	—	—
61	—	—	—	—	—	—
62	—	—	—	—	—	—
63	—	—	—	—	—	—
64	—	11.94	—	11.46	—	11.01
65	0.98	10.96	0.97	10.48	0.97	10.04
66	1.91	10.03	1.90	9.56	1.89	9.12
67	2.79	9.14	2.77	8.68	2.75	8.25
68	3.63	8.30	3.60	7.86	3.56	7.44
69	4.42	7.51	4.37	7.08	4.32	6.68
70	5.17	6.77	5.10	6.36	5.03	5.98
71	5.87	6.06	5.78	5.68	5.69	5.32
72	6.53	5.41	6.41	5.04	6.30	4.71
73	7.14	4.80	7.00	4.46	6.86	4.15
74	7.71	4.23	7.54	3.92	7.38	3.63
75	8.23	3.71	8.04	3.42	7.85	3.16

Males aged 65

Retirement age	2.5% pa Life multiplier—11.49 *Earnings multiplier*	*Pensions multiplier*	3% pa Life multiplier—11.04 *Earnings multiplier*	*Pensions multiplier*	3.5% pa Life multiplier—10.62 *Earnings multiplier*	*Pensions multiplier*
50	—	—	—	—	—	—
51	—	—	—	—	—	—
52	—	—	—	—	—	—
53	—	—	—	—	—	—
54	—	—	—	—	—	—
55	—	—	—	—	—	—
56	—	—	—	—	—	—
57	—	—	—	—	—	—
58	—	—	—	—	—	—
59	—	—	—	—	—	—
60	—	—	—	—	—	—
61	—	—	—	—	—	—
62	—	—	—	—	—	—
63	—	—	—	—	—	—
64	—	—	—	—	—	—
65	—	11.49	—	11.04	—	10.62
66	0.98	10.51	0.97	10.07	0.97	9.65
67	1.90	9.58	1.89	9.14	1.89	8.74
68	2.78	8.70	2.76	8.28	2.74	7.88
69	3.61	7.87	3.58	7.46	3.55	7.07
70	4.40	7.09	4.35	6.69	4.30	6.33
71	5.13	6.36	5.06	5.98	4.99	5.63
72	5.82	5.67	5.73	5.31	5.64	4.98
73	6.46	5.03	6.34	4.69	6.23	4.39
74	7.05	4.43	6.91	4.13	6.78	3.84
75	7.60	3.89	7.44	3.60	7.28	3.34

Males aged 66

Retirement age	2.5% pa Life multiplier—11.04 Earnings multiplier	Pensions multiplier	3% pa Life multiplier—10.63 Earnings multiplier	Pensions multiplier	3.5% pa Life multiplier—10.24 Earnings multiplier	Pensions multiplier
50	—	—	—	—	—	—
51	—	—	—	—	—	—
52	—	—	—	—	—	—
53	—	—	—	—	—	—
54	—	—	—	—	—	—
55	—	—	—	—	—	—
56	—	—	—	—	—	—
57	—	—	—	—	—	—
58	—	—	—	—	—	—
59	—	—	—	—	—	—
60	—	—	—	—	—	—
61	—	—	—	—	—	—
62	—	—	—	—	—	—
63	—	—	—	—	—	—
64	—	—	—	—	—	—
65	—	—	—	—	—	—
66	—	11.04	—	10.63	—	10.24
67	0.97	10.07	0.97	9.66	0.97	9.27
68	1.90	9.14	1.89	8.74	1.88	8.36
69	2.77	8.27	2.75	7.88	2.73	7.51
70	3.59	7.45	3.56	7.07	3.53	6.71
71	4.37	6.68	4.32	6.31	4.27	5.97
72	5.09	5.96	5.02	5.61	4.95	5.29
73	5.76	5.28	5.67	4.96	5.58	4.66
74	6.38	4.66	6.27	4.36	6.16	4.08
75	6.96	4.08	6.82	3.80	6.69	3.55

Males aged 67

	2.5% pa Life multiplier—10.61		**3% pa Life multiplier—10.22**		**3.5% pa Life multiplier—9.86**	
Retirement age	*Earnings multiplier*	*Pensions multiplier*	*Earnings multiplier*	*Pensions multiplier*	*Earnings multiplier*	*Pensions multiplier*
50	—	—	—	—	—	—
51	—	—	—	—	—	—
52	—	—	—	—	—	—
53	—	—	—	—	—	—
54	—	—	—	—	—	—
55	—	—	—	—	—	—
56	—	—	—	—	—	—
57	—	—	—	—	—	—
58	—	—	—	—	—	—
59	—	—	—	—	—	—
60	—	—	—	—	—	—
61	—	—	—	—	—	—
62	—	—	—	—	—	—
63	—	—	—	—	—	—
64	—	—	—	—	—	—
65	—	—	—	—	—	—
66	—	—	—	—	—	—
67	—	10.61	—	10.22	—	9.86
68	0.97	9.63	0.97	9.25	0.97	8.89
69	1.89	8.72	1.88	8.34	1.87	7.98
70	2.76	7.85	2.74	7.48	2.72	7.14
71	3.57	7.04	3.54	6.68	3.51	6.35
72	4.33	6.27	4.28	5.94	4.24	5.62
73	5.04	5.57	4.97	5.25	4.91	4.95
74	5.70	4.91	5.61	4.61	5.52	4.34
75	6.31	4.30	6.19	4.03	6.09	3.77

Males aged 68

Retirement age	2.5% pa Life multiplier—10.18 Earnings multiplier	2.5% pa Pensions multiplier	3% pa Life multiplier—9.82 Earnings multiplier	3% pa Pensions multiplier	3.5% pa Life multiplier—9.49 Earnings multiplier	3.5% pa Pensions multiplier
50	—	—	—	—	—	—
51	—	—	—	—	—	—
52	—	—	—	—	—	—
53	—	—	—	—	—	—
54	—	—	—	—	—	—
55	—	—	—	—	—	—
56	—	—	—	—	—	—
57	—	—	—	—	—	—
58	—	—	—	—	—	—
59	—	—	—	—	—	—
60	—	—	—	—	—	—
61	—	—	—	—	—	—
62	—	—	—	—	—	—
63	—	—	—	—	—	—
64	—	—	—	—	—	—
65	—	—	—	—	—	—
66	—	—	—	—	—	—
67	—	—	—	—	—	—
68	—	10.18	—	9.82	—	9.49
69	0.97	9.21	0.97	8.85	0.97	8.52
70	1.89	8.29	1.88	7.94	1.87	7.62
71	2.75	7.43	2.73	7.10	2.71	6.78
72	3.55	6.63	3.52	6.31	3.49	6.00
73	4.30	5.88	4.25	5.57	4.20	5.28
74	4.99	5.19	4.93	4.90	4.86	4.63
75	5.63	4.55	5.55	4.28	5.46	4.02

Males aged 69

	2.5% pa Life multiplier—9.76		**3% pa Life multiplier—9.43**		**3.5% pa Life multiplier—9.12**	
Retirement age	*Earnings multiplier*	*Pensions multiplier*	*Earnings multiplier*	*Pensions multiplier*	*Earnings multiplier*	*Pensions multiplier*
50	—	—	—	—	—	—
51	—	—	—	—	—	—
52	—	—	—	—	—	—
53	—	—	—	—	—	—
54	—	—	—	—	—	—
55	—	—	—	—	—	—
56	—	—	—	—	—	—
57	—	—	—	—	—	—
58	—	—	—	—	—	—
59	—	—	—	—	—	—
60	—	—	—	—	—	—
61	—	—	—	—	—	—
62	—	—	—	—	—	—
63	—	—	—	—	—	—
64	—	—	—	—	—	—
65	—	—	—	—	—	—
66	—	—	—	—	—	—
67	—	—	—	—	—	—
68	—	—	—	—	—	—
69	—	9.76	—	9.43	—	9.12
70	0.97	8.79	0.97	8.46	0.97	8.15
71	1.88	7.88	1.87	7.56	1.86	7.25
72	2.73	7.03	2.71	6.72	2.70	6.42
73	3.53	6.23	3.49	5.94	3.46	5.66
74	4.26	5.50	4.21	5.22	4.17	4.95
75	4.94	4.82	4.88	4.55	4.81	4.31

Males aged 70

Retirement age	2.5% pa Life multiplier—9.35		3% pa Life multiplier—9.04		3.5% pa Life multiplier—8.75	
	Earnings multiplier	*Pensions multiplier*	*Earnings multiplier*	*Pensions multiplier*	*Earnings multiplier*	*Pensions multiplier*
50	—	—	—	—	—	—
51	—	—	—	—	—	—
52	—	—	—	—	—	—
53	—	—	—	—	—	—
54	—	—	—	—	—	—
55	—	—	—	—	—	—
56	—	—	—	—	—	—
57	—	—	—	—	—	—
58	—	—	—	—	—	—
59	—	—	—	—	—	—
60	—	—	—	—	—	—
61	—	—	—	—	—	—
62	—	—	—	—	—	—
63	—	—	—	—	—	—
64	—	—	—	—	—	—
65	—	—	—	—	—	—
66	—	—	—	—	—	—
67	—	—	—	—	—	—
68	—	—	—	—	—	—
69	—	—	—	—	—	—
70	—	9.35	—	9.04	—	8.75
71	0.97	8.38	0.97	8.07	0.96	7.79
72	1.87	7.47	1.87	7.18	1.86	6.90
73	2.72	6.63	2.70	6.34	2.68	6.07
74	3.50	5.85	3.47	5.57	3.44	5.32
75	4.22	5.12	4.18	4.87	4.13	4.62

Males aged 71

Retirement age	2.5% pa Life multiplier—8.94		3% pa Life multiplier—8.66		3.5% pa Life multiplier—8.39	
	Earnings multiplier	*Pensions multiplier*	*Earnings multiplier*	*Pensions multiplier*	*Earnings multiplier*	*Pensions multiplier*
50	—	—	—	—	—	—
51	—	—	—	—	—	—
52	—	—	—	—	—	—
53	—	—	—	—	—	—
54	—	—	—	—	—	—
55	—	—	—	—	—	—
56	—	—	—	—	—	—
57	—	—	—	—	—	—
58	—	—	—	—	—	—
59	—	—	—	—	—	—
60	—	—	—	—	—	—
61	—	—	—	—	—	—
62	—	—	—	—	—	—
63	—	—	—	—	—	—
64	—	—	—	—	—	—
65	—	—	—	—	—	—
66	—	—	—	—	—	—
67	—	—	—	—	—	—
68	—	—	—	—	—	—
69	—	—	—	—	—	—
70	—	—	—	—	—	—
71	—	8.94	—	8.66	—	8.39
72	0.97	7.97	0.96	7.69	0.96	7.43
73	1.87	7.07	1.86	6.80	1.85	6.54
74	2.70	6.24	2.68	5.97	2.66	5.73
75	3.47	5.47	3.44	5.22	3.41	4.98

Males aged 72

Retirement age	2.5% pa Life multiplier—8.54 Earnings multiplier	Pensions multiplier	3% pa Life multiplier—8.28 Earnings multiplier	Pensions multiplier	3.5% pa Life multiplier—8.04 Earnings multiplier	Pensions multiplier
50	—	—	—	—	—	—
51	—	—	—	—	—	—
52	—	—	—	—	—	—
53	—	—	—	—	—	—
54	—	—	—	—	—	—
55	—	—	—	—	—	—
56	—	—	—	—	—	—
57	—	—	—	—	—	—
58	—	—	—	—	—	—
59	—	—	—	—	—	—
60	—	—	—	—	—	—
61	—	—	—	—	—	—
62	—	—	—	—	—	—
63	—	—	—	—	—	—
64	—	—	—	—	—	—
65	—	—	—	—	—	—
66	—	—	—	—	—	—
67	—	—	—	—	—	—
68	—	—	—	—	—	—
69	—	—	—	—	—	—
70	—	—	—	—	—	—
71	—	—	—	—	—	—
72	—	8.54	—	8.28	—	8.04
73	0.96	7.58	0.96	7.32	0.96	7.08
74	1.86	6.68	1.85	6.43	1.84	6.19
75	2.68	5.86	2.66	5.62	2.65	5.39

Males aged 73

Retirement age	2.5% pa Life multiplier—8.15		3% pa Life multiplier—7.91		3.5% pa Life multiplier—7.69	
	Earnings multiplier	*Pensions multiplier*	*Earnings multiplier*	*Pensions multiplier*	*Earnings multiplier*	*Pensions multiplier*
50	—	—	—	—	—	—
51	—	—	—	—	—	—
52	—	—	—	—	—	—
53	—	—	—	—	—	—
54	—	—	—	—	—	—
55	—	—	—	—	—	—
56	—	—	—	—	—	—
57	—	—	—	—	—	—
58	—	—	—	—	—	—
59	—	—	—	—	—	—
60	—	—	—	—	—	—
61	—	—	—	—	—	—
62	—	—	—	—	—	—
63	—	—	—	—	—	—
64	—	—	—	—	—	—
65	—	—	—	—	—	—
66	—	—	—	—	—	—
67	—	—	—	—	—	—
68	—	—	—	—	—	—
69	—	—	—	—	—	—
70	—	—	—	—	—	—
71	—	—	—	—	—	—
72	—	—	—	—	—	—
73	—	8.15	—	7.91	—	7.69
74	0.96	7.19	0.96	6.95	0.96	6.73
75	1.85	6.30	1.84	6.07	1.83	5.86

Males aged 74

Retirement age	2.5% pa Life multiplier—7.77		3% pa Life multiplier—7.56		3.5% pa Life multiplier—7.35	
	Earnings multiplier	*Pensions multiplier*	*Earnings multiplier*	*Pensions multiplier*	*Earnings multiplier*	*Pensions multiplier*
50	—	—	—	—	—	—
51	—	—	—	—	—	—
52	—	—	—	—	—	—
53	—	—	—	—	—	—
54	—	—	—	—	—	—
55	—	—	—	—	—	—
56	—	—	—	—	—	—
57	—	—	—	—	—	—
58	—	—	—	—	—	—
59	—	—	—	—	—	—
60	—	—	—	—	—	—
61	—	—	—	—	—	—
62	—	—	—	—	—	—
63	—	—	—	—	—	—
64	—	—	—	—	—	—
65	—	—	—	—	—	—
66	—	—	—	—	—	—
67	—	—	—	—	—	—
68	—	—	—	—	—	—
69	—	—	—	—	—	—
70	—	—	—	—	—	—
71	—	—	—	—	—	—
72	—	—	—	—	—	—
73	—	—	—	—	—	—
74	—	7.77	—	7.56	—	7.35
75	0.96	6.81	0.96	6.60	0.96	6.39

Males aged 75

	2.5% pa Life multiplier—7.41		**3% pa Life multiplier—7.21**		**3.5% pa Life multiplier—7.02**	
Retirement age	*Earnings multiplier*	*Pensions multiplier*	*Earnings multiplier*	*Pensions multiplier*	*Earnings multiplier*	*Pensions multiplier*
50	—	—	—	—	—	—
51	—	—	—	—	—	—
52	—	—	—	—	—	—
53	—	—	—	—	—	—
54	—	—	—	—	—	—
55	—	—	—	—	—	—
56	—	—	—	—	—	—
57	—	—	—	—	—	—
58	—	—	—	—	—	—
59	—	—	—	—	—	—
60	—	—	—	—	—	—
61	—	—	—	—	—	—
62	—	—	—	—	—	—
63	—	—	—	—	—	—
64	—	—	—	—	—	—
65	—	—	—	—	—	—
66	—	—	—	—	—	—
67	—	—	—	—	—	—
68	—	—	—	—	—	—
69	—	—	—	—	—	—
70	—	—	—	—	—	—
71	—	—	—	—	—	—
72	—	—	—	—	—	—
73	—	—	—	—	—	—
74	—	—	—	—	—	—
75	—	7.41	—	7.21	—	7.02

Males aged 76–100

Age	2.5% pa *Life/pensions multiplier*	3% pa *Life/pensions multiplier*	3.5% pa *Life/pensions multiplier*
76	7.05	6.87	6.69
77	6.70	6.53	6.37
78	6.36	6.21	6.07
79	6.04	5.90	5.77
80	5.73	5.61	5.49
81	5.43	5.32	5.21
82	5.14	5.04	4.94
83	4.86	4.77	4.68
84	4.60	4.52	4.44
85	4.35	4.27	4.20
86	4.10	4.04	3.97
87	3.88	3.82	3.76
88	3.67	3.61	3.56
89	3.47	3.42	3.37
90	3.27	3.23	3.18
91	3.07	3.03	3.00
92	2.88	2.85	2.81
93	2.70	2.67	2.64
94	2.54	2.52	2.49
95	2.40	2.37	2.35
96	2.26	2.24	2.22
97	2.14	2.12	2.10
98	2.02	2.00	1.98
99	1.91	1.89	1.87
100	1.80	1.78	1.77

Females aged 1

Retirement age	2.5% pa Life multiplier—34.27						
	E.M. 16	*E.M. 18*	*E.M. 21*	*E.M. 24*	*P.M.*	*E.M. 16*	*E.M. 18*
50	15.73	14.39	12.49	10.74	6.03	13.63	12.39
51	16.01	14.67	12.78	11.02	5.74	13.86	12.62
52	16.29	14.95	13.05	11.30	5.47	14.08	12.83
53	16.56	15.22	13.32	11.57	5.20	14.28	13.04
54	16.82	15.48	13.59	11.83	4.93	14.49	13.25
55	17.08	15.73	13.84	12.08	4.68	14.68	13.44
56	17.32	15.98	14.09	12.33	4.43	14.87	13.63
57	17.56	16.22	14.33	12.57	4.19	15.06	13.81
58	17.80	16.45	14.56	12.80	3.96	15.23	13.99
59	18.02	16.68	14.79	13.03	3.73	15.40	14.16
60	18.24	16.90	15.00	13.25	3.52	15.57	14.33
61	18.45	17.11	15.22	13.46	3.30	15.73	14.48
62	18.66	17.31	15.42	13.66	3.10	15.88	14.64
63	18.85	17.51	15.62	13.86	2.90	16.03	14.78
64	19.04	17.70	15.81	14.05	2.71	16.17	14.92
65	19.23	17.89	15.99	14.24	2.53	16.30	15.06
66	19.41	18.06	16.17	14.41	2.35	16.43	15.19
67	19.58	18.23	16.34	14.58	2.18	16.55	15.31
68	19.74	18.40	16.50	14.75	2.02	16.67	15.43
69	19.90	18.55	16.66	14.90	1.86	16.79	15.54
70	20.05	18.70	16.81	15.05	1.71	16.89	15.65
71	20.19	18.85	16.95	15.20	1.57	16.99	15.75
72	20.33	18.98	17.09	15.33	1.43	17.09	15.85
73	20.46	19.11	17.22	15.46	1.30	17.18	15.94
74	20.58	19.24	17.34	15.59	1.18	17.27	16.03
75	20.69	19.35	17.46	15.70	1.06	17.35	16.11

3% pa Life multiplier—30.16			**3.5% pa Life multiplier—26.83**				
E.M. 21	*E.M. 24*	*P.M.*	*E.M. 16*	*E.M. 18*	*E.M. 21*	*E.M. 24*	*P.M.*
10.66	9.08	4.43	11.85	10.70	9.12	7.70	3.27
10.89	9.30	4.21	12.03	10.88	9.30	7.87	3.10
11.10	9.52	3.99	12.20	11.05	9.47	8.04	2.93
11.31	9.73	3.78	12.36	11.21	9.63	8.20	2.76
11.52	9.93	3.58	12.52	11.37	9.79	8.36	2.61
11.71	10.13	3.38	12.67	11.52	9.94	8.51	2.46
11.90	10.32	3.19	12.82	11.67	10.08	8.66	2.31
12.08	10.50	3.01	12.96	11.81	10.22	8.80	2.17
12.26	10.68	2.83	13.09	11.94	10.36	8.93	2.04
12.43	10.85	2.66	13.22	12.07	10.49	9.06	1.91
12.60	11.01	2.50	13.34	12.19	10.61	9.19	1.78
12.75	11.17	2.34	13.46	12.31	10.73	9.31	1.66
12.91	11.32	2.19	13.58	12.43	10.84	9.42	1.55
13.05	11.47	2.04	13.68	12.54	10.95	9.53	1.44
13.19	11.61	1.90	13.79	12.64	11.06	9.63	1.34
13.33	11.75	1.77	13.89	12.74	11.16	9.73	1.24
13.46	11.88	1.64	13.98	12.83	11.25	9.83	1.14
13.58	12.00	1.51	14.07	12.92	11.34	9.92	1.05
13.70	12.12	1.40	14.16	13.01	11.43	10.00	0.97
13.81	12.23	1.28	14.24	13.09	11.51	10.08	0.89
13.92	12.34	1.18	14.32	13.17	11.59	10.16	0.81
14.02	12.44	1.07	14.39	13.24	11.66	10.23	0.74
14.12	12.54	0.98	14.46	13.31	11.73	10.30	0.67
14.21	12.63	0.88	14.52	13.37	11.79	10.37	0.60
14.30	12.72	0.80	14.58	13.43	11.85	10.43	0.54
14.38	12.80	0.72	14.64	13.49	11.91	10.48	0.49

Females aged 2

Retirement age	2.5% pa Life multiplier—34.14						
	E.M. 16	*E.M. 18*	*E.M. 21*	*E.M. 24*	*P.M.*	*E.M. 16*	*E.M. 18*
50	16.13	14.75	12.81	11.01	6.18	14.05	12.77
51	16.42	15.05	13.10	11.30	5.89	14.28	13.00
52	16.71	15.33	13.39	11.59	5.61	14.51	13.22
53	16.98	15.61	13.66	11.86	5.33	14.72	13.44
54	17.25	15.87	13.93	12.13	5.06	14.93	13.65
55	17.51	16.14	14.19	12.39	4.80	15.13	13.85
56	17.77	16.39	14.45	12.65	4.55	15.33	14.05
57	18.01	16.64	14.69	12.89	4.30	15.52	14.24
58	18.25	16.87	14.93	13.13	4.06	15.70	14.42
59	18.48	17.11	15.16	13.36	3.83	15.87	14.59
60	18.71	17.33	15.39	13.59	3.61	16.04	14.76
61	18.92	17.55	15.61	13.80	3.39	16.21	14.93
62	19.13	17.76	15.81	14.01	3.18	16.36	15.08
63	19.34	17.96	16.02	14.22	2.98	16.52	15.23
64	19.53	18.15	16.21	14.41	2.78	16.66	15.38
65	19.72	18.34	16.40	14.60	2.59	16.80	15.52
66	19.90	18.52	16.58	14.78	2.41	16.93	15.65
67	20.08	18.70	16.76	14.96	2.24	17.06	15.78
68	20.24	18.87	16.93	15.12	2.07	17.18	15.90
69	20.40	19.03	17.09	15.29	1.91	17.30	16.02
70	20.56	19.18	17.24	15.44	1.75	17.41	16.13
71	20.71	19.33	17.39	15.59	1.61	17.51	16.23
72	20.85	19.47	17.53	15.73	1.47	17.61	16.33
73	20.98	19.60	17.66	15.86	1.33	17.71	16.43
74	21.10	19.73	17.79	15.98	1.21	17.80	16.52
75	21.22	19.85	17.90	16.10	1.09	17.88	16.60

3% pa Life multiplier—30.07			**3.5% pa Life multiplier—26.76**				
E.M. 21	*E.M. 24*	*P.M.*	*E.M. 16*	*E.M. 18*	*E.M. 21*	*E.M. 24*	*P.M.*
10.99	9.36	4.57	12.27	11.08	9.45	7.97	3.39
11.22	9.59	4.34	12.46	11.27	9.63	8.15	3.21
11.44	9.81	4.11	12.63	11.44	9.80	8.33	3.03
11.66	10.03	3.90	12.80	11.61	9.97	8.50	2.86
11.87	10.24	3.69	12.96	11.77	10.14	8.66	2.70
12.07	10.44	3.49	13.12	11.93	10.29	8.82	2.54
12.26	10.63	3.29	13.27	12.08	10.44	8.97	2.39
12.45	10.82	3.10	13.42	12.23	10.59	9.11	2.25
12.64	11.01	2.92	13.56	12.37	10.73	9.25	2.11
12.81	11.18	2.75	13.69	12.50	10.86	9.38	1.97
12.98	11.35	2.58	13.82	12.63	10.99	9.51	1.85
13.14	11.51	2.41	13.94	12.75	11.11	9.64	1.72
13.30	11.67	2.26	14.06	12.87	11.23	9.75	1.61
13.45	11.82	2.10	14.17	12.98	11.34	9.87	1.49
13.60	11.97	1.96	14.28	13.09	11.45	9.97	1.39
13.74	12.11	1.82	14.38	13.19	11.55	10.08	1.28
13.87	12.24	1.69	14.48	13.29	11.65	10.18	1.18
14.00	12.37	1.56	14.57	13.38	11.74	10.27	1.09
14.12	12.49	1.44	14.66	13.47	11.83	10.36	1.00
14.24	12.61	1.32	14.75	13.56	11.92	10.44	0.92
14.35	12.72	1.21	14.83	13.64	12.00	10.52	0.84
14.45	12.82	1.11	14.90	13.71	12.07	10.60	0.76
14.55	12.92	1.01	14.97	13.78	12.14	10.67	0.69
14.65	13.02	0.91	15.04	13.85	12.21	10.73	0.62
14.73	13.10	0.82	15.10	13.91	12.27	10.80	0.56
14.82	13.19	0.74	15.16	13.97	12.33	10.86	0.50

Females aged 3

Retirement age	2.5% pa Life multiplier—33.99						
	E.M. 16	*E.M. 18*	*E.M. 21*	*E.M. 24*	*P.M.*	*E.M. 16*	*E.M. 18*
50	16.54	15.13	13.14	11.29	6.34	14.48	13.16
51	16.84	15.43	13.44	11.59	6.04	14.72	13.40
52	17.13	15.72	13.73	11.88	5.75	14.95	13.63
53	17.41	16.00	14.01	12.16	5.46	15.17	13.85
54	17.69	16.28	14.29	12.44	5.19	15.38	14.06
55	17.96	16.54	14.55	12.71	4.92	15.59	14.27
56	18.22	16.80	14.81	12.97	4.66	15.79	14.47
57	18.47	17.06	15.07	13.22	4.41	15.99	14.67
58	18.71	17.30	15.31	13.46	4.16	16.17	14.86
59	18.95	17.54	15.55	13.70	3.93	16.36	15.04
60	19.18	17.77	15.78	13.93	3.70	16.53	15.21
61	19.40	17.99	16.00	14.15	3.47	16.70	15.38
62	19.62	18.21	16.22	14.37	3.26	16.86	15.54
63	19.83	18.41	16.42	14.58	3.05	17.02	15.70
64	20.03	18.61	16.62	14.78	2.85	17.17	15.85
65	20.22	18.81	16.82	14.97	2.66	17.31	15.99
66	20.41	18.99	17.00	15.16	2.47	17.45	16.13
67	20.58	19.17	17.18	15.34	2.29	17.58	16.26
68	20.76	19.34	17.35	15.51	2.12	17.70	16.38
69	20.92	19.51	17.52	15.67	1.96	17.82	16.50
70	21.08	19.67	17.68	15.83	1.80	17.94	16.62
71	21.23	19.82	17.83	15.98	1.65	18.05	16.73
72	21.37	19.96	17.97	16.12	1.50	18.15	16.83
73	21.51	20.10	18.11	16.26	1.37	18.25	16.93
74	21.64	20.23	18.24	16.39	1.24	18.34	17.02
75	21.76	20.35	18.36	16.51	1.12	18.42	17.10

3% pa Life multiplier—29.97			3.5% pa Life multiplier—26.69				
E.M. 21	*E.M. 24*	*P.M.*	*E.M. 16*	*E.M. 18*	*E.M. 21*	*E.M. 24*	*P.M.*
11.32	9.64	4.71	12.71	11.47	9.78	8.25	3.51
11.56	9.88	4.47	12.90	11.66	9.97	8.44	3.32
11.79	10.11	4.24	13.08	11.85	10.15	8.62	3.14
12.01	10.33	4.02	13.25	12.02	10.32	8.80	2.96
12.23	10.55	3.80	13.42	12.19	10.49	8.97	2.80
12.44	10.76	3.59	13.58	12.35	10.66	9.13	2.63
12.64	10.96	3.39	13.74	12.51	10.81	9.28	2.48
12.83	11.15	3.20	13.89	12.66	10.96	9.43	2.33
13.02	11.34	3.01	14.04	12.80	11.11	9.58	2.18
13.20	11.52	2.83	14.17	12.94	11.24	9.72	2.04
13.37	11.69	2.65	14.31	13.07	11.38	9.85	1.91
13.54	11.86	2.49	14.43	13.20	11.50	9.98	1.78
13.70	12.02	2.32	14.56	13.32	11.63	10.10	1.66
13.86	12.18	2.17	14.67	13.44	11.74	10.21	1.55
14.01	12.33	2.02	14.78	13.55	11.85	10.33	1.43
14.15	12.47	1.88	14.89	13.66	11.96	10.43	1.33
14.29	12.61	1.74	14.99	13.76	12.06	10.53	1.23
14.42	12.74	1.61	15.09	13.86	12.16	10.63	1.13
14.55	12.87	1.48	15.18	13.95	12.25	10.72	1.04
14.67	12.99	1.36	15.27	14.03	12.34	10.81	0.95
14.78	13.10	1.25	15.35	14.12	12.42	10.89	0.87
14.89	13.21	1.14	15.43	14.20	12.50	10.97	0.79
14.99	13.31	1.04	15.50	14.27	12.57	11.04	0.72
15.09	13.41	0.94	15.57	14.34	12.64	11.11	0.65
15.18	13.50	0.85	15.64	14.40	12.71	11.18	0.58
15.27	13.59	0.76	15.70	14.46	12.77	11.24	0.52

Females aged 4

Retirement age	2.5% pa Life multiplier—33.83						
	E.M. 16	*E.M. 18*	*E.M. 21*	*E.M. 24*	*P.M.*	*E.M. 16*	*E.M. 18*
50	16.96	15.51	13.47	11.57	6.50	14.91	13.56
51	17.26	15.82	13.78	11.88	6.19	15.16	13.80
52	17.56	16.11	14.07	12.18	5.89	15.40	14.04
53	17.85	16.40	14.36	12.47	5.60	15.63	14.27
54	18.14	16.69	14.65	12.75	5.32	15.85	14.49
55	18.41	16.96	14.92	13.03	5.05	16.06	14.70
56	18.68	17.23	15.19	13.29	4.78	16.27	14.91
57	18.93	17.49	15.45	13.55	4.52	16.47	15.11
58	19.19	17.74	15.70	13.80	4.27	16.66	15.30
59	19.43	17.98	15.94	14.05	4.03	16.85	15.49
60	19.66	18.22	16.18	14.28	3.79	17.03	15.67
61	19.89	18.44	16.40	14.51	3.56	17.20	15.84
62	20.11	18.66	16.62	14.73	3.34	17.37	16.01
63	20.33	18.88	16.84	14.94	3.13	17.53	16.17
64	20.53	19.08	17.04	15.15	2.92	17.68	16.33
65	20.73	19.28	17.24	15.35	2.72	17.83	16.47
66	20.92	19.47	17.43	15.54	2.53	17.97	16.61
67	21.10	19.66	17.62	15.72	2.35	18.11	16.75
68	21.28	19.83	17.79	15.90	2.17	18.24	16.88
69	21.45	20.00	17.96	16.07	2.01	18.36	17.00
70	21.61	20.16	18.12	16.23	1.84	18.48	17.12
71	21.76	20.32	18.28	16.38	1.69	18.59	17.23
72	21.91	20.46	18.42	16.53	1.54	18.70	17.34
73	22.05	20.60	18.56	16.67	1.40	18.80	17.44
74	22.18	20.74	18.70	16.80	1.27	18.89	17.53
75	22.31	20.86	18.82	16.93	1.14	18.98	17.62

3% pa Life multiplier—29.86			**3.5% pa Life multiplier—26.61**				
E.M. 21	*E.M. 24*	*P.M.*	*E.M. 16*	*E.M. 18*	*E.M. 21*	*E.M. 24*	*P.M.*
11.66	9.93	4.85	13.16	11.88	10.12	8.54	3.63
11.91	10.18	4.60	13.35	12.07	10.32	8.74	3.44
12.15	10.42	4.37	13.54	12.26	10.51	8.93	3.25
12.37	10.64	4.14	13.72	12.44	10.69	9.11	3.07
12.60	10.87	3.92	13.90	12.62	10.86	9.28	2.89
12.81	11.08	3.70	14.06	12.79	11.03	9.45	2.73
13.02	11.29	3.49	14.23	12.95	11.19	9.61	2.56
13.22	11.49	3.29	14.38	13.10	11.35	9.77	2.41
13.41	11.68	3.10	14.53	13.25	11.50	9.92	2.26
13.60	11.87	2.91	14.67	13.40	11.64	10.06	2.12
13.78	12.05	2.73	14.81	13.53	11.78	10.20	1.98
13.95	12.22	2.56	14.94	13.67	11.91	10.33	1.85
14.12	12.39	2.39	15.07	13.79	12.04	10.45	1.72
14.28	12.55	2.23	15.19	13.91	12.16	10.57	1.60
14.43	12.70	2.08	15.30	14.03	12.27	10.69	1.48
14.58	12.85	1.93	15.41	14.14	12.38	10.80	1.37
14.72	12.99	1.79	15.52	14.24	12.49	10.91	1.27
14.86	13.13	1.66	15.62	14.34	12.59	11.01	1.17
14.99	13.26	1.53	15.71	14.44	12.68	11.10	1.07
15.11	13.38	1.40	15.81	14.53	12.77	11.19	0.98
15.23	13.50	1.29	15.89	14.61	12.86	11.28	0.90
15.34	13.61	1.17	15.97	14.70	12.94	11.36	0.82
15.45	13.71	1.07	16.05	14.77	13.02	11.43	0.74
15.55	13.82	0.97	16.12	14.84	13.09	11.51	0.67
15.64	13.91	0.87	16.19	14.91	13.16	11.57	0.60
15.73	14.00	0.78	16.25	14.97	13.22	11.64	0.54

Females aged 5

Retirement age	2.5% pa Life multiplier—33.67						
	E.M. 16	*E.M. 18*	*E.M. 21*	*E.M. 24*	*P.M.*	*E.M. 16*	*E.M. 18*
50	17.38	15.90	13.81	11.87	6.66	15.37	13.96
51	17.70	16.21	14.12	12.18	6.35	15.62	14.22
52	18.00	16.52	14.43	12.49	6.04	15.86	14.46
53	18.30	16.82	14.73	12.79	5.74	16.10	14.70
54	18.59	17.11	15.02	13.07	5.45	16.33	14.93
55	18.87	17.39	15.30	13.36	5.17	16.55	15.15
56	19.15	17.66	15.57	13.63	4.90	16.76	15.36
57	19.41	17.93	15.83	13.89	4.63	16.97	15.57
58	19.67	18.18	16.09	14.15	4.38	17.17	15.77
59	19.92	18.43	16.34	14.40	4.13	17.36	15.96
60	20.16	18.67	16.58	14.64	3.89	17.54	16.14
61	20.39	18.91	16.82	14.88	3.65	17.72	16.32
62	20.62	19.13	17.04	15.10	3.43	17.89	16.49
63	20.84	19.35	17.26	15.32	3.21	18.06	16.66
64	21.05	19.56	17.47	15.53	3.00	18.22	16.82
65	21.25	19.77	17.68	15.73	2.79	18.37	16.97
66	21.45	19.96	17.87	15.93	2.60	18.52	17.12
67	21.64	20.15	18.06	16.12	2.41	18.66	17.26
68	21.82	20.33	18.24	16.30	2.23	18.79	17.39
69	21.99	20.50	18.41	16.47	2.06	18.92	17.52
70	22.15	20.67	18.58	16.64	1.89	19.04	17.64
71	22.31	20.83	18.74	16.80	1.73	19.15	17.75
72	22.46	20.98	18.89	16.95	1.58	19.26	17.86
73	22.61	21.12	19.03	17.09	1.44	19.36	17.96
74	22.74	21.26	19.17	17.23	1.30	19.46	18.06
75	22.87	21.39	19.30	17.35	1.17	19.55	18.15

3% pa Life multiplier—29.75			3.5% pa Life multiplier—26.53				
E.M. 21	*E.M. 24*	*P.M.*	*E.M. 16*	*E.M. 18*	*E.M. 21*	*E.M. 24*	*P.M.*
12.02	10.23	5.00	13.62	12.30	10.48	8.84	3.76
12.27	10.49	4.74	13.82	12.50	10.68	9.04	3.56
12.51	10.73	4.50	14.02	12.69	10.88	9.24	3.36
12.75	10.97	4.26	14.20	12.88	11.06	9.43	3.18
12.98	11.19	4.03	14.38	13.06	11.25	9.61	3.00
13.20	11.42	3.81	14.56	13.24	11.42	9.78	2.82
13.41	11.63	3.60	14.73	13.40	11.59	9.95	2.65
13.62	11.84	3.39	14.89	13.57	11.75	10.11	2.49
13.82	12.03	3.19	15.04	13.72	11.90	10.26	2.34
14.01	12.23	3.00	15.19	13.87	12.05	10.41	2.19
14.19	12.41	2.82	15.33	14.01	12.19	10.55	2.05
14.37	12.59	2.64	15.47	14.15	12.33	10.69	1.91
14.54	12.76	2.47	15.60	14.28	12.46	10.82	1.78
14.71	12.93	2.30	15.72	14.40	12.58	10.95	1.66
14.87	13.09	2.14	15.84	14.52	12.70	11.07	1.54
15.02	13.24	1.99	15.96	14.64	12.82	11.18	1.42
15.17	13.38	1.85	16.07	14.74	12.93	11.29	1.31
15.31	13.52	1.71	16.17	14.85	13.03	11.39	1.21
15.44	13.66	1.57	16.27	14.95	13.13	11.49	1.11
15.57	13.78	1.45	16.36	15.04	13.22	11.58	1.02
15.69	13.90	1.32	16.45	15.13	13.31	11.67	0.93
15.80	14.02	1.21	16.53	15.21	13.39	11.76	0.85
15.91	14.13	1.10	16.61	15.29	13.47	11.84	0.77
16.01	14.23	1.00	16.69	15.37	13.55	11.91	0.69
16.11	14.33	0.90	16.76	15.44	13.62	11.98	0.62
16.20	14.42	0.81	16.82	15.50	13.68	12.05	0.56

Females aged 6

Retirement age	2.5% pa Life multiplier—33.51						
	E.M. 16	*E.M. 18*	*E.M. 21*	*E.M. 24*	*P.M.*	*E.M. 16*	*E.M. 18*
50	17.82	16.30	14.15	12.17	6.83	15.83	14.39
51	18.14	16.62	14.48	12.49	6.51	16.09	14.65
52	18.46	16.94	14.79	12.80	6.19	16.34	14.90
53	18.76	17.24	15.10	13.11	5.89	16.58	15.14
54	19.06	17.54	15.39	13.40	5.59	16.82	15.38
55	19.35	17.83	15.68	13.69	5.30	17.05	15.60
56	19.63	18.11	15.96	13.97	5.02	17.27	15.82
57	19.90	18.38	16.23	14.24	4.75	17.48	16.04
58	20.16	18.64	16.50	14.51	4.49	17.68	16.24
59	20.42	18.90	16.75	14.76	4.23	17.88	16.44
60	20.67	19.14	17.00	15.01	3.98	18.07	16.63
61	20.91	19.38	17.24	15.25	3.74	18.26	16.81
62	21.14	19.62	17.47	15.48	3.51	18.43	16.99
63	21.36	19.84	17.70	15.71	3.29	18.60	17.16
64	21.58	20.06	17.91	15.92	3.07	18.77	17.33
65	21.79	20.26	18.12	16.13	2.86	18.92	17.48
66	21.99	20.47	18.32	16.33	2.66	19.07	17.63
67	22.18	20.66	18.51	16.52	2.47	19.22	17.78
68	22.37	20.84	18.70	16.71	2.29	19.36	17.91
69	22.54	21.02	18.88	16.89	2.11	19.49	18.04
70	22.71	21.19	19.05	17.06	1.94	19.61	18.17
71	22.87	21.35	19.21	17.22	1.78	19.73	18.29
72	23.03	21.51	19.36	17.37	1.62	19.84	18.40
73	23.18	21.65	19.51	17.52	1.47	19.95	18.51
74	23.32	21.79	19.65	17.66	1.33	20.05	18.61
75	23.45	21.93	19.78	17.79	1.20	20.14	18.70

3% pa Life multiplier—29.63			**3.5% pa Life multiplier—26.45**				
E.M. 21	*E.M. 24*	*P.M.*	*E.M. 16*	*E.M. 18*	*E.M. 21*	*E.M. 24*	*P.M.*
12.38	10.54	5.15	14.10	12.73	10.85	9.15	3.89
12.64	10.80	4.89	14.31	12.94	11.06	9.36	3.68
12.89	11.05	4.64	14.51	13.14	11.26	9.56	3.48
13.13	11.30	4.39	14.70	13.34	11.45	9.76	3.29
13.37	11.53	4.16	14.89	13.52	11.64	9.95	3.10
13.60	11.76	3.93	15.07	13.70	11.82	10.13	2.92
13.82	11.98	3.71	15.24	13.88	11.99	10.30	2.75
14.03	12.19	3.50	15.41	14.04	12.16	10.47	2.58
14.23	12.40	3.29	15.57	14.20	12.32	10.63	2.42
14.43	12.60	3.09	15.72	14.36	12.47	10.78	2.27
14.62	12.79	2.90	15.87	14.50	12.62	10.93	2.12
14.81	12.97	2.72	16.01	14.64	12.76	11.07	1.98
14.98	13.15	2.54	16.15	14.78	12.90	11.20	1.84
15.15	13.32	2.37	16.28	14.91	13.03	11.33	1.71
15.32	13.48	2.21	16.40	15.03	13.15	11.46	1.59
15.47	13.64	2.05	16.52	15.15	13.27	11.57	1.47
15.62	13.79	1.90	16.63	15.26	13.38	11.69	1.36
15.77	13.93	1.76	16.74	15.37	13.49	11.79	1.25
15.90	14.07	1.62	16.84	15.47	13.59	11.90	1.15
16.04	14.20	1.49	16.94	15.57	13.69	11.99	1.05
16.16	14.32	1.36	17.03	15.66	13.78	12.08	0.96
16.28	14.44	1.25	17.11	15.75	13.87	12.17	0.88
16.39	14.55	1.13	17.20	15.83	13.95	12.25	0.79
16.50	14.66	1.03	17.27	15.91	14.02	12.33	0.72
16.60	14.76	0.93	17.35	15.98	14.10	12.40	0.64
16.69	14.86	0.83	17.41	16.05	14.16	12.47	0.58

Females aged 7

Retirement age	2.5% pa Life multiplier—33.34						
	E.M. 16	*E.M. 18*	*E.M. 21*	*E.M. 24*	*P.M.*	*E.M. 16*	*E.M. 18*
50	18.27	16.71	14.51	12.47	7.00	16.31	14.82
51	18.60	17.04	14.84	12.80	6.67	16.57	15.09
52	18.92	17.36	15.16	13.12	6.35	16.83	15.35
53	19.23	17.67	15.48	13.44	6.04	17.08	15.60
54	19.54	17.98	15.78	13.74	5.73	17.33	15.84
55	19.83	18.27	16.08	14.04	5.44	17.56	16.07
56	20.12	18.56	16.36	14.32	5.15	17.79	16.30
57	20.40	18.84	16.64	14.60	4.87	18.01	16.52
58	20.67	19.11	16.91	14.87	4.60	18.22	16.73
59	20.93	19.37	17.17	15.13	4.34	18.42	16.94
60	21.19	19.63	17.43	15.39	4.08	18.62	17.13
61	21.43	19.87	17.67	15.63	3.84	18.81	17.32
62	21.67	20.11	17.91	15.87	3.60	18.99	17.50
63	21.90	20.34	18.14	16.10	3.37	19.17	17.68
64	22.12	20.56	18.36	16.32	3.15	19.33	17.85
65	22.33	20.77	18.58	16.54	2.94	19.50	18.01
66	22.54	20.98	18.78	16.74	2.73	19.65	18.16
67	22.74	21.18	18.98	16.94	2.53	19.80	18.31
68	22.93	21.37	19.17	17.13	2.34	19.94	18.45
69	23.11	21.55	19.35	17.31	2.16	20.07	18.59
70	23.28	21.72	19.53	17.49	1.99	20.20	18.72
71	23.45	21.89	19.69	17.65	1.82	20.32	18.84
72	23.61	22.05	19.85	17.81	1.66	20.44	18.95
73	23.76	22.20	20.00	17.96	1.51	20.55	19.06
74	23.90	22.34	20.14	18.10	1.37	20.65	19.17
75	24.04	22.48	20.28	18.24	1.23	20.75	19.26

3% pa Life multiplier—29.51			3.5% pa Life multiplier—26.36				
E.M. 21	*E.M. 24*	*P.M.*	*E.M. 16*	*E.M. 18*	*E.M. 21*	*E.M. 24*	*P.M.*
12.75	10.86	5.30	14.59	13.18	11.23	9.47	4.03
13.02	11.13	5.03	14.81	13.39	11.45	9.69	3.81
13.28	11.39	4.78	15.02	13.60	11.66	9.90	3.60
13.53	11.64	4.52	15.22	13.80	11.86	10.10	3.40
13.77	11.88	4.28	15.41	14.00	12.05	10.30	3.21
14.01	12.11	4.05	15.60	14.18	12.24	10.48	3.02
14.23	12.34	3.82	15.78	14.36	12.42	10.66	2.84
14.45	12.56	3.60	15.95	14.54	12.59	10.83	2.67
14.66	12.77	3.39	16.12	14.70	12.75	11.00	2.51
14.87	12.98	3.19	16.28	14.86	12.91	11.16	2.35
15.06	13.17	2.99	16.43	15.01	13.07	11.31	2.20
15.25	13.36	2.80	16.57	15.16	13.21	11.46	2.05
15.44	13.54	2.62	16.71	15.30	13.35	11.60	1.91
15.61	13.72	2.44	16.85	15.43	13.49	11.73	1.77
15.78	13.89	2.27	16.98	15.56	13.61	11.86	1.65
15.94	14.05	2.11	17.10	15.68	13.74	11.98	1.52
16.09	14.20	1.96	17.22	15.80	13.85	12.10	1.41
16.24	14.35	1.81	17.33	15.91	13.96	12.21	1.30
16.38	14.49	1.67	17.43	16.02	14.07	12.31	1.19
16.52	14.63	1.53	17.53	16.12	14.17	12.41	1.09
16.65	14.76	1.41	17.63	16.21	14.26	12.51	1.00
16.77	14.88	1.28	17.72	16.30	14.35	12.60	0.91
16.89	14.99	1.17	17.80	16.39	14.44	12.68	0.82
16.99	15.10	1.06	17.88	16.47	14.52	12.76	0.74
17.10	15.21	0.95	17.96	16.54	14.59	12.84	0.67
17.20	15.30	0.86	18.03	16.61	14.66	12.91	0.60

Females aged 8

Retirement age	2.5% pa Life multiplier—33.16						
	E.M. 16	*E.M. 18*	*E.M. 21*	*E.M. 24*	*P.M.*	*E.M. 16*	*E.M. 18*
50	18.73	17.13	14.88	12.78	7.18	16.80	15.27
51	19.07	17.47	15.21	13.12	6.84	17.07	15.54
52	19.40	17.80	15.54	13.45	6.51	17.34	15.81
53	19.72	18.12	15.87	13.77	6.19	17.60	16.07
54	20.03	18.43	16.18	14.09	5.88	17.85	16.32
55	20.33	18.73	16.48	14.39	5.57	18.09	16.56
56	20.63	19.03	16.77	14.68	5.28	18.32	16.79
57	20.91	19.31	17.06	14.97	4.99	18.55	17.02
58	21.19	19.59	17.34	15.25	4.72	18.77	17.24
59	21.46	19.86	17.61	15.51	4.45	18.98	17.45
60	21.72	20.12	17.87	15.78	4.19	19.18	17.65
61	21.97	20.37	18.12	16.03	3.93	19.37	17.84
62	22.21	20.62	18.36	16.27	3.69	19.56	18.03
63	22.45	20.85	18.60	16.51	3.46	19.74	18.21
64	22.68	21.08	18.82	16.73	3.23	19.92	18.39
65	22.90	21.30	19.04	16.95	3.01	20.08	18.55
66	23.11	21.51	19.25	17.16	2.80	20.24	18.71
67	23.31	21.71	19.46	17.37	2.60	20.39	18.86
68	23.50	21.90	19.65	17.56	2.40	20.54	19.01
69	23.69	22.09	19.84	17.75	2.22	20.68	19.15
70	23.87	22.27	20.02	17.93	2.04	20.81	19.28
71	24.04	22.44	20.19	18.10	1.87	20.94	19.41
72	24.20	22.60	20.35	18.26	1.70	21.06	19.53
73	24.36	22.76	20.50	18.41	1.55	21.17	19.64
74	24.50	22.90	20.65	18.56	1.40	21.28	19.74
75	24.64	23.04	20.79	18.70	1.26	21.38	19.85

3% pa Life multiplier—29.38			**3.5% pa Life multiplier—26.27**				
E.M. 21	*E.M. 24*	*P.M.*	*E.M. 16*	*E.M. 18*	*E.M. 21*	*E.M. 24*	*P.M.*
13.14	11.19	5.46	15.11	13.64	11.62	9.81	4.17
13.41	11.46	5.19	15.33	13.86	11.85	10.03	3.95
13.68	11.73	4.92	15.55	14.08	12.06	10.25	3.73
13.94	11.99	4.66	15.75	14.29	12.27	10.46	3.52
14.19	12.24	4.41	15.96	14.49	12.47	10.66	3.32
14.43	12.48	4.17	16.15	14.68	12.67	10.85	3.13
14.66	12.71	3.94	16.33	14.87	12.85	11.04	2.94
14.89	12.94	3.71	16.51	15.05	13.03	11.21	2.77
15.10	13.16	3.49	16.68	15.22	13.20	11.39	2.59
15.31	13.37	3.28	16.85	15.38	13.37	11.55	2.43
15.52	13.57	3.08	17.01	15.54	13.52	11.71	2.27
15.71	13.76	2.88	17.16	15.69	13.68	11.86	2.12
15.90	13.95	2.70	17.30	15.84	13.82	12.00	1.98
16.08	14.13	2.52	17.44	15.98	13.96	12.14	1.84
16.25	14.31	2.34	17.57	16.11	14.09	12.27	1.70
16.42	14.47	2.18	17.70	16.23	14.22	12.40	1.58
16.58	14.63	2.02	17.82	16.35	14.34	12.52	1.46
16.73	14.78	1.86	17.94	16.47	14.45	12.64	1.34
16.88	14.93	1.72	18.04	16.58	14.56	12.75	1.23
17.02	15.07	1.58	18.15	16.68	14.67	12.85	1.13
17.15	15.20	1.45	18.25	16.78	14.76	12.95	1.03
17.28	15.33	1.32	18.34	16.87	14.86	13.04	0.94
17.39	15.45	1.20	18.43	16.96	14.95	13.13	0.85
17.51	15.56	1.09	18.51	17.04	15.03	13.21	0.77
17.61	15.67	0.98	18.59	17.12	15.11	13.29	0.69
17.71	15.77	0.88	18.66	17.19	15.18	13.36	0.62

Females aged 9

Retirement age	2.5% pa Life multiplier—32.98						
	E.M. 16	*E.M. 18*	*E.M. 21*	*E.M. 24*	*P.M.*	*E.M. 16*	*E.M. 18*
50	19.20	17.56	15.25	13.11	7.36	17.30	15.73
51	19.55	17.91	15.60	13.45	7.01	17.59	16.01
52	19.89	18.25	15.94	13.79	6.67	17.86	16.29
53	20.21	18.57	16.26	14.12	6.34	18.13	16.55
54	20.53	18.89	16.58	14.44	6.02	18.39	16.81
55	20.84	19.20	16.89	14.75	5.71	18.64	17.06
56	21.15	19.51	17.20	15.05	5.41	18.88	17.30
57	21.44	19.80	17.49	15.35	5.12	19.11	17.53
58	21.72	20.08	17.77	15.63	4.83	19.33	17.76
59	22.00	20.36	18.05	15.90	4.56	19.55	17.97
60	22.26	20.63	18.32	16.17	4.29	19.76	18.18
61	22.52	20.88	18.57	16.43	4.03	19.96	18.38
62	22.77	21.13	18.82	16.68	3.78	20.15	18.58
63	23.01	21.37	19.06	16.92	3.54	20.34	18.76
64	23.25	21.61	19.30	17.15	3.31	20.52	18.94
65	23.47	21.83	19.52	17.38	3.09	20.69	19.11
66	23.69	22.05	19.74	17.59	2.87	20.85	19.28
67	23.90	22.26	19.95	17.80	2.66	21.01	19.43
68	24.09	22.46	20.15	18.00	2.46	21.16	19.58
69	24.29	22.65	20.34	18.19	2.27	21.30	19.73
70	24.47	22.83	20.52	18.38	2.09	21.44	19.86
71	24.64	23.00	20.69	18.55	1.91	21.57	19.99
72	24.81	23.17	20.86	18.72	1.75	21.69	20.11
73	24.97	23.33	21.02	18.88	1.59	21.81	20.23
74	25.12	23.48	21.17	19.03	1.44	21.92	20.34
75	25.26	23.62	21.31	19.17	1.30	22.02	20.44

3% pa Life multiplier—29.25			3.5% pa Life multiplier—26.17				
E.M. 21	*E.M. 24*	*P.M.*	*E.M. 16*	*E.M. 18*	*E.M. 21*	*E.M. 24*	*P.M.*
13.53	11.52	5.63	15.64	14.12	12.03	10.15	4.32
13.82	11.81	5.34	15.87	14.35	12.27	10.38	4.09
14.09	12.08	5.07	16.09	14.58	12.49	10.61	3.86
14.36	12.35	4.80	16.31	14.79	12.70	10.82	3.65
14.61	12.61	4.54	16.52	15.00	12.91	11.03	3.44
14.86	12.86	4.29	16.72	15.20	13.11	11.23	3.24
15.10	13.10	4.05	16.91	15.39	13.30	11.42	3.05
15.34	13.33	3.82	17.09	15.58	13.49	11.61	2.86
15.56	13.55	3.60	17.27	15.75	13.67	11.79	2.69
15.78	13.77	3.38	17.44	15.92	13.84	11.96	2.52
15.99	13.98	3.17	17.60	16.09	14.00	12.12	2.35
16.19	14.18	2.97	17.76	16.24	14.16	12.28	2.20
16.38	14.37	2.78	17.91	16.39	14.31	12.43	2.05
16.57	14.56	2.59	18.05	16.54	14.45	12.57	1.90
16.74	14.74	2.41	18.19	16.67	14.59	12.71	1.76
16.92	14.91	2.24	18.32	16.80	14.72	12.84	1.63
17.08	15.07	2.08	18.45	16.93	14.84	12.96	1.51
17.24	15.23	1.92	18.57	17.05	14.96	13.08	1.39
17.39	15.38	1.77	18.68	17.16	15.07	13.19	1.28
17.53	15.52	1.63	18.79	17.27	15.18	13.30	1.17
17.67	15.66	1.49	18.89	17.37	15.28	13.40	1.07
17.80	15.79	1.36	18.98	17.47	15.38	13.50	0.97
17.92	15.91	1.24	19.07	17.56	15.47	13.59	0.88
18.03	16.03	1.12	19.16	17.64	15.56	13.68	0.80
18.14	16.14	1.01	19.24	17.72	15.64	13.76	0.72
18.25	16.24	0.91	19.32	17.80	15.71	13.83	0.64

Females aged 10

Retirement age	2.5% pa Life multiplier—32.80						
	E.M. 16	*E.M. 18*	*E.M. 21*	*E.M. 24*	*P.M.*	*E.M. 16*	*E.M. 18*
50	19.68	18.00	15.63	13.44	7.54	17.83	16.20
51	20.04	18.36	15.99	13.79	7.19	18.12	16.49
52	20.39	18.70	16.34	14.14	6.84	18.40	16.78
53	20.72	19.04	16.67	14.48	6.50	18.68	17.05
54	21.05	19.37	17.00	14.80	6.17	18.94	17.32
55	21.37	19.69	17.32	15.12	5.86	19.20	17.57
56	21.68	20.00	17.63	15.43	5.55	19.44	17.82
57	21.98	20.30	17.93	15.73	5.25	19.68	18.06
58	22.27	20.59	18.22	16.02	4.96	19.92	18.29
59	22.55	20.87	18.50	16.30	4.67	20.14	18.51
60	22.82	21.14	18.78	16.58	4.40	20.35	18.73
61	23.09	21.41	19.04	16.84	4.14	20.56	18.94
62	23.35	21.66	19.30	17.10	3.88	20.76	19.14
63	23.59	21.91	19.54	17.35	3.63	20.95	19.33
64	23.83	22.15	19.78	17.59	3.39	21.14	19.51
65	24.06	22.38	20.01	17.82	3.16	21.31	19.69
66	24.28	22.60	20.23	18.04	2.94	21.48	19.86
67	24.50	22.82	20.45	18.25	2.73	21.64	20.02
68	24.70	23.02	20.65	18.45	2.52	21.80	20.17
69	24.90	23.22	20.85	18.65	2.33	21.94	20.32
70	25.08	23.40	21.03	18.84	2.14	22.08	20.46
71	25.26	23.58	21.21	19.02	1.96	22.22	20.59
72	25.43	23.75	21.38	19.19	1.79	22.34	20.72
73	25.60	23.92	21.55	19.35	1.63	22.46	20.84
74	25.75	24.07	21.70	19.50	1.47	22.58	20.95
75	25.90	24.21	21.85	19.65	1.33	22.68	21.06

3% pa Life multiplier—29.12			3.5% pa Life multiplier—26.08				
E.M. 21	*E.M. 24*	*P.M.*	*E.M. 16*	*E.M. 18*	*E.M. 21*	*E.M. 24*	*P.M.*
13.94	11.87	5.80	16.19	14.62	12.46	10.51	4.47
14.23	12.16	5.50	16.43	14.86	12.70	10.75	4.23
14.52	12.45	5.22	16.66	15.09	12.93	10.98	4.00
14.79	12.72	4.95	16.88	15.31	13.15	11.20	3.78
15.05	12.99	4.68	17.10	15.53	13.37	11.42	3.56
15.31	13.24	4.42	17.30	15.73	13.57	11.63	3.35
15.56	13.49	4.18	17.50	15.93	13.77	11.82	3.15
15.80	13.73	3.94	17.69	16.12	13.96	12.02	2.96
16.03	13.96	3.71	17.88	16.31	14.15	12.20	2.78
16.25	14.18	3.48	18.05	16.48	14.32	12.38	2.60
16.47	14.40	3.27	18.22	16.65	14.49	12.54	2.43
16.67	14.61	3.06	18.38	16.81	14.65	12.71	2.27
16.87	14.81	2.86	18.54	16.97	14.81	12.86	2.12
17.06	15.00	2.67	18.69	17.12	14.96	13.01	1.97
17.25	15.18	2.49	18.83	17.26	15.10	13.15	1.83
17.43	15.36	2.31	18.97	17.40	15.24	13.29	1.69
17.59	15.53	2.14	19.09	17.52	15.36	13.42	1.56
17.76	15.69	1.98	19.22	17.65	15.49	13.54	1.44
17.91	15.84	1.82	19.33	17.76	15.60	13.66	1.32
18.06	15.99	1.68	19.45	17.88	15.72	13.77	1.21
18.20	16.13	1.54	19.55	17.98	15.82	13.87	1.11
18.33	16.26	1.40	19.65	18.08	15.92	13.97	1.01
18.46	16.39	1.28	19.74	18.17	16.01	14.07	0.91
18.58	16.51	1.16	19.83	18.26	16.10	14.16	0.82
18.69	16.62	1.04	19.92	18.35	16.19	14.24	0.74
18.80	16.73	0.94	19.99	18.42	16.26	14.32	0.66

Females aged 11

Retirement age	2.5% pa Life multiplier—32.61						
	E.M. 16	*E.M. 18*	*E.M. 21*	*E.M. 24*	*P.M.*	*E.M. 16*	*E.M. 18*
50	20.18	18.45	16.03	13.77	7.73	18.36	16.69
51	20.54	18.82	16.39	14.14	7.37	18.66	16.99
52	20.90	19.17	16.75	14.49	7.01	18.96	17.28
53	21.24	19.52	17.09	14.84	6.67	19.24	17.56
54	21.58	19.86	17.43	15.18	6.33	19.51	17.84
55	21.91	20.18	17.75	15.50	6.00	19.78	18.10
56	22.22	20.50	18.07	15.82	5.69	20.03	18.36
57	22.53	20.81	18.38	16.13	5.38	20.28	18.60
58	22.83	21.11	18.68	16.43	5.08	20.52	18.84
59	23.12	21.40	18.97	16.71	4.79	20.75	19.07
60	23.40	21.68	19.25	17.00	4.51	20.97	19.29
61	23.67	21.95	19.52	17.27	4.24	21.18	19.51
62	23.93	22.21	19.78	17.53	3.98	21.39	19.71
63	24.19	22.46	20.03	17.78	3.72	21.58	19.91
64	24.43	22.71	20.28	18.03	3.48	21.77	20.10
65	24.67	22.94	20.52	18.26	3.24	21.95	20.28
66	24.89	23.17	20.74	18.49	3.02	22.13	20.45
67	25.11	23.39	20.96	18.71	2.80	22.29	20.62
68	25.32	23.60	21.17	18.92	2.59	22.45	20.78
69	25.52	23.80	21.37	19.12	2.39	22.61	20.93
70	25.71	23.99	21.56	19.31	2.19	22.75	21.08
71	25.90	24.18	21.75	19.49	2.01	22.89	21.21
72	26.07	24.35	21.92	19.67	1.84	23.02	21.34
73	26.24	24.52	22.09	19.84	1.67	23.14	21.47
74	26.40	24.67	22.25	19.99	1.51	23.26	21.58
75	26.55	24.82	22.40	20.14	1.36	23.37	21.69

3% pa Life multiplier—28.98			3.5% pa Life multiplier—25.97				
E.M. 21	*E.M. 24*	*P.M.*	*E.M. 16*	*E.M. 18*	*E.M. 21*	*E.M. 24*	*P.M.*
14.36	12.23	5.97	16.75	15.13	12.89	10.88	4.63
14.66	12.53	5.67	17.00	15.38	13.14	11.13	4.38
14.95	12.82	5.38	17.24	15.62	13.38	11.37	4.14
15.23	13.10	5.09	17.47	15.85	13.61	11.60	3.91
15.51	13.38	4.82	17.70	16.07	13.84	11.82	3.69
15.77	13.64	4.56	17.91	16.29	14.05	12.03	3.47
16.03	13.90	4.30	18.12	16.49	14.26	12.24	3.27
16.27	14.14	4.06	18.31	16.69	14.45	12.44	3.07
16.51	14.38	3.82	18.50	16.88	14.64	12.63	2.88
16.74	14.61	3.59	18.69	17.06	14.83	12.81	2.70
16.96	14.83	3.37	18.86	17.24	15.00	12.99	2.52
17.18	15.05	3.15	19.03	17.40	15.17	13.15	2.35
17.38	15.25	2.95	19.19	17.57	15.33	13.31	2.19
17.58	15.45	2.75	19.34	17.72	15.48	13.47	2.04
17.77	15.64	2.56	19.49	17.87	15.63	13.62	1.89
17.95	15.82	2.38	19.63	18.01	15.77	13.76	1.75
18.12	15.99	2.20	19.77	18.14	15.90	13.89	1.62
18.29	16.16	2.04	19.89	18.27	16.03	14.02	1.49
18.45	16.32	1.88	20.01	18.39	16.15	14.14	1.37
18.60	16.47	1.73	20.13	18.50	16.27	14.25	1.25
18.75	16.62	1.58	20.24	18.61	16.38	14.36	1.14
18.88	16.75	1.45	20.34	18.72	16.48	14.46	1.04
19.02	16.88	1.31	20.44	18.81	16.58	14.56	0.94
19.14	17.01	1.19	20.53	18.90	16.67	14.65	0.85
19.25	17.12	1.08	20.62	18.99	16.75	14.74	0.77
19.36	17.23	0.97	20.70	19.07	16.83	14.82	0.69

Females aged 12

Retirement age	2.5% pa Life multiplier—32.42						
	E.M. 16	*E.M. 18*	*E.M. 21*	*E.M. 24*	*P.M.*	*E.M. 16*	*E.M. 18*
50	20.68	18.92	16.43	14.12	7.93	18.92	17.19
51	21.06	19.29	16.80	14.49	7.55	19.23	17.50
52	21.42	19.66	17.17	14.86	7.19	19.53	17.80
53	21.78	20.01	17.52	15.21	6.83	19.82	18.09
54	22.12	20.36	17.87	15.56	6.49	20.10	18.38
55	22.46	20.69	18.20	15.89	6.15	20.37	18.65
56	22.78	21.01	18.53	16.22	5.83	20.63	18.91
57	23.10	21.33	18.84	16.53	5.51	20.89	19.16
58	23.40	21.64	19.15	16.84	5.21	21.13	19.41
59	23.70	21.93	19.44	17.13	4.91	21.37	19.65
60	23.99	22.22	19.73	17.42	4.62	21.60	19.87
61	24.26	22.50	20.01	17.70	4.35	21.82	20.09
62	24.53	22.77	20.28	17.97	4.08	22.03	20.31
63	24.79	23.03	20.54	18.23	3.82	22.23	20.51
64	25.04	23.28	20.79	18.48	3.57	22.43	20.70
65	25.29	23.52	21.03	18.72	3.32	22.62	20.89
66	25.52	23.75	21.26	18.96	3.09	22.80	21.07
67	25.74	23.98	21.49	19.18	2.87	22.97	21.24
68	25.96	24.19	21.70	19.39	2.65	23.13	21.41
69	26.16	24.40	21.91	19.60	2.45	23.29	21.56
70	26.36	24.59	22.11	19.80	2.25	23.44	21.71
71	26.55	24.78	22.29	19.98	2.06	23.58	21.85
72	26.73	24.96	22.47	20.16	1.88	23.71	21.99
73	26.90	25.13	22.64	20.33	1.71	23.84	22.12
74	27.06	25.29	22.81	20.50	1.55	23.96	22.24
75	27.21	25.45	22.96	20.65	1.40	24.07	22.35

3% pa Life multiplier—28.84			3.5% pa Life multiplier—25.87				
E.M. 21	*E.M. 24*	*P.M.*	*E.M. 16*	*E.M. 18*	*E.M. 21*	*E.M. 24*	*P.M.*
14.79	12.60	6.15	17.34	15.66	13.35	11.26	4.79
15.10	12.91	5.84	17.60	15.92	13.60	11.52	4.53
15.40	13.21	5.54	17.85	16.17	13.85	11.77	4.28
15.69	13.50	5.25	18.09	16.41	14.09	12.01	4.05
15.98	13.78	4.97	18.32	16.64	14.32	12.24	3.82
16.25	14.05	4.69	18.54	16.86	14.54	12.46	3.59
16.51	14.32	4.43	18.75	17.07	14.76	12.67	3.38
16.76	14.57	4.18	18.96	17.28	14.96	12.88	3.18
17.01	14.82	3.93	19.16	17.47	15.16	13.07	2.98
17.25	15.05	3.70	19.34	17.66	15.35	13.26	2.79
17.47	15.28	3.47	19.53	17.84	15.53	13.44	2.61
17.69	15.50	3.25	19.70	18.02	15.70	13.62	2.44
17.91	15.71	3.04	19.87	18.18	15.87	13.78	2.27
18.11	15.91	2.83	20.02	18.34	16.03	13.94	2.11
18.30	16.11	2.64	20.18	18.49	16.18	14.09	1.96
18.49	16.30	2.45	20.32	18.64	16.32	14.24	1.81
18.67	16.48	2.27	20.46	18.78	16.46	14.38	1.67
18.84	16.65	2.10	20.59	18.91	16.59	14.51	1.54
19.01	16.81	1.94	20.72	19.04	16.72	14.63	1.42
19.16	16.97	1.78	20.84	19.15	16.84	14.75	1.30
19.31	17.12	1.63	20.95	19.27	16.95	14.87	1.18
19.45	17.26	1.49	21.06	19.37	17.06	14.97	1.08
19.59	17.39	1.35	21.16	19.47	17.16	15.07	0.98
19.72	17.52	1.23	21.25	19.57	17.25	15.17	0.88
19.84	17.64	1.11	21.34	19.66	17.34	15.26	0.79
19.95	17.75	0.99	21.42	19.74	17.43	15.34	0.71

Females aged 13

Retirement age	2.5% pa Life multiplier—32.22						
	E.M. 16	*E.M. 18*	*E.M. 21*	*E.M. 24*	*P.M.*	*E.M. 16*	*E.M. 18*
50	21.20	19.39	16.84	14.47	8.13	19.49	17.71
51	21.59	19.78	17.23	14.86	7.74	19.81	18.03
52	21.96	20.15	17.60	15.23	7.37	20.12	18.34
53	22.32	20.51	17.96	15.60	7.01	20.42	18.64
54	22.68	20.87	18.32	15.95	6.65	20.71	18.93
55	23.02	21.21	18.66	16.29	6.31	20.99	19.21
56	23.35	21.54	18.99	16.62	5.98	21.26	19.48
57	23.68	21.87	19.32	16.95	5.65	21.52	19.74
58	23.99	22.18	19.63	17.26	5.34	21.77	20.00
59	24.30	22.48	19.93	17.57	5.03	22.01	20.24
60	24.59	22.78	20.23	17.86	4.74	22.25	20.47
61	24.88	23.06	20.51	18.15	4.45	22.48	20.70
62	25.15	23.34	20.79	18.42	4.18	22.69	20.92
63	25.42	23.61	21.06	18.69	3.91	22.90	21.13
64	25.67	23.86	21.31	18.95	3.66	23.10	21.33
65	25.92	24.11	21.56	19.19	3.41	23.30	21.52
66	26.16	24.35	21.80	19.43	3.17	23.48	21.71
67	26.39	24.58	22.03	19.66	2.94	23.66	21.88
68	26.61	24.80	22.25	19.88	2.72	23.83	22.05
69	26.82	25.01	22.46	20.09	2.51	23.99	22.21
70	27.02	25.21	22.66	20.29	2.31	24.14	22.37
71	27.22	25.41	22.85	20.49	2.11	24.29	22.51
72	27.40	25.59	23.04	20.67	1.93	24.43	22.65
73	27.58	25.77	23.21	20.85	1.75	24.56	22.78
74	27.74	25.93	23.38	21.01	1.59	24.68	22.91
75	27.90	26.09	23.54	21.17	1.43	24.80	23.02

3% pa Life multiplier—28.69			3.5% pa Life multiplier—25.76				
E.M. 21	*E.M. 24*	*P.M.*	*E.M. 16*	*E.M. 18*	*E.M. 21*	*E.M. 24*	*P.M.*
15.24	12.98	6.34	17.95	16.21	13.82	11.66	4.96
15.56	13.30	6.02	18.22	16.48	14.08	11.92	4.69
15.87	13.61	5.71	18.48	16.74	14.34	12.18	4.43
16.17	13.91	5.41	18.72	16.98	14.59	12.43	4.19
16.46	14.20	5.12	18.96	17.22	14.82	12.67	3.95
16.74	14.48	4.84	19.19	17.45	15.05	12.90	3.72
17.01	14.75	4.57	19.41	17.67	15.27	13.12	3.50
17.27	15.01	4.30	19.62	17.88	15.49	13.33	3.29
17.52	15.26	4.05	19.83	18.09	15.69	13.53	3.08
17.77	15.51	3.81	20.02	18.28	15.89	13.73	2.89
18.00	15.74	3.57	20.21	18.47	16.07	13.91	2.70
18.23	15.97	3.35	20.39	18.65	16.25	14.09	2.52
18.45	16.19	3.13	20.56	18.82	16.43	14.27	2.35
18.65	16.39	2.92	20.73	18.99	16.59	14.43	2.18
18.86	16.60	2.72	20.89	19.14	16.75	14.59	2.03
19.05	16.79	2.52	21.04	19.29	16.90	14.74	1.88
19.23	16.97	2.34	21.18	19.44	17.04	14.88	1.73
19.41	17.15	2.16	21.32	19.57	17.18	15.02	1.60
19.58	17.32	1.99	21.45	19.70	17.31	15.15	1.47
19.74	17.48	1.83	21.57	19.83	17.43	15.27	1.34
19.89	17.63	1.68	21.69	19.94	17.55	15.39	1.23
20.04	17.78	1.53	21.80	20.05	17.66	15.50	1.12
20.18	17.92	1.40	21.90	20.16	17.76	15.60	1.01
20.31	18.05	1.26	22.00	20.26	17.86	15.70	0.91
20.43	18.17	1.14	22.09	20.35	17.95	15.79	0.82
20.55	18.29	1.02	22.18	20.44	18.04	15.88	0.74

Females aged 14

Retirement age	2.5% pa Life multiplier—32.02 E.M. 16	E.M. 18	E.M. 21	E.M. 24	P.M.	E.M. 16	E.M. 18
50	21.74	19.88	17.27	14.84	8.33	20.07	18.24
51	22.13	20.27	17.66	15.23	7.94	20.40	18.57
52	22.51	20.66	18.04	15.62	7.55	20.72	18.89
53	22.89	21.03	18.41	15.99	7.18	21.03	19.20
54	23.25	21.39	18.78	16.35	6.82	21.33	19.50
55	23.60	21.74	19.13	16.70	6.47	21.62	19.79
56	23.94	22.09	19.47	17.04	6.13	21.90	20.07
57	24.27	22.42	19.80	17.37	5.79	22.17	20.34
58	24.59	22.74	20.12	17.70	5.47	22.43	20.60
59	24.91	23.05	20.43	18.01	5.16	22.68	20.85
60	25.21	23.35	20.74	18.31	4.86	22.92	21.09
61	25.50	23.64	21.03	18.60	4.57	23.15	21.32
62	25.78	23.93	21.31	18.88	4.28	23.38	21.55
63	26.06	24.20	21.58	19.16	4.01	23.59	21.76
64	26.32	24.46	21.85	19.42	3.75	23.80	21.97
65	26.57	24.72	22.10	19.68	3.49	24.00	22.17
66	26.82	24.96	22.35	19.92	3.25	24.19	22.36
67	27.05	25.20	22.58	20.16	3.01	24.37	22.54
68	27.28	25.42	22.81	20.38	2.79	24.55	22.72
69	27.50	25.64	23.02	20.60	2.57	24.71	22.88
70	27.70	25.85	23.23	20.81	2.36	24.87	23.04
71	27.90	26.05	23.43	21.00	2.17	25.02	23.19
72	28.09	26.23	23.62	21.19	1.98	25.16	23.33
73	28.27	26.41	23.80	21.37	1.80	25.30	23.47
74	28.44	26.58	23.97	21.54	1.63	25.43	23.60
75	28.60	26.74	24.13	21.70	1.47	25.55	23.72

3% pa Life multiplier—28.54			3.5% pa Life multiplier—25.65				
E.M. 21	*E.M. 24*	*P.M.*	*E.M. 16*	*E.M. 18*	*E.M. 21*	*E.M. 24*	*P.M.*
15.70	13.37	6.53	18.58	16.78	14.30	12.07	5.13
16.03	13.70	6.20	18.86	17.06	14.58	12.34	4.86
16.35	14.02	5.88	19.13	17.32	14.84	12.61	4.59
16.65	14.33	5.57	19.38	17.58	15.10	12.86	4.33
16.95	14.62	5.27	19.63	17.83	15.35	13.11	4.09
17.24	14.91	4.98	19.87	18.06	15.58	13.35	3.85
17.52	15.19	4.70	20.10	18.29	15.81	13.58	3.62
17.79	15.46	4.43	20.31	18.51	16.03	13.80	3.40
18.05	15.72	4.17	20.53	18.72	16.24	14.01	3.19
18.30	15.97	3.92	20.73	18.92	16.44	14.21	2.99
18.54	16.22	3.68	20.92	19.12	16.64	14.40	2.80
18.78	16.45	3.45	21.11	19.31	16.82	14.59	2.61
19.00	16.67	3.22	21.29	19.48	17.00	14.77	2.43
19.22	16.89	3.01	21.46	19.65	17.17	14.94	2.26
19.42	17.10	2.80	21.62	19.82	17.34	15.10	2.10
19.62	17.29	2.60	21.78	19.97	17.49	15.26	1.94
19.81	17.49	2.41	21.92	20.12	17.64	15.41	1.79
20.00	17.67	2.23	22.07	20.26	17.78	15.55	1.65
20.17	17.84	2.05	22.20	20.40	17.92	15.68	1.52
20.34	18.01	1.89	22.33	20.52	18.04	15.81	1.39
20.49	18.17	1.73	22.45	20.65	18.16	15.93	1.27
20.64	18.32	1.58	22.56	20.76	18.28	16.04	1.16
20.79	18.46	1.44	22.67	20.87	18.39	16.15	1.05
20.92	18.59	1.30	22.77	20.97	18.49	16.25	0.95
21.05	18.72	1.18	22.87	21.06	18.58	16.35	0.85
21.17	18.84	1.06	22.96	21.15	18.67	16.44	0.76

Females aged 15

Retirement age	2.5% pa Life multiplier—31.81						
	E.M. 16	*E.M. 18*	*E.M. 21*	*E.M. 24*	*P.M.*	*E.M. 16*	*E.M. 18*
50	22.28	20.38	17.70	15.21	8.54	20.68	18.80
51	22.69	20.79	18.10	15.62	8.14	21.02	19.13
52	23.08	21.18	18.50	16.01	7.74	21.35	19.46
53	23.46	21.56	18.88	16.39	7.36	21.67	19.78
54	23.83	21.93	19.25	16.76	6.99	21.97	20.09
55	24.19	22.29	19.61	17.12	6.63	22.27	20.39
56	24.54	22.64	19.96	17.47	6.28	22.56	20.67
57	24.88	22.98	20.30	17.81	5.94	22.84	20.95
58	25.21	23.31	20.63	18.14	5.61	23.10	21.22
59	25.53	23.63	20.95	18.46	5.29	23.36	21.48
60	25.84	23.94	21.26	18.77	4.98	23.61	21.73
61	26.14	24.24	21.56	19.07	4.68	23.85	21.97
62	26.43	24.53	21.85	19.36	4.39	24.08	22.20
63	26.71	24.81	22.13	19.64	4.11	24.31	22.42
64	26.98	25.08	22.40	19.91	3.84	24.52	22.64
65	27.24	25.34	22.66	20.17	3.58	24.72	22.84
66	27.49	25.59	22.91	20.42	3.33	24.92	23.04
67	27.74	25.83	23.15	20.66	3.09	25.11	23.22
68	27.97	26.06	23.38	20.89	2.86	25.29	23.40
69	28.19	26.29	23.60	21.12	2.64	25.46	23.57
70	28.40	26.50	23.82	21.33	2.42	25.62	23.74
71	28.60	26.70	24.02	21.53	2.22	25.78	23.89
72	28.80	26.89	24.21	21.73	2.03	25.92	24.04
73	28.98	27.08	24.40	21.91	1.84	26.06	24.18
74	29.16	27.25	24.57	22.08	1.67	26.19	24.31
75	29.32	27.42	24.74	22.25	1.50	26.32	24.43

3% pa Life multiplier—28.39			3.5% pa Life multiplier—25.54				
E.M. 21	*E.M. 24*	*P.M.*	*E.M. 16*	*E.M. 18*	*E.M. 21*	*E.M. 24*	*P.M.*
16.17	13.77	6.72	19.24	17.37	14.80	12.49	5.31
16.51	14.11	6.38	19.52	17.66	15.09	12.78	5.03
16.84	14.44	6.06	19.80	17.93	15.37	13.05	4.75
17.16	14.76	5.74	20.07	18.20	15.63	13.32	4.49
17.47	15.07	5.43	20.32	18.45	15.89	13.57	4.23
17.76	15.36	5.13	20.57	18.70	16.13	13.82	3.99
18.05	15.65	4.85	20.80	18.94	16.37	14.05	3.75
18.33	15.93	4.57	21.03	19.16	16.60	14.28	3.52
18.60	16.20	4.30	21.25	19.38	16.81	14.50	3.30
18.85	16.46	4.04	21.46	19.59	17.02	14.71	3.09
19.10	16.71	3.79	21.66	19.79	17.22	14.91	2.89
19.34	16.95	3.55	21.85	19.98	17.42	15.10	2.70
19.58	17.18	3.32	22.04	20.17	17.60	15.29	2.52
19.80	17.40	3.10	22.21	20.35	17.78	15.46	2.34
20.01	17.61	2.88	22.38	20.51	17.95	15.63	2.17
20.22	17.82	2.68	22.54	20.68	18.11	15.79	2.01
20.41	18.01	2.48	22.70	20.83	18.26	15.95	1.86
20.60	18.20	2.30	22.84	20.98	18.41	16.09	1.71
20.78	18.38	2.12	22.98	21.11	18.55	16.23	1.57
20.95	18.55	1.95	23.11	21.25	18.68	16.37	1.44
21.11	18.71	1.78	23.24	21.37	18.80	16.49	1.31
21.27	18.87	1.63	23.36	21.49	18.92	16.61	1.20
21.41	19.02	1.48	23.47	21.60	19.03	16.72	1.08
21.55	19.15	1.34	23.57	21.71	19.14	16.83	0.98
21.68	19.29	1.21	23.67	21.81	19.24	16.92	0.88
21.81	19.41	1.09	23.76	21.90	19.33	17.02	0.79

Females aged 16

Retirement age	2.5% pa Life multiplier—31.60		3% pa Life multiplier—28.23		3.5% pa Life multiplier—25.42	
	Earnings multiplier	*Pensions multiplier*	*Earnings multiplier*	*Pensions multiplier*	*Earnings multiplier*	*Pensions multiplier*
50	22.85	8.76	21.30	6.93	19.92	5.50
51	23.26	8.34	21.65	6.58	20.21	5.20
52	23.66	7.94	21.99	6.24	20.50	4.92
53	24.05	7.55	22.32	5.91	20.77	4.65
54	24.44	7.17	22.64	5.59	21.04	4.38
55	24.80	6.80	22.94	5.29	21.29	4.13
56	25.16	6.44	23.24	4.99	21.54	3.88
57	25.51	6.09	23.53	4.71	21.77	3.65
58	25.85	5.75	23.80	4.43	22.00	3.42
59	26.18	5.42	24.07	4.16	22.21	3.20
60	26.50	5.11	24.33	3.91	22.42	3.00
61	26.80	4.80	24.57	3.66	22.62	2.80
62	27.10	4.50	24.81	3.42	22.81	2.61
63	27.39	4.22	25.04	3.19	22.99	2.42
64	27.66	3.94	25.26	2.97	23.17	2.25
65	27.93	3.67	25.47	2.76	23.34	2.08
66	28.19	3.41	25.67	2.56	23.50	1.92
67	28.44	3.17	25.87	2.36	23.65	1.77
68	28.67	2.93	26.05	2.18	23.79	1.63
69	28.90	2.70	26.23	2.00	23.93	1.49
70	29.12	2.48	26.40	1.84	24.06	1.36
71	29.33	2.28	26.56	1.68	24.18	1.24
72	29.52	2.08	26.71	1.53	24.29	1.12
73	29.71	1.89	26.85	1.38	24.40	1.01
74	29.89	1.71	26.98	1.25	24.51	0.91
75	30.06	1.54	27.11	1.12	24.60	0.82

Females aged 17

	2.5% pa Life multiplier—31.39		3% pa Life multiplier—28.07		3.5% pa Life multiplier—25.30	
Retirement age	*Earnings multiplier*	*Pensions multiplier*	*Earnings multiplier*	*Pensions multiplier*	*Earnings multiplier*	*Pensions multiplier*
50	22.41	8.98	20.93	7.14	19.60	5.69
51	22.84	8.55	21.30	6.78	19.91	5.39
52	23.25	8.14	21.64	6.43	20.20	5.09
53	23.65	7.74	21.98	6.09	20.49	4.81
54	24.04	7.35	22.31	5.76	20.76	4.54
55	24.42	6.97	22.62	5.45	21.02	4.27
56	24.79	6.60	22.93	5.14	21.28	4.02
57	25.14	6.24	23.22	4.85	21.52	3.78
58	25.49	5.90	23.51	4.56	21.75	3.54
59	25.83	5.56	23.78	4.29	21.98	3.32
60	26.15	5.24	24.05	4.02	22.19	3.10
61	26.47	4.92	24.30	3.77	22.40	2.89
62	26.77	4.62	24.55	3.52	22.60	2.70
63	27.07	4.32	24.78	3.29	22.79	2.51
64	27.35	4.04	25.01	3.06	22.97	2.33
65	27.62	3.76	25.23	2.84	23.14	2.15
66	27.89	3.50	25.44	2.64	23.31	1.99
67	28.14	3.25	25.64	2.44	23.46	1.83
68	28.38	3.00	25.83	2.25	23.61	1.68
69	28.62	2.77	26.01	2.06	23.75	1.54
70	28.84	2.55	26.18	1.89	23.89	1.41
71	29.05	2.33	26.34	1.73	24.01	1.28
72	29.26	2.13	26.50	1.57	24.13	1.16
73	29.45	1.94	26.65	1.42	24.25	1.05
74	29.63	1.75	26.79	1.29	24.35	0.94
75	29.81	1.58	26.92	1.15	24.45	0.84

Females aged 18

Retirement age	2.5% pa Life multiplier—31.17 Earnings multiplier	Pensions multiplier	3% pa Life multiplier—27.91 Earnings multiplier	Pensions multiplier	3.5% pa Life multiplier—25.17 Earnings multiplier	Pensions multiplier
50	21.97	9.20	20.55	7.35	19.28	5.90
51	22.40	8.77	20.93	6.98	19.59	5.58
52	22.82	8.35	21.29	6.62	19.90	5.27
53	23.24	7.93	21.63	6.27	20.19	4.98
54	23.64	7.53	21.97	5.94	20.48	4.70
55	24.02	7.15	22.29	5.61	20.75	4.42
56	24.40	6.77	22.61	5.30	21.01	4.16
57	24.77	6.40	22.91	5.00	21.26	3.91
58	25.12	6.05	23.21	4.70	21.51	3.67
59	25.47	5.70	23.49	4.42	21.74	3.43
60	25.80	5.37	23.76	4.15	21.96	3.21
61	26.12	5.05	24.02	3.88	22.17	3.00
62	26.44	4.73	24.28	3.63	22.38	2.79
63	26.74	4.43	24.52	3.39	22.58	2.60
64	27.03	4.14	24.75	3.15	22.76	2.41
65	27.31	3.86	24.98	2.93	22.94	2.23
66	27.58	3.59	25.19	2.72	23.11	2.06
67	27.84	3.33	25.40	2.51	23.27	1.90
68	28.09	3.08	25.59	2.31	23.43	1.74
69	28.33	2.84	25.78	2.13	23.57	1.60
70	28.56	2.61	25.96	1.95	23.71	1.46
71	28.78	2.39	26.13	1.78	23.85	1.33
72	28.99	2.18	26.29	1.62	23.97	1.20
73	29.18	1.99	26.44	1.47	24.09	1.09
74	29.37	1.80	26.58	1.32	24.20	0.98
75	29.55	1.62	26.72	1.19	24.30	0.87

Females aged 19

	2.5% pa Life multiplier—30.95		3% pa Life multiplier—27.74		3.5% pa Life multiplier—25.04	
Retirement age	*Earnings multiplier*	*Pensions multiplier*	*Earnings multiplier*	*Pensions multiplier*	*Earnings multiplier*	*Pensions multiplier*
50	21.51	9.44	20.16	7.58	18.94	6.10
51	21.96	8.99	20.54	7.19	19.27	5.78
52	22.39	8.56	20.92	6.82	19.58	5.46
53	22.81	8.14	21.27	6.47	19.89	5.15
54	23.22	7.73	21.62	6.12	20.18	4.86
55	23.62	7.33	21.96	5.78	20.46	4.58
56	24.01	6.94	22.28	5.46	20.74	4.31
57	24.38	6.56	22.59	5.15	21.00	4.05
58	24.75	6.20	22.89	4.84	21.25	3.80
59	25.10	5.85	23.19	4.55	21.49	3.56
60	25.44	5.50	23.47	4.27	21.72	3.32
61	25.77	5.17	23.74	4.00	21.94	3.10
62	26.09	4.85	24.00	3.74	22.15	2.89
63	26.40	4.54	24.25	3.49	22.36	2.69
64	26.70	4.25	24.49	3.25	22.55	2.49
65	26.99	3.96	24.72	3.02	22.73	2.31
66	27.27	3.68	24.94	2.80	22.91	2.13
67	27.53	3.41	25.15	2.59	23.08	1.96
68	27.79	3.16	25.35	2.38	23.24	1.80
69	28.03	2.91	25.55	2.19	23.39	1.65
70	28.27	2.68	25.73	2.01	23.53	1.51
71	28.49	2.45	25.90	1.83	23.67	1.37
72	28.71	2.24	26.07	1.67	23.80	1.25
73	28.91	2.04	26.23	1.51	23.92	1.12
74	29.10	1.84	26.37	1.36	24.03	1.01
75	29.28	1.66	26.51	1.23	24.14	0.90

Females aged 20

Retirement age	2.5% pa Life multiplier—30.72		3% pa Life multiplier—27.57		3.5% pa Life multiplier—24.91	
	Earnings multiplier	*Pensions multiplier*	*Earnings multiplier*	*Pensions multiplier*	*Earnings multiplier*	*Pensions multiplier*
50	21.04	9.68	19.76	7.81	18.59	6.32
51	21.50	9.22	20.15	7.41	18.93	5.98
52	21.94	8.77	20.53	7.03	19.26	5.65
53	22.38	8.34	20.90	6.66	19.57	5.34
54	22.80	7.92	21.26	6.30	19.88	5.03
55	23.21	7.51	21.61	5.96	20.17	4.74
56	23.60	7.12	21.94	5.62	20.45	4.46
57	23.99	6.73	22.26	5.30	20.72	4.19
58	24.36	6.36	22.57	4.99	20.98	3.93
59	24.72	6.00	22.87	4.69	21.23	3.68
60	25.07	5.64	23.16	4.40	21.47	3.44
61	25.41	5.30	23.44	4.12	21.70	3.21
62	25.74	4.98	23.71	3.85	21.92	2.99
63	26.06	4.66	23.97	3.60	22.13	2.78
64	26.37	4.35	24.22	3.35	22.33	2.58
65	26.66	4.06	24.45	3.11	22.52	2.39
66	26.95	3.77	24.68	2.88	22.70	2.21
67	27.22	3.50	24.90	2.66	22.88	2.03
68	27.48	3.24	25.11	2.46	23.04	1.87
69	27.73	2.99	25.31	2.26	23.20	1.71
70	27.97	2.75	25.50	2.07	23.35	1.56
71	28.20	2.52	25.68	1.89	23.49	1.42
72	28.42	2.30	25.85	1.72	23.62	1.29
73	28.63	2.09	26.01	1.56	23.75	1.16
74	28.83	1.89	26.16	1.41	23.86	1.05
75	29.01	1.70	26.30	1.26	23.97	0.94

Females aged 21

	2.5% pa Life multiplier—30.48		**3% pa Life multiplier—27.39**		**3.5% pa Life multiplier—24.77**	
Retirement age	*Earnings multiplier*	*Pensions multiplier*	*Earnings multiplier*	*Pensions multiplier*	*Earnings multiplier*	*Pensions multiplier*
50	20.56	9.92	19.34	8.04	18.23	6.54
51	21.03	9.45	19.75	7.64	18.58	6.19
52	21.49	9.00	20.14	7.24	18.92	5.85
53	21.93	8.55	20.52	6.86	19.25	5.53
54	22.36	8.12	20.89	6.50	19.56	5.21
55	22.78	7.70	21.25	6.14	19.86	4.91
56	23.19	7.30	21.59	5.80	20.16	4.62
57	23.58	6.90	21.92	5.46	20.44	4.34
58	23.97	6.52	22.24	5.14	20.70	4.07
59	24.34	6.15	22.55	4.83	20.96	3.81
60	24.70	5.79	22.85	4.53	21.21	3.56
61	25.04	5.44	23.14	4.25	21.45	3.33
62	25.38	5.10	23.41	3.97	21.67	3.10
63	25.71	4.78	23.68	3.71	21.89	2.88
64	26.02	4.46	23.94	3.45	22.10	2.67
65	26.32	4.16	24.18	3.20	22.30	2.48
66	26.61	3.87	24.42	2.97	22.49	2.29
67	26.89	3.59	24.64	2.75	22.67	2.11
68	27.16	3.32	24.85	2.53	22.84	1.93
69	27.42	3.06	25.06	2.33	23.00	1.77
70	27.67	2.82	25.25	2.13	23.16	1.62
71	27.90	2.58	25.44	1.95	23.30	1.47
72	28.13	2.36	25.61	1.77	23.44	1.33
73	28.34	2.14	25.78	1.60	23.57	1.21
74	28.54	1.94	25.94	1.45	23.69	1.08
75	28.74	1.75	26.08	1.30	23.80	0.97

Females aged 22

Retirement age	2.5% pa Life multiplier—30.24		3% pa Life multiplier—27.20		3.5% pa Life multiplier—24.63	
	Earnings multiplier	*Pensions multiplier*	*Earnings multiplier*	*Pensions multiplier*	*Earnings multiplier*	*Pensions multiplier*
50	20.07	10.17	18.91	8.29	17.86	6.77
51	20.55	9.69	19.33	7.87	18.22	6.41
52	21.02	9.22	19.74	7.46	18.57	6.06
53	21.47	8.77	20.13	7.07	18.91	5.72
54	21.92	8.33	20.51	6.69	19.24	5.40
55	22.35	7.90	20.88	6.33	19.55	5.08
56	22.76	7.48	21.23	5.97	19.85	4.78
57	23.17	7.08	21.57	5.63	20.14	4.49
58	23.56	6.68	21.90	5.30	20.42	4.21
59	23.94	6.30	22.22	4.98	20.69	3.95
60	24.31	5.93	22.53	4.67	20.94	3.69
61	24.67	5.58	22.82	4.38	21.19	3.44
62	25.01	5.23	23.11	4.09	21.42	3.21
63	25.35	4.90	23.38	3.82	21.65	2.98
64	25.67	4.58	23.65	3.55	21.86	2.77
65	25.98	4.27	23.90	3.30	22.07	2.56
66	26.28	3.97	24.14	3.06	22.26	2.37
67	26.56	3.68	24.37	2.83	22.45	2.18
68	26.84	3.40	24.59	2.61	22.63	2.00
69	27.10	3.14	24.80	2.40	22.80	1.83
70	27.36	2.89	25.00	2.20	22.96	1.68
71	27.60	2.65	25.20	2.01	23.11	1.52
72	27.83	2.41	25.38	1.82	23.25	1.38
73	28.05	2.20	25.55	1.65	23.38	1.25
74	28.25	1.99	25.71	1.49	23.51	1.12
75	28.45	1.79	25.86	1.34	23.63	1.00

Females aged 23

Retirement age	2.5% pa Life multiplier—30.00 *Earnings multiplier*	*Pensions multiplier*	3% pa Life multiplier—27.01 *Earnings multiplier*	*Pensions multiplier*	3.5% pa Life multiplier—24.48 *Earnings multiplier*	*Pensions multiplier*
50	19.57	10.43	18.47	8.54	17.47	7.01
51	20.06	9.94	18.90	8.11	17.85	6.64
52	20.54	9.46	19.32	7.69	18.21	6.27
53	21.01	8.99	19.73	7.29	18.56	5.92
54	21.46	8.54	20.12	6.90	18.90	5.59
55	21.90	8.10	20.49	6.52	19.22	5.26
56	22.33	7.67	20.86	6.15	19.53	4.95
57	22.74	7.26	21.21	5.80	19.83	4.65
58	23.14	6.85	21.55	5.46	20.12	4.36
59	23.53	6.46	21.88	5.13	20.40	4.09
60	23.91	6.08	22.20	4.81	20.66	3.82
61	24.28	5.72	22.50	4.51	20.92	3.57
62	24.63	5.36	22.80	4.22	21.16	3.32
63	24.97	5.02	23.08	3.93	21.40	3.09
64	25.30	4.69	23.35	3.66	21.62	2.87
65	25.62	4.37	23.61	3.40	21.83	2.65
66	25.93	4.07	23.86	3.15	22.03	2.45
67	26.22	3.77	24.10	2.91	22.23	2.26
68	26.51	3.49	24.32	2.69	22.41	2.07
69	26.78	3.22	24.54	2.47	22.58	1.90
70	27.04	2.96	24.75	2.26	22.75	1.73
71	27.28	2.71	24.94	2.07	22.91	1.58
72	27.52	2.48	25.13	1.88	23.05	1.43
73	27.75	2.25	25.31	1.70	23.19	1.29
74	27.96	2.04	25.47	1.54	23.32	1.16
75	28.16	1.84	25.63	1.38	23.44	1.04

Females aged 24

Retirement age	2.5% pa Life multiplier—29.74 Earnings multiplier	Pensions multiplier	3% pa Life multiplier—26.82 Earnings multiplier	Pensions multiplier	3.5% pa Life multiplier—24.33 Earnings multiplier	Pensions multiplier
50	19.05	10.69	18.02	8.80	17.07	7.26
51	19.56	10.19	18.46	8.35	17.46	6.87
52	20.05	9.70	18.89	7.92	17.84	6.49
53	20.52	9.22	19.31	7.51	18.20	6.13
54	20.99	8.75	19.71	7.10	18.55	5.78
55	21.44	8.30	20.10	6.72	18.88	5.45
56	21.88	7.86	20.48	6.34	19.21	5.12
57	22.30	7.44	20.84	5.98	19.52	4.81
58	22.72	7.03	21.19	5.63	19.82	4.52
59	23.12	6.63	21.53	5.29	20.10	4.23
60	23.51	6.24	21.86	4.96	20.38	3.95
61	23.88	5.86	22.17	4.65	20.64	3.69
62	24.24	5.50	22.47	4.34	20.89	3.44
63	24.59	5.15	22.76	4.05	21.13	3.20
64	24.93	4.81	23.04	3.77	21.36	2.97
65	25.26	4.48	23.31	3.51	21.58	2.75
66	25.57	4.17	23.57	3.25	21.79	2.54
67	25.88	3.87	23.81	3.00	21.99	2.34
68	26.17	3.58	24.05	2.77	22.18	2.15
69	26.44	3.30	24.27	2.54	22.36	1.97
70	26.71	3.03	24.48	2.33	22.54	1.80
71	26.96	2.78	24.69	2.13	22.70	1.63
72	27.21	2.54	24.88	1.94	22.85	1.48
73	27.44	2.31	25.06	1.76	22.99	1.34
74	27.65	2.09	25.23	1.58	23.13	1.20
75	27.86	1.88	25.39	1.42	23.25	1.08

Females aged 25

	2.5% pa Life multiplier—29.49		3% pa Life multiplier—26.61		3.5% pa Life multiplier—24.17	
Retirement age	*Earnings multiplier*	*Pensions multiplier*	*Earnings multiplier*	*Pensions multiplier*	*Earnings multiplier*	*Pensions multiplier*
50	18.52	10.97	17.55	9.06	16.66	7.52
51	19.04	10.45	18.01	8.61	17.06	7.11
52	19.54	9.94	18.45	8.16	17.45	6.72
53	20.03	9.45	18.88	7.73	17.82	6.35
54	20.51	8.98	19.29	7.32	18.19	5.99
55	20.97	8.51	19.70	6.92	18.53	5.64
56	21.42	8.06	20.08	6.53	18.87	5.31
57	21.86	7.63	20.46	6.16	19.19	4.98
58	22.28	7.20	20.82	5.80	19.50	4.68
59	22.69	6.79	21.17	5.45	19.79	4.38
60	23.09	6.40	21.50	5.11	20.08	4.09
61	23.47	6.01	21.83	4.79	20.35	3.82
62	23.85	5.64	22.14	4.48	20.61	3.56
63	24.21	5.28	22.44	4.18	20.86	3.31
64	24.55	4.93	22.73	3.89	21.10	3.07
65	24.89	4.60	23.00	3.61	21.33	2.84
66	25.21	4.28	23.27	3.35	21.55	2.63
67	25.52	3.97	23.52	3.09	21.75	2.42
68	25.82	3.67	23.76	2.85	21.95	2.22
69	26.10	3.38	23.99	2.62	22.14	2.04
70	26.37	3.11	24.21	2.40	22.31	1.86
71	26.63	2.85	24.42	2.19	22.48	1.69
72	26.88	2.60	24.62	2.00	22.64	1.53
73	27.12	2.37	24.81	1.81	22.79	1.38
74	27.34	2.14	24.98	1.63	22.93	1.25
75	27.55	1.93	25.15	1.47	23.06	1.11

Females aged 26

	2.5% pa Life multiplier—29.22		3% pa Life multiplier—26.41		3.5% pa Life multiplier—24.01	
Retirement age	*Earnings multiplier*	*Pensions multiplier*	*Earnings multiplier*	*Pensions multiplier*	*Earnings multiplier*	*Pensions multiplier*
50	17.98	11.24	17.07	9.34	16.23	7.78
51	18.51	10.71	17.54	8.87	16.65	7.37
52	19.02	10.20	18.00	8.41	17.05	6.96
53	19.53	9.69	18.44	7.97	17.44	6.57
54	20.02	9.20	18.86	7.54	17.81	6.20
55	20.49	8.73	19.28	7.13	18.17	5.84
56	20.95	8.27	19.68	6.73	18.52	5.49
57	21.40	7.82	20.06	6.34	18.85	5.16
58	21.83	7.39	20.44	5.97	19.17	4.84
59	22.25	6.97	20.79	5.61	19.48	4.53
60	22.66	6.56	21.14	5.27	19.77	4.24
61	23.06	6.16	21.47	4.93	20.05	3.96
62	23.44	5.78	21.80	4.61	20.32	3.69
63	23.81	5.41	22.10	4.30	20.58	3.43
64	24.16	5.06	22.40	4.01	20.83	3.18
65	24.51	4.71	22.69	3.72	21.07	2.94
66	24.84	4.38	22.96	3.45	21.29	2.72
67	25.15	4.07	23.22	3.19	21.51	2.51
68	25.46	3.76	23.47	2.94	21.71	2.30
69	25.75	3.47	23.71	2.70	21.90	2.11
70	26.03	3.19	23.93	2.48	22.09	1.92
71	26.30	2.92	24.15	2.26	22.26	1.75
72	26.55	2.67	24.35	2.06	22.42	1.59
73	26.79	2.43	24.54	1.86	22.58	1.43
74	27.02	2.20	24.73	1.68	22.72	1.29
75	27.24	1.98	24.90	1.51	22.86	1.15

Females aged 27

Retirement age	2.5% pa Life multiplier—28.95 *Earnings multiplier*	*Pensions multiplier*	3% pa Life multiplier—26.19 *Earnings multiplier*	*Pensions multiplier*	3.5% pa Life multiplier—23.84 *Earnings multiplier*	*Pensions multiplier*
50	17.42	11.53	16.57	9.62	15.78	8.06
51	17.96	10.98	17.06	9.14	16.22	7.63
52	18.49	10.45	17.53	8.67	16.63	7.21
53	19.01	9.94	17.98	8.21	17.04	6.81
54	19.51	9.44	18.42	7.77	17.42	6.42
55	20.00	8.95	18.85	7.35	17.80	6.05
56	20.47	8.48	19.26	6.93	18.15	5.69
57	20.93	8.02	19.66	6.54	18.50	5.34
58	21.37	7.57	20.04	6.15	18.83	5.01
59	21.81	7.14	20.41	5.78	19.15	4.69
60	22.22	6.72	20.77	5.43	19.45	4.39
61	22.63	6.32	21.11	5.08	19.75	4.10
62	23.02	5.93	21.44	4.75	20.03	3.82
63	23.40	5.55	21.76	4.43	20.29	3.55
64	23.76	5.19	22.07	4.13	20.55	3.29
65	24.11	4.83	22.36	3.83	20.79	3.05
66	24.45	4.50	22.64	3.55	21.03	2.82
67	24.78	4.17	22.91	3.29	21.25	2.59
68	25.09	3.86	23.17	3.03	21.46	2.38
69	25.39	3.56	23.41	2.78	21.66	2.18
70	25.68	3.27	23.64	2.55	21.85	1.99
71	25.95	3.00	23.86	2.33	22.03	1.81
72	26.21	2.74	24.07	2.12	22.20	1.64
73	26.46	2.49	24.27	1.92	22.36	1.48
74	26.69	2.25	24.46	1.73	22.51	1.33
75	26.92	2.03	24.64	1.56	22.65	1.19

Females aged 28

Retirement age	2.5% pa Life multiplier—28.67 Earnings multiplier	2.5% pa Life multiplier—28.67 Pensions multiplier	3% pa Life multiplier—25.97 Earnings multiplier	3% pa Life multiplier—25.97 Pensions multiplier	3.5% pa Life multiplier—23.67 Earnings multiplier	3.5% pa Life multiplier—23.67 Pensions multiplier
50	16.85	11.82	16.06	9.92	15.32	8.34
51	17.41	11.26	16.56	9.41	15.77	7.90
52	17.95	10.72	17.04	8.93	16.20	7.46
53	18.48	10.19	17.51	8.46	16.62	7.05
54	18.99	9.68	17.97	8.01	17.02	6.65
55	19.49	9.18	18.41	7.57	17.41	6.26
56	19.98	8.69	18.83	7.14	17.78	5.89
57	20.45	8.22	19.24	6.74	18.14	5.53
58	20.90	7.77	19.63	6.34	18.48	5.19
59	21.35	7.32	20.02	5.96	18.81	4.86
60	21.77	6.90	20.38	5.59	19.12	4.54
61	22.19	6.48	20.74	5.24	19.43	4.24
62	22.59	6.08	21.08	4.90	19.72	3.95
63	22.98	5.69	21.41	4.57	19.99	3.67
64	23.35	5.32	21.72	4.25	20.26	3.41
65	23.71	4.96	22.02	3.95	20.51	3.16
66	24.06	4.61	22.31	3.66	20.75	2.92
67	24.39	4.28	22.59	3.38	20.98	2.69
68	24.71	3.96	22.85	3.12	21.20	2.47
69	25.02	3.65	23.11	2.87	21.41	2.26
70	25.32	3.35	23.35	2.63	21.60	2.06
71	25.60	3.07	23.57	2.40	21.79	1.88
72	25.86	2.81	23.79	2.18	21.97	1.70
73	26.12	2.55	24.00	1.98	22.13	1.54
74	26.36	2.31	24.19	1.79	22.29	1.38
75	26.59	2.08	24.37	1.60	22.43	1.24

Females aged 29

	2.5% pa Life multiplier—28.39		**3% pa Life multiplier—25.75**		**3.5% pa Life multiplier—23.49**	
Retirement age	*Earnings multiplier*	*Pensions multiplier*	*Earnings multiplier*	*Pensions multiplier*	*Earnings multiplier*	*Pensions multiplier*
50	16.26	12.12	15.53	10.22	14.85	8.64
51	16.84	11.55	16.05	9.70	15.31	8.17
52	17.39	10.99	16.55	9.20	15.76	7.73
53	17.94	10.45	17.03	8.72	16.19	7.30
54	18.46	9.92	17.50	8.25	16.61	6.88
55	18.97	9.41	17.95	7.80	17.01	6.48
56	19.47	8.91	18.39	7.36	17.39	6.10
57	19.95	8.43	18.81	6.94	17.76	5.73
58	20.42	7.96	19.22	6.53	18.12	5.37
59	20.88	7.51	19.61	6.14	18.46	5.03
60	21.31	7.07	19.99	5.76	18.78	4.71
61	21.74	6.65	20.35	5.40	19.10	4.39
62	22.15	6.23	20.70	5.04	19.40	4.09
63	22.55	5.84	21.04	4.71	19.68	3.80
64	22.93	5.45	21.37	4.38	19.96	3.53
65	23.30	5.08	21.68	4.07	20.22	3.27
66	23.66	4.73	21.98	3.77	20.47	3.02
67	24.00	4.38	22.26	3.49	20.71	2.78
68	24.33	4.06	22.53	3.22	20.93	2.55
69	24.64	3.74	22.79	2.96	21.15	2.34
70	24.95	3.44	23.04	2.71	21.35	2.14
71	25.23	3.15	23.28	2.47	21.54	1.94
72	25.51	2.88	23.50	2.25	21.73	1.76
73	25.77	2.62	23.71	2.04	21.90	1.59
74	26.02	2.37	23.91	1.84	22.06	1.43
75	26.25	2.14	24.10	1.65	22.21	1.28

Females aged 30

Retirement age	2.5% pa Life multiplier—28.09 Earnings multiplier	2.5% pa Life multiplier—28.09 Pensions multiplier	3% pa Life multiplier—25.52 Earnings multiplier	3% pa Life multiplier—25.52 Pensions multiplier	3.5% pa Life multiplier—23.30 Earnings multiplier	3.5% pa Life multiplier—23.30 Pensions multiplier
50	15.66	12.43	14.99	10.53	14.36	8.95
51	16.25	11.84	15.52	10.00	14.84	8.46
52	16.82	11.27	16.04	9.48	15.30	8.00
53	17.38	10.71	16.53	8.98	15.75	7.55
54	17.92	10.17	17.01	8.50	16.18	7.12
55	18.44	9.65	17.48	8.04	16.59	6.71
56	18.95	9.14	17.93	7.59	16.99	6.31
57	19.45	8.65	18.37	7.15	17.37	5.93
58	19.93	8.17	18.79	6.73	17.74	5.56
59	20.39	7.70	19.19	6.33	18.09	5.21
60	20.84	7.25	19.58	5.94	18.43	4.87
61	21.28	6.81	19.96	5.56	18.75	4.55
62	21.70	6.39	20.32	5.20	19.07	4.24
63	22.11	5.98	20.67	4.85	19.36	3.94
64	22.50	5.59	21.00	4.52	19.65	3.66
65	22.88	5.21	21.32	4.19	19.92	3.38
66	23.25	4.85	21.63	3.89	20.18	3.13
67	23.60	4.50	21.92	3.59	20.42	2.88
68	23.93	4.16	22.20	3.31	20.66	2.64
69	24.26	3.84	22.47	3.05	20.88	2.42
70	24.57	3.53	22.73	2.79	21.09	2.21
71	24.86	3.23	22.97	2.55	21.29	2.01
72	25.14	2.95	23.20	2.32	21.48	1.82
73	25.41	2.68	23.42	2.10	21.65	1.65
74	25.66	2.43	23.62	1.90	21.82	1.48
75	25.90	2.19	23.81	1.70	21.98	1.33

Females aged 31

Retirement age	2.5% pa Life multiplier—27.80 Earnings multiplier	Pensions multiplier	3% pa Life multiplier—25.28 Earnings multiplier	Pensions multiplier	3.5% pa Life multiplier—23.11 Earnings multiplier	Pensions multiplier
50	15.05	12.75	14.43	10.85	13.85	9.26
51	15.65	12.14	14.98	10.30	14.35	8.76
52	16.24	11.56	15.51	9.77	14.83	8.28
53	16.81	10.99	16.02	9.26	15.29	7.82
54	17.36	10.43	16.52	8.76	15.73	7.38
55	17.90	9.90	17.00	8.28	16.16	6.95
56	18.42	9.37	17.46	7.82	16.57	6.54
57	18.93	8.87	17.91	7.37	16.97	6.14
58	19.42	8.37	18.34	6.94	17.35	5.76
59	19.90	7.90	18.76	6.52	17.72	5.40
60	20.36	7.43	19.16	6.12	18.07	5.04
61	20.81	6.99	19.55	5.73	18.40	4.71
62	21.24	6.55	19.92	5.36	18.72	4.39
63	21.66	6.14	20.28	5.00	19.03	4.08
64	22.06	5.73	20.62	4.65	19.33	3.78
65	22.45	5.34	20.96	4.32	19.61	3.50
66	22.83	4.97	21.27	4.01	19.87	3.24
67	23.19	4.61	21.57	3.70	20.13	2.98
68	23.53	4.26	21.86	3.41	20.37	2.74
69	23.86	3.93	22.14	3.14	20.60	2.51
70	24.18	3.62	22.40	2.88	20.82	2.29
71	24.48	3.31	22.65	2.63	21.03	2.08
72	24.77	3.03	22.89	2.39	21.22	1.89
73	25.04	2.75	23.11	2.16	21.40	1.71
74	25.30	2.49	23.32	1.95	21.58	1.53
75	25.55	2.25	23.52	1.75	21.74	1.37

Females aged 32

	2.5% pa Life multiplier—27.49		3% pa Life multiplier—25.03		3.5% pa Life multiplier—22.91	
Retirement age	*Earnings multiplier*	*Pensions multiplier*	*Earnings multiplier*	*Pensions multiplier*	*Earnings multiplier*	*Pensions multiplier*
50	14.42	13.07	13.85	11.18	13.32	9.59
51	15.04	12.45	14.42	10.61	13.84	9.08
52	15.64	11.85	14.97	10.07	14.33	8.58
53	16.22	11.27	15.49	9.54	14.81	8.10
54	16.79	10.70	16.01	9.03	15.27	7.64
55	17.34	10.15	16.50	8.53	15.72	7.20
56	17.88	9.61	16.98	8.05	16.14	6.77
57	18.40	9.09	17.44	7.59	16.55	6.36
58	18.90	8.59	17.89	7.15	16.95	5.96
59	19.39	8.10	18.32	6.72	17.33	5.59
60	19.87	7.62	18.73	6.30	17.69	5.22
61	20.33	7.17	19.13	5.90	18.04	4.88
62	20.77	6.72	19.51	5.52	18.37	4.54
63	21.20	6.29	19.88	5.15	18.69	4.22
64	21.61	5.88	20.24	4.79	18.99	3.92
65	22.01	5.48	20.58	4.45	19.28	3.63
66	22.39	5.10	20.91	4.13	19.56	3.35
67	22.76	4.73	21.22	3.82	19.83	3.09
68	23.12	4.37	21.52	3.52	20.08	2.84
69	23.46	4.03	21.80	3.23	20.32	2.60
70	23.78	3.71	22.07	2.96	20.54	2.37
71	24.09	3.40	22.33	2.71	20.75	2.16
72	24.39	3.10	22.57	2.46	20.96	1.96
73	24.67	2.82	22.80	2.23	21.15	1.77
74	24.94	2.55	23.02	2.01	21.32	1.59
75	25.19	2.30	23.23	1.81	21.49	1.42

Females aged 33

Retirement age	2.5% pa Life multiplier—27.18 Earnings multiplier	2.5% pa Life multiplier—27.18 Pensions multiplier	3% pa Life multiplier—24.78 Earnings multiplier	3% pa Life multiplier—24.78 Pensions multiplier	3.5% pa Life multiplier—22.71 Earnings multiplier	3.5% pa Life multiplier—22.71 Pensions multiplier
50	13.78	13.40	13.26	11.52	12.78	9.93
51	14.41	12.77	13.84	10.94	13.31	9.40
52	15.03	12.15	14.41	10.37	13.83	8.88
53	15.63	11.55	14.95	9.83	14.32	8.39
54	16.21	10.97	15.48	9.30	14.80	7.91
55	16.77	10.41	15.99	8.79	15.26	7.45
56	17.32	9.86	16.48	8.30	15.70	7.01
57	17.86	9.32	16.96	7.83	16.12	6.58
58	18.37	8.81	17.42	7.37	16.53	6.18
59	18.88	8.30	17.86	6.92	16.92	5.79
60	19.36	7.82	18.29	6.50	17.30	5.41
61	19.83	7.35	18.70	6.08	17.66	5.05
62	20.29	6.89	19.09	5.69	18.01	4.70
63	20.73	6.45	19.48	5.31	18.34	4.37
64	21.15	6.03	19.84	4.94	18.65	4.06
65	21.56	5.62	20.19	4.59	18.95	3.76
66	21.95	5.23	20.53	4.25	19.24	3.47
67	22.33	4.85	20.85	3.93	19.51	3.20
68	22.70	4.48	21.16	3.63	19.77	2.94
69	23.04	4.14	21.45	3.33	20.02	2.69
70	23.38	3.80	21.73	3.05	20.25	2.46
71	23.70	3.49	21.99	2.79	20.47	2.24
72	24.00	3.18	22.25	2.54	20.68	2.03
73	24.29	2.89	22.48	2.30	20.88	1.83
74	24.56	2.62	22.71	2.07	21.06	1.65
75	24.82	2.36	22.92	1.86	21.24	1.47

Females aged 34

Retirement age	2.5% pa Life multiplier—26.86 *Earnings multiplier*	*Pensions multiplier*	3% pa Life multiplier—24.53 *Earnings multiplier*	*Pensions multiplier*	3.5% pa Life multiplier—22.50 *Earnings multiplier*	*Pensions multiplier*
50	13.12	13.75	12.65	11.87	12.21	10.29
51	13.77	13.10	13.25	11.27	12.77	9.73
52	14.40	12.46	13.83	10.69	13.30	9.20
53	15.01	11.85	14.39	10.13	13.81	8.69
54	15.61	11.25	14.94	9.59	14.31	8.19
55	16.19	10.67	15.46	9.06	14.78	7.72
56	16.75	10.11	15.97	8.55	15.24	7.26
57	17.30	9.56	16.46	8.06	15.68	6.82
58	17.83	9.03	16.93	7.59	16.10	6.40
59	18.35	8.52	17.39	7.13	16.51	5.99
60	18.84	8.02	17.83	6.69	16.90	5.60
61	19.33	7.54	18.26	6.27	17.27	5.23
62	19.79	7.07	18.66	5.86	17.63	4.87
63	20.24	6.62	19.06	5.47	17.97	4.53
64	20.68	6.18	19.43	5.09	18.30	4.20
65	21.10	5.76	19.79	4.73	18.61	3.89
66	21.50	5.36	20.14	4.38	18.91	3.59
67	21.89	4.97	20.47	4.05	19.19	3.31
68	22.26	4.60	20.79	3.74	19.46	3.04
69	22.62	4.24	21.09	3.43	19.71	2.79
70	22.96	3.90	21.38	3.15	19.96	2.54
71	23.29	3.57	21.65	2.87	20.19	2.31
72	23.60	3.26	21.91	2.61	20.40	2.10
73	23.90	2.97	22.16	2.37	20.61	1.89
74	24.18	2.69	22.39	2.14	20.80	1.70
75	24.44	2.42	22.61	1.92	20.98	1.52

Females aged 35

Retirement age	2.5% pa Life multiplier—26.54		3% pa Life multiplier—24.26		3.5% pa Life multiplier—22.28	
	Earnings multiplier	*Pensions multiplier*	*Earnings multiplier*	*Pensions multiplier*	*Earnings multiplier*	*Pensions multiplier*
50	12.44	14.10	12.03	12.24	11.63	10.65
51	13.11	13.43	12.64	11.62	12.21	10.08
52	13.76	12.78	13.24	11.02	12.76	9.53
53	14.39	12.15	13.82	10.44	13.29	9.00
54	15.00	11.54	14.38	9.88	13.80	8.48
55	15.59	10.95	14.92	9.34	14.29	7.99
56	16.17	10.37	15.44	8.82	14.77	7.52
57	16.73	9.81	15.95	8.31	15.22	7.06
58	17.28	9.26	16.44	7.82	15.66	6.62
59	17.80	8.74	16.91	7.35	16.08	6.20
60	18.32	8.22	17.36	6.90	16.48	5.80
61	18.81	7.73	17.80	6.46	16.87	5.42
62	19.29	7.25	18.22	6.04	17.24	5.05
63	19.75	6.79	18.62	5.64	17.59	4.69
64	20.20	6.34	19.01	5.25	17.93	4.35
65	20.63	5.91	19.39	4.88	18.26	4.03
66	21.04	5.50	19.74	4.52	18.56	3.72
67	21.44	5.10	20.08	4.18	18.86	3.43
68	21.82	4.72	20.41	3.85	19.14	3.15
69	22.19	4.35	20.72	3.54	19.40	2.88
70	22.54	4.00	21.02	3.24	19.65	2.63
71	22.87	3.67	21.30	2.96	19.89	2.40
72	23.19	3.35	21.57	2.69	20.11	2.17
73	23.50	3.04	21.82	2.44	20.32	1.96
74	23.78	2.76	22.06	2.20	20.52	1.76
75	24.06	2.48	22.28	1.98	20.71	1.58

Females aged 36

Retirement age	2.5% pa Life multiplier—26.21		3% pa Life multiplier—23.99		3.5% pa Life multiplier—22.06	
	Earnings multiplier	*Pensions multiplier*	*Earnings multiplier*	*Pensions multiplier*	*Earnings multiplier*	*Pensions multiplier*
50	11.75	14.46	11.38	12.61	11.03	11.03
51	12.43	13.78	12.02	11.97	11.62	10.44
52	13.10	13.11	12.63	11.36	12.20	9.87
53	13.74	12.47	13.23	10.76	12.75	9.32
54	14.37	11.84	13.81	10.18	13.28	8.79
55	14.98	11.23	14.36	9.63	13.79	8.28
56	15.57	10.64	14.90	9.09	14.28	7.79
57	16.15	10.06	15.42	8.57	14.75	7.31
58	16.71	9.50	15.93	8.06	15.20	6.86
59	17.25	8.96	16.41	7.58	15.64	6.43
60	17.77	8.44	16.88	7.11	16.05	6.01
61	18.28	7.93	17.33	6.66	16.45	5.61
62	18.77	7.44	17.76	6.23	16.84	5.23
63	19.25	6.96	18.18	5.81	17.20	4.86
64	19.70	6.51	18.58	5.41	17.55	4.51
65	20.14	6.06	18.97	5.03	17.89	4.17
66	20.57	5.64	19.33	4.66	18.21	3.85
67	20.98	5.23	19.69	4.31	18.51	3.55
68	21.37	4.84	20.02	3.97	18.80	3.26
69	21.75	4.46	20.34	3.65	19.07	2.99
70	22.11	4.10	20.65	3.34	19.33	2.73
71	22.45	3.76	20.94	3.05	19.58	2.48
72	22.78	3.43	21.21	2.78	19.81	2.25
73	23.09	3.12	21.47	2.52	20.03	2.03
74	23.38	2.83	21.72	2.27	20.24	1.83
75	23.66	2.55	21.95	2.04	20.43	1.64

Females aged 37

	2.5% pa Life multiplier—25.87		3% pa Life multiplier—23.71		3.5% pa Life multiplier—21.83	
Retirement age	*Earnings multiplier*	*Pensions multiplier*	*Earnings multiplier*	*Pensions multiplier*	*Earnings multiplier*	*Pensions multiplier*
50	11.04	14.83	10.71	13.00	10.41	11.43
51	11.74	14.13	11.37	12.34	11.02	10.81
52	12.42	13.45	12.01	11.71	11.61	10.22
53	13.08	12.79	12.62	11.09	12.18	9.65
54	13.73	12.14	13.22	10.50	12.73	9.10
55	14.35	11.52	13.79	9.92	13.26	8.57
56	14.96	10.91	14.35	9.37	13.77	8.06
57	15.55	10.32	14.88	8.83	14.26	7.58
58	16.13	9.75	15.40	8.31	14.73	7.11
59	16.68	9.19	15.90	7.81	15.18	6.66
60	17.22	8.65	16.38	7.33	15.61	6.22
61	17.74	8.13	16.85	6.87	16.03	5.81
62	18.24	7.63	17.30	6.42	16.42	5.41
63	18.73	7.14	17.73	5.99	16.80	5.03
64	19.20	6.67	18.14	5.58	17.16	4.67
65	19.65	6.22	18.53	5.18	17.51	4.32
66	20.09	5.78	18.91	4.80	17.84	3.99
67	20.51	5.37	19.28	4.44	18.16	3.68
68	20.91	4.96	19.62	4.09	18.46	3.38
69	21.29	4.58	19.95	3.76	18.74	3.09
70	21.66	4.21	20.27	3.45	19.01	2.83
71	22.01	3.86	20.57	3.15	19.26	2.57
72	22.35	3.52	20.85	2.86	19.50	2.33
73	22.67	3.20	21.12	2.59	19.73	2.11
74	22.97	2.90	21.37	2.34	19.94	1.89
75	23.26	2.61	21.61	2.10	20.14	1.69

Females aged 38

Retirement age	2.5% pa Life multiplier—25.53		3% pa Life multiplier—23.43		3.5% pa Life multiplier—21.60	
	Earnings multiplier	*Pensions multiplier*	*Earnings multiplier*	*Pensions multiplier*	*Earnings multiplier*	*Pensions multiplier*
50	10.31	15.22	10.03	13.40	9.76	11.84
51	11.03	14.50	10.71	12.72	10.40	11.20
52	11.73	13.80	11.36	12.07	11.01	10.59
53	12.41	13.12	12.00	11.44	11.60	10.00
54	13.07	12.46	12.61	10.82	12.17	9.43
55	13.71	11.82	13.20	10.23	12.72	8.88
56	14.34	11.19	13.77	9.66	13.25	8.35
57	14.94	10.59	14.33	9.10	13.75	7.85
58	15.53	10.00	14.86	8.57	14.24	7.36
59	16.10	9.43	15.38	8.05	14.70	6.89
60	16.65	8.88	15.87	7.56	15.15	6.45
61	17.18	8.34	16.35	7.08	15.58	6.02
62	17.70	7.83	16.81	6.62	15.99	5.61
63	18.20	7.33	17.26	6.17	16.39	5.21
64	18.68	6.85	17.68	5.75	16.76	4.84
65	19.15	6.38	18.09	5.34	17.12	4.48
66	19.59	5.93	18.48	4.95	17.46	4.14
67	20.02	5.50	18.86	4.57	17.79	3.81
68	20.44	5.09	19.21	4.22	18.10	3.50
69	20.83	4.70	19.55	3.88	18.39	3.21
70	21.21	4.32	19.88	3.55	18.67	2.93
71	21.57	3.96	20.19	3.24	18.94	2.66
72	21.91	3.61	20.48	2.95	19.18	2.41
73	22.24	3.29	20.76	2.67	19.42	2.18
74	22.55	2.97	21.02	2.41	19.64	1.96
75	22.85	2.68	21.26	2.17	19.84	1.75

Females aged 39

Retirement age	2.5% pa Life multiplier—25.18 Earnings multiplier	2.5% pa Life multiplier—25.18 Pensions multiplier	3% pa Life multiplier—23.14 Earnings multiplier	3% pa Life multiplier—23.14 Pensions multiplier	3.5% pa Life multiplier—21.36 Earnings multiplier	3.5% pa Life multiplier—21.36 Pensions multiplier
50	9.56	15.61	9.32	13.82	9.09	12.26
51	10.30	14.87	10.02	13.12	9.75	11.60
52	11.02	14.16	10.70	12.44	10.39	10.97
53	11.72	13.46	11.35	11.79	11.00	10.36
54	12.40	12.78	11.98	11.16	11.59	9.77
55	13.05	12.12	12.59	10.55	12.16	9.20
56	13.69	11.48	13.19	9.95	12.70	8.65
57	14.32	10.86	13.76	9.38	13.23	8.13
58	14.92	10.26	14.31	8.83	13.73	7.63
59	15.50	9.67	14.84	8.30	14.22	7.14
60	16.07	9.11	15.35	7.79	14.68	6.68
61	16.62	8.56	15.84	7.30	15.12	6.23
62	17.15	8.03	16.32	6.82	15.55	5.81
63	17.66	7.52	16.78	6.36	15.96	5.40
64	18.15	7.02	17.21	5.93	16.35	5.01
65	18.63	6.55	17.63	5.51	16.72	4.64
66	19.09	6.09	18.04	5.10	17.07	4.28
67	19.53	5.65	18.42	4.72	17.41	3.95
68	19.95	5.22	18.79	4.35	17.73	3.63
69	20.36	4.82	19.14	4.00	18.04	3.32
70	20.75	4.43	19.48	3.66	18.33	3.03
71	21.12	4.06	19.80	3.34	18.60	2.76
72	21.47	3.71	20.10	3.04	18.86	2.50
73	21.81	3.37	20.38	2.76	19.10	2.26
74	22.12	3.05	20.65	2.49	19.33	2.03
75	22.43	2.75	20.91	2.23	19.54	1.82

Females aged 40

Retirement age	2.5% pa Life multiplier—24.82 Earnings multiplier	Pensions multiplier	3% pa Life multiplier—22.84 Earnings multiplier	Pensions multiplier	3.5% pa Life multiplier—21.11 Earnings multiplier	Pensions multiplier
50	8.80	16.02	8.60	14.24	8.40	12.70
51	9.56	15.26	9.32	13.52	9.09	12.02
52	10.29	14.52	10.01	12.83	9.75	11.36
53	11.01	13.81	10.69	12.15	10.38	10.73
54	11.71	13.11	11.34	11.50	10.99	10.12
55	12.38	12.44	11.97	10.87	11.58	9.53
56	13.04	11.78	12.58	10.26	12.14	8.97
57	13.68	11.14	13.17	9.68	12.69	8.42
58	14.29	10.52	13.73	9.11	13.21	7.90
59	14.89	9.92	14.28	8.56	13.71	7.40
60	15.47	9.34	14.81	8.03	14.19	6.92
61	16.04	8.78	15.32	7.52	14.65	6.46
62	16.58	8.24	15.81	7.03	15.09	6.02
63	17.11	7.71	16.28	6.56	15.51	5.59
64	17.61	7.21	16.73	6.11	15.92	5.19
65	18.10	6.72	17.17	5.68	16.30	4.81
66	18.57	6.25	17.58	5.26	16.67	4.44
67	19.02	5.79	17.98	4.86	17.02	4.09
68	19.46	5.36	18.36	4.48	17.35	3.76
69	19.87	4.94	18.72	4.12	17.67	3.44
70	20.27	4.55	19.07	3.78	17.97	3.14
71	20.65	4.17	19.39	3.45	18.25	2.86
72	21.02	3.80	19.71	3.14	18.52	2.59
73	21.36	3.46	20.00	2.84	18.77	2.34
74	21.69	3.13	20.28	2.56	19.00	2.10
75	22.00	2.82	20.54	2.30	19.23	1.88

Females aged 41

	2.5% pa Life multiplier—24.45		3% pa Life multiplier—22.54		3.5% pa Life multiplier—20.85	
Retirement age	*Earnings multiplier*	*Pensions multiplier*	*Earnings multiplier*	*Pensions multiplier*	*Earnings multiplier*	*Pensions multiplier*
50	8.02	16.44	7.85	14.69	7.69	13.16
51	8.79	15.66	8.59	13.94	8.40	12.45
52	9.55	14.90	9.31	13.23	9.08	11.77
53	10.28	14.17	10.00	12.53	9.74	11.12
54	11.00	13.45	10.68	11.86	10.37	10.48
55	11.69	12.76	11.33	11.21	10.98	9.87
56	12.37	12.09	11.95	10.58	11.56	9.29
57	13.02	11.43	12.56	9.98	12.13	8.73
58	13.65	10.80	13.15	9.39	12.67	8.19
59	14.27	10.18	13.71	8.83	13.19	7.67
60	14.86	9.59	14.26	8.28	13.68	7.17
61	15.44	9.01	14.78	7.76	14.16	6.69
62	16.00	8.45	15.29	7.25	14.62	6.23
63	16.54	7.91	15.77	6.77	15.06	5.80
64	17.06	7.39	16.24	6.30	15.47	5.38
65	17.56	6.89	16.68	5.85	15.87	4.98
66	18.04	6.41	17.11	5.42	16.25	4.60
67	18.51	5.95	17.52	5.01	16.62	4.24
68	18.95	5.50	17.91	4.62	16.96	3.89
69	19.38	5.07	18.29	4.25	17.29	3.56
70	19.79	4.66	18.64	3.89	17.60	3.26
71	20.18	4.27	18.98	3.55	17.89	2.96
72	20.55	3.90	19.30	3.23	18.17	2.69
73	20.90	3.55	19.61	2.93	18.43	2.42
74	21.24	3.21	19.89	2.64	18.67	2.18
75	21.56	2.90	20.16	2.38	18.90	1.95

Females aged 42

Retirement age	2.5% pa Life multiplier—24.08 Earnings multiplier	Pensions multiplier	3% pa Life multiplier—22.22 Earnings multiplier	Pensions multiplier	3.5% pa Life multiplier—20.59 Earnings multiplier	Pensions multiplier
50	7.21	16.87	7.08	15.15	6.95	13.64
51	8.01	16.07	7.84	14.38	7.68	12.91
52	8.79	15.29	8.59	13.64	8.39	12.20
53	9.54	14.54	9.30	12.92	9.07	11.52
54	10.27	13.81	9.99	12.23	9.73	10.86
55	10.98	13.10	10.66	11.56	10.36	10.23
56	11.68	12.40	11.31	10.91	10.96	9.63
57	12.35	11.73	11.94	10.29	11.55	9.04
58	13.00	11.08	12.54	9.68	12.11	8.48
59	13.63	10.45	13.12	9.10	12.65	7.94
60	14.24	9.84	13.69	8.54	13.16	7.43
61	14.83	9.25	14.23	8.00	13.66	6.93
62	15.41	8.67	14.75	7.48	14.13	6.46
63	15.96	8.12	15.25	6.98	14.58	6.01
64	16.49	7.59	15.73	6.50	15.02	5.57
65	17.01	7.07	16.19	6.03	15.43	5.16
66	17.50	6.58	16.63	5.59	15.82	4.77
67	17.98	6.10	17.05	5.17	16.20	4.39
68	18.44	5.64	17.46	4.77	16.56	4.03
69	18.87	5.21	17.84	4.38	16.90	3.69
70	19.29	4.79	18.21	4.01	17.22	3.37
71	19.69	4.39	18.56	3.67	17.52	3.07
72	20.08	4.00	18.89	3.34	17.81	2.78
73	20.44	3.64	19.20	3.02	18.08	2.51
74	20.78	3.30	19.50	2.73	18.33	2.26
75	21.11	2.97	19.78	2.45	18.57	2.02

Females aged 43

Retirement age	2.5% pa Life multiplier—23.70		3% pa Life multiplier—21.91		3.5% pa Life multiplier—20.32	
	Earnings multiplier	*Pensions multiplier*	*Earnings multiplier*	*Pensions multiplier*	*Earnings multiplier*	*Pensions multiplier*
50	6.39	17.31	6.29	15.62	6.18	14.14
51	7.21	16.49	7.07	14.83	6.95	13.37
52	8.00	15.70	7.84	14.07	7.68	12.64
53	8.78	14.92	8.58	13.33	8.38	11.94
54	9.53	14.17	9.29	12.61	9.06	11.26
55	10.26	13.44	9.98	11.92	9.72	10.60
56	10.97	12.73	10.65	11.25	10.34	9.98
57	11.66	12.04	11.30	10.61	10.95	9.37
58	12.33	11.37	11.92	9.99	11.53	8.79
59	12.98	10.73	12.52	9.39	12.09	8.23
60	13.60	10.10	13.10	8.81	12.62	7.70
61	14.21	9.49	13.66	8.25	13.13	7.19
62	14.80	8.90	14.19	7.71	13.63	6.69
63	15.37	8.33	14.71	7.20	14.10	6.22
64	15.91	7.79	15.21	6.70	14.54	5.78
65	16.44	7.26	15.68	6.22	14.97	5.35
66	16.95	6.75	16.14	5.77	15.38	4.94
67	17.44	6.26	16.57	5.33	15.77	4.55
68	17.91	5.79	16.99	4.92	16.14	4.18
69	18.36	5.34	17.39	4.52	16.49	3.83
70	18.79	4.91	17.77	4.14	16.82	3.50
71	19.20	4.50	18.12	3.78	17.14	3.18
72	19.59	4.11	18.47	3.44	17.44	2.88
73	19.96	3.74	18.79	3.12	17.72	2.60
74	20.32	3.38	19.09	2.81	17.98	2.34
75	20.65	3.05	19.38	2.53	18.22	2.10

Females aged 44

Retirement age	2.5% pa Life multiplier—23.31 Earnings multiplier	Pensions multiplier	3% pa Life multiplier—21.58 Earnings multiplier	Pensions multiplier	3.5% pa Life multiplier—20.04 Earnings multiplier	Pensions multiplier
50	5.55	17.77	5.47	16.11	5.39	14.65
51	6.39	16.93	6.28	15.30	6.18	13.86
52	7.20	16.11	7.07	14.51	6.94	13.10
53	8.00	15.32	7.83	13.75	7.67	12.37
54	8.77	14.55	8.57	13.01	8.38	11.67
55	9.52	13.80	9.28	12.30	9.05	10.99
56	10.25	13.07	9.97	11.61	9.70	10.34
57	10.95	12.36	10.64	10.94	10.33	9.71
58	11.64	11.67	11.28	10.30	10.93	9.11
59	12.31	11.01	11.90	9.68	11.51	8.53
60	12.95	10.36	12.49	9.08	12.06	7.98
61	13.57	9.74	13.07	8.51	12.60	7.45
62	14.18	9.14	13.62	7.95	13.10	6.94
63	14.76	8.56	14.16	7.42	13.59	6.45
64	15.32	7.99	14.67	6.91	14.06	5.99
65	15.86	7.45	15.16	6.42	14.50	5.54
66	16.39	6.93	15.63	5.95	14.92	5.12
67	16.89	6.43	16.08	5.50	15.33	4.72
68	17.37	5.95	16.51	5.07	15.71	4.33
69	17.83	5.48	16.92	4.66	16.08	3.97
70	18.27	5.04	17.31	4.27	16.42	3.62
71	18.69	4.62	17.68	3.90	16.75	3.30
72	19.10	4.22	18.03	3.55	17.05	2.99
73	19.48	3.84	18.36	3.21	17.34	2.70
74	19.84	3.47	18.68	2.90	17.62	2.43
75	20.18	3.13	18.97	2.61	17.87	2.17

Females aged 45

	2.5% pa Life multiplier—22.92		3% pa Life multiplier—21.25		3.5% pa Life multiplier—19.76	
Retirement age	*Earnings multiplier*	*Pensions multiplier*	*Earnings multiplier*	*Pensions multiplier*	*Earnings multiplier*	*Pensions multiplier*
50	4.68	18.24	4.63	16.62	4.57	15.19
51	5.54	17.38	5.46	15.78	5.39	14.37
52	6.38	16.54	6.28	14.97	6.18	13.58
53	7.20	15.73	7.06	14.18	6.93	12.83
54	7.99	14.93	7.82	13.42	7.66	12.10
55	8.76	14.16	8.56	12.69	8.37	11.39
56	9.51	13.42	9.27	11.98	9.04	10.72
57	10.23	12.69	9.96	11.29	9.69	10.07
58	10.94	11.99	10.62	10.63	10.31	9.44
59	11.62	11.30	11.26	9.99	10.91	8.85
60	12.28	10.64	11.87	9.37	11.49	8.27
61	12.92	10.00	12.47	8.78	12.04	7.72
62	13.54	9.38	13.04	8.21	12.57	7.19
63	14.14	8.78	13.59	7.66	13.07	6.69
64	14.72	8.21	14.12	7.13	13.55	6.21
65	15.27	7.65	14.62	6.62	14.01	5.75
66	15.81	7.11	15.11	6.14	14.45	5.31
67	16.32	6.60	15.57	5.67	14.87	4.89
68	16.82	6.10	16.01	5.23	15.27	4.49
69	17.29	5.63	16.44	4.81	15.65	4.11
70	17.75	5.18	16.84	4.41	16.00	3.76
71	18.18	4.74	17.22	4.02	16.34	3.42
72	18.59	4.33	17.59	3.66	16.66	3.10
73	18.98	3.94	17.93	3.32	16.96	2.80
74	19.36	3.57	18.25	2.99	17.24	2.52
75	19.71	3.21	18.56	2.69	17.51	2.25

Females aged 46

Retirement age	2.5% pa Life multiplier—22.52 *Earnings multiplier*	*Pensions multiplier*	3% pa Life multiplier—20.91 *Earnings multiplier*	*Pensions multiplier*	3.5% pa Life multiplier—19.47 *Earnings multiplier*	*Pensions multiplier*
50	3.79	18.73	3.76	17.15	3.72	15.75
51	4.68	17.85	4.62	16.28	4.57	14.90
52	5.54	16.98	5.46	15.44	5.39	14.08
53	6.38	16.15	6.27	14.63	6.17	13.30
54	7.19	15.33	7.06	13.85	6.93	12.54
55	7.98	14.54	7.82	13.09	7.66	11.81
56	8.75	13.78	8.55	12.36	8.36	11.11
57	9.49	13.03	9.26	11.65	9.03	10.44
58	10.22	12.31	9.94	10.97	9.68	9.79
59	10.92	11.61	10.60	10.31	10.30	9.17
60	11.60	10.93	11.24	9.67	10.89	8.58
61	12.25	10.27	11.85	9.06	11.46	8.00
62	12.89	9.63	12.44	8.47	12.01	7.46
63	13.50	9.02	13.01	7.90	12.53	6.93
64	14.10	8.43	13.55	7.36	13.03	6.43
65	14.67	7.85	14.07	6.83	13.51	5.96
66	15.22	7.30	14.57	6.33	13.97	5.50
67	15.75	6.78	15.05	5.85	14.40	5.07
68	16.26	6.27	15.51	5.40	14.81	4.66
69	16.74	5.78	15.95	4.96	15.20	4.26
70	17.21	5.32	16.36	4.55	15.57	3.89
71	17.65	4.87	16.76	4.15	15.93	3.54
72	18.08	4.45	17.13	3.78	16.26	3.21
73	18.48	4.04	17.48	3.42	16.57	2.90
74	18.86	3.66	17.82	3.09	16.86	2.61
75	19.22	3.30	18.13	2.77	17.13	2.33

Females aged 47

	2.5% pa Life multiplier—22.12		3% pa Life multiplier—20.56		3.5% pa Life multiplier—19.17	
Retirement age	*Earnings multiplier*	*Pensions multiplier*	*Earnings multiplier*	*Pensions multiplier*	*Earnings multiplier*	*Pensions multiplier*
50	2.88	19.24	2.86	17.70	2.84	16.33
51	3.79	18.33	3.75	16.81	3.72	15.45
52	4.68	17.44	4.62	15.94	4.57	14.61
53	5.54	16.58	5.46	15.10	5.38	13.79
54	6.37	15.75	6.27	14.29	6.17	13.01
55	7.18	14.94	7.05	13.51	6.92	12.25
56	7.97	14.15	7.81	12.75	7.65	11.52
57	8.74	13.38	8.54	12.02	8.35	10.83
58	9.48	12.64	9.24	11.32	9.02	10.16
59	10.20	11.92	9.92	10.64	9.66	9.51
60	10.90	11.22	10.58	9.98	10.28	8.89
61	11.57	10.55	11.21	9.35	10.87	8.30
62	12.23	9.89	11.82	8.74	11.44	7.73
63	12.86	9.26	12.41	8.15	11.98	7.19
64	13.47	8.65	12.97	7.59	12.50	6.67
65	14.05	8.07	13.51	7.05	12.99	6.18
66	14.62	7.50	14.02	6.54	13.47	5.71
67	15.16	6.96	14.52	6.04	13.92	5.26
68	15.68	6.44	14.99	5.57	14.34	4.83
69	16.18	5.94	15.44	5.12	14.75	4.42
70	16.66	5.46	15.87	4.69	15.13	4.04
71	17.12	5.00	16.28	4.28	15.50	3.67
72	17.55	4.57	16.66	3.90	15.84	3.33
73	17.97	4.15	17.03	3.53	16.16	3.01
74	18.36	3.76	17.37	3.19	16.47	2.70
75	18.73	3.39	17.70	2.86	16.75	2.42

Females aged 48

Retirement age	2.5% pa Life multiplier—21.71		3% pa Life multiplier—20.21		3.5% pa Life multiplier—18.87	
	Earnings multiplier	*Pensions multiplier*	*Earnings multiplier*	*Pensions multiplier*	*Earnings multiplier*	*Pensions multiplier*
50	1.95	19.76	1.94	18.27	1.93	16.94
51	2.88	18.83	2.86	17.35	2.84	16.03
52	3.79	17.92	3.75	16.45	3.72	15.15
53	4.67	17.04	4.62	15.59	4.56	14.30
54	5.53	16.18	5.45	14.75	5.38	13.49
55	6.37	15.34	6.26	13.95	6.16	12.71
56	7.18	14.53	7.04	13.16	6.91	11.95
57	7.96	13.75	7.80	12.41	7.64	11.23
58	8.72	12.98	8.53	11.68	8.33	10.53
59	9.46	12.24	9.23	10.98	9.00	9.87
60	10.18	11.53	9.91	10.30	9.64	9.23
61	10.87	10.83	10.56	9.65	10.26	8.61
62	11.55	10.16	11.19	9.02	10.85	8.02
63	12.19	9.51	11.79	8.42	11.41	7.46
64	12.82	8.89	12.37	7.84	11.95	6.92
65	13.42	8.29	12.93	7.28	12.46	6.41
66	14.00	7.71	13.46	6.75	12.95	5.92
67	14.56	7.15	13.97	6.24	13.42	5.45
68	15.10	6.61	14.46	5.75	13.86	5.01
69	15.61	6.10	14.92	5.29	14.28	4.59
70	16.10	5.61	15.36	4.84	14.68	4.19
71	16.57	5.14	15.79	4.42	15.06	3.81
72	17.02	4.69	16.18	4.02	15.41	3.46
73	17.44	4.27	16.56	3.65	15.75	3.12
74	17.85	3.86	16.92	3.29	16.06	2.81
75	18.23	3.48	17.25	2.95	16.36	2.51

Females aged 49

	2.5% pa Life multiplier—21.29		3% pa Life multiplier—19.85		3.5% pa Life multiplier—18.56	
Retirement age	*Earnings multiplier*	*Pensions multiplier*	*Earnings multiplier*	*Pensions multiplier*	*Earnings multiplier*	*Pensions multiplier*
50	0.99	20.30	0.98	18.86	0.98	17.57
51	1.95	19.34	1.94	17.91	1.93	16.63
52	2.88	18.41	2.86	16.99	2.84	15.72
53	3.79	17.50	3.75	16.10	3.72	14.84
54	4.67	16.62	4.61	15.23	4.56	14.00
55	5.53	15.76	5.45	14.40	5.37	13.18
56	6.36	14.93	6.26	13.59	6.15	12.40
57	7.17	14.12	7.03	12.81	6.91	11.65
58	7.95	13.34	7.79	12.06	7.63	10.93
59	8.71	12.58	8.51	11.34	8.32	10.24
60	9.45	11.84	9.21	10.64	8.99	9.57
61	10.16	11.13	9.89	9.96	9.62	8.93
62	10.85	10.44	10.53	9.31	10.23	8.32
63	11.51	9.78	11.16	8.69	10.82	7.74
64	12.16	9.13	11.76	8.09	11.38	7.18
65	12.78	8.51	12.33	7.52	11.91	6.65
66	13.37	7.92	12.88	6.97	12.42	6.14
67	13.95	7.34	13.41	6.44	12.90	5.66
68	14.50	6.79	13.91	5.94	13.36	5.20
69	15.02	6.27	14.39	5.46	13.80	4.76
70	15.53	5.76	14.85	5.00	14.21	4.35
71	16.01	5.28	15.28	4.57	14.60	3.95
72	16.47	4.82	15.69	4.15	14.97	3.59
73	16.91	4.38	16.08	3.76	15.32	3.24
74	17.32	3.97	16.45	3.40	15.65	2.91
75	17.71	3.58	16.80	3.05	15.95	2.61

Females aged 50

Retirement age	2.5% pa Life multiplier—20.87 Earnings multiplier	2.5% pa Pensions multiplier	3% pa Life multiplier—19.48 Earnings multiplier	3% pa Pensions multiplier	3.5% pa Life multiplier—18.24 Earnings multiplier	3.5% pa Pensions multiplier
50	—	20.87	—	19.48	—	18.24
51	0.99	19.88	0.98	18.50	0.98	17.26
52	1.95	18.92	1.94	17.55	1.93	16.31
53	2.88	17.99	2.86	16.62	2.84	15.40
54	3.78	17.08	3.75	15.73	3.71	14.52
55	4.67	16.20	4.61	14.87	4.56	13.68
56	5.52	15.35	5.44	14.04	5.37	12.87
57	6.35	14.52	6.25	13.23	6.15	12.09
58	7.16	13.71	7.02	12.46	6.90	11.34
59	7.94	12.93	7.77	11.71	7.62	10.62
60	8.69	12.17	8.50	10.98	8.31	9.93
61	9.43	11.44	9.19	10.29	8.97	9.27
62	10.14	10.73	9.86	9.62	9.60	8.64
63	10.82	10.05	10.51	8.97	10.21	8.03
64	11.48	9.39	11.13	8.36	10.79	7.45
65	12.12	8.75	11.72	7.76	11.34	6.90
66	12.73	8.14	12.29	7.19	11.87	6.37
67	13.32	7.55	12.83	6.65	12.37	5.87
68	13.89	6.98	13.35	6.13	12.85	5.39
69	14.43	6.44	13.85	5.64	13.30	4.94
70	14.95	5.92	14.32	5.16	13.73	4.51
71	15.44	5.43	14.77	4.72	14.13	4.10
72	15.91	4.95	15.19	4.29	14.52	3.72
73	16.36	4.50	15.59	3.89	14.88	3.36
74	16.79	4.08	15.97	3.51	15.22	3.02
75	17.19	3.68	16.33	3.15	15.53	2.70

Females aged 51

Retirement age	2.5% pa Life multiplier—20.44		3% pa Life multiplier—19.11		3.5% pa Life multiplier—17.91	
	Earnings multiplier	*Pensions multiplier*	*Earnings multiplier*	*Pensions multiplier*	*Earnings multiplier*	*Pensions multiplier*
50	—	—	—	—	—	—
51	—	20.44	—	19.11	—	17.91
52	0.99	19.45	0.98	18.12	0.98	16.93
53	1.95	18.49	1.94	17.17	1.93	15.99
54	2.88	17.56	2.86	16.25	2.84	15.08
55	3.78	16.66	3.75	15.36	3.71	14.20
56	4.66	15.78	4.61	14.50	4.55	13.36
57	5.52	14.92	5.44	13.67	5.36	12.55
58	6.34	14.09	6.24	12.87	6.14	11.77
59	7.15	13.29	7.01	12.09	6.89	11.03
60	7.92	12.51	7.76	11.35	7.60	10.31
61	8.68	11.76	8.48	10.63	8.29	9.62
62	9.41	11.03	9.17	9.94	8.95	8.97
63	10.11	10.33	9.84	9.27	9.58	8.34
64	10.79	9.65	10.48	8.63	10.18	7.74
65	11.44	9.00	11.09	8.02	10.75	7.16
66	12.07	8.37	11.68	7.43	11.30	6.61
67	12.68	7.76	12.24	6.87	11.82	6.09
68	13.26	7.18	12.77	6.33	12.32	5.60
69	13.82	6.62	13.29	5.82	12.79	5.13
70	14.35	6.09	13.77	5.33	13.23	4.68
71	14.86	5.58	14.24	4.87	13.65	4.26
72	15.35	5.09	14.68	4.43	14.05	3.86
73	15.81	4.63	15.09	4.02	14.43	3.49
74	16.25	4.19	15.48	3.62	14.78	3.14
75	16.66	3.78	15.85	3.26	15.11	2.81

Females aged 52

Retirement age	2.5% pa Life multiplier—20.00		3% pa Life multiplier—18.73		3.5% pa Life multiplier—17.58	
	Earnings multiplier	*Pensions multiplier*	*Earnings multiplier*	*Pensions multiplier*	*Earnings multiplier*	*Pensions multiplier*
50	—	—	—	—	—	—
51	—	—	—	—	—	—
52	—	20.00	—	18.73	—	17.58
53	0.99	19.02	0.98	17.75	0.98	16.60
54	1.94	18.06	1.94	16.79	1.93	15.66
55	2.88	17.13	2.86	15.87	2.83	14.75
56	3.78	16.22	3.74	14.99	3.71	13.87
57	4.66	15.35	4.60	14.13	4.55	13.03
58	5.51	14.49	5.43	13.30	5.36	12.23
59	6.34	13.67	6.23	12.50	6.13	11.45
60	7.14	12.87	7.00	11.73	6.88	10.71
61	7.91	12.09	7.75	10.98	7.59	9.99
62	8.66	11.35	8.46	10.27	8.27	9.31
63	9.38	10.62	9.15	9.58	8.92	8.66
64	10.08	9.92	9.81	8.92	9.55	8.03
65	10.75	9.25	10.44	8.29	10.15	7.44
66	11.40	8.60	11.05	7.68	10.71	6.87
67	12.02	7.98	11.63	7.10	11.26	6.33
68	12.62	7.38	12.18	6.55	11.77	5.81
69	13.20	6.81	12.71	6.02	12.26	5.32
70	13.74	6.26	13.22	5.51	12.72	4.86
71	14.27	5.74	13.70	5.03	13.16	4.42
72	14.77	5.24	14.15	4.58	13.57	4.01
73	15.24	4.76	14.58	4.15	13.96	3.62
74	15.69	4.31	14.98	3.74	14.33	3.26
75	16.12	3.89	15.37	3.36	14.67	2.91

Females aged 53

Retirement age	2.5% pa Life multiplier—19.56		3% pa Life multiplier—18.34		3.5% pa Life multiplier—17.24	
	Earnings multiplier	*Pensions multiplier*	*Earnings multiplier*	*Pensions multiplier*	*Earnings multiplier*	*Pensions multiplier*
50	—	—	—	—	—	—
51	—	—	—	—	—	—
52	—	—	—	—	—	—
53	—	19.56	—	18.34	—	17.24
54	0.99	18.58	0.98	17.36	0.98	16.26
55	1.94	17.62	1.93	16.41	1.93	15.32
56	2.87	16.69	2.85	15.49	2.83	14.41
57	3.78	15.79	3.74	14.60	3.71	13.54
58	4.65	14.91	4.60	13.75	4.54	12.70
59	5.50	14.06	5.43	12.92	5.35	11.89
60	6.33	13.24	6.22	12.12	6.12	11.12
61	7.12	12.44	6.99	11.35	6.86	10.38
62	7.89	11.67	7.73	10.61	7.57	9.67
63	8.64	10.93	8.44	9.90	8.25	8.99
64	9.35	10.21	9.12	9.22	8.90	8.34
65	10.05	9.52	9.78	8.57	9.52	7.72
66	10.71	8.85	10.40	7.94	10.11	7.13
67	11.35	8.21	11.00	7.34	10.67	6.57
68	11.97	7.59	11.58	6.77	11.21	6.04
69	12.56	7.00	12.12	6.22	11.71	5.53
70	13.12	6.44	12.65	5.70	12.19	5.05
71	13.66	5.90	13.14	5.20	12.65	4.59
72	14.18	5.39	13.61	4.73	13.08	4.17
73	14.66	4.90	14.05	4.29	13.48	3.76
74	15.13	4.44	14.47	3.87	13.86	3.38
75	15.56	4.00	14.87	3.48	14.22	3.03

Females aged 54

Retirement age	2.5% pa Life multiplier—19.12		3% pa Life multiplier—17.95		3.5% pa Life multiplier—16.90	
	Earnings multiplier	*Pensions multiplier*	*Earnings multiplier*	*Pensions multiplier*	*Earnings multiplier*	*Pensions multiplier*
50	—	—	—	—	—	—
51	—	—	—	—	—	—
52	—	—	—	—	—	—
53	—	—	—	—	—	—
54	—	19.12	—	17.95	—	16.90
55	0.99	18.13	0.98	16.97	0.98	15.92
56	1.94	17.17	1.93	16.02	1.92	14.97
57	2.87	16.24	2.85	15.10	2.83	14.07
58	3.77	15.34	3.74	14.21	3.70	13.19
59	4.65	14.47	4.59	13.36	4.54	12.36
60	5.49	13.62	5.42	12.53	5.34	11.56
61	6.31	12.80	6.21	11.74	6.11	10.79
62	7.11	12.01	6.98	10.98	6.85	10.05
63	7.87	11.24	7.71	10.24	7.55	9.34
64	8.61	10.50	8.42	9.53	8.23	8.67
65	9.32	9.79	9.09	8.86	8.87	8.03
66	10.01	9.11	9.74	8.21	9.48	7.41
67	10.67	8.45	10.36	7.59	10.07	6.83
68	11.30	7.81	10.96	7.00	10.62	6.27
69	11.91	7.21	11.52	6.43	11.15	5.75
70	12.49	6.63	12.06	5.89	11.65	5.25
71	13.04	6.07	12.57	5.38	12.12	4.77
72	13.57	5.54	13.06	4.90	12.57	4.33
73	14.08	5.04	13.52	4.44	12.99	3.91
74	14.55	4.56	13.95	4.00	13.38	3.51
75	15.00	4.11	14.36	3.60	13.75	3.15

Females aged 55

Retirement age	2.5% pa Life multiplier—18.66 Earnings multiplier	2.5% pa Life multiplier—18.66 Pensions multiplier	3% pa Life multiplier—17.55 Earnings multiplier	3% pa Life multiplier—17.55 Pensions multiplier	3.5% pa Life multiplier—16.54 Earnings multiplier	3.5% pa Life multiplier—16.54 Pensions multiplier
50	—	—	—	—	—	—
51	—	—	—	—	—	—
52	—	—	—	—	—	—
53	—	—	—	—	—	—
54	—	—	—	—	—	—
55	—	18.66	—	17.55	—	16.54
56	0.99	17.68	0.98	16.57	0.98	15.56
57	1.94	16.72	1.93	15.62	1.92	14.62
58	2.87	15.79	2.85	14.70	2.83	13.72
59	3.77	14.89	3.73	13.82	3.70	12.85
60	4.64	14.02	4.59	12.97	4.53	12.01
61	5.49	13.18	5.41	12.14	5.33	11.21
62	6.30	12.36	6.20	11.35	6.10	10.45
63	7.09	11.57	6.96	10.59	6.83	9.71
64	7.85	10.81	7.69	9.86	7.53	9.01
65	8.58	10.08	8.39	9.16	8.20	8.34
66	9.29	9.37	9.06	8.49	8.84	7.70
67	9.97	8.70	9.70	7.85	9.45	7.10
68	10.62	8.04	10.32	7.24	10.02	6.52
69	11.24	7.42	10.90	6.65	10.57	5.97
70	11.84	6.82	11.46	6.09	11.09	5.45
71	12.41	6.25	11.99	5.57	11.58	4.96
72	12.96	5.71	12.49	5.06	12.05	4.50
73	13.47	5.19	12.96	4.59	12.48	4.06
74	13.96	4.70	13.41	4.14	12.89	3.65
75	14.43	4.24	13.83	3.72	13.27	3.27

Females aged 56

Retirement age	2.5% pa Life multiplier—18.21		3% pa Life multiplier—17.15		3.5% pa Life multiplier—16.19	
	Earnings multiplier	*Pensions multiplier*	*Earnings multiplier*	*Pensions multiplier*	*Earnings multiplier*	*Pensions multiplier*
50	—	—	—	—	—	—
51	—	—	—	—	—	—
52	—	—	—	—	—	—
53	—	—	—	—	—	—
54	—	—	—	—	—	—
55	—	—	—	—	—	—
56	—	18.21	—	17.15	—	16.19
57	0.99	17.22	0.98	16.16	0.98	15.21
58	1.94	16.27	1.93	15.22	1.92	14.26
59	2.87	15.34	2.85	14.30	2.83	13.36
60	3.77	14.44	3.73	13.42	3.69	12.49
61	4.63	13.57	4.58	12.57	4.53	11.66
62	5.47	12.73	5.40	11.75	5.32	10.86
63	6.29	11.92	6.18	10.96	6.09	10.10
64	7.07	11.14	6.94	10.21	6.81	9.37
65	7.83	10.38	7.66	9.48	7.51	8.68
66	8.55	9.65	8.36	8.79	8.17	8.01
67	9.25	8.96	9.02	8.12	8.80	7.38
68	9.92	8.28	9.66	7.49	9.40	6.78
69	10.57	7.64	10.26	6.88	9.97	6.21
70	11.18	7.03	10.84	6.31	10.51	5.67
71	11.77	6.44	11.39	5.76	11.02	5.16
72	12.33	5.88	11.91	5.24	11.51	4.68
73	12.86	5.34	12.40	4.75	11.96	4.22
74	13.37	4.84	12.86	4.28	12.39	3.80
75	13.84	4.36	13.30	3.85	12.79	3.40

Females aged 57

Retirement age	2.5% pa Life multiplier—17.75		3% pa Life multiplier—16.74		3.5% pa Life multiplier—15.82	
	Earnings multiplier	*Pensions multiplier*	*Earnings multiplier*	*Pensions multiplier*	*Earnings multiplier*	*Pensions multiplier*
50	—	—	—	—	—	—
51	—	—	—	—	—	—
52	—	—	—	—	—	—
53	—	—	—	—	—	—
54	—	—	—	—	—	—
55	—	—	—	—	—	—
56	—	—	—	—	—	—
57	—	17.75	—	16.74	—	15.82
58	0.98	16.76	0.98	15.76	0.98	14.84
59	1.94	15.81	1.93	14.81	1.92	13.90
60	2.86	14.88	2.84	13.89	2.82	13.00
61	3.76	13.99	3.72	13.01	3.69	12.13
62	4.63	13.12	4.57	12.17	4.52	11.30
63	5.46	12.28	5.39	11.35	5.31	10.51
64	6.27	11.48	6.17	10.57	6.07	9.75
65	7.05	10.70	6.92	9.82	6.79	9.03
66	7.80	9.95	7.64	9.10	7.48	8.34
67	8.52	9.23	8.33	8.41	8.14	7.68
68	9.21	8.54	8.98	7.76	8.77	7.06
69	9.87	7.87	9.61	7.13	9.36	6.46
70	10.51	7.24	10.21	6.53	9.92	5.90
71	11.11	6.63	10.77	5.96	10.45	5.37
72	11.69	6.06	11.31	5.43	10.95	4.87
73	12.24	5.51	11.82	4.92	11.42	4.40
74	12.76	4.99	12.30	4.44	11.87	3.95
75	13.25	4.50	12.75	3.99	12.28	3.54

Females aged 58

Retirement age	2.5% pa Life multiplier—17.28 Earnings multiplier	Pensions multiplier	3% pa Life multiplier—16.33 Earnings multiplier	Pensions multiplier	3.5% pa Life multiplier—15.45 Earnings multiplier	Pensions multiplier
50	—	—	—	—	—	—
51	—	—	—	—	—	—
52	—	—	—	—	—	—
53	—	—	—	—	—	—
54	—	—	—	—	—	—
55	—	—	—	—	—	—
56	—	—	—	—	—	—
57	—	—	—	—	—	—
58	—	17.28	—	16.33	—	15.45
59	0.98	16.30	0.98	15.34	0.98	14.47
60	1.94	15.34	1.93	14.40	1.92	13.53
61	2.86	14.42	2.84	13.48	2.82	12.63
62	3.75	13.53	3.72	12.61	3.68	11.77
63	4.62	12.67	4.56	11.76	4.51	10.94
64	5.45	11.83	5.37	10.95	5.30	10.15
65	6.25	11.03	6.15	10.17	6.05	9.40
66	7.03	10.26	6.90	9.43	6.77	8.68
67	7.77	9.51	7.61	8.72	7.46	8.00
68	8.48	8.80	8.29	8.04	8.11	7.35
69	9.16	8.12	8.94	7.39	8.72	6.73
70	9.82	7.46	9.56	6.77	9.31	6.14
71	10.44	6.84	10.15	6.18	9.86	5.59
72	11.04	6.24	10.70	5.62	10.38	5.07
73	11.60	5.68	11.23	5.09	10.87	4.58
74	12.14	5.14	11.73	4.60	11.34	4.12
75	12.65	4.64	12.20	4.13	11.77	3.68

Females aged 59

Retirement age	2.5% pa Life multiplier—16.82		3% pa Life multiplier—15.91		3.5% pa Life multiplier—15.08	
	Earnings multiplier	*Pensions multiplier*	*Earnings multiplier*	*Pensions multiplier*	*Earnings multiplier*	*Pensions multiplier*
50	—	—	—	—	—	—
51	—	—	—	—	—	—
52	—	—	—	—	—	—
53	—	—	—	—	—	—
54	—	—	—	—	—	—
55	—	—	—	—	—	—
56	—	—	—	—	—	—
57	—	—	—	—	—	—
58	—	—	—	—	—	—
59	—	16.82	—	15.91	—	15.08
60	0.98	15.83	0.98	14.93	0.98	14.10
61	1.94	14.88	1.93	13.98	1.92	13.16
62	2.86	13.96	2.84	13.07	2.82	12.26
63	3.75	13.07	3.71	12.20	3.68	11.40
64	4.61	12.21	4.55	11.36	4.50	10.58
65	5.44	11.38	5.36	10.55	5.29	9.79
66	6.23	10.58	6.13	9.78	6.03	9.04
67	7.00	9.82	6.87	9.04	6.75	8.33
68	7.73	9.08	7.58	8.33	7.42	7.65
69	8.44	8.38	8.25	7.66	8.07	7.01
70	9.11	7.70	8.89	7.02	8.68	6.40
71	9.76	7.06	9.50	6.41	9.25	5.83
72	10.37	6.44	10.08	5.83	9.80	5.28
73	10.96	5.86	10.63	5.28	10.31	4.77
74	11.51	5.31	11.14	4.77	10.79	4.29
75	12.03	4.78	11.63	4.28	11.24	3.84

Females aged 60

Retirement age	2.5% pa Life multiplier—16.35 Earnings multiplier	2.5% pa Pensions multiplier	3% pa Life multiplier—15.49 Earnings multiplier	3% pa Pensions multiplier	3.5% pa Life multiplier—14.70 Earnings multiplier	3.5% pa Pensions multiplier
50	—	—	—	—	—	—
51	—	—	—	—	—	—
52	—	—	—	—	—	—
53	—	—	—	—	—	—
54	—	—	—	—	—	—
55	—	—	—	—	—	—
56	—	—	—	—	—	—
57	—	—	—	—	—	—
58	—	—	—	—	—	—
59	—	—	—	—	—	—
60	—	16.35	—	15.49	—	14.70
61	0.98	15.37	0.98	14.51	0.98	13.72
62	1.94	14.41	1.93	13.56	1.92	12.78
63	2.85	13.49	2.83	12.65	2.81	11.89
64	3.74	12.61	3.71	11.78	3.67	11.03
65	4.60	11.75	4.54	10.95	4.49	10.21
66	5.42	10.93	5.34	10.14	5.27	9.43
67	6.21	10.14	6.11	9.38	6.01	8.69
68	6.97	9.38	6.84	8.65	6.72	7.98
69	7.70	8.65	7.54	7.95	7.39	7.31
70	8.40	7.95	8.21	7.28	8.03	6.68
71	9.06	7.29	8.84	6.65	8.63	6.07
72	9.70	6.65	9.44	6.05	9.19	5.51
73	10.30	6.05	10.01	5.48	9.73	4.97
74	10.87	5.48	10.54	4.95	10.23	4.47
75	11.41	4.94	11.05	4.44	10.70	4.00

Females aged 61

	2.5% pa Life multiplier—15.88		**3% pa Life multiplier—15.07**		**3.5% pa Life multiplier—14.32**	
Retirement age	*Earnings multiplier*	*Pensions multiplier*	*Earnings multiplier*	*Pensions multiplier*	*Earnings multiplier*	*Pensions multiplier*
50	—	—	—	—	—	—
51	—	—	—	—	—	—
52	—	—	—	—	—	—
53	—	—	—	—	—	—
54	—	—	—	—	—	—
55	—	—	—	—	—	—
56	—	—	—	—	—	—
57	—	—	—	—	—	—
58	—	—	—	—	—	—
59	—	—	—	—	—	—
60	—	—	—	—	—	—
61	—	15.88	—	15.07	—	14.32
62	0.98	14.90	0.98	14.09	0.98	13.34
63	1.93	13.95	1.92	13.14	1.91	12.41
64	2.85	13.03	2.83	12.24	2.81	11.51
65	3.73	12.15	3.70	11.37	3.66	10.66
66	4.58	11.30	4.53	10.54	4.48	9.84
67	5.40	10.48	5.33	9.74	5.25	9.07
68	6.19	9.69	6.09	8.98	5.99	8.33
69	6.94	8.94	6.81	8.25	6.69	7.63
70	7.66	8.22	7.51	7.56	7.35	6.97
71	8.35	7.53	8.16	6.91	7.98	6.34
72	9.00	6.88	8.78	6.28	8.57	5.75
73	9.63	6.25	9.37	5.69	9.13	5.19
74	10.22	5.66	9.93	5.14	9.65	4.67
75	10.78	5.10	10.45	4.61	10.14	4.18

Females aged 62

Retirement age	2.5% pa Life multiplier—15.41 Earnings multiplier	2.5% pa Life multiplier—15.41 Pensions multiplier	3% pa Life multiplier—14.64 Earnings multiplier	3% pa Life multiplier—14.64 Pensions multiplier	3.5% pa Life multiplier—13.94 Earnings multiplier	3.5% pa Life multiplier—13.94 Pensions multiplier
50	—	—	—	—	—	—
51	—	—	—	—	—	—
52	—	—	—	—	—	—
53	—	—	—	—	—	—
54	—	—	—	—	—	—
55	—	—	—	—	—	—
56	—	—	—	—	—	—
57	—	—	—	—	—	—
58	—	—	—	—	—	—
59	—	—	—	—	—	—
60	—	—	—	—	—	—
61	—	—	—	—	—	—
62	—	15.41	—	14.64	—	13.94
63	0.98	14.43	0.98	13.66	0.98	12.96
64	1.93	13.48	1.92	12.72	1.91	12.02
65	2.85	12.57	2.83	11.82	2.81	11.13
66	3.73	11.69	3.69	10.95	3.66	10.28
67	4.57	10.84	4.52	10.13	4.47	9.47
68	5.38	10.03	5.31	9.33	5.24	8.70
69	6.16	9.25	6.06	8.58	5.97	7.97
70	6.91	8.50	6.78	7.86	6.66	7.28
71	7.62	7.79	7.47	7.18	7.32	6.62
72	8.30	7.11	8.11	6.53	7.93	6.00
73	8.94	6.47	8.73	5.92	8.52	5.42
74	9.55	5.86	9.30	5.34	9.06	4.87
75	10.13	5.28	9.85	4.80	9.57	4.36

Females aged 63

Retirement age	2.5% pa Life multiplier—14.94		3% pa Life multiplier—14.22		3.5% pa Life multiplier—13.55	
	Earnings multiplier	*Pensions multiplier*	*Earnings multiplier*	*Pensions multiplier*	*Earnings multiplier*	*Pensions multiplier*
50	—	—	—	—	—	—
51	—	—	—	—	—	—
52	—	—	—	—	—	—
53	—	—	—	—	—	—
54	—	—	—	—	—	—
55	—	—	—	—	—	—
56	—	—	—	—	—	—
57	—	—	—	—	—	—
58	—	—	—	—	—	—
59	—	—	—	—	—	—
60	—	—	—	—	—	—
61	—	—	—	—	—	—
62	—	—	—	—	—	—
63	—	14.94	—	14.22	—	13.55
64	0.98	13.96	0.98	13.24	0.98	12.57
65	1.93	13.01	1.92	12.30	1.91	11.64
66	2.84	12.10	2.82	11.40	2.80	10.75
67	3.72	11.23	3.68	10.54	3.65	9.90
68	4.56	10.38	4.50	9.71	4.45	9.10
69	5.36	9.58	5.29	8.93	5.22	8.33
70	6.14	8.81	6.04	8.18	5.94	7.61
71	6.87	8.07	6.75	7.47	6.63	6.92
72	7.58	7.37	7.42	6.80	7.27	6.28
73	8.24	6.70	8.06	6.16	7.88	5.67
74	8.88	6.07	8.66	5.56	8.45	5.10
75	9.47	5.47	9.23	4.99	8.99	4.56

Females aged 64

Retirement age	2.5% pa Life multiplier—14.47		3% pa Life multiplier—13.79		3.5% pa Life multiplier—13.16	
	Earnings multiplier	*Pensions multiplier*	*Earnings multiplier*	*Pensions multiplier*	*Earnings multiplier*	*Pensions multiplier*
50	—	—	—	—	—	—
51	—	—	—	—	—	—
52	—	—	—	—	—	—
53	—	—	—	—	—	—
54	—	—	—	—	—	—
55	—	—	—	—	—	—
56	—	—	—	—	—	—
57	—	—	—	—	—	—
58	—	—	—	—	—	—
59	—	—	—	—	—	—
60	—	—	—	—	—	—
61	—	—	—	—	—	—
62	—	—	—	—	—	—
63	—	—	—	—	—	—
64	—	14.47	—	13.79	—	13.16
65	0.98	13.49	0.98	12.81	0.98	12.18
66	1.93	12.55	1.92	11.87	1.91	11.25
67	2.83	11.64	2.81	10.98	2.79	10.37
68	3.71	10.77	3.67	10.12	3.64	9.52
69	4.54	9.93	4.49	9.30	4.44	8.72
70	5.34	9.13	5.27	8.52	5.20	7.97
71	6.11	8.37	6.01	7.78	5.91	7.25
72	6.83	7.64	6.71	7.08	6.59	6.57
73	7.53	6.95	7.38	6.42	7.23	5.93
74	8.18	6.29	8.00	5.79	7.83	5.34
75	8.80	5.67	8.59	5.20	8.39	4.78

Females aged 65

Retirement age	2.5% pa Life multiplier—14.00		3% pa Life multiplier—13.37		3.5% pa Life multiplier—12.77	
	Earnings multiplier	*Pensions multiplier*	*Earnings multiplier*	*Pensions multiplier*	*Earnings multiplier*	*Pensions multiplier*
50	—	—	—	—	—	—
51	—	—	—	—	—	—
52	—	—	—	—	—	—
53	—	—	—	—	—	—
54	—	—	—	—	—	—
55	—	—	—	—	—	—
56	—	—	—	—	—	—
57	—	—	—	—	—	—
58	—	—	—	—	—	—
59	—	—	—	—	—	—
60	—	—	—	—	—	—
61	—	—	—	—	—	—
62	—	—	—	—	—	—
63	—	—	—	—	—	—
64	—	—	—	—	—	—
65	—	14.00	—	13.37	—	12.77
66	0.98	13.02	0.98	12.39	0.98	11.80
67	1.92	12.08	1.91	11.45	1.91	10.87
68	2.83	11.18	2.81	10.56	2.79	9.98
69	3.70	10.31	3.66	9.70	3.63	9.14
70	4.53	9.48	4.47	8.89	4.42	8.35
71	5.32	8.68	5.25	8.12	5.17	7.60
72	6.08	7.93	5.98	7.39	5.88	6.89
73	6.80	7.21	6.67	6.69	6.55	6.22
74	7.48	6.53	7.33	6.04	7.18	5.59
75	8.12	5.89	7.94	5.42	7.77	5.01

Females aged 66

Retirement age	2.5% pa Life multiplier—13.54		3% pa Life multiplier—12.94		3.5% pa Life multiplier—12.38	
	Earnings multiplier	*Pensions multiplier*	*Earnings multiplier*	*Pensions multiplier*	*Earnings multiplier*	*Pensions multiplier*
50	—	—	—	—	—	—
51	—	—	—	—	—	—
52	—	—	—	—	—	—
53	—	—	—	—	—	—
54	—	—	—	—	—	—
55	—	—	—	—	—	—
56	—	—	—	—	—	—
57	—	—	—	—	—	—
58	—	—	—	—	—	—
59	—	—	—	—	—	—
60	—	—	—	—	—	—
61	—	—	—	—	—	—
62	—	—	—	—	—	—
63	—	—	—	—	—	—
64	—	—	—	—	—	—
65	—	—	—	—	—	—
66	—	13.54	—	12.94	—	12.38
67	0.98	12.56	0.98	11.96	0.98	11.41
68	1.92	11.62	1.91	11.03	1.90	10.48
69	2.82	10.72	2.80	10.14	2.78	9.60
70	3.69	9.85	3.65	9.29	3.62	8.77
71	4.51	9.03	4.46	8.48	4.41	7.98
72	5.30	8.24	5.22	7.72	5.15	7.23
73	6.04	7.50	5.95	6.99	5.85	6.53
74	6.75	6.79	6.63	6.31	6.51	5.87
75	7.42	6.12	7.27	5.67	7.13	5.25

Females aged 67

	2.5% pa Life multiplier—13.07		**3% pa Life multiplier—12.51**		**3.5% pa Life multiplier—11.99**	
Retirement age	*Earnings multiplier*	*Pensions multiplier*	*Earnings multiplier*	*Pensions multiplier*	*Earnings multiplier*	*Pensions multiplier*
50	—	—	—	—	—	—
51	—	—	—	—	—	—
52	—	—	—	—	—	—
53	—	—	—	—	—	—
54	—	—	—	—	—	—
55	—	—	—	—	—	—
56	—	—	—	—	—	—
57	—	—	—	—	—	—
58	—	—	—	—	—	—
59	—	—	—	—	—	—
60	—	—	—	—	—	—
61	—	—	—	—	—	—
62	—	—	—	—	—	—
63	—	—	—	—	—	—
64	—	—	—	—	—	—
65	—	—	—	—	—	—
66	—	—	—	—	—	—
67	—	13.07	—	12.51	—	11.99
68	0.98	12.09	0.98	11.53	0.97	11.01
69	1.92	11.15	1.91	10.60	1.90	10.09
70	2.82	10.25	2.80	9.71	2.78	9.21
71	3.67	9.40	3.64	8.87	3.61	8.38
72	4.49	8.58	4.44	8.07	4.39	7.60
73	5.27	7.80	5.20	7.31	5.13	6.86
74	6.01	7.06	5.91	6.60	5.82	6.17
75	6.70	6.37	6.58	5.93	6.47	5.52

Females aged 68

Retirement age	2.5% pa Life multiplier—12.61		3% pa Life multiplier—12.08		3.5% pa Life multiplier—11.59	
	Earnings multiplier	*Pensions multiplier*	*Earnings multiplier*	*Pensions multiplier*	*Earnings multiplier*	*Pensions multiplier*
50	—	—	—	—	—	—
51	—	—	—	—	—	—
52	—	—	—	—	—	—
53	—	—	—	—	—	—
54	—	—	—	—	—	—
55	—	—	—	—	—	—
56	—	—	—	—	—	—
57	—	—	—	—	—	—
58	—	—	—	—	—	—
59	—	—	—	—	—	—
60	—	—	—	—	—	—
61	—	—	—	—	—	—
62	—	—	—	—	—	—
63	—	—	—	—	—	—
64	—	—	—	—	—	—
65	—	—	—	—	—	—
66	—	—	—	—	—	—
67	—	—	—	—	—	—
68	—	12.61	—	12.08	—	11.59
69	0.98	11.63	0.98	11.11	0.97	10.62
70	1.92	10.69	1.91	10.18	1.90	9.70
71	2.81	9.80	2.79	9.29	2.77	8.82
72	3.66	8.94	3.63	8.45	3.59	8.00
73	4.47	8.13	4.42	7.66	4.37	7.22
74	5.24	7.36	5.17	6.91	5.10	6.50
75	5.97	6.64	5.87	6.21	5.78	5.81

Females aged 69

	2.5% pa Life multiplier—12.14		3% pa Life multiplier—11.65		3.5% pa Life multiplier—11.20	
Retirement age	*Earnings multiplier*	*Pensions multiplier*	*Earnings multiplier*	*Pensions multiplier*	*Earnings multiplier*	*Pensions multiplier*
50	—	—	—	—	—	—
51	—	—	—	—	—	—
52	—	—	—	—	—	—
53	—	—	—	—	—	—
54	—	—	—	—	—	—
55	—	—	—	—	—	—
56	—	—	—	—	—	—
57	—	—	—	—	—	—
58	—	—	—	—	—	—
59	—	—	—	—	—	—
60	—	—	—	—	—	—
61	—	—	—	—	—	—
62	—	—	—	—	—	—
63	—	—	—	—	—	—
64	—	—	—	—	—	—
65	—	—	—	—	—	—
66	—	—	—	—	—	—
67	—	—	—	—	—	—
68	—	—	—	—	—	—
69	—	12.14	—	11.65	—	11.20
70	0.98	11.16	0.98	10.68	0.97	10.22
71	1.91	10.23	1.90	9.75	1.89	9.30
72	2.80	9.34	2.78	8.87	2.76	8.44
73	3.65	8.49	3.61	8.04	3.58	7.62
74	4.45	7.69	4.40	7.25	4.35	6.85
75	5.21	6.93	5.14	6.52	5.07	6.13

Females aged 70

Retirement age	2.5% pa Life multiplier—11.68		3% pa Life multiplier—11.23		3.5% pa Life multiplier—10.80	
	Earnings multiplier	*Pensions multiplier*	*Earnings multiplier*	*Pensions multiplier*	*Earnings multiplier*	*Pensions multiplier*
50	—	—	—	—	—	—
51	—	—	—	—	—	—
52	—	—	—	—	—	—
53	—	—	—	—	—	—
54	—	—	—	—	—	—
55	—	—	—	—	—	—
56	—	—	—	—	—	—
57	—	—	—	—	—	—
58	—	—	—	—	—	—
59	—	—	—	—	—	—
60	—	—	—	—	—	—
61	—	—	—	—	—	—
62	—	—	—	—	—	—
63	—	—	—	—	—	—
64	—	—	—	—	—	—
65	—	—	—	—	—	—
66	—	—	—	—	—	—
67	—	—	—	—	—	—
68	—	—	—	—	—	—
69	—	—	—	—	—	—
70	—	11.68	—	11.23	—	10.80
71	0.98	10.70	0.97	10.25	0.97	9.83
72	1.91	9.77	1.90	9.33	1.89	8.91
73	2.79	8.88	2.77	8.45	2.75	8.05
74	3.63	8.04	3.60	7.63	3.57	7.23
75	4.43	7.25	4.38	6.85	4.33	6.48

Females aged 71

Retirement age	2.5% pa Life multiplier—11.21 *Earnings multiplier*	*Pensions multiplier*	3% pa Life multiplier—10.79 *Earnings multiplier*	*Pensions multiplier*	3.5% pa Life multiplier—10.40 *Earnings multiplier*	*Pensions multiplier*
50	—	—	—	—	—	—
51	—	—	—	—	—	—
52	—	—	—	—	—	—
53	—	—	—	—	—	—
54	—	—	—	—	—	—
55	—	—	—	—	—	—
56	—	—	—	—	—	—
57	—	—	—	—	—	—
58	—	—	—	—	—	—
59	—	—	—	—	—	—
60	—	—	—	—	—	—
61	—	—	—	—	—	—
62	—	—	—	—	—	—
63	—	—	—	—	—	—
64	—	—	—	—	—	—
65	—	—	—	—	—	—
66	—	—	—	—	—	—
67	—	—	—	—	—	—
68	—	—	—	—	—	—
69	—	—	—	—	—	—
70	—	—	—	—	—	—
71	—	11.21	—	10.79	—	10.40
72	0.98	10.24	0.97	9.82	0.97	9.43
73	1.90	9.31	1.90	8.90	1.89	8.51
74	2.78	8.43	2.76	8.03	2.74	7.66
75	3.62	7.60	3.58	7.21	3.55	6.85

Females aged 72

Retirement age	2.5% pa Life multiplier—10.75		3% pa Life multiplier—10.36		3.5% pa Life multiplier—10.00	
	Earnings multiplier	*Pensions multiplier*	*Earnings multiplier*	*Pensions multiplier*	*Earnings multiplier*	*Pensions multiplier*
50	—	—	—	—	—	—
51	—	—	—	—	—	—
52	—	—	—	—	—	—
53	—	—	—	—	—	—
54	—	—	—	—	—	—
55	—	—	—	—	—	—
56	—	—	—	—	—	—
57	—	—	—	—	—	—
58	—	—	—	—	—	—
59	—	—	—	—	—	—
60	—	—	—	—	—	—
61	—	—	—	—	—	—
62	—	—	—	—	—	—
63	—	—	—	—	—	—
64	—	—	—	—	—	—
65	—	—	—	—	—	—
66	—	—	—	—	—	—
67	—	—	—	—	—	—
68	—	—	—	—	—	—
69	—	—	—	—	—	—
70	—	—	—	—	—	—
71	—	—	—	—	—	—
72	—	10.75	—	10.36	—	10.00
73	0.97	9.78	0.97	9.39	0.97	9.03
74	1.90	8.85	1.89	8.47	1.88	8.12
75	2.77	7.98	2.75	7.61	2.73	7.27

Females aged 73

	2.5% pa Life multiplier—10.30		3% pa Life multiplier—9.94		3.5% pa Life multiplier—9.60	
Retirement age	*Earnings multiplier*	*Pensions multiplier*	*Earnings multiplier*	*Pensions multiplier*	*Earnings multiplier*	*Pensions multiplier*
50	—	—	—	—	—	—
51	—	—	—	—	—	—
52	—	—	—	—	—	—
53	—	—	—	—	—	—
54	—	—	—	—	—	—
55	—	—	—	—	—	—
56	—	—	—	—	—	—
57	—	—	—	—	—	—
58	—	—	—	—	—	—
59	—	—	—	—	—	—
60	—	—	—	—	—	—
61	—	—	—	—	—	—
62	—	—	—	—	—	—
63	—	—	—	—	—	—
64	—	—	—	—	—	—
65	—	—	—	—	—	—
66	—	—	—	—	—	—
67	—	—	—	—	—	—
68	—	—	—	—	—	—
69	—	—	—	—	—	—
70	—	—	—	—	—	—
71	—	—	—	—	—	—
72	—	—	—	—	—	—
73	—	10.30	—	9.94	—	9.60
74	0.97	9.33	0.97	8.97	0.97	8.63
75	1.89	8.41	1.88	8.06	1.87	7.73

Females aged 74

Retirement age	2.5% pa Life multiplier—9.86 Earnings multiplier	2.5% pa Life multiplier—9.86 Pensions multiplier	3% pa Life multiplier—9.53 Earnings multiplier	3% pa Life multiplier—9.53 Pensions multiplier	3.5% pa Life multiplier—9.21 Earnings multiplier	3.5% pa Life multiplier—9.21 Pensions multiplier
50	—	—	—	—	—	—
51	—	—	—	—	—	—
52	—	—	—	—	—	—
53	—	—	—	—	—	—
54	—	—	—	—	—	—
55	—	—	—	—	—	—
56	—	—	—	—	—	—
57	—	—	—	—	—	—
58	—	—	—	—	—	—
59	—	—	—	—	—	—
60	—	—	—	—	—	—
61	—	—	—	—	—	—
62	—	—	—	—	—	—
63	—	—	—	—	—	—
64	—	—	—	—	—	—
65	—	—	—	—	—	—
66	—	—	—	—	—	—
67	—	—	—	—	—	—
68	—	—	—	—	—	—
69	—	—	—	—	—	—
70	—	—	—	—	—	—
71	—	—	—	—	—	—
72	—	—	—	—	—	—
73	—	—	—	—	—	—
74	—	9.86	—	9.53	—	9.21
75	0.97	8.88	0.97	8.56	0.97	8.25

Females aged 75

Retirement age	2.5% pa Life multiplier—9.42		3% pa Life multiplier—9.11		3.5% pa Life multiplier—8.83	
	Earnings multiplier	*Pensions multiplier*	*Earnings multiplier*	*Pensions multiplier*	*Earnings multiplier*	*Pensions multiplier*
50	—	—	—	—	—	—
51	—	—	—	—	—	—
52	—	—	—	—	—	—
53	—	—	—	—	—	—
54	—	—	—	—	—	—
55	—	—	—	—	—	—
56	—	—	—	—	—	—
57	—	—	—	—	—	—
58	—	—	—	—	—	—
59	—	—	—	—	—	—
60	—	—	—	—	—	—
61	—	—	—	—	—	—
62	—	—	—	—	—	—
63	—	—	—	—	—	—
64	—	—	—	—	—	—
65	—	—	—	—	—	—
66	—	—	—	—	—	—
67	—	—	—	—	—	—
68	—	—	—	—	—	—
69	—	—	—	—	—	—
70	—	—	—	—	—	—
71	—	—	—	—	—	—
72	—	—	—	—	—	—
73	—	—	—	—	—	—
74	—	—	—	—	—	—
75	—	9.42	—	9.11	—	8.83

Females aged 76–100

Age	2.5% pa *Life/pensions multiplier*	3% pa *Life/pensions multiplier*	3.5% pa *Life/pensions multiplier*
76	8.98	8.70	8.44
77	8.54	8.29	8.05
78	8.12	7.89	7.67
79	7.71	7.50	7.30
80	7.31	7.12	6.94
81	6.92	6.75	6.58
82	6.54	6.39	6.24
83	6.18	6.04	5.90
84	5.82	5.69	5.57
85	5.48	5.36	5.26
86	5.15	5.05	4.95
87	4.85	4.76	4.67
88	4.56	4.48	4.40
89	4.27	4.20	4.13
90	4.00	3.94	3.88
91	3.75	3.70	3.64
92	3.52	3.47	3.42
93	3.31	3.26	3.22
94	3.11	3.07	3.03
95	2.92	2.88	2.85
96	2.75	2.72	2.69
97	2.60	2.57	2.54
98	2.45	2.43	2.40
99	2.30	2.28	2.26
100	2.16	2.14	2.12

Fixed term multipliers

0–8 years

Years	Months	*2.5%*	***3.0%***	*3.5%*	Years	Months	*2.5%*	***3.0%***	*3.5%*
0	1	0.08	0.08	0.08	4	2	3.96	3.92	3.88
0	2	0.17	0.17	0.17	4	3	4.03	3.99	3.95
0	3	0.25	0.25	0.25	4	4	4.11	4.07	4.03
0	4	0.33	0.33	0.33	4	5	4.18	4.14	4.10
0	5	0.41	0.41	0.41	4	6	4.26	4.21	4.17
0	6	0.50	0.50	0.50	4	7	4.33	4.29	4.24
0	7	0.58	0.58	0.58	4	8	4.41	4.36	4.31
0	8	0.66	0.66	0.66	4	9	4.48	4.43	4.38
0	9	0.74	0.74	0.74	4	10	4.56	4.50	4.45
0	10	0.82	0.82	0.82	4	11	4.63	4.58	4.52
0	11	0.91	0.90	0.90	**5**	**0**	**4.70**	**4.65**	**4.59**
1	**0**	**0.99**	**0.99**	**0.98**	5	1	4.78	4.72	4.66
1	1	1.07	1.07	1.06	5	2	4.85	4.79	4.73
1	2	1.15	1.15	1.14	5	3	4.92	4.86	4.80
1	3	1.23	1.23	1.22	5	4	5.00	4.93	4.87
1	4	1.31	1.31	1.30	5	5	5.07	5.01	4.94
1	5	1.39	1.39	1.38	5	6	5.14	5.08	5.01
1	6	1.47	1.47	1.46	5	7	5.22	5.15	5.08
1	7	1.55	1.55	1.54	5	8	5.29	5.22	5.15
1	8	1.63	1.63	1.62	5	9	5.36	5.29	5.22
1	9	1.71	1.71	1.70	5	10	5.43	5.36	5.29
1	10	1.79	1.78	1.78	5	11	5.50	5.43	5.35
1	11	1.87	1.86	1.85	**6**	**0**	**5.58**	**5.50**	**5.42**
2	**0**	**1.95**	**1.94**	**1.93**	6	1	5.65	5.57	5.49
2	1	2.03	2.02	2.01	6	2	5.72	5.64	5.56
2	2	2.11	2.10	2.09	6	3	5.79	5.71	5.62
2	3	2.19	2.18	2.17	6	4	5.86	5.78	5.69
2	4	2.27	2.25	2.24	6	5	5.93	5.84	5.76
2	5	2.35	2.33	2.32	6	6	6.01	5.91	5.82
2	6	2.42	2.41	2.40	6	7	6.08	5.98	5.89
2	7	2.50	2.49	2.47	6	8	6.15	6.05	5.96
2	8	2.58	2.56	2.55	6	9	6.22	6.12	6.02
2	9	2.66	2.64	2.62	6	10	6.29	6.19	6.09
2	10	2.74	2.72	2.70	6	11	6.36	6.26	6.16
2	11	2.81	2.79	2.78	**7**	**0**	**6.43**	**6.32**	**6.22**
3	**0**	**2.89**	**2.87**	**2.85**	7	1	6.50	6.39	6.29
3	1	2.97	2.95	2.93	7	2	6.57	6.46	6.35
3	2	3.05	3.02	3.00	7	3	6.64	6.53	6.42
3	3	3.12	3.10	3.07	7	4	6.71	6.59	6.48
3	4	3.20	3.17	3.15	7	5	6.78	6.66	6.55
3	5	3.28	3.25	3.22	7	6	6.85	6.73	6.61
3	6	3.35	3.33	3.30	7	7	6.92	6.79	6.67
3	7	3.43	3.40	3.37	7	8	6.98	6.86	6.74
3	8	3.51	3.47	3.44	7	9	7.05	6.93	6.80
3	9	3.58	3.55	3.52	7	10	7.12	6.99	6.87
3	10	3.66	3.62	3.59	7	11	7.19	7.06	6.93
3	11	3.73	3.70	3.66	**8**	**0**	**7.26**	**7.12**	**6.99**
4	**0**	**3.81**	**3.77**	**3.74**	8	1	7.33	7.19	7.06
4	1	3.88	3.85	3.81	8	2	7.40	7.26	7.12

8–16 years

Years	Months	*2.5%*	***3.0%***	*3.5%*	Years	Months	*2.5%*	***3.0%***	*3.5%*
8	3	7.46	7.32	7.18	12	7	10.82	10.51	10.21
8	4	7.53	7.39	7.25	12	8	10.88	10.57	10.27
8	5	7.60	7.45	7.31	12	9	10.94	10.62	10.32
8	6	7.67	7.52	7.37	12	10	11.00	10.68	10.38
8	7	7.73	7.58	7.43	12	11	11.06	10.74	10.43
8	8	7.80	7.65	7.49	**13**	**0**	**11.12**	**10.79**	**10.48**
8	9	7.87	7.71	7.56	13	1	11.18	10.85	10.54
8	10	7.94	7.77	7.62	13	2	11.24	10.91	10.59
8	11	8.00	7.84	7.68	13	3	11.30	10.96	10.64
9	**0**	**8.07**	**7.90**	**7.74**	13	4	11.36	11.02	10.69
9	1	8.14	7.97	7.80	13	5	11.42	11.08	10.75
9	2	8.20	8.03	7.86	13	6	11.48	11.13	10.80
9	3	8.27	8.09	7.92	13	7	11.54	11.19	10.85
9	4	8.34	8.16	7.98	13	8	11.60	11.24	10.90
9	5	8.40	8.22	8.04	13	9	11.66	11.30	10.96
9	6	8.47	8.28	8.10	13	10	11.72	11.35	11.01
9	7	8.53	8.35	8.16	13	11	11.78	11.41	11.06
9	8	8.60	8.41	8.22	**14**	**0**	**11.84**	**11.46**	**11.11**
9	9	8.67	8.47	8.28	14	1	11.90	11.52	11.16
9	10	8.73	8.53	8.34	14	2	11.95	11.57	11.21
9	11	8.80	8.60	8.40	14	3	12.01	11.63	11.26
10	**0**	**8.86**	**8.66**	**8.46**	14	4	12.07	11.68	11.32
10	1	8.93	8.72	8.52	14	5	12.13	11.74	11.37
10	2	8.99	8.78	8.58	14	6	12.19	11.79	11.42
10	3	9.06	8.84	8.64	14	7	12.25	11.85	11.47
10	4	9.12	8.90	8.70	14	8	12.30	11.90	11.52
10	5	9.18	8.97	8.75	14	9	12.36	11.96	11.57
10	6	9.25	9.03	8.81	14	10	12.42	12.01	11.62
10	7	9.31	9.09	8.87	14	11	12.48	12.06	11.67
10	8	9.38	9.15	8.93	**15**	**0**	**12.54**	**12.12**	**11.72**
10	9	9.44	9.21	8.99	15	1	12.59	12.17	11.77
10	10	9.51	9.27	9.04	15	2	12.65	12.22	11.82
10	11	9.57	9.33	9.10	15	3	12.71	12.28	11.87
11	**0**	**9.63**	**9.39**	**9.16**	15	4	12.76	12.33	11.92
11	1	9.70	9.45	9.22	15	5	12.82	12.38	11.96
11	2	9.76	9.51	9.27	15	6	12.88	12.43	12.01
11	3	9.82	9.57	9.33	15	7	12.94	12.49	12.06
11	4	9.89	9.63	9.39	15	8	12.99	12.54	12.11
11	5	9.95	9.69	9.44	15	9	13.05	12.59	12.16
11	6	10.01	9.75	9.50	15	10	13.11	12.64	12.21
11	7	10.07	9.81	9.55	15	11	13.16	12.70	12.26
11	8	10.14	9.87	9.61	**16**	**0**	**13.22**	**12.75**	**12.30**
11	9	10.20	9.93	9.67	16	1	13.27	12.80	12.35
11	10	10.26	9.99	9.72	16	2	13.33	12.85	12.40
11	11	10.32	10.04	9.78	16	3	13.39	12.90	12.45
12	**0**	**10.39**	**10.10**	**9.83**	16	4	13.44	12.96	12.50
12	1	10.45	10.16	9.89	16	5	13.50	13.01	12.54
12	2	10.51	10.22	9.94	16	6	13.55	13.06	12.59
12	3	10.57	10.28	10.00	16	7	13.61	13.11	12.64
12	4	10.63	10.34	10.05	16	8	13.66	13.16	12.68
12	5	10.69	10.39	10.11	16	9	13.72	13.21	12.73
12	6	10.75	10.45	10.16	16	10	13.77	13.26	12.78

16–25 years

Years	Months	*2.5%*	***3.0%***	*3.5%*	Years	Months	*2.5%*	***3.0%***	*3.5%*
16	11	13.83	13.31	12.82	21	3	16.53	15.78	15.07
17	**0**	**13.88**	**13.36**	**12.87**	21	4	16.58	15.82	15.11
17	1	13.94	13.41	12.92	21	5	16.63	15.87	15.15
17	2	13.99	13.46	12.96	21	6	16.68	15.91	15.19
17	3	14.05	13.51	13.01	21	7	16.73	15.96	15.23
17	4	14.10	13.56	13.06	21	8	16.78	16.00	15.27
17	5	14.16	13.61	13.10	21	9	16.83	16.04	15.31
17	6	14.21	13.66	13.15	21	10	16.88	16.09	15.35
17	7	14.26	13.71	13.19	21	11	16.93	16.13	15.39
17	8	14.32	13.76	13.24	**22**	**0**	**16.97**	**16.17**	**15.43**
17	9	14.37	13.81	13.28	22	1	17.02	16.22	15.47
17	10	14.42	13.86	13.33	22	2	17.07	16.26	15.51
17	11	14.48	13.91	13.37	22	3	17.12	16.30	15.55
18	**0**	**14.53**	**13.96**	**13.42**	22	4	17.17	16.35	15.59
18	1	14.59	14.01	13.46	22	5	17.21	16.39	15.63
18	2	14.64	14.06	13.51	22	6	17.26	16.43	15.66
18	3	14.69	14.11	13.55	22	7	17.31	16.48	15.70
18	4	14.74	14.15	13.60	22	8	17.36	16.52	15.74
18	5	14.80	14.20	13.64	22	9	17.41	16.56	15.78
18	6	14.85	14.25	13.69	22	10	17.45	16.60	15.82
18	7	14.90	14.30	13.73	22	11	17.50	16.65	15.85
18	8	14.96	14.35	13.77	**23**	**0**	**17.55**	**16.69**	**15.89**
18	9	15.01	14.39	13.82	23	1	17.60	16.73	15.93
18	10	15.06	14.44	13.86	23	2	17.64	16.77	15.97
18	11	15.11	14.49	13.90	23	3	17.69	16.82	16.01
19	**0**	**15.17**	**14.54**	**13.95**	23	4	17.74	16.86	16.04
19	1	15.22	14.59	13.99	23	5	17.78	16.90	16.08
19	2	15.27	14.63	14.03	23	6	17.83	16.94	16.12
19	3	15.32	14.68	14.08	23	7	17.88	16.98	16.15
19	4	15.37	14.73	14.12	23	8	17.92	17.02	16.19
19	5	15.42	14.77	14.16	23	9	17.97	17.06	16.23
19	6	15.48	14.82	14.21	23	10	18.02	17.11	16.26
19	7	15.53	14.87	14.25	23	11	18.06	17.15	16.30
19	8	15.58	14.91	14.29	**24**	**0**	**18.11**	**17.19**	**16.34**
19	9	15.63	14.96	14.33	24	1	18.15	17.23	16.37
19	10	15.68	15.01	14.38	24	2	18.20	17.27	16.41
19	11	15.73	15.05	14.42	24	3	18.25	17.31	16.45
20	**0**	**15.78**	**15.10**	**14.46**	24	4	18.29	17.35	16.48
20	1	15.83	15.15	14.50	24	5	18.34	17.39	16.52
20	2	15.88	15.19	14.54	24	6	18.38	17.43	16.55
20	3	15.94	15.24	14.58	24	7	18.43	17.47	16.59
20	4	15.99	15.28	14.63	24	8	18.47	17.51	16.63
20	5	16.04	15.33	14.67	24	9	18.52	17.55	16.66
20	6	16.09	15.37	14.71	24	10	18.56	17.59	16.70
20	7	16.14	15.42	14.75	24	11	18.61	17.63	16.73
20	8	16.19	15.47	14.79	**25**	**0**	**18.65**	**17.67**	**16.77**
20	9	16.24	15.51	14.83	25	1	18.70	17.71	16.80
20	10	16.29	15.56	14.87	25	2	18.74	17.75	16.84
20	11	16.34	15.60	14.91	25	3	18.79	17.79	16.87
21	**0**	**16.39**	**15.65**	**14.95**	25	4	18.83	17.83	16.91
21	1	16.44	15.69	14.99	25	5	18.88	17.87	16.94
21	2	16.49	15.73	15.03	25	6	18.92	17.91	16.98

25–34 years

Years	Months	*2.5%*	***3.0%***	*3.5%*
25	7	18.97	17.95	17.01
25	8	19.01	17.99	17.05
25	9	19.05	18.03	17.08
25	10	19.10	18.07	17.12
25	11	19.14	18.10	17.15
26	**0**	**19.19**	**18.14**	**17.18**
26	1	19.23	18.18	17.22
26	2	19.27	18.22	17.25
26	3	19.32	18.26	17.29
26	4	19.36	18.30	17.32
26	5	19.40	18.34	17.35
26	6	19.45	18.37	17.39
26	7	19.49	18.41	17.42
26	8	19.53	18.45	17.45
26	9	19.58	18.49	17.49
26	10	19.62	18.53	17.52
26	11	19.66	18.56	17.55
27	**0**	**19.71**	**18.60**	**17.59**
27	1	19.75	18.64	17.62
27	2	19.79	18.68	17.65
27	3	19.83	18.71	17.68
27	4	19.88	18.75	17.72
27	5	19.92	18.79	17.75
27	6	19.96	18.82	17.78
27	7	20.00	18.86	17.81
27	8	20.05	18.90	17.85
27	9	20.09	18.93	17.88
27	10	20.13	18.97	17.91
27	11	20.17	19.01	17.94
28	**0**	**20.21**	**19.04**	**17.97**
28	1	20.26	19.08	18.01
28	2	20.30	19.12	18.04
28	3	20.34	19.15	18.07
28	4	20.38	19.19	18.10
28	5	20.42	19.23	18.13
28	6	20.46	19.26	18.16
28	7	20.50	19.30	18.19
28	8	20.54	19.33	18.23
28	9	20.59	19.37	18.26
28	10	20.63	19.40	18.29
28	11	20.67	19.44	18.32
29	**0**	**20.71**	**19.47**	**18.35**
29	1	20.75	19.51	18.38
29	2	20.79	19.55	18.41
29	3	20.83	19.58	18.44
29	4	20.87	19.62	18.47
29	5	20.91	19.65	18.50
29	6	20.95	19.69	18.53
29	7	20.99	19.72	18.56
29	8	21.03	19.75	18.59
29	9	21.07	19.79	18.62
29	10	21.11	19.82	18.65
29	11	21.15	19.86	18.68
30	**0**	**21.19**	**19.89**	**18.71**
30	1	21.23	19.93	18.74
30	2	21.27	19.96	18.77
30	3	21.31	20.00	18.80
30	4	21.35	20.03	18.83
30	5	21.39	20.06	18.86
30	6	21.43	20.10	18.89
30	7	21.47	20.13	18.92
30	8	21.51	20.16	18.95
30	9	21.55	20.20	18.98
30	10	21.58	20.23	19.00
30	11	21.62	20.27	19.03
31	**0**	**21.66**	**20.30**	**19.06**
31	1	21.70	20.33	19.09
31	2	21.74	20.37	19.12
31	3	21.78	20.40	19.15
31	4	21.82	20.43	19.18
31	5	21.85	20.46	19.20
31	6	21.89	20.50	19.23
31	7	21.93	20.53	19.26
31	8	21.97	20.56	19.29
31	9	22.01	20.60	19.32
31	10	22.05	20.63	19.35
31	11	22.08	20.66	19.37
32	**0**	**22.12**	**20.69**	**19.40**
32	1	22.16	20.73	19.43
32	2	22.20	20.76	19.46
32	3	22.23	20.79	19.48
32	4	22.27	20.82	19.51
32	5	22.31	20.85	19.54
32	6	22.35	20.89	19.57
32	7	22.38	20.92	19.59
32	8	22.42	20.95	19.62
32	9	22.46	20.98	19.65
32	10	22.50	21.01	19.67
32	11	22.53	21.04	19.70
33	**0**	**22.57**	**21.08**	**19.73**
33	1	22.61	21.11	19.75
33	2	22.64	21.14	19.78
33	3	22.68	21.17	19.81
33	4	22.72	21.20	19.83
33	5	22.75	21.23	19.86
33	6	22.79	21.26	19.89
33	7	22.83	21.29	19.91
33	8	22.86	21.32	19.94
33	9	22.90	21.36	19.97
33	10	22.93	21.39	19.99
33	11	22.97	21.42	20.02
34	**0**	**23.01**	**21.45**	**20.04**
34	1	23.04	21.48	20.07
34	2	23.08	21.51	20.10

34–42 years

Years	Months	*2.5%*	***3.0%***	*3.5%*	Years	Months	*2.5%*	***3.0%***	*3.5%*
34	3	23.11	21.54	20.12	38	7	24.88	23.02	21.36
34	4	23.15	21.57	20.15	38	8	24.91	23.04	21.38
34	5	23.19	21.60	20.17	38	9	24.94	23.07	21.40
34	6	23.22	21.63	20.20	38	10	24.97	23.10	21.43
34	7	23.26	21.66	20.22	38	11	25.01	23.12	21.45
34	8	23.29	21.69	20.25	**39**	**0**	**25.04**	**23.15**	**21.47**
34	9	23.33	21.72	20.27	39	1	25.07	23.17	21.49
34	10	23.36	21.75	20.30	39	2	25.10	23.20	21.51
34	11	23.40	21.78	20.32	39	3	25.13	23.23	21.53
35	**0**	**23.43**	**21.81**	**20.35**	39	4	25.16	23.25	21.56
35	1	23.47	21.84	20.37	39	5	25.20	23.28	21.58
35	2	23.50	21.87	20.40	39	6	25.23	23.31	21.60
35	3	23.54	21.90	20.42	39	7	25.26	23.33	21.62
35	4	23.57	21.93	20.45	39	8	25.29	23.36	21.64
35	5	23.61	21.96	20.47	39	9	25.32	23.38	21.66
35	6	23.64	21.98	20.50	39	10	25.35	23.41	21.68
35	7	23.68	22.01	20.52	39	11	25.38	23.43	21.71
35	8	23.71	22.04	20.55	**40**	**0**	**25.42**	**23.46**	**21.73**
35	9	23.75	22.07	20.57	40	1	25.45	23.49	21.75
35	10	23.78	22.10	20.60	40	2	25.48	23.51	21.77
35	11	23.82	22.13	20.62	40	3	25.51	23.54	21.79
36	**0**	**23.85**	**22.16**	**20.64**	40	4	25.54	23.56	21.81
36	1	23.88	22.19	20.67	40	5	25.57	23.59	21.83
36	2	23.92	22.22	20.69	40	6	25.60	23.61	21.85
36	3	23.95	22.24	20.72	40	7	25.63	23.64	21.87
36	4	23.99	22.27	20.74	40	8	25.66	23.66	21.89
36	5	24.02	22.30	20.76	40	9	25.69	23.69	21.91
36	6	24.05	22.33	20.79	40	10	25.72	23.71	21.93
36	7	24.09	22.36	20.81	40	11	25.75	23.74	21.95
36	8	24.12	22.39	20.83	**41**	**0**	**25.78**	**23.76**	**21.97**
36	9	24.15	22.41	20.86	41	1	25.81	23.79	22.00
36	10	24.19	22.44	20.88	41	2	25.84	23.81	22.02
36	11	24.22	22.47	20.91	41	3	25.87	23.84	22.04
37	**0**	**24.26**	**22.50**	**20.93**	41	4	25.90	23.86	22.06
37	1	24.29	22.53	20.95	41	5	25.93	23.89	22.08
37	2	24.32	22.55	20.97	41	6	25.96	23.91	22.10
37	3	24.36	22.58	21.00	41	7	25.99	23.93	22.12
37	4	24.39	22.61	21.02	41	8	26.02	23.96	22.14
37	5	24.42	22.64	21.04	41	9	26.05	23.98	22.16
37	6	24.45	22.66	21.07	41	10	26.08	24.01	22.18
37	7	24.49	22.69	21.09	41	11	26.11	24.03	22.20
37	8	24.52	22.72	21.11	**42**	**0**	**26.14**	**24.06**	**22.21**
37	9	24.55	22.75	21.14	42	1	26.17	24.08	22.23
37	10	24.59	22.77	21.16	42	2	26.20	24.10	22.25
37	11	24.62	22.80	21.18	42	3	26.23	24.13	22.27
38	**0**	**24.65**	**22.83**	**21.20**	42	4	26.26	24.15	22.29
38	1	24.68	22.86	21.23	42	5	26.29	24.17	22.31
38	2	24.72	22.88	21.25	42	6	26.32	24.20	22.33
38	3	24.75	22.91	21.27	42	7	26.35	24.22	22.35
38	4	24.78	22.94	21.29	42	8	26.38	24.25	22.37
38	5	24.81	22.96	21.32	42	9	26.41	24.27	22.39
38	6	24.85	22.99	21.34	42	10	26.43	24.29	22.41

42–51 years

Years	Months	*2.5%*	***3.0%***	*3.5%*
42	11	26.46	24.32	22.43
43	**0**	**26.49**	**24.34**	**22.45**
43	1	26.52	24.36	22.47
43	2	26.55	24.39	22.48
43	3	26.58	24.41	22.50
43	4	26.61	24.43	22.52
43	5	26.64	24.46	22.54
43	6	26.66	24.48	22.56
43	7	26.69	24.50	22.58
43	8	26.72	24.53	22.60
43	9	26.75	24.55	22.62
43	10	26.78	24.57	22.63
43	11	26.81	24.59	22.65
44	**0**	**26.83**	**24.62**	**22.67**
44	1	26.86	24.64	22.69
44	2	26.89	24.66	22.71
44	3	26.92	24.68	22.73
44	4	26.95	24.71	22.74
44	5	26.97	24.73	22.76
44	6	27.00	24.75	22.78
44	7	27.03	24.77	22.80
44	8	27.06	24.80	22.82
44	9	27.08	24.82	22.83
44	10	27.11	24.84	22.85
44	11	27.14	24.86	22.87
45	**0**	**27.17**	**24.88**	**22.89**
45	1	27.19	24.91	22.90
45	2	27.22	24.93	22.92
45	3	27.25	24.95	22.94
45	4	27.28	24.97	22.96
45	5	27.30	24.99	22.97
45	6	27.33	25.02	22.99
45	7	27.36	25.04	23.01
45	8	27.38	25.06	23.03
45	9	27.41	25.08	23.04
45	10	27.44	25.10	23.06
45	11	27.47	25.12	23.08
46	**0**	**27.49**	**25.15**	**23.10**
46	1	27.52	25.17	23.11
46	2	27.55	25.19	23.13
46	3	27.57	25.21	23.15
46	4	27.60	25.23	23.16
46	5	27.63	25.25	23.18
46	6	27.65	25.27	23.20
46	7	27.68	25.29	23.21
46	8	27.70	25.31	23.23
46	9	27.73	25.34	23.25
46	10	27.76	25.36	23.26
46	11	27.78	25.38	23.28
47	**0**	**27.81**	**25.40**	**23.30**
47	1	27.84	25.42	23.31
47	2	27.86	25.44	23.33
47	3	27.89	25.46	23.35
47	4	27.91	25.48	23.36
47	5	27.94	25.50	23.38
47	6	27.97	25.52	23.40
47	7	27.99	25.54	23.41
47	8	28.02	25.56	23.43
47	9	28.04	25.58	23.44
47	10	28.07	25.60	23.46
47	11	28.09	25.62	23.48
48	**0**	**28.12**	**25.64**	**23.49**
48	1	28.14	25.66	23.51
48	2	28.17	25.68	23.52
48	3	28.20	25.70	23.54
48	4	28.22	25.72	23.56
48	5	28.25	25.74	23.57
48	6	28.27	25.76	23.59
48	7	28.30	25.78	23.60
48	8	28.32	25.80	23.62
48	9	28.35	25.82	23.64
48	10	28.37	25.84	23.65
48	11	28.40	25.86	23.67
49	**0**	**28.42**	**25.88**	**23.68**
49	1	28.45	25.90	23.70
49	2	28.47	25.92	23.71
49	3	28.50	25.94	23.73
49	4	28.52	25.96	23.74
49	5	28.54	25.98	23.76
49	6	28.57	26.00	23.77
49	7	28.59	26.02	23.79
49	8	28.62	26.04	23.80
49	9	28.64	26.06	23.82
49	10	28.67	26.08	23.83
49	11	28.69	26.09	23.85
50	**0**	**28.72**	**26.11**	**23.86**
50	1	28.74	26.13	23.88
50	2	28.76	26.15	23.89
50	3	28.79	26.17	23.91
50	4	28.81	26.19	23.92
50	5	28.84	26.21	23.94
50	6	28.86	26.23	23.95
50	7	28.88	26.25	23.97
50	8	28.91	26.26	23.98
50	9	28.93	26.28	24.00
50	10	28.96	26.30	24.01
50	11	28.98	26.32	24.03
51	**0**	**29.00**	**26.34**	**24.04**
51	1	29.03	26.36	24.05
51	2	29.05	26.38	24.07
51	3	29.07	26.39	24.08
51	4	29.10	26.41	24.10
51	5	29.12	26.43	24.11
51	6	29.14	26.45	24.13

51–60 years

Years	Months	*2.5%*	***3.0%***	*3.5%*	Years	Months	*2.5%*	***3.0%***	*3.5%*
51	7	29.17	26.47	24.14	55	11	30.32	27.35	24.82
51	8	29.19	26.48	24.15	**56**	**0**	**30.34**	**27.37**	**24.83**
51	9	29.21	26.50	24.17	56	1	30.36	27.38	24.85
51	10	29.24	26.52	24.18	56	2	30.38	27.40	24.86
51	11	29.26	26.54	24.20	56	3	30.40	27.42	24.87
52	**0**	**29.28**	**26.56**	**24.21**	56	4	30.42	27.43	24.88
52	1	29.31	26.57	24.22	56	5	30.44	27.45	24.89
52	2	29.33	26.59	24.24	56	6	30.46	27.46	24.91
52	3	29.35	26.61	24.25	56	7	30.48	27.48	24.92
52	4	29.38	26.63	24.27	56	8	30.50	27.49	24.93
52	5	29.40	26.65	24.28	56	9	30.52	27.51	24.94
52	6	29.42	26.66	24.29	56	10	30.54	27.53	24.95
52	7	29.44	26.68	24.31	56	11	30.57	27.54	24.97
52	8	29.47	26.70	24.32	**57**	**0**	**30.59**	**27.56**	**24.98**
52	9	29.49	26.72	24.33	57	1	30.61	27.57	24.99
52	10	29.51	26.73	24.35	57	2	30.63	27.59	25.00
52	11	29.53	26.75	24.36	57	3	30.65	27.60	25.01
53	**0**	**29.56**	**26.77**	**24.37**	57	4	30.67	27.62	25.02
53	1	29.58	26.79	24.39	57	5	30.69	27.63	25.04
53	2	29.60	26.80	24.40	57	6	30.71	27.65	25.05
53	3	29.62	26.82	24.41	57	7	30.73	27.66	25.06
53	4	29.65	26.84	24.43	57	8	30.75	27.68	25.07
53	5	29.67	26.86	24.44	57	9	30.77	27.69	25.08
53	6	29.69	26.87	24.45	57	10	30.79	27.71	25.09
53	7	29.71	26.89	24.47	57	11	30.81	27.72	25.10
53	8	29.74	26.91	24.48	**58**	**0**	**30.83**	**27.74**	**25.12**
53	9	29.76	26.92	24.49	58	1	30.85	27.75	25.13
53	10	29.78	26.94	24.51	58	2	30.87	27.77	25.14
53	11	29.80	26.96	24.52	58	3	30.89	27.78	25.15
54	**0**	**29.82**	**26.97**	**24.53**	58	4	30.91	27.80	25.16
54	1	29.85	26.99	24.55	58	5	30.93	27.81	25.17
54	2	29.87	27.01	24.56	58	6	30.95	27.83	25.18
54	3	29.89	27.02	24.57	58	7	30.97	27.84	25.19
54	4	29.91	27.04	24.58	58	8	30.99	27.86	25.21
54	5	29.93	27.06	24.60	58	9	31.00	27.87	25.22
54	6	29.95	27.07	24.61	58	10	31.02	27.89	25.23
54	7	29.98	27.09	24.62	58	11	31.04	27.90	25.24
54	8	30.00	27.11	24.64	**59**	**0**	**31.06**	**27.92**	**25.25**
54	9	30.02	27.12	24.65	59	1	31.08	27.93	25.26
54	10	30.04	27.14	24.66	59	2	31.10	27.95	25.27
54	11	30.06	27.16	24.67	59	3	31.12	27.96	25.28
55	**0**	**30.08**	**27.17**	**24.69**	59	4	31.14	27.97	25.29
55	1	30.11	27.19	24.70	59	5	31.16	27.99	25.30
55	2	30.13	27.21	24.71	59	6	31.18	28.00	25.31
55	3	30.15	27.22	24.72	59	7	31.20	28.02	25.33
55	4	30.17	27.24	24.74	59	8	31.22	28.03	25.34
55	5	30.19	27.26	24.75	59	9	31.24	28.05	25.35
55	6	30.21	27.27	24.76	59	10	31.26	28.06	25.36
55	7	30.23	27.29	24.77	59	11	31.27	28.07	25.37
55	8	30.25	27.30	24.79	**60**	**0**	**31.29**	**28.09**	**25.38**
55	9	30.27	27.32	24.80	60	1	31.31	28.10	25.39
55	10	30.30	27.34	24.81	60	2	31.33	28.12	25.40

60–68 years

Years	Months	*2.5%*	***3.0%***	*3.5%*	Years	Months	*2.5%*	***3.0%***	*3.5%*
60	3	31.35	28.13	25.41	64	7	32.28	28.82	25.92
60	4	31.37	28.14	25.42	64	8	32.30	28.83	25.93
60	5	31.39	28.16	25.43	64	9	32.31	28.84	25.94
60	6	31.41	28.17	25.44	64	10	32.33	28.85	25.94
60	7	31.43	28.19	25.45	64	11	32.35	28.87	25.95
60	8	31.44	28.20	25.46	**65**	**0**	**32.36**	**28.88**	**25.96**
60	9	31.46	28.21	25.47	65	1	32.38	28.89	25.97
60	10	31.48	28.23	25.48	65	2	32.40	28.90	25.98
60	11	31.50	28.24	25.49	65	3	32.41	28.91	25.99
61	**0**	**31.52**	**28.26**	**25.50**	65	4	32.43	28.93	26.00
61	1	31.54	28.27	25.51	65	5	32.45	28.94	26.01
61	2	31.55	28.28	25.52	65	6	32.46	28.95	26.01
61	3	31.57	28.30	25.53	65	7	32.48	28.96	26.02
61	4	31.59	28.31	25.54	65	8	32.50	28.97	26.03
61	5	31.61	28.32	25.55	65	9	32.51	28.99	26.04
61	6	31.63	28.34	25.56	65	10	32.53	29.00	26.05
61	7	31.65	28.35	25.57	65	11	32.54	29.01	26.06
61	8	31.66	28.36	25.58	**66**	**0**	**32.56**	**29.02**	**26.07**
61	9	31.68	28.38	25.59	66	1	32.58	29.03	26.08
61	10	31.70	28.39	25.60	66	2	32.59	29.05	26.08
61	11	31.72	28.40	25.61	66	3	32.61	29.06	26.09
62	**0**	**31.74**	**28.42**	**25.62**	66	4	32.63	29.07	26.10
62	1	31.75	28.43	25.63	66	5	32.64	29.08	26.11
62	2	31.77	28.44	25.64	66	6	32.66	29.09	26.12
62	3	31.79	28.46	25.65	66	7	32.67	29.10	26.13
62	4	31.81	28.47	25.66	66	8	32.69	29.12	26.13
62	5	31.83	28.48	25.67	66	9	32.71	29.13	26.14
62	6	31.84	28.50	25.68	66	10	32.72	29.14	26.15
62	7	31.86	28.51	25.69	66	11	32.74	29.15	26.16
62	8	31.88	28.52	25.70	**67**	**0**	**32.75**	**29.16**	**26.17**
62	9	31.90	28.54	25.71	67	1	32.77	29.17	26.18
62	10	31.92	28.55	25.72	67	2	32.79	29.18	26.18
62	11	31.93	28.56	25.73	67	3	32.80	29.20	26.19
63	**0**	**31.95**	**28.58**	**25.74**	67	4	32.82	29.21	26.20
63	1	31.97	28.59	25.75	67	5	32.83	29.22	26.21
63	2	31.99	28.60	25.76	67	6	32.85	29.23	26.22
63	3	32.00	28.61	25.77	67	7	32.87	29.24	26.23
63	4	32.02	28.63	25.78	67	8	32.88	29.25	26.23
63	5	32.04	28.64	25.79	67	9	32.90	29.26	26.24
63	6	32.06	28.65	25.80	67	10	32.91	29.28	26.25
63	7	32.07	28.67	25.81	67	11	32.93	29.29	26.26
63	8	32.09	28.68	25.82	**68**	**0**	**32.94**	**29.30**	**26.27**
63	9	32.11	28.69	25.83	68	1	32.96	29.31	26.27
63	10	32.12	28.70	25.83	68	2	32.97	29.32	26.28
63	11	32.14	28.72	25.84	68	3	32.99	29.33	26.29
64	**0**	**32.16**	**28.73**	**25.85**	68	4	33.01	29.34	26.30
64	1	32.18	28.74	25.86	68	5	33.02	29.35	26.31
64	2	32.19	28.75	25.87	68	6	33.04	29.36	26.31
64	3	32.21	28.77	25.88	68	7	33.05	29.38	26.32
64	4	32.23	28.78	25.89	68	8	33.07	29.39	26.33
64	5	32.24	28.79	25.90	68	9	33.08	29.40	26.34
64	6	32.26	28.80	25.91	68	10	33.10	29.41	26.35

68–77 years

Years	Months	*2.5%*	***3.0%***	*3.5%*	Years	Months	*2.5%*	***3.0%***	*3.5%*
68	11	33.11	29.42	26.35	73	3	33.86	29.95	26.73
69	**0**	**33.13**	**29.43**	**26.36**	73	4	33.88	29.96	26.74
69	1	33.14	29.44	26.37	73	5	33.89	29.97	26.74
69	2	33.16	29.45	26.38	73	6	33.90	29.98	26.75
69	3	33.17	29.46	26.38	73	7	33.92	29.99	26.76
69	4	33.19	29.47	26.39	73	8	33.93	30.00	26.76
69	5	33.20	29.48	26.40	73	9	33.94	30.01	26.77
69	6	33.22	29.49	26.41	73	10	33.96	30.02	26.78
69	7	33.23	29.51	26.42	73	11	33.97	30.03	26.78
69	8	33.25	29.52	26.42	**74**	**0**	**33.98**	**30.03**	**26.79**
69	9	33.26	29.53	26.43	74	1	34.00	30.04	26.80
69	10	33.28	29.54	26.44	74	2	34.01	30.05	26.80
69	11	33.29	29.55	26.45	74	3	34.02	30.06	26.81
70	**0**	**33.31**	**29.56**	**26.45**	74	4	34.04	30.07	26.82
70	1	33.32	29.57	26.46	74	5	34.05	30.08	26.82
70	2	33.34	29.58	26.47	74	6	34.06	30.09	26.83
70	3	33.35	29.59	26.48	74	7	34.08	30.10	26.83
70	4	33.37	29.60	26.48	74	8	34.09	30.11	26.84
70	5	33.38	29.61	26.49	74	9	34.10	30.12	26.85
70	6	33.40	29.62	26.50	74	10	34.12	30.13	26.85
70	7	33.41	29.63	26.50	74	11	34.13	30.14	26.86
70	8	33.42	29.64	26.51	**75**	**0**	**34.14**	**30.15**	**26.87**
70	9	33.44	29.65	26.52	75	1	34.16	30.15	26.87
70	10	33.45	29.66	26.53	75	2	34.17	30.16	26.88
70	11	33.47	29.67	26.53	75	3	34.18	30.17	26.89
71	**0**	**33.48**	**29.68**	**26.54**	75	4	34.19	30.18	26.89
71	1	33.50	29.69	26.55	75	5	34.21	30.19	26.90
71	2	33.51	29.70	26.56	75	6	34.22	30.20	26.90
71	3	33.53	29.71	26.56	75	7	34.23	30.21	26.91
71	4	33.54	29.72	26.57	75	8	34.25	30.22	26.92
71	5	33.55	29.73	26.58	75	9	34.26	30.23	26.92
71	6	33.57	29.74	26.58	75	10	34.27	30.23	26.93
71	7	33.58	29.75	26.59	75	11	34.28	30.24	26.93
71	8	33.60	29.76	26.60	**76**	**0**	**34.30**	**30.25**	**26.94**
71	9	33.61	29.77	26.61	76	1	34.31	30.26	26.95
71	10	33.63	29.78	26.61	76	2	34.32	30.27	26.95
71	11	33.64	29.79	26.62	76	3	34.34	30.28	26.96
72	**0**	**33.65**	**29.80**	**26.63**	76	4	34.35	30.29	26.96
72	1	33.67	29.81	26.63	76	5	34.36	30.30	26.97
72	2	33.68	29.82	26.64	76	6	34.37	30.31	26.98
72	3	33.70	29.83	26.65	76	7	34.39	30.31	26.98
72	4	33.71	29.84	26.65	76	8	34.40	30.32	26.99
72	5	33.72	29.85	26.66	76	9	34.41	30.33	26.99
72	6	33.74	29.86	26.67	76	10	34.42	30.34	27.00
72	7	33.75	29.87	26.68	76	11	34.44	30.35	27.01
72	8	33.77	29.88	26.68	**77**	**0**	**34.45**	**30.36**	**27.01**
72	9	33.78	29.89	26.69	77	1	34.46	30.37	27.02
72	10	33.79	29.90	26.70	77	2	34.47	30.37	27.02
72	11	33.81	29.91	26.70	77	3	34.49	30.38	27.03
73	**0**	**33.82**	**29.92**	**26.71**	77	4	34.50	30.39	27.04
73	1	33.83	29.93	26.72	77	5	34.51	30.40	27.04
73	2	33.85	29.94	26.72	77	6	34.52	30.41	27.05

77–86 years

Years	Months	*2.5%*	***3.0%***	*3.5%*
77	7	34.54	30.42	27.05
77	8	34.55	30.42	27.06
77	9	34.56	30.43	27.06
77	10	34.57	30.44	27.07
77	11	34.58	30.45	27.08
78	**0**	**34.60**	**30.46**	**27.08**
78	1	34.61	30.47	27.09
78	2	34.62	30.47	27.09
78	3	34.63	30.48	27.10
78	4	34.64	30.49	27.10
78	5	34.66	30.50	27.11
78	6	34.67	30.51	27.12
78	7	34.68	30.52	27.12
78	8	34.69	30.52	27.13
78	9	34.70	30.53	27.13
78	10	34.72	30.54	27.14
78	11	34.73	30.55	27.14
79	**0**	**34.74**	**30.56**	**27.15**
79	1	34.75	30.56	27.15
79	2	34.76	30.57	27.16
79	3	34.78	30.58	27.17
79	4	34.79	30.59	27.17
79	5	34.80	30.60	27.18
79	6	34.81	30.60	27.18
79	7	34.82	30.61	27.19
79	8	34.83	30.62	27.19
79	9	34.85	30.63	27.20
79	10	34.86	30.64	27.20
79	11	34.87	30.64	27.21
80	**0**	**34.88**	**30.65**	**27.21**
80	1	34.89	30.66	27.22
80	2	34.90	30.67	27.22
80	3	34.92	30.67	27.23
80	4	34.93	30.68	27.24
80	5	34.94	30.69	27.24
80	6	34.95	30.70	27.25
80	7	34.96	30.71	27.25
80	8	34.97	30.71	27.26
80	9	34.98	30.72	27.26
80	10	35.00	30.73	27.27
80	11	35.01	30.74	27.27
81	**0**	**35.02**	**30.74**	**27.28**
81	1	35.03	30.75	27.28
81	2	35.04	30.76	27.29
81	3	35.05	30.77	27.29
81	4	35.06	30.77	27.30
81	5	35.07	30.78	27.30
81	6	35.08	30.79	27.31
81	7	35.10	30.80	27.31
81	8	35.11	30.80	27.32
81	9	35.12	30.81	27.32
81	10	35.13	30.82	27.33
81	11	35.14	30.83	27.33
82	**0**	**35.15**	**30.83**	**27.34**
82	1	35.16	30.84	27.34
82	2	35.17	30.85	27.35
82	3	35.18	30.86	27.35
82	4	35.20	30.86	27.36
82	5	35.21	30.87	27.36
82	6	35.22	30.88	27.37
82	7	35.23	30.89	27.37
82	8	35.24	30.89	27.38
82	9	35.25	30.90	27.38
82	10	35.26	30.91	27.39
82	11	35.27	30.91	27.39
83	**0**	**35.28**	**30.92**	**27.40**
83	1	35.29	30.93	27.40
83	2	35.30	30.94	27.41
83	3	35.31	30.94	27.41
83	4	35.32	30.95	27.42
83	5	35.34	30.96	27.42
83	6	35.35	30.96	27.42
83	7	35.36	30.97	27.43
83	8	35.37	30.98	27.43
83	9	35.38	30.99	27.44
83	10	35.39	30.99	27.44
83	11	35.40	31.00	27.45
84	**0**	**35.41**	**31.01**	**27.45**
84	1	35.42	31.01	27.46
84	2	35.43	31.02	27.46
84	3	35.44	31.03	27.47
84	4	35.45	31.03	27.47
84	5	35.46	31.04	27.48
84	6	35.47	31.05	27.48
84	7	35.48	31.05	27.48
84	8	35.49	31.06	27.49
84	9	35.50	31.07	27.49
84	10	35.51	31.07	27.50
84	11	35.52	31.08	27.50
85	**0**	**35.53**	**31.09**	**27.51**
85	1	35.54	31.10	27.51
85	2	35.55	31.10	27.52
85	3	35.56	31.11	27.52
85	4	35.57	31.12	27.53
85	5	35.58	31.12	27.53
85	6	35.59	31.13	27.53
85	7	35.60	31.14	27.54
85	8	35.61	31.14	27.54
85	9	35.62	31.15	27.55
85	10	35.63	31.16	27.55
85	11	35.64	31.16	27.56
86	**0**	**35.65**	**31.17**	**27.56**
86	1	35.66	31.17	27.56
86	2	35.67	31.18	27.57

86–94 years

Years	Months	*2.5%*	***3.0%***	*3.5%*
86	3	35.68	31.19	27.57
86	4	35.69	31.19	27.58
86	5	35.70	31.20	27.58
86	6	35.71	31.21	27.59
86	7	35.72	31.21	27.59
86	8	35.73	31.22	27.59
86	9	35.74	31.23	27.60
86	10	35.75	31.23	27.60
86	11	35.76	31.24	27.61
87	**0**	**35.77**	**31.25**	**27.61**
87	1	35.78	31.25	27.62
87	2	35.79	31.26	27.62
87	3	35.80	31.26	27.62
87	4	35.81	31.27	27.63
87	5	35.82	31.28	27.63
87	6	35.83	31.28	27.64
87	7	35.84	31.29	27.64
87	8	35.85	31.30	27.64
87	9	35.86	31.30	27.65
87	10	35.87	31.31	27.65
87	11	35.88	31.31	27.66
88	**0**	**35.89**	**31.32**	**27.66**
88	1	35.90	31.33	27.66
88	2	35.91	31.33	27.67
88	3	35.92	31.34	27.67
88	4	35.93	31.35	27.68
88	5	35.93	31.35	27.68
88	6	35.94	31.36	27.68
88	7	35.95	31.36	27.69
88	8	35.96	31.37	27.69
88	9	35.97	31.38	27.70
88	10	35.98	31.38	27.70
88	11	35.99	31.39	27.70
89	**0**	**36.00**	**31.39**	**27.71**
89	1	36.01	31.40	27.71
89	2	36.02	31.41	27.72
89	3	36.03	31.41	27.72
89	4	36.04	31.42	27.72
89	5	36.05	31.42	27.73
89	6	36.06	31.43	27.73
89	7	36.06	31.44	27.73
89	8	36.07	31.44	27.74
89	9	36.08	31.45	27.74
89	10	36.09	31.45	27.75
89	11	36.10	31.46	27.75
90	**0**	**36.11**	**31.47**	**27.75**
90	1	36.12	31.47	27.76
90	2	36.13	31.48	27.76
90	3	36.14	31.48	27.77
90	4	36.15	31.49	27.77
90	5	36.15	31.49	27.77
90	6	36.16	31.50	27.78
90	7	36.17	31.51	27.78
90	8	36.18	31.51	27.78
90	9	36.19	31.52	27.79
90	10	36.20	31.52	27.79
90	11	36.21	31.53	27.79
91	**0**	**36.22**	**31.53**	**27.80**
91	1	36.23	31.54	27.80
91	2	36.23	31.55	27.81
91	3	36.24	31.55	27.81
91	4	36.25	31.56	27.81
91	5	36.26	31.56	27.82
91	6	36.27	31.57	27.82
91	7	36.28	31.57	27.82
91	8	36.29	31.58	27.83
91	9	36.30	31.58	27.83
91	10	36.30	31.59	27.83
91	11	36.31	31.60	27.84
92	**0**	**36.32**	**31.60**	**27.84**
92	1	36.33	31.61	27.84
92	2	36.34	31.61	27.85
92	3	36.35	31.62	27.85
92	4	36.36	31.62	27.86
92	5	36.36	31.63	27.86
92	6	36.37	31.63	27.86
92	7	36.38	31.64	27.87
92	8	36.39	31.64	27.87
92	9	36.40	31.65	27.87
92	10	36.41	31.66	27.88
92	11	36.41	31.66	27.88
93	**0**	**36.42**	**31.67**	**27.88**
93	1	36.43	31.67	27.89
93	2	36.44	31.68	27.89
93	3	36.45	31.68	27.89
93	4	36.46	31.69	27.90
93	5	36.46	31.69	27.90
93	6	36.47	31.70	27.90
93	7	36.48	31.70	27.91
93	8	36.49	31.71	27.91
93	9	36.50	31.71	27.91
93	10	36.51	31.72	27.92
93	11	36.51	31.72	27.92
94	**0**	**36.52**	**31.73**	**27.92**
94	1	36.53	31.73	27.93
94	2	36.54	31.74	27.93
94	3	36.55	31.74	27.93
94	4	36.56	31.75	27.94
94	5	36.56	31.75	27.94
94	6	36.57	31.76	27.94
94	7	36.58	31.76	27.95
94	8	36.59	31.77	27.95
94	9	36.60	31.78	27.95
94	10	36.60	31.78	27.96

94–100 years

Years	Months	*2.5%*	***3.0%***	*3.5%*	Years	Months	*2.5%*	***3.0%***	*3.5%*
94	11	36.61	31.79	27.96	97	6	36.85	31.94	28.05
95	**0**	**36.62**	**31.79**	**27.96**	97	7	36.86	31.94	28.06
95	1	36.63	31.80	27.96	97	8	36.87	31.94	28.06
95	2	36.64	31.80	27.97	97	9	36.87	31.95	28.06
95	3	36.64	31.81	27.97	97	10	36.88	31.95	28.06
95	4	36.65	31.81	27.97	97	11	36.89	31.96	28.07
95	5	36.66	31.82	27.98	**98**	**0**	**36.90**	**31.96**	**28.07**
95	6	36.67	31.82	27.98	98	1	36.90	31.97	28.07
95	7	36.67	31.83	27.98	98	2	36.91	31.97	28.08
95	8	36.68	31.83	27.99	98	3	36.92	31.98	28.08
95	9	36.69	31.83	27.99	98	4	36.93	31.98	28.08
95	10	36.70	31.84	27.99	98	5	36.93	31.99	28.08
95	11	36.71	31.84	28.00	98	6	36.94	31.99	28.09
96	**0**	**36.71**	**31.85**	**28.00**	98	7	36.95	32.00	28.09
96	1	36.72	31.85	28.00	98	8	36.96	32.00	28.09
96	2	36.73	31.86	28.01	98	9	36.96	32.00	28.10
96	3	36.74	31.86	28.01	98	10	36.97	32.01	28.10
96	4	36.75	31.87	28.01	98	11	36.98	32.01	28.10
96	5	36.75	31.87	28.01	**99**	**0**	**36.98**	**32.02**	**28.10**
96	6	36.76	31.88	28.02	99	1	36.99	32.02	28.11
96	7	36.77	31.88	28.02	99	2	37.00	32.03	28.11
96	8	36.78	31.89	28.02	99	3	37.01	32.03	28.11
96	9	36.78	31.89	28.03	99	4	37.01	32.04	28.12
96	10	36.79	31.90	28.03	99	5	37.02	32.04	28.12
96	11	36.80	31.90	28.03	99	6	37.03	32.04	28.12
97	**0**	**36.81**	**31.91**	**28.04**	99	7	37.03	32.05	28.12
97	1	36.81	31.91	28.04	99	8	37.04	32.05	28.13
97	2	36.82	31.92	28.04	99	9	37.05	32.06	28.13
97	3	36.83	31.92	28.04	99	10	37.06	32.06	28.13
97	4	36.84	31.93	28.05	99	11	37.06	32.07	28.13
97	5	36.84	31.93	28.05	**100**	**0**	**37.07**	**32.07**	**28.14**

Consolidated Compound Interest Tables

Showing the present value of £1 discounted at an annual rate of:

Years	Months	*2.5%*	***3.0%***	*3.5%*
0	1	0.997944	0.997540	0.997137
0	2	0.995893	0.995086	0.994283
0	3	0.993846	0.992638	0.991437
0	4	0.991803	0.990195	0.988598
0	5	0.989764	0.987759	0.985768
0	6	0.987730	0.985329	0.982946
0	7	0.985699	0.982905	0.980133
0	8	0.983673	0.980487	0.977327
0	9	0.981651	0.978075	0.974529
0	10	0.979633	0.975669	0.971739
0	11	0.977619	0.973268	0.968957
1	**0**	**0.975610**	**0.970874**	**0.966184**
1	1	0.973604	0.968485	0.963418
1	2	0.971603	0.966103	0.960660
1	3	0.969606	0.963726	0.957910
1	4	0.967613	0.961355	0.955167
1	5	0.965624	0.958990	0.952433
1	6	0.963639	0.956630	0.949707
1	7	0.961658	0.954277	0.946988
1	8	0.959681	0.951929	0.944277
1	9	0.957708	0.949587	0.941574
1	10	0.955740	0.947251	0.938878
1	11	0.953775	0.944921	0.936191
2	**0**	**0.951814**	**0.942596**	**0.933511**
2	1	0.949858	0.940277	0.930838
2	2	0.947905	0.937964	0.928174
2	3	0.945957	0.935656	0.925517
2	4	0.944012	0.933354	0.922867
2	5	0.942072	0.931058	0.920225
2	6	0.940135	0.928767	0.917591
2	7	0.938203	0.926482	0.914964
2	8	0.936274	0.924203	0.912345
2	9	0.934350	0.921929	0.909733
2	10	0.932429	0.919661	0.907129
2	11	0.930512	0.917399	0.904532
3	**0**	**0.928599**	**0.915142**	**0.901943**
3	1	0.926691	0.912890	0.899361
3	2	0.924786	0.910644	0.896786
3	3	0.922885	0.908404	0.894219
3	4	0.920988	0.906169	0.891659
3	5	0.919094	0.903940	0.889107
3	6	0.917205	0.901716	0.886561
3	7	0.915320	0.899497	0.884023
3	8	0.913438	0.897285	0.881493
3	9	0.911561	0.895077	0.878969
3	10	0.909687	0.892875	0.876453
3	11	0.907817	0.890678	0.873944
4	**0**	**0.905951**	**0.888487**	**0.871442**
4	1	0.904088	0.886301	0.868948

Years	Months	*2.5%*	***3.0%***	*3.5%*
4	2	0.902230	0.884121	0.866460
4	3	0.900375	0.881946	0.863980
4	4	0.898524	0.879776	0.861506
4	5	0.896677	0.877611	0.859040
4	6	0.894834	0.875452	0.856581
4	7	0.892995	0.873299	0.854129
4	8	0.891159	0.871150	0.851684
4	9	0.889327	0.869007	0.849246
4	10	0.887499	0.866869	0.846815
4	11	0.885675	0.864736	0.844390
5	**0**	**0.883854**	**0.862609**	**0.841973**
5	1	0.882037	0.860487	0.839563
5	2	0.880224	0.858370	0.837159
5	3	0.878415	0.856258	0.834763
5	4	0.876609	0.854151	0.832373
5	5	0.874807	0.852050	0.829990
5	6	0.873009	0.849954	0.827614
5	7	0.871214	0.847863	0.825245
5	8	0.869424	0.845777	0.822883
5	9	0.867636	0.843696	0.820527
5	10	0.865853	0.841620	0.818178
5	11	0.864073	0.839550	0.815836
6	**0**	**0.862297**	**0.837484**	**0.813501**
6	1	0.860524	0.835424	0.811172
6	2	0.858755	0.833369	0.808850
6	3	0.856990	0.831318	0.806534
6	4	0.855229	0.829273	0.804225
6	5	0.853471	0.827233	0.801923
6	6	0.851716	0.825198	0.799628
6	7	0.849965	0.823168	0.797338
6	8	0.848218	0.821142	0.795056
6	9	0.846475	0.819122	0.792780
6	10	0.844735	0.817107	0.790510
6	11	0.842998	0.815097	0.788247
7	**0**	**0.841265**	**0.813092**	**0.785991**
7	1	0.839536	0.811091	0.783741
7	2	0.837810	0.809096	0.781497
7	3	0.836088	0.807105	0.779260
7	4	0.834369	0.805120	0.777029
7	5	0.832654	0.803139	0.774805
7	6	0.830943	0.801163	0.772587
7	7	0.829234	0.799192	0.770375
7	8	0.827530	0.797226	0.768170
7	9	0.825829	0.795264	0.765971
7	10	0.824131	0.793308	0.763778
7	11	0.822437	0.791356	0.761592
8	**0**	**0.820747**	**0.789409**	**0.759412**
8	1	0.819059	0.787467	0.757238
8	2	0.817376	0.785530	0.755070
8	3	0.815696	0.783597	0.752908
8	4	0.814019	0.781669	0.750753
8	5	0.812346	0.779746	0.748604
8	6	0.810676	0.777828	0.746461
8	7	0.809009	0.775914	0.744324

Years	Months	*2.5%*	***3.0%***	*3.5%*
8	8	0.807346	0.774006	0.742193
8	9	0.805687	0.772101	0.740069
8	10	0.804031	0.770202	0.737950
8	11	0.802378	0.768307	0.735837
9	**0**	**0.800728**	**0.766417**	**0.733731**
9	1	0.799082	0.764531	0.731631
9	2	0.797440	0.762650	0.729536
9	3	0.795801	0.760774	0.727448
9	4	0.794165	0.758902	0.725365
9	5	0.792532	0.757035	0.723289
9	6	0.790903	0.755173	0.721218
9	7	0.789277	0.753315	0.719154
9	8	0.787655	0.751462	0.717095
9	9	0.786036	0.749613	0.715042
9	10	0.784420	0.747769	0.712995
9	11	0.782808	0.745929	0.710954
10	**0**	**0.781198**	**0.744094**	**0.708919**
10	1	0.779593	0.742263	0.706889
10	2	0.777990	0.740437	0.704866
10	3	0.776391	0.738616	0.702848
10	4	0.774795	0.736798	0.700836
10	5	0.773202	0.734986	0.698830
10	6	0.771613	0.733178	0.696829
10	7	0.770027	0.731374	0.694834
10	8	0.768444	0.729574	0.692845
10	9	0.766864	0.727780	0.690862
10	10	0.765288	0.725989	0.688884
10	11	0.763715	0.724203	0.686912
11	**0**	**0.762145**	**0.722421**	**0.684946**
11	1	0.760578	0.720644	0.682985
11	2	0.759015	0.718871	0.681030
11	3	0.757454	0.717102	0.679080
11	4	0.755897	0.715338	0.677136
11	5	0.754344	0.713578	0.675198
11	6	0.752793	0.711823	0.673265
11	7	0.751246	0.710072	0.671338
11	8	0.749701	0.708325	0.669416
11	9	0.748160	0.706582	0.667499
11	10	0.746622	0.704844	0.665589
11	11	0.745087	0.703110	0.663683
12	**0**	**0.743556**	**0.701380**	**0.661783**
12	1	0.742027	0.699654	0.659889
12	2	0.740502	0.697933	0.658000
12	3	0.738980	0.696216	0.656116
12	4	0.737461	0.694503	0.654238
12	5	0.735945	0.692795	0.652365
12	6	0.734432	0.691090	0.650497
12	7	0.732922	0.689390	0.648635
12	8	0.731416	0.687694	0.646778
12	9	0.729912	0.686002	0.644927
12	10	0.728412	0.684314	0.643081
12	11	0.726915	0.682631	0.641240
13	**0**	**0.725420**	**0.680951**	**0.639404**
13	1	0.723929	0.679276	0.637574

Years	Months	*2.5%*	***3.0%***	*3.5%*
13	2	0.722441	0.677605	0.635749
13	3	0.720956	0.675938	0.633929
13	4	0.719474	0.674275	0.632114
13	5	0.717995	0.672616	0.630304
13	6	0.716519	0.670961	0.628500
13	7	0.715046	0.669311	0.626701
13	8	0.713576	0.667664	0.624907
13	9	0.712110	0.666021	0.623118
13	10	0.710646	0.664383	0.621334
13	11	0.709185	0.662748	0.619555
14	**0**	**0.707727**	**0.661118**	**0.617782**
14	1	0.706272	0.659491	0.616013
14	2	0.704821	0.657869	0.614250
14	3	0.703372	0.656250	0.612491
14	4	0.701926	0.654636	0.610738
14	5	0.700483	0.653025	0.608990
14	6	0.699043	0.651419	0.607246
14	7	0.697606	0.649816	0.605508
14	8	0.696172	0.648217	0.603775
14	9	0.694741	0.646623	0.602046
14	10	0.693313	0.645032	0.600323
14	11	0.691888	0.643445	0.598604
15	**0**	**0.690466**	**0.641862**	**0.596891**
15	1	0.689046	0.640283	0.595182
15	2	0.687630	0.638708	0.593478
15	3	0.686216	0.637136	0.591779
15	4	0.684806	0.635569	0.590085
15	5	0.683398	0.634005	0.588396
15	6	0.681993	0.632445	0.586711
15	7	0.680591	0.630889	0.585032
15	8	0.679192	0.629337	0.583357
15	9	0.677796	0.627789	0.581687
15	10	0.676403	0.626245	0.580022
15	11	0.675012	0.624704	0.578362
16	**0**	**0.673625**	**0.623167**	**0.576706**
16	1	0.672240	0.621634	0.575055
16	2	0.670858	0.620104	0.573409
16	3	0.669479	0.618579	0.571767
16	4	0.668103	0.617057	0.570131
16	5	0.666730	0.615539	0.568498
16	6	0.665359	0.614025	0.566871
16	7	0.663992	0.612514	0.565248
16	8	0.662627	0.611007	0.563630
16	9	0.661265	0.609504	0.562017
16	10	0.659905	0.608004	0.560408
16	11	0.658549	0.606509	0.558803
17	**0**	**0.657195**	**0.605016**	**0.557204**
17	1	0.655844	0.603528	0.555609
17	2	0.654496	0.602043	0.554018
17	3	0.653151	0.600562	0.552432
17	4	0.651808	0.599085	0.550851
17	5	0.650468	0.597611	0.549274
17	6	0.649131	0.596140	0.547701
17	7	0.647797	0.594674	0.546134

Years	Months	*2.5%*	***3.0%***	*3.5%*
17	8	0.646465	0.593211	0.544570
17	9	0.645136	0.591751	0.543011
17	10	0.643810	0.590296	0.541457
17	11	0.642487	0.588843	0.539907
18	**0**	**0.641166**	**0.587395**	**0.538361**
18	1	0.639848	0.585950	0.536820
18	2	0.638533	0.584508	0.535283
18	3	0.637220	0.583070	0.533751
18	4	0.635910	0.581635	0.532223
18	5	0.634603	0.580205	0.530699
18	6	0.633299	0.578777	0.529180
18	7	0.631997	0.577353	0.527665
18	8	0.630698	0.575933	0.526155
18	9	0.629401	0.574516	0.524649
18	10	0.628107	0.573102	0.523147
18	11	0.626816	0.571693	0.521649
19	**0**	**0.625528**	**0.570286**	**0.520156**
19	1	0.624242	0.568883	0.518667
19	2	0.622959	0.567483	0.517182
19	3	0.621678	0.566087	0.515701
19	4	0.620400	0.564695	0.514225
19	5	0.619125	0.563305	0.512753
19	6	0.617852	0.561920	0.511285
19	7	0.616582	0.560537	0.509822
19	8	0.615315	0.559158	0.508362
19	9	0.614050	0.557782	0.506907
19	10	0.612788	0.556410	0.505456
19	11	0.611528	0.555041	0.504009
20	**0**	**0.610271**	**0.553676**	**0.502566**
20	1	0.609016	0.552314	0.501127
20	2	0.607765	0.550955	0.499693
20	3	0.606515	0.549599	0.498262
20	4	0.605269	0.548247	0.496836
20	5	0.604024	0.546898	0.495414
20	6	0.602783	0.545553	0.493995
20	7	0.601544	0.544211	0.492581
20	8	0.600307	0.542872	0.491171
20	9	0.599073	0.541536	0.489765
20	10	0.597842	0.540204	0.488363
20	11	0.596613	0.538875	0.486965
21	**0**	**0.595386**	**0.537549**	**0.485571**
21	1	0.594162	0.536227	0.484181
21	2	0.592941	0.534908	0.482795
21	3	0.591722	0.533592	0.481413
21	4	0.590506	0.532279	0.480035
21	5	0.589292	0.530969	0.478660
21	6	0.588081	0.529663	0.477290
21	7	0.586872	0.528360	0.475924
21	8	0.585665	0.527060	0.474561
21	9	0.584462	0.525763	0.473203
21	10	0.583260	0.524470	0.471848
21	11	0.582061	0.523180	0.470498
22	**0**	**0.580865**	**0.521893**	**0.469151**
22	1	0.579671	0.520609	0.467808

Years	Months	*2.5%*	***3.0%***	*3.5%*
22	2	0.578479	0.519328	0.466468
22	3	0.577290	0.518050	0.465133
22	4	0.576103	0.516776	0.463802
22	5	0.574919	0.515504	0.462474
22	6	0.573737	0.514236	0.461150
22	7	0.572558	0.512971	0.459830
22	8	0.571381	0.511709	0.458513
22	9	0.570206	0.510450	0.457201
22	10	0.569034	0.509194	0.455892
22	11	0.567865	0.507941	0.454587
23	**0**	**0.566697**	**0.506692**	**0.453286**
23	1	0.565532	0.505445	0.451988
23	2	0.564370	0.504202	0.450694
23	3	0.563210	0.502961	0.449404
23	4	0.562052	0.501724	0.448117
23	5	0.560897	0.500490	0.446835
23	6	0.559744	0.499258	0.445555
23	7	0.558593	0.498030	0.444280
23	8	0.557445	0.496805	0.443008
23	9	0.556299	0.495582	0.441740
23	10	0.555155	0.494363	0.440475
23	11	0.554014	0.493147	0.439214
24	**0**	**0.552875**	**0.491934**	**0.437957**
24	1	0.551739	0.490723	0.436703
24	2	0.550605	0.489516	0.435453
24	3	0.549473	0.488312	0.434207
24	4	0.548343	0.487111	0.432964
24	5	0.547216	0.485912	0.431724
24	6	0.546091	0.484717	0.430488
24	7	0.544969	0.483524	0.429256
24	8	0.543849	0.482335	0.428027
24	9	0.542731	0.481148	0.426802
24	10	0.541615	0.479964	0.425580
24	11	0.540502	0.478783	0.424362
25	**0**	**0.539391**	**0.477606**	**0.423147**
25	1	0.538282	0.476431	0.421936
25	2	0.537175	0.475258	0.420728
25	3	0.536071	0.474089	0.419523
25	4	0.534969	0.472923	0.418322
25	5	0.533869	0.471759	0.417125
25	6	0.532772	0.470599	0.415931
25	7	0.531677	0.469441	0.414740
25	8	0.530584	0.468286	0.413553
25	9	0.529493	0.467134	0.412369
25	10	0.528405	0.465985	0.411189
25	11	0.527319	0.464838	0.410011
26	**0**	**0.526235**	**0.463695**	**0.408838**
26	1	0.525153	0.462554	0.407667
26	2	0.524073	0.461416	0.406500
26	3	0.522996	0.460281	0.405337
26	4	0.521921	0.459148	0.404176
26	5	0.520848	0.458019	0.403019
26	6	0.519778	0.456892	0.401866
26	7	0.518709	0.455768	0.400715

Years	Months	*2.5%*	***3.0%***	*3.5%*
26	8	0.517643	0.454647	0.399568
26	9	0.516579	0.453528	0.398424
26	10	0.515517	0.452412	0.397284
26	11	0.514457	0.451299	0.396146
27	**0**	**0.513400**	**0.450189**	**0.395012**
27	1	0.512344	0.449082	0.393881
27	2	0.511291	0.447977	0.392754
27	3	0.510240	0.446875	0.391630
27	4	0.509191	0.445775	0.390508
27	5	0.508145	0.444678	0.389391
27	6	0.507100	0.443584	0.388276
27	7	0.506058	0.442493	0.387164
27	8	0.505017	0.441405	0.386056
27	9	0.503979	0.440319	0.384951
27	10	0.502943	0.439235	0.383849
27	11	0.501910	0.438155	0.382750
28	**0**	**0.500878**	**0.437077**	**0.381654**
28	1	0.499848	0.436001	0.380562
28	2	0.498821	0.434929	0.379472
28	3	0.497795	0.433859	0.378386
28	4	0.496772	0.432791	0.377303
28	5	0.495751	0.431727	0.376223
28	6	0.494732	0.430665	0.375146
28	7	0.493715	0.429605	0.374072
28	8	0.492700	0.428548	0.373001
28	9	0.491687	0.427494	0.371933
28	10	0.490676	0.426442	0.370868
28	11	0.489668	0.425393	0.369807
29	**0**	**0.488661**	**0.424346**	**0.368748**
29	1	0.487657	0.423302	0.367693
29	2	0.486654	0.422261	0.366640
29	3	0.485654	0.421222	0.365590
29	4	0.484656	0.420186	0.364544
29	5	0.483659	0.419152	0.363500
29	6	0.482665	0.418121	0.362460
29	7	0.481673	0.417092	0.361422
29	8	0.480683	0.416066	0.360387
29	9	0.479695	0.415042	0.359356
29	10	0.478709	0.414021	0.358327
29	11	0.477725	0.413003	0.357301
30	**0**	**0.476743**	**0.411987**	**0.356278**
30	1	0.475763	0.410973	0.355259
30	2	0.474785	0.409962	0.354242
30	3	0.473809	0.408954	0.353227
30	4	0.472835	0.407947	0.352216
30	5	0.471863	0.406944	0.351208
30	6	0.470893	0.405943	0.350203
30	7	0.469925	0.404944	0.349200
30	8	0.468959	0.403948	0.348200
30	9	0.467995	0.402954	0.347204
30	10	0.467033	0.401963	0.346210
30	11	0.466073	0.400974	0.345219
31	**0**	**0.465115**	**0.399987**	**0.344230**
31	1	0.464159	0.399003	0.343245

Years	Months	*2.5%*	***3.0%***	*3.5%*
31	2	0.463205	0.398021	0.342262
31	3	0.462252	0.397042	0.341283
31	4	0.461302	0.396065	0.340306
31	5	0.460354	0.395091	0.339331
31	6	0.459408	0.394119	0.338360
31	7	0.458463	0.393149	0.337391
31	8	0.457521	0.392182	0.336426
31	9	0.456580	0.391217	0.335462
31	10	0.455642	0.390255	0.334502
31	11	0.454705	0.389295	0.333545
32	**0**	**0.453771**	**0.388337**	**0.332590**
32	1	0.452838	0.387382	0.331638
32	2	0.451907	0.386429	0.330688
32	3	0.450978	0.385478	0.329742
32	4	0.450051	0.384530	0.328798
32	5	0.449126	0.383584	0.327856
32	6	0.448203	0.382640	0.326918
32	7	0.447281	0.381698	0.325982
32	8	0.446362	0.380759	0.325049
32	9	0.445444	0.379823	0.324118
32	10	0.444529	0.378888	0.323190
32	11	0.443615	0.377956	0.322265
33	**0**	**0.442703**	**0.377026**	**0.321343**
33	1	0.441793	0.376099	0.320423
33	2	0.440885	0.375173	0.319506
33	3	0.439979	0.374250	0.318591
33	4	0.439074	0.373330	0.317679
33	5	0.438172	0.372411	0.316769
33	6	0.437271	0.371495	0.315863
33	7	0.436372	0.370581	0.314958
33	8	0.435475	0.369669	0.314057
33	9	0.434580	0.368760	0.313158
33	10	0.433686	0.367853	0.312261
33	11	0.432795	0.366948	0.311367
34	**0**	**0.431905**	**0.366045**	**0.310476**
34	1	0.431018	0.365144	0.309587
34	2	0.430132	0.364246	0.308701
34	3	0.429247	0.363350	0.307817
34	4	0.428365	0.362456	0.306936
34	5	0.427484	0.361564	0.306057
34	6	0.426606	0.360675	0.305181
34	7	0.425729	0.359787	0.304308
34	8	0.424854	0.358902	0.303437
34	9	0.423980	0.358019	0.302568
34	10	0.423109	0.357139	0.301702
34	11	0.422239	0.356260	0.300838
35	**0**	**0.421371**	**0.355383**	**0.299977**
35	1	0.420505	0.354509	0.299118
35	2	0.419641	0.353637	0.298262
35	3	0.418778	0.352767	0.297408
35	4	0.417917	0.351899	0.296557
35	5	0.417058	0.351033	0.295708
35	6	0.416201	0.350170	0.294861
35	7	0.415345	0.349308	0.294017

Years	Months	*2.5%*	***3.0%***	*3.5%*
35	8	0.414491	0.348449	0.293175
35	9	0.413639	0.347592	0.292336
35	10	0.412789	0.346736	0.291499
35	11	0.411941	0.345883	0.290665
36	**0**	**0.411094**	**0.345032**	**0.289833**
36	1	0.410249	0.344184	0.289003
36	2	0.409405	0.343337	0.288176
36	3	0.408564	0.342492	0.287351
36	4	0.407724	0.341650	0.286528
36	5	0.406886	0.340809	0.285708
36	6	0.406049	0.339971	0.284890
36	7	0.405215	0.339134	0.284074
36	8	0.404382	0.338300	0.283261
36	9	0.403551	0.337468	0.282450
36	10	0.402721	0.336637	0.281642
36	11	0.401893	0.335809	0.280836
37	**0**	**0.401067**	**0.334983**	**0.280032**
37	1	0.400243	0.334159	0.279230
37	2	0.399420	0.333337	0.278431
37	3	0.398599	0.332517	0.277634
37	4	0.397779	0.331699	0.276839
37	5	0.396962	0.330883	0.276046
37	6	0.396146	0.330069	0.275256
37	7	0.395331	0.329256	0.274468
37	8	0.394519	0.328446	0.273682
37	9	0.393708	0.327638	0.272899
37	10	0.392899	0.326832	0.272118
37	11	0.392091	0.326028	0.271339
38	**0**	**0.391285**	**0.325226**	**0.270562**
38	1	0.390481	0.324426	0.269787
38	2	0.389678	0.323628	0.269015
38	3	0.388877	0.322832	0.268245
38	4	0.388078	0.322037	0.267477
38	5	0.387280	0.321245	0.266711
38	6	0.386484	0.320455	0.265948
38	7	0.385689	0.319666	0.265187
38	8	0.384896	0.318880	0.264427
38	9	0.384105	0.318096	0.263670
38	10	0.383316	0.317313	0.262916
38	11	0.382528	0.316532	0.262163
39	**0**	**0.381741**	**0.315754**	**0.261413**
39	1	0.380957	0.314977	0.260664
39	2	0.380174	0.314202	0.259918
39	3	0.379392	0.313429	0.259174
39	4	0.378612	0.312658	0.258432
39	5	0.377834	0.311889	0.257692
39	6	0.377057	0.311121	0.256954
39	7	0.376282	0.310356	0.256219
39	8	0.375509	0.309592	0.255485
39	9	0.374737	0.308831	0.254754
39	10	0.373967	0.308071	0.254025
39	11	0.373198	0.307313	0.253298
40	**0**	**0.372431**	**0.306557**	**0.252572**
40	1	0.371665	0.305803	0.251849

Years	Months	*2.5%*	***3.0%***	*3.5%*
40	2	0.370901	0.305050	0.251128
40	3	0.370139	0.304300	0.250410
40	4	0.369378	0.303551	0.249693
40	5	0.368618	0.302804	0.248978
40	6	0.367861	0.302059	0.248265
40	7	0.367105	0.301316	0.247554
40	8	0.366350	0.300575	0.246846
40	9	0.365597	0.299836	0.246139
40	10	0.364845	0.299098	0.245435
40	11	0.364095	0.298362	0.244732
41	**0**	**0.363347**	**0.297628**	**0.244031**
41	1	0.362600	0.296896	0.243333
41	2	0.361855	0.296165	0.242636
41	3	0.361111	0.295437	0.241942
41	4	0.360369	0.294710	0.241249
41	5	0.359628	0.293985	0.240558
41	6	0.358889	0.293262	0.239870
41	7	0.358151	0.292540	0.239183
41	8	0.357415	0.291820	0.238498
41	9	0.356680	0.291102	0.237816
41	10	0.355947	0.290386	0.237135
41	11	0.355215	0.289672	0.236456
42	**0**	**0.354485**	**0.288959**	**0.235779**
42	1	0.353756	0.288248	0.235104
42	2	0.353029	0.287539	0.234431
42	3	0.352303	0.286832	0.233760
42	4	0.351579	0.286126	0.233091
42	5	0.350856	0.285422	0.232424
42	6	0.350135	0.284720	0.231758
42	7	0.349415	0.284020	0.231095
42	8	0.348697	0.283321	0.230433
42	9	0.347980	0.282624	0.229774
42	10	0.347265	0.281928	0.229116
42	11	0.346551	0.281235	0.228460
43	**0**	**0.345839**	**0.280543**	**0.227806**
43	1	0.345128	0.279853	0.227154
43	2	0.344419	0.279164	0.226503
43	3	0.343711	0.278477	0.225855
43	4	0.343004	0.277792	0.225209
43	5	0.342299	0.277109	0.224564
43	6	0.341595	0.276427	0.223921
43	7	0.340893	0.275747	0.223280
43	8	0.340192	0.275069	0.222641
43	9	0.339493	0.274392	0.222003
43	10	0.338795	0.273717	0.221368
43	11	0.338099	0.273044	0.220734
44	**0**	**0.337404**	**0.272372**	**0.220102**
44	1	0.336710	0.271702	0.219472
44	2	0.336018	0.271033	0.218844
44	3	0.335327	0.270366	0.218217
44	4	0.334638	0.269701	0.217593
44	5	0.333950	0.269038	0.216970
44	6	0.333264	0.268376	0.216349
44	7	0.332579	0.267716	0.215729

Years	Months	*2.5%*	***3.0%***	*3.5%*
44	8	0.331895	0.267057	0.215112
44	9	0.331213	0.266400	0.214496
44	10	0.330532	0.265745	0.213882
44	11	0.329852	0.265091	0.213270
45	**0**	**0.329174**	**0.264439**	**0.212659**
45	1	0.328498	0.263788	0.212050
45	2	0.327822	0.263139	0.211443
45	3	0.327149	0.262492	0.210838
45	4	0.326476	0.261846	0.210235
45	5	0.325805	0.261202	0.209633
45	6	0.325135	0.260559	0.209033
45	7	0.324467	0.259918	0.208434
45	8	0.323800	0.259279	0.207838
45	9	0.323134	0.258641	0.207243
45	10	0.322470	0.258004	0.206649
45	11	0.321807	0.257370	0.206058
46	**0**	**0.321146**	**0.256737**	**0.205468**
46	1	0.320486	0.256105	0.204880
46	2	0.319827	0.255475	0.204293
46	3	0.319169	0.254846	0.203708
46	4	0.318513	0.254219	0.203125
46	5	0.317859	0.253594	0.202544
46	6	0.317205	0.252970	0.201964
46	7	0.316553	0.252348	0.201386
46	8	0.315902	0.251727	0.200809
46	9	0.315253	0.251108	0.200234
46	10	0.314605	0.250490	0.199661
46	11	0.313958	0.249874	0.199090
47	**0**	**0.313313**	**0.249259**	**0.198520**
47	1	0.312669	0.248646	0.197951
47	2	0.312026	0.248034	0.197385
47	3	0.311385	0.247424	0.196820
47	4	0.310745	0.246815	0.196256
47	5	0.310106	0.246208	0.195694
47	6	0.309468	0.245602	0.195134
47	7	0.308832	0.244998	0.194576
47	8	0.308197	0.244395	0.194019
47	9	0.307564	0.243794	0.193463
47	10	0.306932	0.243194	0.192909
47	11	0.306301	0.242596	0.192357
48	**0**	**0.305671**	**0.241999**	**0.191806**
48	1	0.305043	0.241403	0.191257
48	2	0.304416	0.240810	0.190710
48	3	0.303790	0.240217	0.190164
48	4	0.303166	0.239626	0.189620
48	5	0.302542	0.239037	0.189077
48	6	0.301920	0.238449	0.188535
48	7	0.301300	0.237862	0.187996
48	8	0.300680	0.237277	0.187458
48	9	0.300062	0.236693	0.186921
48	10	0.299446	0.236111	0.186386
48	11	0.298830	0.235530	0.185852
49	**0**	**0.298216**	**0.234950**	**0.185320**
49	1	0.297603	0.234372	0.184790

Years	Months	*2.5%*	***3.0%***	*3.5%*
49	2	0.296991	0.233796	0.184261
49	3	0.296381	0.233220	0.183733
49	4	0.295771	0.232647	0.183207
49	5	0.295163	0.232074	0.182683
49	6	0.294557	0.231503	0.182160
49	7	0.293951	0.230934	0.181638
49	8	0.293347	0.230366	0.181118
49	9	0.292744	0.229799	0.180600
49	10	0.292142	0.229234	0.180083
49	11	0.291542	0.228670	0.179567
50	**0**	**0.290942**	**0.228107**	**0.179053**
50	1	0.290344	0.227546	0.178541
50	2	0.289747	0.226986	0.178030
50	3	0.289152	0.226428	0.177520
50	4	0.288557	0.225871	0.177012
50	5	0.287964	0.225315	0.176505
50	6	0.287372	0.224761	0.176000
50	7	0.286782	0.224208	0.175496
50	8	0.286192	0.223656	0.174994
50	9	0.285604	0.223106	0.174493
50	10	0.285017	0.222557	0.173993
50	11	0.284431	0.222009	0.173495
51	**0**	**0.283846**	**0.221463**	**0.172998**
51	1	0.283263	0.220918	0.172503
51	2	0.282680	0.220375	0.172009
51	3	0.282099	0.219833	0.171517
51	4	0.281519	0.219292	0.171026
51	5	0.280941	0.218752	0.170536
51	6	0.280363	0.218214	0.170048
51	7	0.279787	0.217677	0.169561
51	8	0.279212	0.217142	0.169076
51	9	0.278638	0.216608	0.168592
51	10	0.278065	0.216075	0.168109
51	11	0.277493	0.215543	0.167628
52	**0**	**0.276923**	**0.215013**	**0.167148**
52	1	0.276354	0.214484	0.166670
52	2	0.275786	0.213956	0.166193
52	3	0.275219	0.213430	0.165717
52	4	0.274653	0.212905	0.165242
52	5	0.274088	0.212381	0.164769
52	6	0.273525	0.211858	0.164298
52	7	0.272963	0.211337	0.163827
52	8	0.272402	0.210817	0.163358
52	9	0.271842	0.210299	0.162891
52	10	0.271283	0.209781	0.162424
52	11	0.270725	0.209265	0.161960
53	**0**	**0.270169**	**0.208750**	**0.161496**
53	1	0.269613	0.208237	0.161034
53	2	0.269059	0.207724	0.160573
53	3	0.268506	0.207213	0.160113
53	4	0.267954	0.206704	0.159655
53	5	0.267403	0.206195	0.159198
53	6	0.266854	0.205688	0.158742
53	7	0.266305	0.205182	0.158287

Years	Months	*2.5%*	***3.0%***	*3.5%*
53	8	0.265758	0.204677	0.157834
53	9	0.265211	0.204173	0.157382
53	10	0.264666	0.203671	0.156932
53	11	0.264122	0.203170	0.156483
54	**0**	**0.263579**	**0.202670**	**0.156035**
54	1	0.263037	0.202172	0.155588
54	2	0.262497	0.201674	0.155143
54	3	0.261957	0.201178	0.154698
54	4	0.261419	0.200683	0.154256
54	5	0.260881	0.200189	0.153814
54	6	0.260345	0.199697	0.153374
54	7	0.259810	0.199206	0.152935
54	8	0.259276	0.198715	0.152497
54	9	0.258743	0.198227	0.152060
54	10	0.258211	0.197739	0.151625
54	11	0.257680	0.197252	0.151191
55	**0**	**0.257151**	**0.196767**	**0.150758**
55	1	0.256622	0.196283	0.150327
55	2	0.256094	0.195800	0.149896
55	3	0.255568	0.195318	0.149467
55	4	0.255043	0.194838	0.149039
55	5	0.254518	0.194359	0.148613
55	6	0.253995	0.193880	0.148187
55	7	0.253473	0.193403	0.147763
55	8	0.252952	0.192928	0.147340
55	9	0.252432	0.192453	0.146918
55	10	0.251913	0.191980	0.146498
55	11	0.251395	0.191507	0.146078
56	**0**	**0.250879**	**0.191036**	**0.145660**
56	1	0.250363	0.190566	0.145243
56	2	0.249848	0.190097	0.144827
56	3	0.249335	0.189630	0.144413
56	4	0.248822	0.189163	0.143999
56	5	0.248311	0.188698	0.143587
56	6	0.247800	0.188233	0.143176
56	7	0.247291	0.187770	0.142766
56	8	0.246782	0.187308	0.142357
56	9	0.246275	0.186848	0.141950
56	10	0.245769	0.186388	0.141544
56	11	0.245264	0.185929	0.141138
57	**0**	**0.244760**	**0.185472**	**0.140734**
57	1	0.244256	0.185016	0.140331
57	2	0.243754	0.184560	0.139930
57	3	0.243253	0.184106	0.139529
57	4	0.242753	0.183653	0.139130
57	5	0.242254	0.183202	0.138731
57	6	0.241756	0.182751	0.138334
57	7	0.241259	0.182301	0.137938
57	8	0.240763	0.181853	0.137543
57	9	0.240268	0.181405	0.137150
57	10	0.239775	0.180959	0.136757
57	11	0.239282	0.180514	0.136366
58	**0**	**0.238790**	**0.180070**	**0.135975**
58	1	0.238299	0.179627	0.135586

Years	Months	*2.5%*	***3.0%***	*3.5%*
58	2	0.237809	0.179185	0.135198
58	3	0.237320	0.178744	0.134811
58	4	0.236832	0.178304	0.134425
58	5	0.236346	0.177866	0.134040
58	6	0.235860	0.177428	0.133656
58	7	0.235375	0.176992	0.133274
58	8	0.234891	0.176556	0.132892
58	9	0.234408	0.176122	0.132512
58	10	0.233926	0.175688	0.132132
58	11	0.233446	0.175256	0.131754
59	**0**	**0.232966**	**0.174825**	**0.131377**
59	1	0.232487	0.174395	0.131001
59	2	0.232009	0.173966	0.130626
59	3	0.231532	0.173538	0.130252
59	4	0.231056	0.173111	0.129879
59	5	0.230581	0.172685	0.129507
59	6	0.230107	0.172260	0.129137
59	7	0.229634	0.171836	0.128767
59	8	0.229162	0.171414	0.128398
59	9	0.228691	0.170992	0.128031
59	10	0.228221	0.170571	0.127664
59	11	0.227752	0.170152	0.127299
60	**0**	**0.227284**	**0.169733**	**0.126934**
60	1	0.226816	0.169316	0.126571
60	2	0.226350	0.168899	0.126209
60	3	0.225885	0.168483	0.125847
60	4	0.225421	0.168069	0.125487
60	5	0.224957	0.167655	0.125128
60	6	0.224495	0.167243	0.124770
60	7	0.224033	0.166832	0.124412
60	8	0.223573	0.166421	0.124056
60	9	0.223113	0.166012	0.123701
60	10	0.222655	0.165603	0.123347
60	11	0.222197	0.165196	0.122994
61	**0**	**0.221740**	**0.164789**	**0.122642**
61	1	0.221284	0.164384	0.122291
61	2	0.220829	0.163980	0.121941
61	3	0.220375	0.163576	0.121592
61	4	0.219922	0.163174	0.121244
61	5	0.219470	0.162772	0.120896
61	6	0.219019	0.162372	0.120550
61	7	0.218569	0.161972	0.120205
61	8	0.218120	0.161574	0.119861
61	9	0.217671	0.161176	0.119518
61	10	0.217224	0.160780	0.119176
61	11	0.216777	0.160384	0.118835
62	**0**	**0.216332**	**0.159990**	**0.118495**
62	1	0.215887	0.159596	0.118155
62	2	0.215443	0.159203	0.117817
62	3	0.215000	0.158812	0.117480
62	4	0.214559	0.158421	0.117144
62	5	0.214117	0.158031	0.116808
62	6	0.213677	0.157643	0.116474
62	7	0.213238	0.157255	0.116140

Years	Months	*2.5%*	***3.0%***	*3.5%*
62	8	0.212800	0.156868	0.115808
62	9	0.212362	0.156482	0.115476
62	10	0.211926	0.156097	0.115146
62	11	0.211490	0.155713	0.114816
63	**0**	**0.211055**	**0.155330**	**0.114487**
63	1	0.210622	0.154948	0.114160
63	2	0.210189	0.154566	0.113833
63	3	0.209757	0.154186	0.113507
63	4	0.209325	0.153807	0.113182
63	5	0.208895	0.153428	0.112858
63	6	0.208466	0.153051	0.112535
63	7	0.208037	0.152674	0.112213
63	8	0.207610	0.152299	0.111892
63	9	0.207183	0.151924	0.111571
63	10	0.206757	0.151550	0.111252
63	11	0.206332	0.151178	0.110933
64	**0**	**0.205908**	**0.150806**	**0.110616**
64	1	0.205484	0.150435	0.110299
64	2	0.205062	0.150065	0.109984
64	3	0.204641	0.149695	0.109669
64	4	0.204220	0.149327	0.109355
64	5	0.203800	0.148960	0.109042
64	6	0.203381	0.148593	0.108730
64	7	0.202963	0.148228	0.108418
64	8	0.202546	0.147863	0.108108
64	9	0.202130	0.147499	0.107798
64	10	0.201714	0.147136	0.107490
64	11	0.201299	0.146774	0.107182
65	**0**	**0.200886**	**0.146413**	**0.106875**
65	1	0.200473	0.146053	0.106569
65	2	0.200061	0.145694	0.106264
65	3	0.199649	0.145335	0.105960
65	4	0.199239	0.144978	0.105657
65	5	0.198829	0.144621	0.105354
65	6	0.198421	0.144265	0.105053
65	7	0.198013	0.143910	0.104752
65	8	0.197606	0.143556	0.104452
65	9	0.197200	0.143203	0.104153
65	10	0.196794	0.142851	0.103855
65	11	0.196390	0.142499	0.103558
66	**0**	**0.195986**	**0.142149**	**0.103261**
66	1	0.195583	0.141799	0.102966
66	2	0.195181	0.141450	0.102671
66	3	0.194780	0.141102	0.102377
66	4	0.194379	0.140755	0.102084
66	5	0.193980	0.140409	0.101792
66	6	0.193581	0.140063	0.101500
66	7	0.193183	0.139719	0.101210
66	8	0.192786	0.139375	0.100920
66	9	0.192390	0.139032	0.100631
66	10	0.191994	0.138690	0.100343
66	11	0.191600	0.138349	0.100056
67	**0**	**0.191206**	**0.138009**	**0.099769**
67	1	0.190813	0.137669	0.099484

Years	Months	*2.5%*	***3.0%***	*3.5%*
67	2	0.190421	0.137330	0.099199
67	3	0.190029	0.136992	0.098915
67	4	0.189638	0.136655	0.098632
67	5	0.189249	0.136319	0.098349
67	6	0.188860	0.135984	0.098068
67	7	0.188471	0.135649	0.097787
67	8	0.188084	0.135316	0.097507
67	9	0.187697	0.134983	0.097228
67	10	0.187312	0.134651	0.096950
67	11	0.186926	0.134319	0.096672
68	**0**	**0.186542**	**0.133989**	**0.096395**
68	1	0.186159	0.133659	0.096119
68	2	0.185776	0.133330	0.095844
68	3	0.185394	0.133002	0.095570
68	4	0.185013	0.132675	0.095296
68	5	0.184633	0.132349	0.095024
68	6	0.184253	0.132023	0.094751
68	7	0.183875	0.131698	0.094480
68	8	0.183497	0.131374	0.094210
68	9	0.183119	0.131051	0.093940
68	10	0.182743	0.130729	0.093671
68	11	0.182367	0.130407	0.093403
69	**0**	**0.181992**	**0.130086**	**0.093136**
69	1	0.181618	0.129766	0.092869
69	2	0.181245	0.129447	0.092603
69	3	0.180872	0.129129	0.092338
69	4	0.180501	0.128811	0.092074
69	5	0.180130	0.128494	0.091810
69	6	0.179759	0.128178	0.091547
69	7	0.179390	0.127862	0.091285
69	8	0.179021	0.127548	0.091024
69	9	0.178653	0.127234	0.090763
69	10	0.178286	0.126921	0.090504
69	11	0.177919	0.126609	0.090244
70	**0**	**0.177554**	**0.126297**	**0.089986**
70	1	0.177189	0.125987	0.089729
70	2	0.176824	0.125677	0.089472
70	3	0.176461	0.125368	0.089216
70	4	0.176098	0.125059	0.088960
70	5	0.175736	0.124751	0.088705
70	6	0.175375	0.124444	0.088452
70	7	0.175014	0.124138	0.088198
70	8	0.174655	0.123833	0.087946
70	9	0.174296	0.123528	0.087694
70	10	0.173937	0.123224	0.087443
70	11	0.173580	0.122921	0.087193
71	**0**	**0.173223**	**0.122619**	**0.086943**
71	1	0.172867	0.122317	0.086694
71	2	0.172512	0.122016	0.086446
71	3	0.172157	0.121716	0.086199
71	4	0.171803	0.121417	0.085952
71	5	0.171450	0.121118	0.085706
71	6	0.171097	0.120820	0.085460
71	7	0.170746	0.120523	0.085216

Years	Months	*2.5%*	***3.0%***	*3.5%*
71	8	0.170395	0.120226	0.084972
71	9	0.170045	0.119930	0.084729
71	10	0.169695	0.119635	0.084486
71	11	0.169346	0.119341	0.084244
72	**0**	**0.168998**	**0.119047**	**0.084003**
72	1	0.168651	0.118754	0.083763
72	2	0.168304	0.118462	0.083523
72	3	0.167958	0.118171	0.083284
72	4	0.167613	0.117880	0.083045
72	5	0.167268	0.117590	0.082808
72	6	0.166924	0.117301	0.082570
72	7	0.166581	0.117012	0.082334
72	8	0.166239	0.116724	0.082098
72	9	0.165897	0.116437	0.081863
72	10	0.165556	0.116151	0.081629
72	11	0.165216	0.115865	0.081395
73	**0**	**0.164876**	**0.115580**	**0.081162**
73	1	0.164537	0.115296	0.080930
73	2	0.164199	0.115012	0.080698
73	3	0.163861	0.114729	0.080467
73	4	0.163525	0.114447	0.080237
73	5	0.163189	0.114165	0.080007
73	6	0.162853	0.113884	0.079778
73	7	0.162518	0.113604	0.079550
73	8	0.162184	0.113325	0.079322
73	9	0.161851	0.113046	0.079095
73	10	0.161518	0.112768	0.078869
73	11	0.161186	0.112490	0.078643
74	**0**	**0.160855**	**0.112214**	**0.078418**
74	1	0.160524	0.111938	0.078193
74	2	0.160194	0.111662	0.077969
74	3	0.159865	0.111387	0.077746
74	4	0.159536	0.111113	0.077524
74	5	0.159208	0.110840	0.077302
74	6	0.158881	0.110567	0.077080
74	7	0.158554	0.110295	0.076860
74	8	0.158229	0.110024	0.076640
74	9	0.157903	0.109753	0.076420
74	10	0.157579	0.109483	0.076202
74	11	0.157255	0.109214	0.075983
75	**0**	**0.156931**	**0.108945**	**0.075766**
75	1	0.156609	0.108677	0.075549
75	2	0.156287	0.108410	0.075333
75	3	0.155966	0.108143	0.075117
75	4	0.155645	0.107877	0.074902
75	5	0.155325	0.107612	0.074688
75	6	0.155006	0.107347	0.074474
75	7	0.154687	0.107083	0.074261
75	8	0.154369	0.106819	0.074048
75	9	0.154052	0.106557	0.073836
75	10	0.153735	0.106294	0.073625
75	11	0.153419	0.106033	0.073414
76	**0**	**0.153104**	**0.105772**	**0.073204**
76	1	0.152789	0.105512	0.072994

Years	Months	2.5%	**3.0%**	3.5%
76	2	0.152475	0.105252	0.072785
76	3	0.152162	0.104993	0.072577
76	4	0.151849	0.104735	0.072369
76	5	0.151537	0.104477	0.072162
76	6	0.151225	0.104220	0.071955
76	7	0.150914	0.103964	0.071749
76	8	0.150604	0.103708	0.071544
76	9	0.150295	0.103453	0.071339
76	10	0.149986	0.103198	0.071135
76	11	0.149677	0.102945	0.070931
77	**0**	**0.149370**	**0.102691**	**0.070728**
77	1	0.149063	0.102439	0.070526
77	2	0.148756	0.102187	0.070324
77	3	0.148450	0.101935	0.070123
77	4	0.148145	0.101684	0.069922
77	5	0.147841	0.101434	0.069722
77	6	0.147537	0.101185	0.069522
77	7	0.147234	0.100936	0.069323
77	8	0.146931	0.100688	0.069125
77	9	0.146629	0.100440	0.068927
77	10	0.146327	0.100193	0.068729
77	11	0.146027	0.099946	0.068533
78	**0**	**0.145726**	**0.099700**	**0.068337**
78	1	0.145427	0.099455	0.068141
78	2	0.145128	0.099210	0.067946
78	3	0.144830	0.098966	0.067751
78	4	0.144532	0.098723	0.067557
78	5	0.144235	0.098480	0.067364
78	6	0.143938	0.098238	0.067171
78	7	0.143642	0.097996	0.066979
78	8	0.143347	0.097755	0.066787
78	9	0.143053	0.097514	0.066596
78	10	0.142758	0.097274	0.066405
78	11	0.142465	0.097035	0.066215
79	**0**	**0.142172**	**0.096796**	**0.066026**
79	1	0.141880	0.096558	0.065837
79	2	0.141588	0.096321	0.065648
79	3	0.141297	0.096084	0.065460
79	4	0.141007	0.095847	0.065273
79	5	0.140717	0.095612	0.065086
79	6	0.140428	0.095376	0.064900
79	7	0.140139	0.095142	0.064714
79	8	0.139851	0.094908	0.064529
79	9	0.139563	0.094674	0.064344
79	10	0.139277	0.094441	0.064160
79	11	0.138990	0.094209	0.063976
80	**0**	**0.138705**	**0.093977**	**0.063793**
80	1	0.138419	0.093746	0.063610
80	2	0.138135	0.093515	0.063428
80	3	0.137851	0.093285	0.063247
80	4	0.137568	0.093056	0.063066
80	5	0.137285	0.092827	0.062885
80	6	0.137003	0.092598	0.062705
80	7	0.136721	0.092371	0.062525

Years	Months	*2.5%*	***3.0%***	*3.5%*
80	8	0.136440	0.092143	0.062346
80	9	0.136159	0.091917	0.062168
80	10	0.135880	0.091691	0.061990
80	11	0.135600	0.091465	0.061813
81	**0**	**0.135322**	**0.091240**	**0.061636**
81	1	0.135043	0.091015	0.061459
81	2	0.134766	0.090792	0.061283
81	3	0.134489	0.090568	0.061108
81	4	0.134212	0.090345	0.060933
81	5	0.133936	0.090123	0.060758
81	6	0.133661	0.089901	0.060584
81	7	0.133386	0.089680	0.060411
81	8	0.133112	0.089460	0.060238
81	9	0.132839	0.089239	0.060066
81	10	0.132565	0.089020	0.059894
81	11	0.132293	0.088801	0.059722
82	**0**	**0.132021**	**0.088582**	**0.059551**
82	1	0.131750	0.088365	0.059381
82	2	0.131479	0.088147	0.059211
82	3	0.131209	0.087930	0.059041
82	4	0.130939	0.087714	0.058872
82	5	0.130670	0.087498	0.058704
82	6	0.130401	0.087283	0.058536
82	7	0.130133	0.087068	0.058368
82	8	0.129866	0.086854	0.058201
82	9	0.129599	0.086640	0.058034
82	10	0.129332	0.086427	0.057868
82	11	0.129066	0.086214	0.057703
83	**0**	**0.128801**	**0.086002**	**0.057538**
83	1	0.128536	0.085791	0.057373
83	2	0.128272	0.085580	0.057209
83	3	0.128008	0.085369	0.057045
83	4	0.127745	0.085159	0.056881
83	5	0.127483	0.084950	0.056719
83	6	0.127221	0.084741	0.056556
83	7	0.126959	0.084532	0.056394
83	8	0.126698	0.084324	0.056233
83	9	0.126438	0.084117	0.056072
83	10	0.126178	0.083910	0.055911
83	11	0.125918	0.083703	0.055751
84	**0**	**0.125659**	**0.083497**	**0.055592**
84	1	0.125401	0.083292	0.055433
84	2	0.125143	0.083087	0.055274
84	3	0.124886	0.082883	0.055116
84	4	0.124629	0.082679	0.054958
84	5	0.124373	0.082475	0.054801
84	6	0.124118	0.082272	0.054644
84	7	0.123862	0.082070	0.054487
84	8	0.123608	0.081868	0.054331
84	9	0.123354	0.081667	0.054176
84	10	0.123100	0.081466	0.054021
84	11	0.122847	0.081265	0.053866
85	**0**	**0.122595**	**0.081065**	**0.053712**
85	1	0.122343	0.080866	0.053558

Years	Months	*2.5%*	***3.0%***	*3.5%*
85	2	0.122091	0.080667	0.053405
85	3	0.121840	0.080469	0.053252
85	4	0.121590	0.080271	0.053099
85	5	0.121340	0.080073	0.052947
85	6	0.121090	0.079876	0.052796
85	7	0.120841	0.079680	0.052645
85	8	0.120593	0.079484	0.052494
85	9	0.120345	0.079288	0.052344
85	10	0.120098	0.079093	0.052194
85	11	0.119851	0.078898	0.052045
86	**0**	**0.119605**	**0.078704**	**0.051896**
86	1	0.119359	0.078511	0.051747
86	2	0.119113	0.078318	0.051599
86	3	0.118868	0.078125	0.051451
86	4	0.118624	0.077933	0.051304
86	5	0.118380	0.077741	0.051157
86	6	0.118137	0.077550	0.051011
86	7	0.117894	0.077359	0.050864
86	8	0.117652	0.077169	0.050719
86	9	0.117410	0.076979	0.050574
86	10	0.117169	0.076789	0.050429
86	11	0.116928	0.076600	0.050285
87	**0**	**0.116687**	**0.076412**	**0.050141**
87	1	0.116447	0.076224	0.049997
87	2	0.116208	0.076036	0.049854
87	3	0.115969	0.075849	0.049711
87	4	0.115731	0.075663	0.049569
87	5	0.115493	0.075477	0.049427
87	6	0.115256	0.075291	0.049286
87	7	0.115019	0.075106	0.049144
87	8	0.114782	0.074921	0.049004
87	9	0.114546	0.074737	0.048863
87	10	0.114311	0.074553	0.048724
87	11	0.114076	0.074369	0.048584
88	**0**	**0.113841**	**0.074186**	**0.048445**
88	1	0.113607	0.074004	0.048306
88	2	0.113374	0.073822	0.048168
88	3	0.113141	0.073640	0.048030
88	4	0.112908	0.073459	0.047893
88	5	0.112676	0.073278	0.047756
88	6	0.112444	0.073098	0.047619
88	7	0.112213	0.072918	0.047483
88	8	0.111983	0.072739	0.047347
88	9	0.111752	0.072560	0.047211
88	10	0.111523	0.072381	0.047076
88	11	0.111293	0.072203	0.046941
89	**0**	**0.111065**	**0.072026**	**0.046807**
89	1	0.110836	0.071848	0.046673
89	2	0.110609	0.071672	0.046539
89	3	0.110381	0.071495	0.046406
89	4	0.110154	0.071319	0.046273
89	5	0.109928	0.071144	0.046141
89	6	0.109702	0.070969	0.046009
89	7	0.109476	0.070794	0.045877

Years	Months	*2.5%*	***3.0%***	*3.5%*
89	8	0.109251	0.070620	0.045746
89	9	0.109027	0.070446	0.045615
89	10	0.108803	0.070273	0.045484
89	11	0.108579	0.070100	0.045354
90	**0**	**0.108356**	**0.069928**	**0.045224**
90	1	0.108133	0.069756	0.045094
90	2	0.107911	0.069584	0.044965
90	3	0.107689	0.069413	0.044837
90	4	0.107468	0.069242	0.044708
90	5	0.107247	0.069072	0.044580
90	6	0.107026	0.068902	0.044453
90	7	0.106806	0.068732	0.044325
90	8	0.106587	0.068563	0.044199
90	9	0.106368	0.068395	0.044072
90	10	0.106149	0.068226	0.043946
90	11	0.105931	0.068058	0.043820
91	**0**	**0.105713**	**0.067891**	**0.043695**
91	1	0.105496	0.067724	0.043570
91	2	0.105279	0.067557	0.043445
91	3	0.105062	0.067391	0.043320
91	4	0.104846	0.067225	0.043196
91	5	0.104631	0.067060	0.043073
91	6	0.104416	0.066895	0.042949
91	7	0.104201	0.066730	0.042827
91	8	0.103987	0.066566	0.042704
91	9	0.103773	0.066403	0.042582
91	10	0.103560	0.066239	0.042460
91	11	0.103347	0.066076	0.042338
92	**0**	**0.103135**	**0.065914**	**0.042217**
92	1	0.102923	0.065751	0.042096
92	2	0.102711	0.065590	0.041976
92	3	0.102500	0.065428	0.041856
92	4	0.102289	0.065267	0.041736
92	5	0.102079	0.065107	0.041616
92	6	0.101869	0.064947	0.041497
92	7	0.101660	0.064787	0.041378
92	8	0.101451	0.064627	0.041260
92	9	0.101242	0.064468	0.041142
92	10	0.101034	0.064310	0.041024
92	11	0.100826	0.064152	0.040907
93	**0**	**0.100619**	**0.063994**	**0.040789**
93	1	0.100412	0.063836	0.040673
93	2	0.100206	0.063679	0.040556
93	3	0.100000	0.063523	0.040440
93	4	0.099794	0.063366	0.040324
93	5	0.099589	0.063211	0.040209
93	6	0.099384	0.063055	0.040094
93	7	0.099180	0.062900	0.039979
93	8	0.098976	0.062745	0.039865
93	9	0.098773	0.062591	0.039750
93	10	0.098570	0.062437	0.039637
93	11	0.098367	0.062283	0.039523
94	**0**	**0.098165**	**0.062130**	**0.039410**
94	1	0.097963	0.061977	0.039297

Years	Months	*2.5%*	***3.0%***	*3.5%*
94	2	0.097762	0.061825	0.039185
94	3	0.097561	0.061673	0.039073
94	4	0.097360	0.061521	0.038961
94	5	0.097160	0.061369	0.038849
94	6	0.096960	0.061218	0.038738
94	7	0.096761	0.061068	0.038627
94	8	0.096562	0.060918	0.038517
94	9	0.096364	0.060768	0.038406
94	10	0.096166	0.060618	0.038296
94	11	0.095968	0.060469	0.038187
95	**0**	**0.095771**	**0.060320**	**0.038077**
95	1	0.095574	0.060172	0.037968
95	2	0.095377	0.060024	0.037860
95	3	0.095181	0.059876	0.037751
95	4	0.094986	0.059729	0.037643
95	5	0.094790	0.059582	0.037535
95	6	0.094596	0.059435	0.037428
95	7	0.094401	0.059289	0.037321
95	8	0.094207	0.059143	0.037214
95	9	0.094013	0.058998	0.037107
95	10	0.093820	0.058853	0.037001
95	11	0.093627	0.058708	0.036895
96	**0**	**0.093435**	**0.058563**	**0.036790**
96	1	0.093243	0.058419	0.036684
96	2	0.093051	0.058276	0.036579
96	3	0.092860	0.058132	0.036475
96	4	0.092669	0.057989	0.036370
96	5	0.092478	0.057847	0.036266
96	6	0.092288	0.057704	0.036162
96	7	0.092099	0.057562	0.036059
96	8	0.091909	0.057421	0.035956
96	9	0.091720	0.057279	0.035853
96	10	0.091532	0.057138	0.035750
96	11	0.091344	0.056998	0.035648
97	**0**	**0.091156**	**0.056858**	**0.035546**
97	1	0.090969	0.056718	0.035444
97	2	0.090782	0.056578	0.035342
97	3	0.090595	0.056439	0.035241
97	4	0.090409	0.056300	0.035140
97	5	0.090223	0.056162	0.035040
97	6	0.090037	0.056024	0.034939
97	7	0.089852	0.055886	0.034839
97	8	0.089668	0.055748	0.034740
97	9	0.089483	0.055611	0.034640
97	10	0.089299	0.055474	0.034541
97	11	0.089116	0.055338	0.034442
98	**0**	**0.088933**	**0.055202**	**0.034344**
98	1	0.088750	0.055066	0.034245
98	2	0.088567	0.054930	0.034147
98	3	0.088385	0.054795	0.034049
98	4	0.088204	0.054660	0.033952
98	5	0.088022	0.054526	0.033855
98	6	0.087841	0.054392	0.033758
98	7	0.087661	0.054258	0.033661

Years	Months	*2.5%*	***3.0%***	*3.5%*
98	8	0.087481	0.054124	0.033565
98	9	0.087301	0.053991	0.033469
98	10	0.087121	0.053859	0.033373
98	11	0.086942	0.053726	0.033277
99	**0**	**0.086764**	**0.053594**	**0.033182**
99	1	0.086585	0.053462	0.033087
99	2	0.086407	0.053330	0.032993
99	3	0.086230	0.053199	0.032898
99	4	0.086052	0.053068	0.032804
99	5	0.085875	0.052938	0.032710
99	6	0.085699	0.052808	0.032616
99	7	0.085523	0.052678	0.032523
99	8	0.085347	0.052548	0.032430
99	9	0.085172	0.052419	0.032337
99	10	0.084996	0.052290	0.032244
99	11	0.084822	0.052161	0.032152
100	**0**	**0.084647**	**0.052033**	**0.032060**

Appendix 1

English Life Tables No 15, 1990–92

SERIES DS no 14

OFFICE FOR
NATIONAL
STATISTICS

1990–
1992

English Life Tables
No 15

England & Wales

A publication of the Government Statistical Service

Office for National Statistics

Series DS No 14

English Life Tables No 15

LONDON: The Stationery Office

Foreword

These English Life Tables (number fifteen in the series) together with associated supplementary tables and commentary, were prepared by Chris Daykin of the Government Actuary's Department, at the invitation of the Registrar General for England and Wales, who is also Director of the Office for National Statistics.

The series of English Life Tables has now been prepared for over 150 years. The idea was conceived by Dr William Farr, first Medical Statistician at the General Register Office, who himself produced numbers 1, 2 and 3 between 1843 and 1864. The GRO continued to produce subsequent Tables until after the 1911 Census, when the Registrar General invited Mr George King, a former Vice-President of the Institute of Actuaries, to prepare Tables 7 and 8, which incorporated important advances in principles and methods. Since then the English Life Tables have been prepared by the Government Actuary of the time, at the invitation of the Registrar General.

The current tables are based on mortality experience in England and Wales during the years 1990, 1991 and 1992. This volume is generally similar to its predecessor, English Life Tables No 14, and continues the use of rates based on mid-year population estimates rather than the census.

On behalf of the Registrar General, I wish to record our appreciation of the considerable work carried out to provide the accompanying commentary and tables, including the contribution of Professor Stephen Haberman in graduating mortality rates.

A J Fox
Director, Census, Population and Health Group
Office for National Statistics

Contents

* Of this book.

List of Figures and Tables

Report on English Life Tables No 15 by the Government Actuary

Dr T Holt
Registrar General for England and Wales
Office for National Statistics
1 Drummond Gate
London SW1V 2QQ

Sir,

Life tables for males and for females have been constructed based on the mortality experience of the population of England and Wales during the three years 1990, 1991 and 1992. These tables, (denoted briefly as ELT 15), are the fifteenth in a series known as the English Life Tables which are associated with decennial population censuses, beginning with the census of 1841.

Reports on the life tables have traditionally contained (i) a record of the mortality rates at each age, calculated as accurately as possible from death registration data and population numbers and (ii) a graduated set of those rates which, together with the resulting life tables, have been used as a standard for various purposes. These period life tables show the increasing longevity of the population of England and Wales over a long period, and they can be compared with the experience of other countries and other groups of people.

Data used in constructing the tables

The period 1990–92 was chosen because it is centred on the census year, 1991. A three-year period is normally of sufficient length to smooth out most of the effect if the mortality experience of the census year itself happens not to be typical of the general level of mortality at the beginning of the decade.

Apart from the calculation of the rates for mortality during the first year of life and at ages 90 and over, the average population numbers at each age during the three years 1990–92 were taken as the mean of the mid-year estimates[1] published by the Office of Population Censuses and Surveys (now merged with the Central Statistical Office to form the Office for National Statistics) for those years, which take into account the results from the 1991 census. The reason for treating ages 90 and over differently is the problem of age mis-statement of elderly people in censuses. Further information about the data used in constructing ELT 15 is given in Appendix A to this report.

Crude rates of mortality for each age (denoted by m_x) were obtained by dividing the total deaths in each of the three calendar years 1990, 1991 and 1992 by an exposed-to-risk derived from the mid-year population estimates for the three years added together, as explained in Appendix A. These crude death rates, given in Appendix A, are not suitable as the basis for a standard life table because they tend to vary erratically from age to age owing to the small numbers of deaths involved. This is particularly so in childhood and at very advanced ages. Errors are also present in the data because no census is perfectly accurate or complete and neither are the mid-year estimates of the population. Errors arising because of the small numbers of deaths, and, to some extent, other types of error, can be reduced by a process of smoothing these crude death rates.

Graduation

For the English Life Tables, the intention of this smoothing (or 'graduation', as it is called by mathematicians) is to replace the crude rates by a series of graduated rates which, while forming a smooth progression over the whole age range covered, still preserves the general shape of the mortality curve. Various means of carrying out this smoothing have been applied in constructing the English Life Tables in the past. For the current graduation, experiments using differing methods of graduation were carried out, both within the Government Actuary's Department and by Professor Steven Haberman at City University, London. From the results of these, it was decided to employ a variant of the cubic spline fitting method used in English Life Table No 14, with knots taken at each age from 1 to 103 for males and 1 to 104 for females. The graduated death rates are then converted into initial rates of mortality q_x, which give the probability of a person aged exactly x dying before reaching age $(x+1)$.

It is necessary to complete the graduation by obtaining initial rates of mortality at the youngest and oldest ages. The values of q_x were obtained directly from the records of births and deaths at age 0 in the years 1990 to 1992. For the oldest ages, the rates were found by extrapolation from the values of q_x, obtained for ages 85 to 103 for males and to 104 for females. Professor Haberman's description of the methodology used is given in Appendix B. The resulting English Life Tables No 15 appear on pages 2 and 3 of this report. Definitions of the symbols used in the Life Tables and elsewhere in this report are given in Appendix D. I am grateful to Professor Steven Haberman for his assistance in preparing these Tables.

English Life Table No 15.1

Age	Males			Females		
x	l_x	q_x	$\mathring{e}_x$	l_x	q_x	$\mathring{e}_x$
0	100000	.00814	73.413	100000	.00632	78.956
1	99186	.00062	73.019	99368	.00055	78.462
2	99124	.00038	72.064	99313	.00030	77.505
3	99086	.00030	71.091	99283	.00022	76.528
4	99056	.00024	70.113	99261	.00018	75.545
5	99032	.00022	69.130	99243	.00016	74.559
6	99010	.00020	68.145	99228	.00015	73.570
7	98990	.00019	67.158	99213	.00014	72.581
8	98972	.00018	66.171	99199	.00014	71.591
9	98953	.00018	65.183	99185	.00013	70.601
10	98935	.00018	64.195	99172	.00013	69.610
11	98917	.00018	63.206	99159	.00014	68.620
12	98899	.00019	62.218	99145	.00014	67.629
13	98880	.00023	61.230	99131	.00015	66.638
14	98857	.00029	60.244	99116	.00018	65.649
15	98828	.00040	59.261	99098	.00022	64.660
16	98789	.00052	58.285	99077	.00026	63.674
17	98737	.00075	57.315	99051	.00031	62.691
18	98663	.00087	56.358	99020	.00031	61.710
19	98577	.00083	55.406	98989	.00032	60.729
20	98496	.00084	54.452	98957	.00031	59.748
21	98413	.00086	53.497	98926	.00032	58.767
22	98328	.00089	52.543	98894	.00033	57.786
23	98241	.00089	51.589	98862	.00033	56.805
24	98154	.00088	50.635	98829	.00033	55.823
25	98067	.00086	49.679	98797	.00034	54.842
26	97983	.00085	48.721	98763	.00035	53.860
27	97900	.00085	47.762	98729	.00036	52.878
28	97817	.00087	46.802	98694	.00038	51.897
29	97732	.00090	45.842	98656	.00040	50.917
30	97645	.00091	44.883	98617	.00043	49.937
31	97556	.00094	43.923	98574	.00047	48.958
32	97465	.00097	42.964	98528	.00052	47.981
33	97370	.00099	42.005	98477	.00057	47.006
34	97273	.00106	41.046	98420	.00063	46.032
35	97170	.00116	40.090	98359	.00069	45.061
36	97057	.00127	39.136	98291	.00075	44.092
37	96933	.00138	38.185	98217	.00082	43.124
38	96800	.00149	37.237	98136	.00090	42.160
39	96655	.00160	36.292	98048	.00098	41.197
40	96500	.00172	35.349	97952	.00107	40.237
41	96334	.00186	34.409	97847	.00117	39.279
42	96155	.00201	33.473	97733	.00129	38.325
43	95961	.00219	32.539	97607	.00142	37.374
44	95751	.00240	31.609	97469	.00158	36.426

English Life Table No 15.1 *continued*

Age	Males			Females		
x	l_x	q_x	$\mathring{e}_x$	l_x	q_x	$\mathring{e}_x$
45	95521	.00266	30.684	97315	.00177	35.483
46	95266	.00297	29.765	97142	.00198	34.545
47	94983	.00332	28.852	96950	.00219	33.612
48	94668	.00371	27.947	96738	.00241	32.685
49	94316	.00415	27.049	96504	.00266	31.763
50	93925	.00464	26.159	96247	.00294	30.846
51	93489	.00519	25.279	95964	.00326	29.936
52	93004	.00577	24.408	95652	.00357	29.032
53	92467	.00642	23.547	95310	.00390	28.134
54	91873	.00714	22.696	94938	.00428	27.242
55	91217	.00797	21.856	94532	.00475	26.357
56	90490	.00890	21.027	94082	.00531	25.481
57	89684	.00995	20.211	93583	.00592	24.614
58	88792	.01112	19.409	93029	.00660	23.757
59	87805	.01243	18.622	92415	.00739	22.912
60	86714	.01392	17.850	91732	.00830	22.079
61	85507	.01560	17.095	90971	.00922	21.259
62	84173	.01749	16.357	90132	.01015	20.452
63	82701	.01965	15.640	89217	.01129	19.657
64	81076	.02199	14.943	88210	.01266	18.875
65	79293	.02447	14.267	87093	.01339	18.111
66	77353	.02711	13.612	85875	.01523	17.361
67	75256	.02997	12.978	84567	.01676	16.621
68	73001	.03292	12.363	83150	.01844	15.896
69	70598	.03602	11.767	81617	.02017	15.185
70	68055	.03930	11.187	79970	.02190	14.487
71	65381	.04311	10.624	78219	.02399	13.800
72	62562	.04745	10.080	76343	.02693	13.127
73	59593	.05217	9.557	74287	.03014	12.476
74	56484	.05697	9.056	72048	.03284	11.848
75	53266	.06197	8.572	69682	.03569	11.234
76	49965	.06777	8.106	67195	.03919	10.631
77	46579	.07418	7.658	64561	.04356	10.044
78	43124	.08101	7.232	61749	.04833	9.478
79	39630	.08838	6.825	58765	.05373	8.934
80	36128	.09616	6.438	55607	.05961	8.413
81	32654	.10411	6.070	52293	.06568	7.914
82	29254	.11279	5.718	48858	.07216	7.435
83	25954	.12235	5.382	45332	.07933	6.974
84	22779	.13270	5.063	41736	.08757	6.532
85	19756	.14372	4.762	38081	.09731	6.111
86	16917	.15585	4.478	34375	.10833	5.715
87	14280	.16848	4.213	30651	.11859	5.349
88	11874	.18061	3.968	27017	.12860	5.002
89	9730	.19246	3.734	23542	.14146	4.667

English Life Table No 15.1 *continued*

Age	Males			Females		
x	l_x	q_x	$\mathring{e}_x$	l_x	q_x	$\mathring{e}_x$
90	7857	.20465	3.508	20212	.15550	4.354
91	6249	.21911	3.285	17069	.17006	4.065
92	4880	.23655	3.071	14166	.18573	3.797
93	3726	.25575	2.872	11535	.20126	3.551
94	2773	.27483	2.693	9214	.21790	3.322
95	2011	.29311	2.531	7206	.23619	3.112
96	1421	.31104	2.383	5504	.25344	2.925
97	979	.32919	2.244	4109	.26820	2.754
98	657	.34783	2.114	3007	.28352	2.588
99	428	.36712	1.991	2154	.30331	2.422
100	271	.38705	1.874	1501	.32489	2.269
101	166	.40760	1.764	1013	.34562	2.133
102	98	.42870	1.660	663	.36186	2.011
103	56	.45030	1.562	423	.37992	1.887
104	31	.47428	1.468	262	.40045	1.758
105	16	.49634	1.384	157	.43618	1.621
106	8	.51841	1.306	89	.45994	1.518
107	4	.54041	1.234	48	.48389	1.425
108	2	.56225	1.166	25	.50791	1.338
109	1	.58385	1.104	12	.53190	1.257
110				6	.55574	1.183
111				3	.57932	1.114
112				1	.60255	1.050
113						
114						

English Life Table No 15.2

Age	Males			Females		
x	d_x	T_x	μ_x	d_x	T_x	μ_x
0	814	7341337		632	7895613	
1	62	7242424	.00080	55	7796600	.00073
2	38	7143272	.00043	30	7697262	.00035
3	30	7044168	00033	22	7597965	.00025
4	24	6945097	.00027	18	7498693	.00020
5	22	6846053	.00023	15	7399441	.00017
6	20	6747032	.00021	15	7300206	.00015
7	18	6648032	.00019	14	7200986	.00014
8	19	6549051	.00018	14	7101780	.00014
9	18	6450088	.00018	13	7002588	.00014
10	18	6351144	.00018	13	6903409	.00013
11	18	6252218	.00018	14	6804244	.00014
12	19	6153309	.00019	14	6705092	.00014
13	23	6054419	.00021	15	6605953	.00014
14	29	5955550	.00026	18	6506829	.00017
15	39	5856707	.00034	21	6407722	.00020
16	52	5757897	.00045	26	6308634	.00024
17	74	5659132	.00064	31	6209570	.00029
18	86	5560431	.00083	31	6110535	.00031
19	81	5461810	.00085	32	6011530	.00032
20	83	5363274	.00083	31	5912557	.00032
21	85	5264819	.00085	32	5813615	.00032
22	87	5166448	.00088	32	5714704	.00032
23	87	5068163	.00089	33	5615826	.00033
24	87	4969966	.00089	32	5516980	.00033
25	84	4871856	.00087	34	5418167	.00033
26	83	4773831	.00085	34	5319387	.00034
27	83	4675889	.00084	35	5220641	.00035
28	85	4578030	.00086	38	5121929	.00037
29	87	4480255	.00088	39	5023254	.00039
30	89	4382566	.00090	43	4924617	.00042
31	91	4284966	.00092	46	4826021	.00045
32	95	4187455	.00096	51	4727470	.00050
33	97	4090037	.00098	57	4628967	.00054
34	103	3992715	.00102	61	4530518	.00060
35	113	3895493	.00111	68	4432128	.00066
36	124	3798379	.00122	74	4333803	.00072
37	133	3701383	.00133	81	4235549	.00079
38	145	3604515	.00144	88	4137372	.00086
39	155	3507787	.00155	96	4039279	.00094
40	166	3411208	.00166	105	3941278	.00102
41	179	3314791	.00179	114	3843377	.00112
42	194	3218545	.00193	126	3745586	.00123
43	210	3122486	.00210	138	3647916	.00135
44	230	3026629	.00229	154	3550377	.00149

English Life Table No 15.2 *continued*

Age	Males			Females		
x	d_x	T_x	μ_x	d_x	T_x	μ_x
45	255	2930992	.00253	173	3452984	.00167
46	283	2835596	.00281	192	3355754	.00187
47	315	2740469	.00314	212	3258706	.00208
48	352	2645640	.00352	234	3161861	.00230
49	391	2551145	.00393	257	3065238	.00253
50	436	2457021	.00440	283	2968860	.00280
51	485	2363311	.00492	312	2872752	.00310
52	537	2270060	.00549	342	2776942	.00342
53	594	2177320	.00610	372	2681459	.00374
54	656	2085145	.00679	406	2586332	.00408
55	727	1993595	.00757	450	2491594	.00451
56	806	1902735	.00845	499	2397283	.00503
57	892	1812641	.00945	554	2303446	.00562
58	987	1723395	.01057	614	2210135	.00626
59	1091	1635088	.01182	683	2117408	.00700
60	1207	1547820	.01323	761	2025328	.00786
61	1334	1461700	.01483	839	1933970	.00880
62	1472	1376849	.01664	915	1843412	.00972
63	1625	1293400	.01870	1007	1753731	.01074
64	1783	1211498	.02101	1117	1665008	.01203
65	1940	1131301	.02348	1218	1577348	.01342
66	2097	1052965	.02610	1308	1490856	.01470
67	2255	976647	.02893	1417	1405626	.01609
68	2403	902506	.03192	1533	1321758	.01774
69	2543	830695	.03505	1647	1239366	.01949
70	2674	761357	.03833	1751	1158563	.02123
71	2819	694628	.04198	1876	1079459	.02311
72	2969	630644	.04626	2056	1002166	.02569
73	3109	569554	.05105	2239	926835	.02897
74	3218	511505	.05609	2366	853654	.03203
75	3301	456622	.06123	2487	782780	.03480
76	3386	404999	.06694	2634	714331	.03803
77	3455	356720	.07352	2812	648439	.04214
78	3494	311864	.08068	2984	585270	.04694
79	3502	270485	.08840	3158	524998	.05228
80	3474	232607	.09675	3314	467798	.05827
81	3400	198221	.10544	3435	413837	.06464
82	3300	167274	.11464	3526	363253	.07131
83	3175	139679	.12491	3596	316152	.07861
84	3023	115324	.13627	3655	272612	.08691
85	2839	94071	.14857	3706	232699	.09674
86	2637	75751	.16208	3724	196467	.10841
87	2406	60170	.17689	3634	163956	.12052
88	2144	47113	.19190	3475	135134	.13174
89	1873	36334	.20647	3330	109867	.14462

English Life Table No 15.2 *continued*

Age	Males			Females		
x	d_x	T_x	μ_x	d_x	T_x	μ_x
90	1608	27563	.22114	3143	88003	.16053
91	1369	20530	.23754	2903	69381	.17751
92	1154	14985	.25793	2631	53784	.19573
93	953	10699	.28226	2321	40958	.21498
94	762	7466	.30837	2008	30610	.23490
95	590	5090	.33424	1702	22426	.25732
96	442	3387	.35974	1395	16097	.28114
97	322	2198	.38579	1102	11316	.30267
98	229	1389	.41313	853	7781	.32241
99	157	853	.44216	653	5219	.34628
100	105	508	.47312	488	3406	.37671
101	68	293	.50609	350	2161	.40887
102	42	163	.54117	240	1334	.43769
103	25	88	.57832	161	798	.46273
104	15	45	.61901	105	461	.49300
105	8	22	.66418	68	255	.53729
106	4	11	.70630	41	135	.59908
107	2	5	.75111	23	68	.63785
108	1	2	.79741	13	33	.68388
109	1	1	.84499	6	15	.73191
110				3	7	.78181
111				2	3	.83337
112				1	1	.88629
113						
114						

As well as the normal life tables constructed from single sex mortality rates, a life table for persons has been calculated and is given in Appendix C. This notional life table has been constructed assuming that 100,000 persons born are divided in the ratio 105:100 between males and females and that the resulting male and female populations develop in line with the respective single sex life tables. The ratio has been selected as being the average sex ratio of births in the late 1980s and early 1990s[2]. This procedure was followed by William Farr in his 1864 report on ELT No 3 and for constructing the life table for persons given in ELT No 14. Such a table is useful for both historical and international comparisons where there are no separate figures for males and females. Appendix C cannot be used to derive mortality rates for persons which would have any general application, since they would only reflect the mortality of a population which at any particular age has the same ratio of males to females as underlies the 'persons' table. For example, the mortality rate for age 80 would be (3395 ÷ 45629) = 0.07440 from the 'persons' life table, whilst for a group consisting of equal numbers of men and women, the corresponding 'persons' rate would be $\frac{1}{2} \times$ (0.09616 + 0.05961)=0.07788, some $4\frac{1}{2}$ per cent more.

Comparison with earlier English Life Tables

A picture of changes in mortality over a period of 80 years can be obtained by comparing ELT 15 with the seven previous sets. Table 1 shows the rates of mortality (q_x), for each tenth year of age for males and females, given by each of these eight sets of tables, and in Table 2 the changes in the rates since 1911 are shown by expressing the rates from the seven later tables as percentages of those from English Life Table No 8. Figure 1 shows the ratios graphically, for ages up to 70.

The percentages in Table 2 and the graphs in Figure 1 give a broad picture of the secular trend of mortality from 1911 to 1991. The figures for ages 80 and 90 should, however, be treated with some caution. Mortality at these older ages is much more affected than at younger ages by the incidence of epidemics or severe winter weather, so that even the experience of a three-year period may differ considerably from the general trend. The uncertainty is greater at age 90 than at age 80, since the data are relatively scanty. Examination of the data suggests that there may have been some misstatement of age in extreme old age. In addition, changes in the graduation method from one table to another may affect the comparison at these very old ages.

Tables 1 and 2 show that there has been great improvement in mortality over the period since 1911. The percentage improvement has, however, varied considerably.

Over the 80-year period infant mortality has reduced to less than one-tenth of its level in 1910–1912 for both sexes. For females the relatively consistent degree of reduction at all ages up to 30 noted in ELT No 14 has continued. Although the percentage improvement lessens with age thereafter, it is now at least 50 per cent up to age 80 and there has been a reduction of about 35 per cent in the death rate at age 90. For males, improvement at every age has been less than for females. Even so, mortality rates for males in 1990–92 were less than 50 per cent of those in 1910–12 up to age 60. Even at age 90 where the improvements have been slowest, death rates have now fallen by about 25 per cent. The lower reductions in mortality for both males and females at ages 80 and 90 over the 80 year period is a reflection mainly of the lack of any change in the first forty years compared to the improvements registered at younger ages over those years.

The graphs in Figure 1 show similar rates of improvement in mortality for males and females for children and for age 50. For ages 20, 30 and 40 the rate of improvement for men has been lower than for women since 1951. It is interesting to note that, as in previous ELTs, there continues to be less improvement in mortality rates for men aged 20 than for men aged 30 and 40. On the other hand, at ages 60 and 70 the rate of improvement for men, having been lower than that for women over the period 1911–1971, has been higher since 1971. For men in their eighties the improvement during the 1980s has been much higher than the previous trend.

The changes between 1981 and 1991 are examined in more detail in Table 3 in which the 1990–92 rates, at every fifth age, are expressed as percentages of the 1980–82 rates. Table 3 also gives, for both 1980–82 and 1990–92, the ratio of male mortality rates to female rates at the same age.

In general the rate of improvement in mortality between 1981 and 1991 was not as high as in the previous decade, or was the same order of magnitude, for men and women aged 45 or younger (with the exception of girls in their early teens and women aged around 30). Of particular interest in comparison to previous ELTs is the flattening of the hump of increased mortality experienced by males in their late teens (see Figures A1(a) and A1(b) in Appendix A). This has been noted in other developed countries also. such as Australia[3]. This flattening, combined with an increase in the mortality of males in their late twenties and early thirties since 1981, mainly due to deaths associated with AIDS and increasing numbers of suicides more than offsetting decreases in deaths due to other causes, has led to the appearance of a plateau in the mortality curve for males from the late teens to the early thirties. This feature also appears for female mortality, although the effect is not quite as pronounced as for males. Conversely the rate of mortality improvement has been greater between 1981 and 1991 than in the previous decade for both men and women at most ages over 45. This is most notably the case for men and women in their fifties and early sixties, for men in their eighties and women around age 90.

The last three columns in Table 3 show that male mortality continues to be higher than that of females at every age. The excess ranges from about 30 per cent in infancy to a peak of 171 per cent at age 20 (where it is mainly due to heavier male mortality from accidents, suicides and deaths associated with AIDS). Men's mortality is over 50 per cent higher than women's at almost every age from 15 to 80. Another way of expressing the excess is to say that women's mortality at ages 45 to 65 is no higher than that of men four or five years younger than themselves. The difference widens to about 6 years for women in their seventies, before falling to 4 years at age 90.

Figure 1 Rates of mortality expressed as percentages of 1911 rates (logarithmic scale)

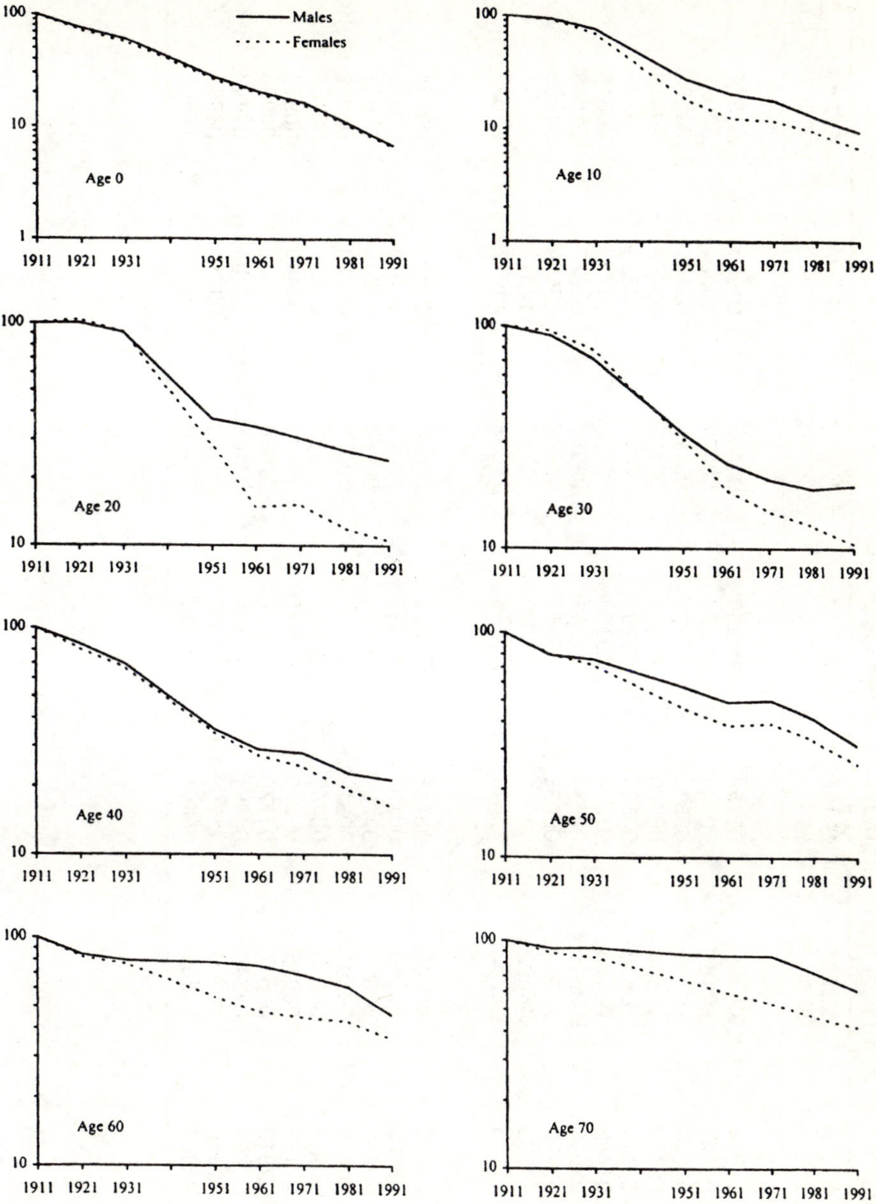

Table 1 Rates of mortality (q_x) from English Life Tables Nos 8 to 15

Age *x*	*ELT 8* *(1910–12)*	*ELT 9* *(1920–22)*	*ELT10* *(1930–32)*	*ELT 11* *(1950–52)*	*ELT 12* *(1960–62)*	*ELT 13* *(1970–72)*	*ELT 14* *(I980–82)*	*ELT 15* *(1990–92)*
Males								
0	.12044	.08996	.07186	.03266	.02449	.01980	.01271	.00814
10	.00193	.00181	.00146	.00052	.00039	.00034	.00024	.00018
20	.00348	.00349	.00316	.00129	.00119	.00106	.00093	.00084
30	.00478	.00434	.00340	.00157	.00115	.00097	.00088	.00091
40	.00811	.00688	.00562	.00290	.00235	.00226	.00184	.00172
50	.01482	.01179	.01128	.00850	.00728	.00739	.00615	.00464
60	.03042	.02561	.02415	.02369	.02287	.02075	.01843	.01392
70	.06470	.05997	.06035	.05651	.05566	.05546	.04703	.03930
80	.14299	.14002	.14500	.13629	.12747	.12019	.11334	.09616
90	.27395	.26752	.28614	.29255	.25593	.24077	.22693	.20465
Females								
0	.09767	.06942	.05455	.02510	.01896	.01523	.00984	.00632
10	.00196	.00180	.00134	.00035	.00024	.00023	.00018	.00013
20	.00295	.00306	.00268	.00083	.00044	.00045	.00035	.00031
30	.00411	.00392	.00319	.00127	.00075	.00060	.00052	.00043
40	00660	.00532	.00440	.00227	.00180	.00160	.00127	.00107
50	.01140	.00915	.00816	.00524	.00439	.00449	.00378	.00294
60	.02310	.01897	.01770	.01271	.01088	.01025	.00986	.00830
70	.05259	.04646	.04451	.03532	.03104	.02784	.02443	.02190
80	.12419	.11766	.11858	.10466	.09108	.08014	.06982	.05961
90	.23826	.23852	.25061	.24146	.22128	.19805	.18468	.15550

Table 2 Rates of mortality (q_x) expressed as percentage of English Life Tables No 8 rates

Age *x*	*ELT 8* *(1910–12)*	*ELT 9* *(1920–22)*	*ELT10* *(1930–32)*	*ELT 11* *(1950–52)*	*ELT 12* *(1960–62)*	*ELT 13* *(1970–72)*	*ELT 14* *(1980–82)*	*ELT 15* *(1990–92)*
Males								
0	100	75	60	27	20	16	11	7
10	100	94	76	27	20	18	12	9
20	100	100	91	37	34	30	27	24
30	100	91	71	33	24	20	18	19
40	100	85	69	36	29	28	23	21
50	100	80	76	57	49	50	41	31
60	100	84	79	78	75	68	61	46
70	100	93	93	87	86	86	73	61
80	100	98	101	95	89	84	79	67
90	100	98	104	107	93	88	83	75
Females								
0	100	71	56	26	19	16	10	7
10	100	92	68	18	12	12	9	7
20	100	104	91	28	15	15	12	11
30	100	95	78	31	18	15	13	10
40	100	81	67	34	27	24	19	16
50	100	80	72	46	39	39	33	26
60	100	82	77	55	47	44	43	36
70	100	88	85	67	59	53	46	42
80	100	95	95	84	73	65	56	48
90	100	100	105	101	93	83	78	65

Table 3 Rates of mortality as percentages of rates ten years earlier, and male mortality rates as percentages of female rates

Age	Males		Females		Male mortality rates as percentages of female rates		
	1990–92 (as percentage of 1980–82)	*1980–82 (as percentage of 1970–72)*	*1990–92 (as percentage of 1980–82)*	*1980–82 (as percentage of 1970–72)*	*1990–92*	*1980–82*	*1970–72*
0	64	64	64	65	129	129	130
5	69	68	73	65	138	145	138
10	75	71	72	78	138	133	148
15	98	73	85	90	182	158	193
20	90	88	89	78	271	266	236
25	106	92	87	87	253	208	196
30	103	91	83	87	212	169	162
35	103	84	88	84	168	145	144
40	93	81	84	79	161	145	141
45	80	80	81	78	150	152	148
50	75	83	78	84	158	163	165
55	73	88	76	92	168	176	185
60	76	89	84	96	168	187	202
65	83	85	92	93	175	193	210
70	84	85	90	88	179	193	199
75	84	90	87	86	174	180	173
80	85	94	85	87	161	162	150
85	87	96	82	92	148	139	134
90	90	94	84	93	132	123	122

Table 4 Expectation of life ($\mathring{e}_x$) from English Life Tablet Nos 8 to 15

Age *x*	*ELT8* *(1910–12)*	*ELT10* *(1930–32)*	*ELT11* *(1950–52)*	*ELT13* *(1970–72)*	*ELT14* *(1980–82)*	*ELT15* *(1990–92)*
Males						
0	51.50	58.74	66.42	69.00	71.04	73.41
10	53.08	55.79	59.24	60.74	62.19	64.20
20	44.21	46.81	49.64	51.08	52.50	54.45
30	35.81	38.21	40.27	41.51	42.90	44.88
40	27.74	29.62	30.98	32.01	33.34	35.35
50	20.29	21.60	22.23	23.11	24.26	26.16
60	13.78	14.43	14.79	15.41	16.38	17.85
65	10.99	11.30	11.69	12.18	13.04	14.27
70	8.53	8.62	9.00	9.50	10.12	11.19
Females						
0	55.35	62.88	71.54	75.25	77.00	78.96
10	55.91	58.87	63.87	66.71	67.97	69.61
20	47.10	49.88	54.17	56.89	58.12	59.75
30	38.54	41.22	44.68	47.13	48.34	49.94
40	30.30	32.55	35.32	37.52	38.67	40.24
50	22.52	24.18	26.34	28.41	29.39	30.85
60	15.48	16.50	18.07	19.98	20.89	22.08
70	9.58	10.02	10.97	12.56	13.41	14.49

Figure 2 Expectation of life at birth, period basis

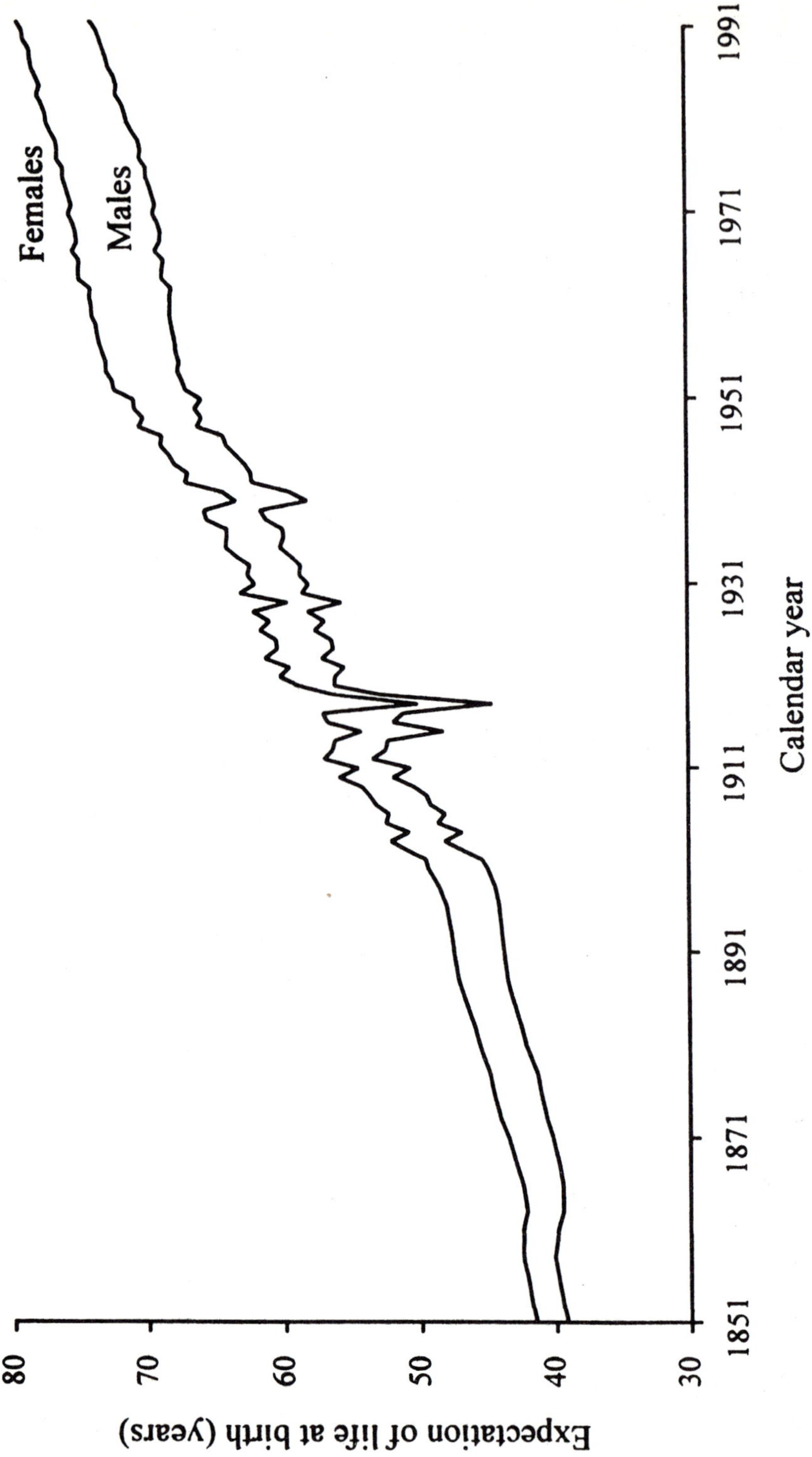

Expectation of life

Another way of illustrating the reductions in death rates is to show the increase in expectation of life at birth, calculating it either from the death rates of particular calendar years, or taking the rates over time applicable to people born in a particular year. The latter can, however, only be done for generations not yet extinct by making assumptions about future death rates.

The data presented in the English Life Tables represents a snapshot of the mortality of the community at a particular point in time; they do not purport to show the likely experience of any particular generation. However, in spite of this, expectations of life based on such period measures form a convenient summary measure of the overall effects of changes in mortality. Table 4 sets out the expectations of life at various ages for mortality based on the years 1910–12 and at twenty year intervals thereafter until 1970–72, together with those for 1980–82 and 1990–92. The figures are compiled from the English Life Tables derived from the mortality experience in these periods.

Over the 80 years covered by Table 4 the expectation of life at birth, measured in this way, has increased by nearly 22 years for a boy and by just over 23½ years for a girl. The improvement in the decade 1981 to 1991 has been about 2.4 years for boys and 2.0 years for girls. A large part of the improvement since 1911 has been due to reductions in mortality in infancy and childhood hut this is not the only cause, as is shown by the fact that the expectation for a man aged 20 has increased by 10¼ years and for a women aged 20 by nearly 12¾ years. At age 60 the increase in expectation is just over 4 years for males and just over 6½ years for females. The expectation of life of a woman at the current state pension age of 60 had reached 22 years in 1990–92 whereas, for a man at age 65, the male state pension age, the expectation of life had reached 14¼ years.

Figure 2 shows the expectation of life at birth on a period basis for the years 1851 to 1991. The chart shows that the period measure of expectation of life at birth is currently increasing by about two years in each decade. Other features shown by the chart are the rapid variations in the period rates between 1910 and 1950. These are due to the effects of two world wars and the 1919 influenza pandemic. The curves are smoother before 1910 only because detailed information about individual years before then has not yet been analysed.

The above expectations of life, and the corresponding life tables, represent a secular cross-section of the experience of those born during a century or so prior to the respective periods. If the mortality rates for each age assumed for English Life Tables No 15 continued unaltered in future years, the expectation of life at birth would be 73.41 years for males and 78.96 years for females for any year in the future.

It is also possible to calculate expectations of life applicable to people born in a particular year (often referred to as cohort expectations of life). Figure 3 shows the expectations of life at birth calculated on a cohort basis. In order

Figure 3 Expectation of life at birth, cohort basis

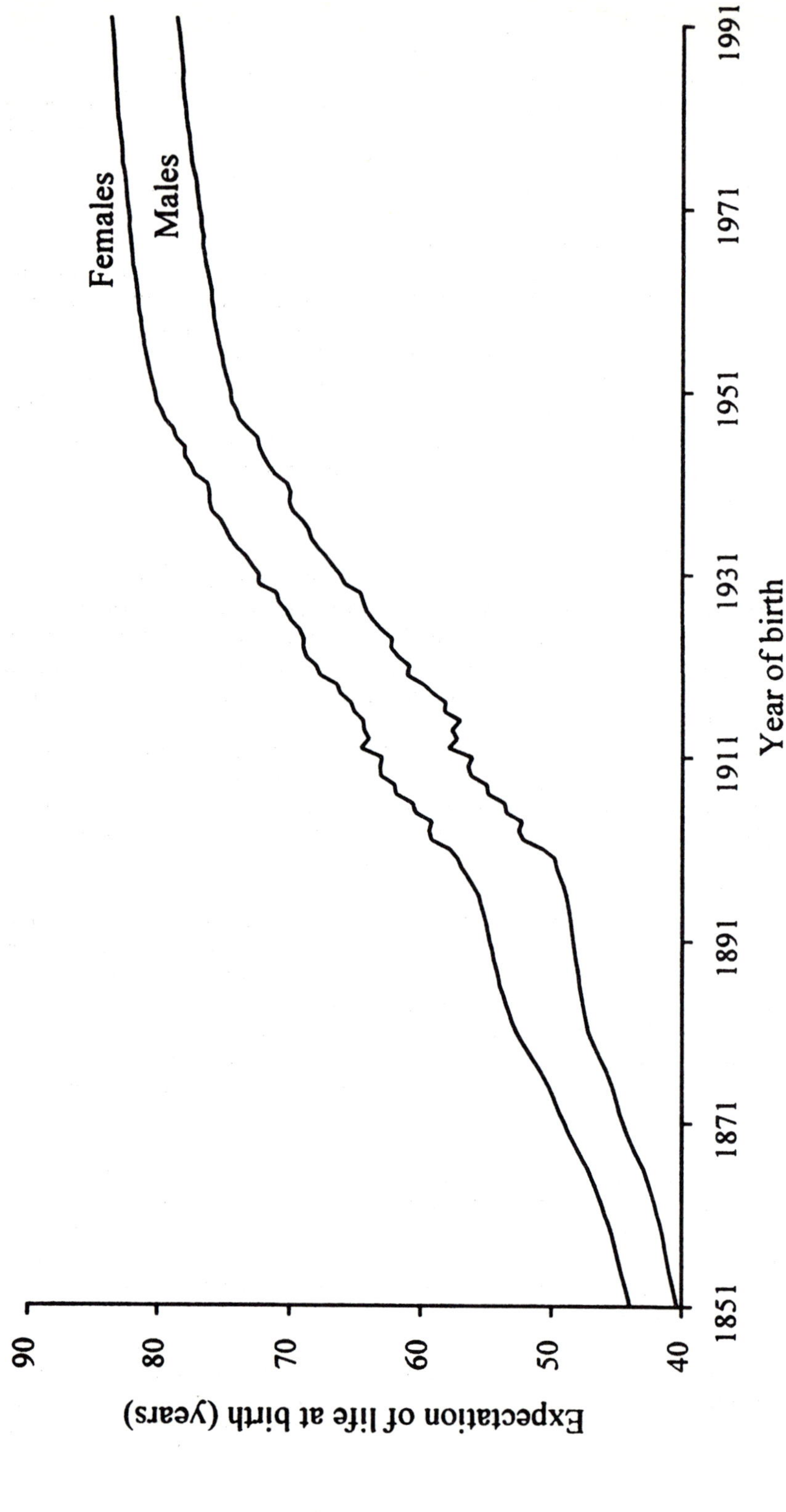

to estimate cohort expectation of life, mortality rates for years beyond 1994 have been taken from the Government Actuary's 1994-based projections for England and Wales. The chart shows, for example, that the average number of years that a new-born boy could expect to live rose from 40 in 1851 to about 78½ in 1991. The 1851 child had only a 65 percent chance of reaching age 20 and those reaching this age on average lived only to age 60. Of the generation born in 1971 only 3 per cent failed to reach age 20. The cohort expectation of life of 78½ years for a boy born in 1991 is calculated on the assumption that death rates will continue to fall, but at a diminishing rate.

A comparison of the expectation of life at birth in Figures 2 and 3 shows that the cohort expectation of life is longer than the period expectation of life for all years of birth since 1851 for both males and females. This is because the cohort calculation takes into account changes in the actual (or projected) mortality rates in years succeeding the year of birth whereas the period calculation uses mortality rates applicable in the year under consideration. Since, in general, mortality rates have been improving in successive years at most ages, the cohort expectation of life assumes lower mortality than the period expectation of life.

Table 5 Expectation of life (allowing for future improvement in mortality) for selected ages in 1991

Age in 1991	Expectation of life	
	Male	*Female*
0	78.4	83.5
10	69.0	74.0
20	59.0	64.0
30	49.0	53.8
40	38.9	43.5
50	28.8	33.3
60	19.3	23.3
70	11.7	14.9
80	6.6	8.6

Table 5 shows the cohort expectations of life in 1991 for various attained ages in 1991 assuming that the future improvements in mortality assumed in the 1994-based population projections for England and Wales actually occur.

Interim Life Tables and future developments

The English Life Tables provide a valuable time series which can be used to monitor trends in mortality in England and Wales. However, these tables are only calculated once every ten years and the graduation process carried out is usually complex. The Government Actuary's Department also produce annual life tables, known as Interim Life Tables, for each constituent country of the United Kingdom, together with life tables for England and Wales combined, Great Britain, and the United Kingdom as a whole. Two sets of interim life tables are produced, one based on mortality data for a single calendar year and one based on mortality data for three consecutive calendar years combined (as for the English Life Tables). These interim life tables are available on request from the Government Actuary's Department.

In order to produce these interim life tables quickly, once the relevant data is available, the mortality rates used in these tables are not graduated. As mentioned in Appendix B, one of the reasons for the choice of the graduation method used for the English Life Tables No 15 is that the method is simpler and more flexible to apply than methods used for previous English Life Tables. It is intended to adapt the current methodology for use in constructing future interim life tables so that a series of graduated mortality rates can be produced for each future year using a consistent methodology.

CHRIS DAYKIN
Government Actuary's Department
London
December 1996

Appendix A

Calculation of the 'exposed to risk' and the central rates of mortality, England and Wales, 1990–92

As stated earlier in the report, the estimates of the 'central exposed to risk of death' have been derived from the ONS (formerly OPCS) estimates of the home population (that is, the persons usually resident in England and Wales, excluding foreign visitors and UK Armed Forces stationed elsewhere, but including civilian residents temporarily elsewhere, and all Armed Forces stationed in England and Wales). However, these estimates do not normally give estimates of the number of men and women at individual ages over 90. Neither do population censuses provide reliable estimates of peoples' ages over 90, due largely to the difficulty of obtaining accurate information from very elderly people (or those caring for them) as to their date of birth. Subsequent death registrations, however, are believed to be generally more accurate in reporting age at death. Thus, accurate mortality rates can only be calculated for advanced ages when a population has become extinct. Population numbers can then be obtained by accumulating registered deaths backwards in time, assuming that ages at death have been accurately registered and that international migration is negligible at these ages. The methodology described later in this Appendix draws on work carried out on mortality at high ages in England and Wales by A R Thatcher[4].

Although generations cannot be regarded as extinct until well over a hundred years after their date of birth, in practice sufficiently accurate population numbers for ages 90 and over in 1990, 1991 and 1992 can be obtained by extrapolating the numbers of deaths in future years from numbers of deaths already registered, using the method of reverse survival rates that is described below. In this process. it is assumed that the trend in declining death rates will continue. The resulting age distribution for those aged 90 and over obtained by this method for each of the years 1990, 1991 and 1992 was then applied to the ONS estimate of total numbers aged 90 and over for the relevant year to obtain the revised population numbers at each of these ages. The method also gives population estimates for ages below 90 which are close to those published by ONS for 1991, 50 that the change in the methods used at older ages should not affect the graduation of the life table.

The method of reverse survival rates involved firstly calculating, for each age x for each calendar year up to and including 1993, the ratio of the numbers of deaths at ages $(x-2)$ to age $(x+2)$ in the calendar year to the numbers of death aged $(x-3)$ to age $(x-1)$ in the previous year. These ratios were then extrapolated into future years. The estimated numbers of deaths at each age x in the years from 1994 onwards were then obtained by applying the appropriate projected ratios of deaths at age x in the year to the number of deaths at age $(x-1)$ in the preceding calendar year. The population numbers aged 90 and over in 1990, 1991 and 1992 were then obtained by summing the deaths backwards along a cohort from the future year in which deaths for the cohort are projected to be negligible.

Having obtained mid-year estimates of the population at individual ages 90 and over to supplement those for younger ages taken directly from the ONS estimates, the "central exposed to risk of death" was then derived for each age as follows.

Let $P_{t,x}$ be the home population of a particular sex t years after 1 January 1990, for a particular age group, represented by x. Then, for the particular age group x let the mid year home population estimates at 30 June 1990, 1991 and 1992 be $P_{\frac{1}{2},x}$, $P_{1\frac{1}{2},x}$, $P_{2\frac{1}{2},x}$ respectively.

For the age group x the central exposed to risk of death E_x is defined as

$$E_x = \int_0^3 P_{t,x} dt = \left(P_{\frac{1}{2},x} + P_{1\frac{1}{2},x} + P_{2\frac{1}{2},x}\right)$$

on the assumption that $P_{t,x}$ is a linear function of t (for each age group) over each of the individual years represented by the t values 0–1, 1–2 and 2–3.

This methodology differs from that used for ELT 14 where a quadratic (rather than linear) polynomial assumption was used. This had the presentational disadvantage of leading to a formula that placed least weight on the mid-year estimate $P_{1\frac{1}{2},x}$ which was nearest in time to the Census date and would hence be the most reliable. The numerical differences between the two approaches are of minor significance. The above approach has been chosen on the grounds of simplicity and because it avoids the above-mentioned peculiarity whilst following conventional actuarial methodology.

For ELT 14, special treatment was given to the cohorts born between 1915 and 1923, when the pattern of births was severely disrupted by the separation of families during the First World War and by subsequent epidemics. Adjustments were made to the exposed to risk formula to take account of the uneven distribution of births in these calendar years and the impact on those surviving to 1980–82. The magnitude of such adjustments would now be smaller and it has been decided to dispense with these ad hoc adjustments for ELT 15.

The number of deaths used in constructing the tables are those published by ONS. These include all deaths registered in England and Wales. including those of residents from abroad whose deaths are registered here. It is assumed that inclusion of deaths of abroad-residents approximately compensates for the exclusion of deaths abroad of residents of England and Wales.

Figure A1(a) ELT 15 – Graph of $\log_{10}(m_x)$

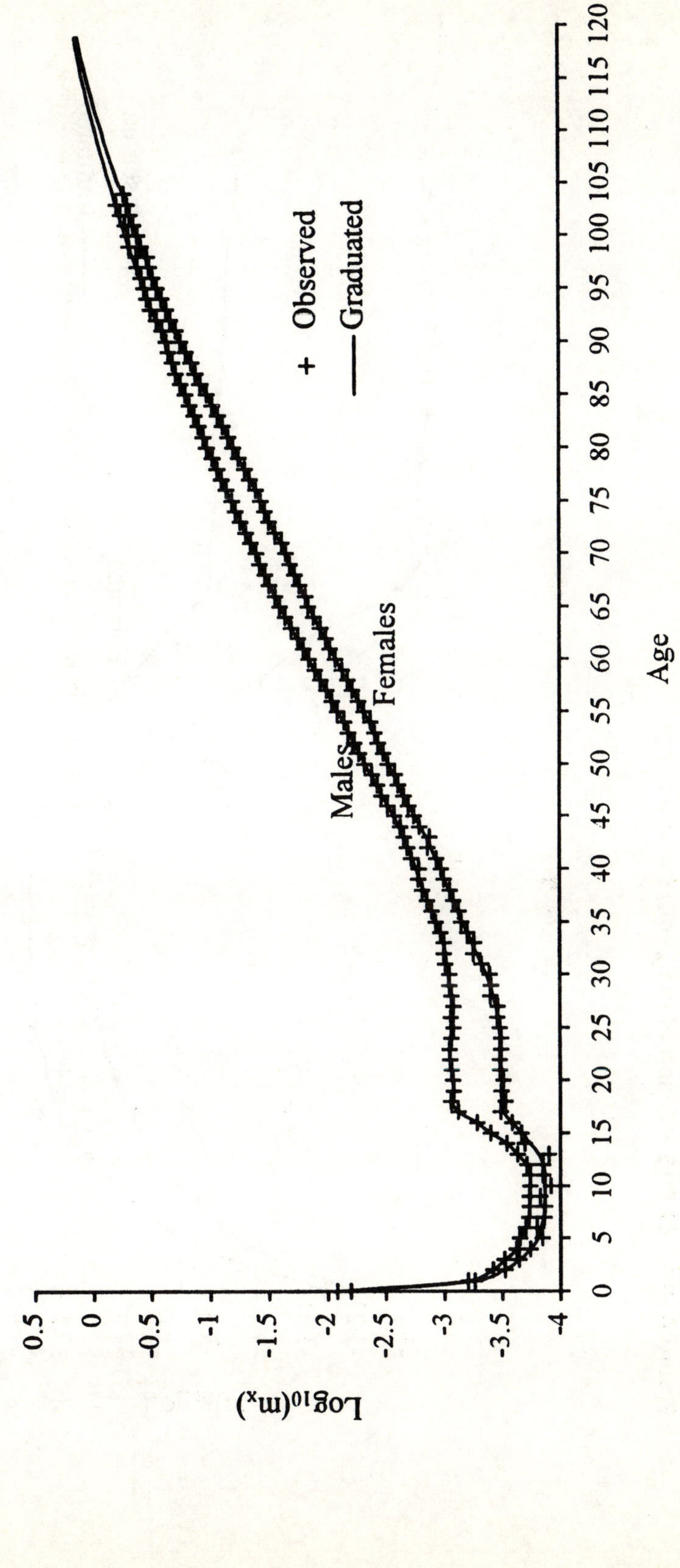

Figure A1(b) ELT 15 – Graph of $\log_{10}(m_x)$ for young ages

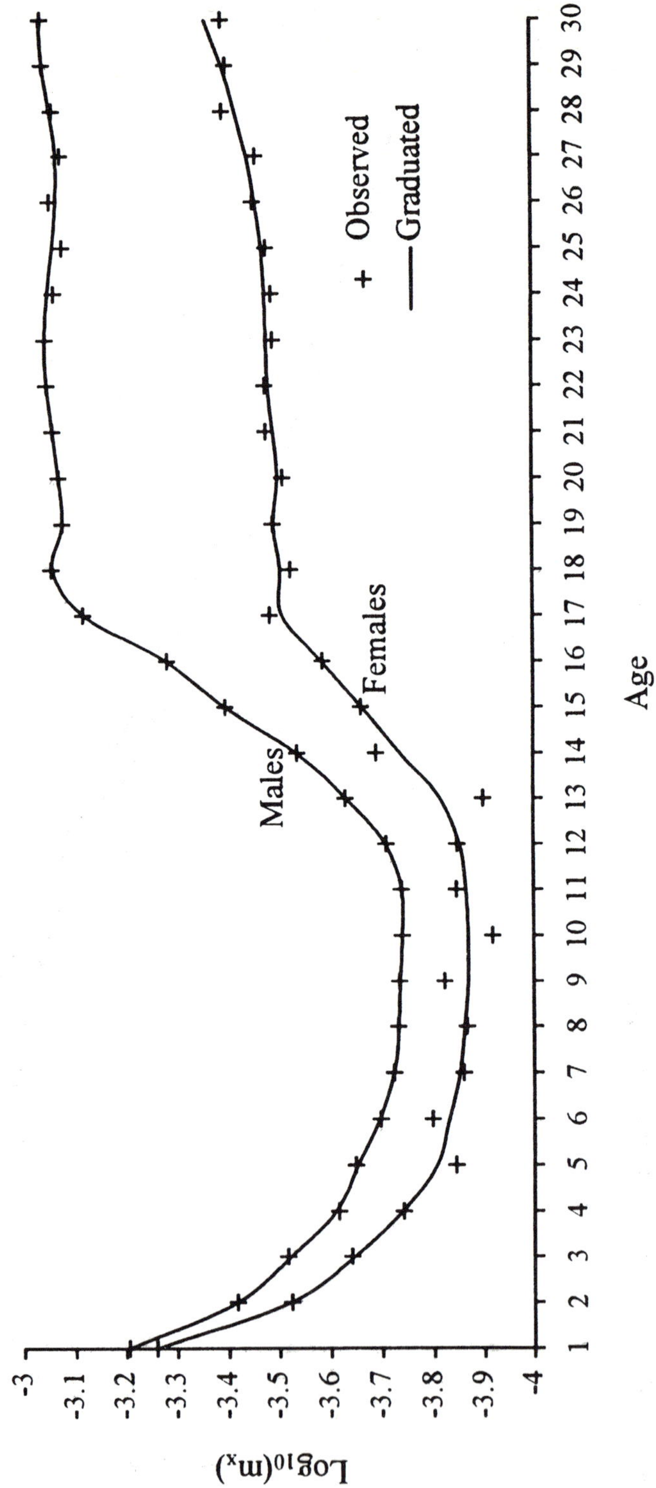

Let $\theta_{k,x}$ represent the deaths of a particular sex in calendar year 1990+k at attained age x, with k = 0, 1 and 2. Then the crude central rates of mortality at that age are given by

$$\mathring{m}_x = \frac{\theta_{0,x} + \theta_{1,x} + \theta_{2,x}}{E_x} = \frac{\theta_{0,x} + \theta_{1,x} + \theta_{2,x}}{P_{\frac{1}{2},x} + P_{1\frac{1}{2},x} + P_{2\frac{1}{2},x}}$$

The resulting crude central rates of mortality (rounded to five decimal places) are set out in Table A1. These crude rates were then graduated to run smoothly from age to age by the method described in Appendix B (these graduated central mortality rates are also shown in Table A1). Finally, the graduated central rates of mortality (m_x) were converted to initial rates (q_x) for the purposes of the life tables by the formula

$$q_x = \frac{m_x\left(1-\frac{1}{2}m_{x-1}\right)}{\left(1+\frac{5}{12}\left(m_x - m_{x-1}\right)-\frac{1}{6}m_{x-1}.m_x\right)}$$

as described in detail in Appendix B.

Different methods were used at the extreme ages. At these ages the initial rate of mortality (q_x) was calculated directly. The calculation of the infant mortality rate (corresponding to x=0) took into account the distribution of births and deaths by month during the period 1990–92 to allow for the uneven incidence of death during this first year of life and the variation in the flow of births over time. The initial rates of mortality for the oldest ages (104 and above for men, 105 and above for women) were obtained by extrapolation of the values of q_x derived from the above formula, by the method described in Appendix B.

Figure A1(a) shows the graduated curves of the central rates of mortality m_x, superimposed on the actual crude rates for each age, Figure A1(b) shows a magnified portion of the curves for ages 1 to 30. Figure A2 shows the graph of the values of q_x derived from the graduated values of m_x using the above formula.

Figure A2 **ELT 15 – Graph of $\log_{10}(q_x)$**

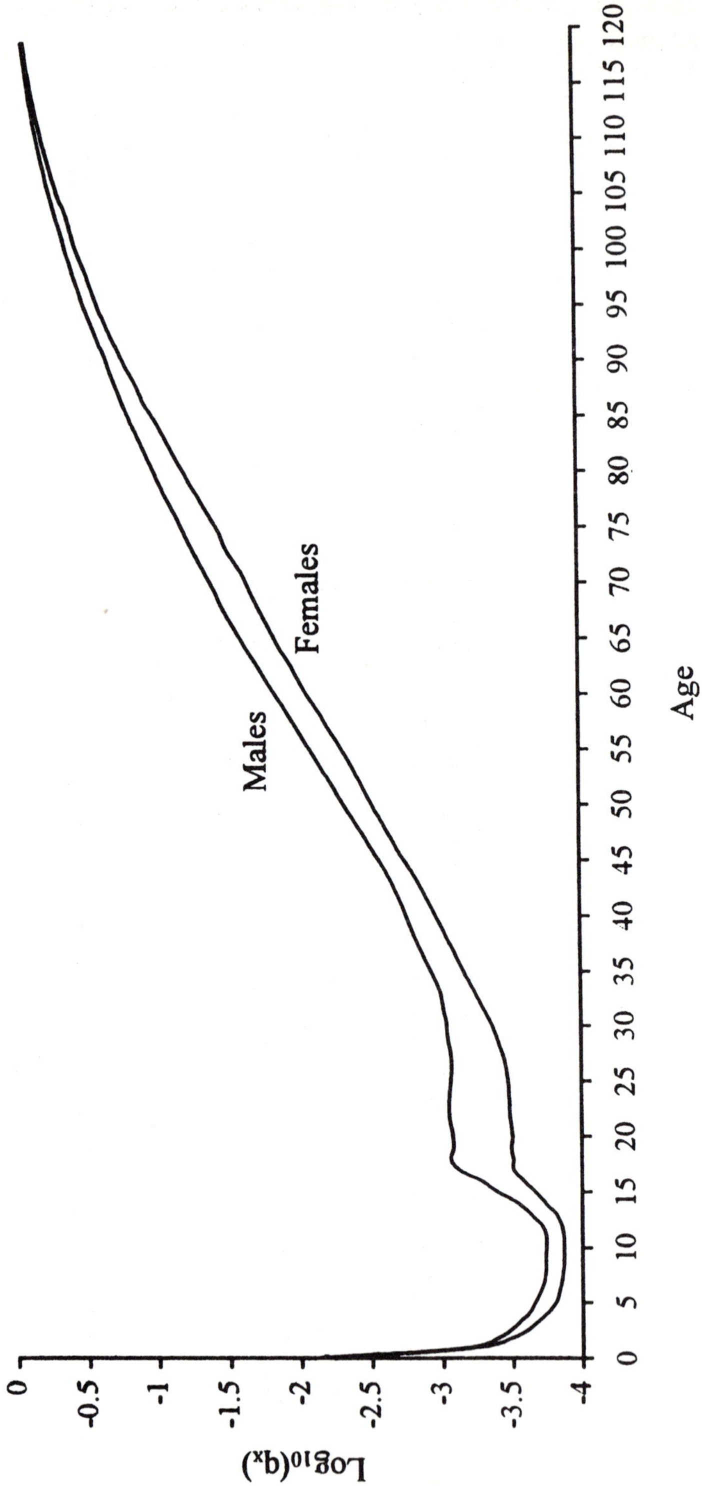

Table A1 Derivation of central rates of mortality (m_x) for 1990–92

(a) Males

Age *x*	*Exposed to risk*	*Deaths 1990–92*	*Crude death rate per 100,000*	*Graduated death rate per 100,000*
0	1066867	8779	823	
1	1059343	661	62	62
2	1054256	403	38	38
3	1047298	319	30	30
4	1037973	251	24	25
5	1022032	229	22	22
6	1003486	201	20	20
7	989008	186	19	19
8	976049	180	18	18
9	981422	180	18	18
10	988020	179	18	18
11	984778	179	18	18
12	950853	185	19	20
13	909437	212	23	23
14	891556	259	29	29
15	913423	366	40	40
16	954339	496	52	52
17	1002077	758	76	76
18	1057508	922	87	87
19	1124668	930	83	83
20	1163581	979	84	84
21	1195366	1030	86	86
22	1210521	1073	89	89
23	1238979	1105	89	89
24	1263313	1083	86	88
25	1296300	1068	82	86
26	1313794	1145	87	85
27	1311662	1090	83	85
28	1291017	1110	86	87
29	1259644	1129	90	90
30	1219278	1101	90	91
31	1176120	1144	97	94
32	1135091	1128	99	97
33	1103162	1095	99	100
34	1071474	1142	107	107
35	1035587	1218	118	116
36	1017422	1291	127	127
37	1010544	1399	138	138
38	1006929	1536	153	149
39	1006500	1660	165	161
40	1016727	1662	163	173
41	1046632	1967	188	186
42	1092927	2240	205	202
43	1167798	2543	218	219
44	1134652	2656	234	241
45	1071729	2836	265	267
46	974301	2930	301	298
47	955329	3251	340	333
48	914107	3354	367	372
49	848419	3489	411	416
50	815653	3836	470	466
51	811134	4251	524	520
52	827414	4781	578	579

Table A1 Derivation of central rates of mortality (m_x) for 1990–92 *continued*

(a) Males

Age *x*	*Exposed to risk*	*Deaths 1990–92*	*Crude death rate per 100,000*	*Graduated death rate per 100,000*
53	822603	5324	647	644
54	810731	5723	706	717
55	794930	6411	806	800
56	775350	6925	893	894
57	759747	7592	999	1000
58	755475	8477	1122	1118
59	761913	9484	1245	1251
60	764497	10735	1404	1402
61	753706	11880	1576	1572
62	736868	12871	1747	1764
63	725679	14463	1993	1984
64	721743	16094	2230	2223
65	713576	17704	2481	2477
66	700666	19097	2726	2748
67	681977	20930	3069	3042
68	676972	22507	3325	3346
69	678157	25127	3705	3668
70	684764	27159	3966	4008
71	600343	26508	4415	4405
72	504808	24443	4842	4859
73	422817	22792	5391	5356
74	422480	24921	5899	5863
75	431321	27286	6326	6395
76	422822	29712	7027	7013
77	399257	30856	7728	7703
78	365168	30744	8419	8442
79	328386	30334	9237	9247
80	293014	29788	10166	10103
81	260517	28483	10933	10985
82	229149	27399	11957	11957
83	197322	25697	13023	13038
84	165896	23717	14296	14222
85	136103	20930	15378	15497
86	110565	18689	16903	16920
87	87989	16370	18605	18424
88	68443	13571	19828	19894
89	52151	11284	21637	21350
90	40257	9061	22508	22869
91	29000	7032	24248	24695
92	20124	5405	26858	26941
93	13406	4057	30263	29478
94	9392	3069	32677	32074
95	6446	2219	34424	34635
96	4384	1578	35995	37215
97	2795	1091	39034	39895
98	1761	701	39807	42729
99	1059	489	46176	45754
100	624	292	46795	48988
101	359	178	49582	52449
102	216	118	54630	56154
103	107	63	58879	60120

Table A1 Derivation of central rates of mortality (m_x) for 1990–92

(b) Females

Age x	*Exposed to risk*	*Deaths 1990–92*	*Crude death rate per 100,000*	*Graduated death rate per 100,000*
0	1015568	6482	638	
1	1007142	555	55	55
2	1000153	300	30	30
3	993334	227	23	23
4	982837	178	18	18
5	967204	138	14	16
6	949488	151	16	15
7	935871	129	14	14
8	922706	125	14	14
9	928413	139	15	14
10	934699	113	12	14
11	931265	132	14	14
12	896626	127	14	14
13	856001	108	13	15
14	839834	171	20	18
15	860194	187	22	22
16	895867	232	26	26
17	942984	308	33	31
18	997909	297	30	31
19	1063585	342	32	32
20	1103895	340	31	32
21	1138661	377	33	32
22	1156956	384	33	33
23	1191215	382	32	33
24	1215921	392	32	33
25	1245809	412	33	34
26	1262210	441	35	35
27	1262043	436	35	36
28	1244680	498	40	38
29	1215063	479	39	40
30	1177166	473	40	43
31	1141825	541	47	47
32	1110745	617	56	52
33	1086408	597	55	57
34	1055913	659	62	63
35	1022392	724	71	69
36	1006861	750	74	75
37	1002263	829	83	82
38	1002142	883	88	90
39	1001695	1004	100	98
40	1012808	1067	105	107
41	1041532	1201	115	117
42	1090422	1490	137	129
43	1161886	1536	132	142
44	1129852	1811	160	158
45	1067124	1908	179	177
46	972362	1935	199	198
47	952436	2087	219	219
48	909991	2217	244	242
49	845304	2203	261	266
50	812892	2412	297	295
51	810640	2650	327	326
52	827403	3000	363	358

Table A1 Derivation of central rates of mortality (m_x) for 1990–92 *continued*

(b) Females

Age *x*	*Exposed to risk*	*Deaths 1990–92*	*Crude death rate per 100,000*	*Graduated death rate per 100,000*
53	822948	3200	389	391
54	811339	3430	423	429
55	796199	3823	480	477
56	779464	4134	530	532
57	767152	4597	599	594
58	767566	5043	657	662
59	782447	5780	739	742
60	796900	6661	836	833
61	799178	7485	937	927
62	790358	7989	1011	1020
63	783428	8827	1127	1135
64	784779	10060	1282	1274
65	787473	11195	1422	1409
66	789269	11951	1514	1535
67	789788	13422	1699	1690
68	801015	14871	1857	1861
69	822377	16827	2046	2038
70	850456	18832	2214	2214
71	768613	18529	2411	2428
72	667010	18199	2728	2729
73	576708	17820	3090	3060
74	592654	19703	3325	3338
75	625559	22735	3634	3634
76	635837	25340	3985	3997
77	622573	27799	4465	4452
78	590340	29187	4944	4952
79	554162	30590	5520	5520
80	521694	32073	6148	6143
81	491652	33378	6789	6790
82	460135	34440	7485	7485
83	422854	34924	8259	8259
84	379994	34790	9155	9157
85	336228	34326	10209	10228
86	292832	33617	11480	11453
87	253334	32018	12639	12609
88	214461	29331	13677	13751
89	176475	26944	15268	15231
90	144765	24454	16892	16875
91	114830	21315	18562	18611
92	88458	18206	20582	20511
93	66750	14956	22406	22434
94	49528	12102	24435	24532
95	36285	9781	26956	26890
96	25458	7476	29366	29177
97	17654	5523	31285	31188
98	11821	3837	32459	33305
99	7761	2848	36696	36084
100	4768	1865	39115	39225
101	2939	1248	42463	42367
102	1754	795	45325	44948
103	1010	481	47624	47839
104	575	292	50783	51228

Appendix B

Smoothing spline graduation of the crude data for the English Life Tables No 15

by Professor Steven Haberman MA, PhD, FIA, FSS

Method of smoothing splines

The graduation method used for ELT No 13 and No 14 was based on the method of cubic spline fitting. For ELT 14, a technique for choosing the optimum number of knots and their location was successfully implemented.

For the production of ELT 15, it was decided to introduce an established variant of the cubic spline method that does not require the optimal choice of knots.

The smoothed curve consists of a series of cubic curves, selected so that one cubic runs smoothly into the next. However, whereas the ELT 14 graduations (for each sex) used only nine or ten such cubics, the ELT 15 graduations require separate cubics for each year of age between the first and 103rd birthdays (for males: 104th for females – see later). The results obtained are similar to those that would be obtained using the earlier methodology but the process is simpler to apply and has the advantage of flexibility. This would mean that the method could be used more easily and extensively, in particular outside of the confines of the Decennial Supplement. Thus, it is proposed to use this method for the future construction of interim or abridged life tables and it has been used elsewhere for the graduation of fertility data (see Papaleonides[5]).

The graduation method proposed is the method of smoothing splines and is described in detail elsewhere (de Boor[6]; Green and Silverman[7]). For completeness, however, we give below a brief summary of the method as applied to the present work.

The method of smoothing splines explicitly considers the two conflicting goals of graduation: (a) obtaining a good fit to the observed data and (b) obtaining a curve that is smooth ie does not display too much rapid fluctuation.

Considering (b), if we are given a curve g on an interval $[a, b]$, there are many different ways of measuring how "rough" or "unsmooth" the curve g is. An intuitively appealing approach to measuring roughness (or lack of smoothness) of a twice-differentiable curve g is to calculate its integrated squared second derivative

$$\int_a^b [g''(t)]^2 dt$$

Green and Silverman[7] provide a variety of reasons for using this measure.

We now consider the formal statement of the problem. We wish to construct an estimate of a curve of mortality rates (possibly transformed) whose values are subject to random error. We shall find it convenient to work with the commonly used log transform of the crude central mortality rates.

Suppose that $x_1, x_2, \ldots, x_n$ are age points in the range $[a, b]$ satisfying a $<x_1 <x_2 <, \ldots, <x_n <b$ at which the crude data have been collected and that the transformed crude mortality rates are

$$Y_i = log\left(\overset{\circ}{m}_{x_i}\right) \text{for } i = 1, 2, \ldots, n.$$

For any function g (with certain technical properties ie differentiable on $[a, b]$ with absolutely continuous first derivative), we consider the penalized sum of squares defined by

$$S(g) = p\sum_{i=1}^{n}\left(Y_i - g(x_i)\right)^2 + (1-p)\int_a^b [g'' (t)]^2 dt$$

with positive smoothing parameter p, $0 <p <1$. And we let $\hat{g}$ be the *minimizing* choice of g over the class of curves with the above properties (i.e sufficiently smooth curves). The two terms in $S(g)$ correspond to the conflicting criteria mentioned earlier of goodness of fit and smoothness and these have been combined together as a weighted average with coefficients p and $(1-p)$ respectively.

It is then possible to show that the minimizing choice $\hat{g}$ is unique and is a natural cubic spline with knots automatically at each of the data points x_i. We thus see how the difficulty of finding the optimal position of the knots is avoided.

In the implementation of this method, two modifications have been made to the first term of $S(g)$ allowing the introduction of weights[7]. This has been done in two stages. The first stage deals with the feature that the data are such that the y_i (the underlying random variable corresponding to the crude values Y_i) have unequal variances: in this case, it is a natural step in statistical modelling to use weights that are inversely proportional to the variances of the observations (or their transformation). Then the data points with the lowest variance will make the greatest contribution to the sum of squares term in $S(g)$. The second stage involves a set of weights $\{w_i\}$being introduced so that the graduator can use his/her judgement in respect of those parts of the age range where he/she would like to see the closest fit, for sound *a priori* reasons. Thus, $S(g)$ becomes

$$S(g) = p\sum_{i=1}^{n} w_i \frac{(Y_i - g(x_i))^2}{Var\ y_i} + (1-p)\int_a^b [g^{\shortparallel}(t)]^2 dt$$

If we assume that the number of deaths occurring follows a Poisson distribution, then an approximation to the Var y_i term can be obtained. In this case, we find that the reciprocal of Var y_i is approximately equal to the observed deaths at age x_i and this has been used in the formula for $S(g)$.

The parameters at the disposal of the graduator are p and the set of $\{w_i\}$. A choice of $p = 0$ would lead to $\hat{g}$ being the straight line that most nearly fits the (transformed) data ie the "ultimate" perfectly smooth curve. A choice of p=1 would lead to a curve $\hat{y}$ that passes through all the (transformed) data points. In practice, by choosing an intermediate value of p, we select a compromise curve that minimizes this weighted sum of goodness of fit and overall smoothness with weights determined by the choice of p. With an intermediate value of p, ($0<p<1$), careful choice of the set of weights $\{w_i\}$ can ensure that key features in the crude data are retained by the graduating curve $\hat{g}$.

The selection of p and $\{w_i\}$ are considered later in this Appendix.

Minimization procedure

To carry out the minimization we have used the well-established algorithm of Reinsch[8]. The main idea is to set up a non-singular system of linear equations for the second derivatives γ_i of $\hat{g}$ at the knots x_i. These equations are presented in matrix form and can then be solved efficiently because the matrices involved are band matrices (ie the non-zero entries are concentrated on a small number of diagonals), and use can be made of the well-known Cholesky decomposition (from linear algebra). The values of γ_i are then used to determine $\hat{g}$. This procedure has been implemented using the Excel spreadsheet package.

Choice of *p* and weights

As we have seen, the selection of p determines the degree of emphasis that we place on goodness of fit relative to smoothness. A number of procedures (some automatic) have been proposed for the estimation of p, including cross validation: readers are referred to Green and Silverman for further discussion of this methodology[7].

We have adopted a more pragmatic approach and followed the original proposal of Reinsch[8] and have chosen p so that the first term of $S(g)$

$$S_1(g) = \sum_{i=1}^{n} \frac{w_i(Y_i - g(x_i))^2}{Var\ y_i}$$

lies in the interval $(n-\sqrt{2n}, n+\sqrt{2n})$ Reinsch proposed this range (for the case where w_i=1) on the grounds that it represented a confidence interval for S_1, by analogy with the chi squared distribution.

This gives a range of values (p_1, p_2) for p and then experiments with different values of p have been undertaken and the resulting $\hat{g}$ subjected to the conventional battery of graduation tests to ensure a satisfactory fit. It was found helpful to plot $S_1(g)$ as a function of p to test its sensitivity to different values within the range advocated by Reinsch. The values of w_i have been chosen to ensure that key features of the observations are preserved in the graduation: what the actuarial literature[9] refers to as "intrinsic roughness": for example the peak in the rates for males at ages 17–19. The choice is somewhat arbitrary and requires a certain amount of judgement. The final values chosen are of the following form:

MALES

$w_i >$ 1 for ages 1–23, 27–35 (with peak values at 1–17, 19–20, 22–23, 29)

$w_i <$ 1 for ages ≥ 95

$w_i =$ 1 elsewhere.

FEMALES

$w_i >$ 1 for ages 1–21 (with peak values at 1, 2, 16, 19)

$w_i =$ 1 elsewhere.

The graduation for males caused more difficulty in the sense of obtaining a good progression without too many undulations.

Extreme ages

The severe curvature in the curve of mortality rates in the first year of life places a heavy constraint on the fitting procedure. It was decided to omit age 0 from the fitting procedure and so choose the minimum age as 1 and to utilise the crude value at age 0 without modification.

At the highest ages, the available data are suspect and at these ages the crude mortality rates have a somewhat uneven progression with age. For practical purposes the inclusion in the curve-fitting process of these data points at the highest ages is of little significance *providing* that care is taken regarding the cut-off point. In particular it is necessary to ensure that for the ages included there is a monotonic (upward) progression in the crude rates otherwise the graduating spline may turn downwards. With this guidance, the maximum age was chosen to be 103 for males and 104 for females.

Tests of graduation

The resulting graduations were tested for goodness of fit and smoothness. To test for goodness of fit, the standard procedures were used: plots of residuals versus age and fitted values, standardised deviations test, cumulative deviations test, serial correlations test, signs test, changes of sign test and grouping of signs test[9].

Extrapolation of the mortality rates to the highest ages

A number of different methods have been tried for the extrapolation of the mortality rates beyond ages 103 for males and 104 for females. For ELT 14, a cubic polynomial was fitted to the last 3 spline values and an arbitrary fixed value; this approach was not adopted for FLT 15 because it was found that the resulting extrapolated values depended critically on the arbitrarily chosen fixed value and the initial conditions. Experiments for ELT 15 were undertaken using straight line extrapolation of the graduated m_x (or implied q_x) and of suitable transforms of these rates. The most satisfactory results (judged on the basis of the age-to-age progression of the rates and the relationship between the extrapolated male and female rates) were obtained by using a regression line fitted to the values of the function $\log(q_x/(1-q_x))$ from ages 85 to 103 for males (104 for females) and then extrapolated beyond. The extrapolated values of $\log(q_x/(1-q_x))$ for the ages beyond 103/104 were then converted back to give values of q_x directly.

Construction of the Life Tables from the graduated rates of mortality

In order to produce the final life tables for males and females, it was necessary to calculate values of q_x from the graduated central mortality rates, m_x. The available information is

(i) value of q_0 derived directly from the data
(ii) graduated central mortality rates m_x for $x = 1, \ldots, 103$ (104 for females)
(iii) φ_0 the average age at death for those dying in the first year of life, assumed to be 0.15 for males and 0.16 for females as for ELT 14
(iv) the limiting age ω. The method chosen for the extrapolation of q_x beyond age 103 (104 for females) implies that q_x will approach, but never quite reach, the value of 1 as age increases. In order to calculate the expectation of life it was decided to choose an arbitrary upper age, ω, such that $q_{\omega-l} = 1$. If we assume the life table function l_x is linear over the year of age $(\omega-l, \omega)$ then this implies $m_{\omega-l} = 2$. ω was set to equal 121 for males and for females.

The mathematical procedure for determining the rates of mortality is then:

(a) $$m_o = \frac{q_o}{1-(1-\varphi_o)q_o}$$

(b) $$q_1 = m_1\left[\frac{1+\frac{1}{2}\ m_2}{1+\frac{1}{12}\ (7m_1+5m_2)+\frac{1}{3}\ m_1m_2}\right]$$

(c) $$q_x = m_x\left[\frac{1-\frac{1}{2}\ m_{x-1}}{1+\frac{5}{12}(m_x - m_{x-1})-\frac{1}{6}\ m_xm_{x-1}}\right]$$

for $x = 2, 3, \ldots, 103$ (for males) or 104 (for females)

(d) $$q_{\omega-l} - 1$$

where ω = 121 for both males and females.

The formula in (b) holds if l_t is quadratic over the age interval [1,3] and in (c) holds if l_t is quadratic over the age interval $[x-l, x+l]$[10].

These assumptions having been made, the arrays (m_x) and (q_x) are completely determined for $x = 0, 1, \ldots, \omega-l$. The values of l_x were found successively from the radix l_0 as

$$1_{x+l} = l_x(1-q_x).$$

The values for the complete expectation of life at each age, $\mathring{e}_x$, was calculated as

$$\mathring{e}_x = \sum_{t=1}^{w-x-1} \frac{l_{x+t}}{l_x} + \tfrac{1}{2} - \tfrac{1}{12}\ \mu_x$$

The value of μ_x, the force of mortality at age x, is calculated as

$$\left(11l_x - 18l_{x+1} + 9l_{x+2} - 2l_{x+3}\right)/6l_x \text{ if } x = 1 \text{ or } 2,$$

and

$$\left(-l_{x-2} + 8l_{x-1} - 8l_{x+1} + l_{x+2}\right)/12l_x \text{ otherwise}$$

The value of T_x, the number of years that the survivors to age x will collectively survive thereafter, is calculated as $l_x\mathring{e}_x$.

STEVEN HABERMAN
The City University
London
December 1996

Appendix C

Persons Life Table*

Age	l_x			d_x		
x	*Males*	*Females*	*Persons*	*Males*	*Females*	*Persons*
0	51220	48780	100000	417	308	725
1	50803	48472	99275	32	26	58
2	50771	48446	99217	20	15	35
3	50751	48431	99182	15	11	26
4	50736	48420	99156	12	9	21
5	50724	48411	99135	11	7	18
6	50713	48404	99117	11	7	18
7	50702	48397	99099	9	7	16
8	50693	48390	99083	10	7	17
9	50683	48383	99066	9	6	15
10	50674	48377	99051	9	7	16
11	50665	48370	99035	9	6	15
12	50656	48364	99020	10	7	17
13	50646	48357	99003	12	8	20
14	50634	48349	98983	15	8	23
15	50619	48341	98960	20	11	31
16	50599	48330	98929	26	13	39
17	50573	48317	98890	38	15	53
18	50535	48302	98837	44	15	59
19	50491	48287	98778	42	15	57
20	50449	48272	98721	42	15	57
21	50407	48257	98664	44	16	60
22	50363	48241	98604	44	16	60
23	50319	48225	98544	45	16	61
24	50274	48209	98483	44	16	60
25	50230	48193	98423	44	16	60
26	50186	48177	98363	42	16	58
27	50144	48161	98305	42	18	60
28	50102	48143	98245	44	18	62
29	50058	48125	98183	45	19	64
30	50013	48106	98119	45	21	66
31	49968	48085	98053	47	23	70
32	49921	48062	97983	48	25	73
33	49873	48037	97910	50	27	77
34	49823	48010	97833	53	30	83
35	49770	47980	97750	58	33	91
36	49712	47947	97659	63	36	99
37	49649	47911	97560	69	40	109
38	49580	47871	97451	74	43	117
39	49506	47828	97334	79	46	125

Age	l_x			d_x		
x	*Males*	*Females*	*Persons*	*Males*	*Females*	*Persons*
40	49427	47782	97209	85	52	137
41	49342	47730	97072	92	55	147
42	49250	47675	96925	99	62	161
43	49151	47613	96764	108	67	175
44	49043	47546	96589	118	75	193
45	48925	47471	96396	130	85	215
46	48795	47386	96181	145	93	238
47	48650	47293	95943	162	104	266
48	48488	47189	95677	180	114	294
49	48308	47075	95383	200	125	325
50	48108	46950	95058	224	138	362
51	47884	46812	94696	248	153	401
52	47636	46659	94295	275	166	441
53	47361	46493	93854	304	182	486
54	47057	46311	93368	336	198	534
55	46721	46113	92834	373	219	592
56	46348	45894	92242	412	244	656
57	45936	45650	91586	457	270	727
58	45479	45380	90859	506	299	805
59	44973	45081	90054	559	334	893
60	44414	44747	89161	618	371	989
61	43796	44376	88172	683	409	1092
62	43113	43967	87080	754	446	1200
63	42359	43521	85880	832	492	1324
64	41527	43029	84556	913	544	1457
65	40614	42485	83099	994	595	1589
66	39620	41890	81510	1074	638	1712
67	38546	41252	79798	1155	691	1846
68	37391	40561	77952	1231	748	1979
69	36160	39813	75973	1303	803	2106
70	34857	39010	73867	1369	854	2223
71	33488	38156	71644	1444	916	2360
72	32044	37240	69284	1521	1002	2523
73	30523	36238	66761	1592	1093	2685
74	28931	35145	64076	1648	1154	2802
75	27283	33991	61274	1691	1213	2904
76	25592	32778	58370	1734	1285	3019
77	23858	31493	55351	1770	1372	3142
78	22088	30121	55029	1789	1455	3244
79	20299	28666	48965	1795	1541	3336
80	18504	27125	45629	1779	1616	3395
81	16725	25509	42234	1741	1676	3417
82	14984	23833	38817	1690	1720	3410
83	13294	22113	35407	1627	1754	3381
84	11667	20359	32026	1548	1783	3331
85	10119	18576	28695	1454	1808	3262
86	8665	16768	25433	1351	1816	3167
87	7314	14952	22266	1232	1773	3005
88	6082	13179	19261	1098	1695	2793
89	4984	11484	16468	960	1624	2584

Age	l_x			d_x		
x	Males	Females	Persons	Males	Females	Persons
90	4024	9860	13884	823	1534	2357
91	3201	8326	11527	701	1416	2117
92	2500	6910	9410	592	1283	1875
93	1908	5627	7535	488	1133	1621
94	1420	4494	5914	390	979	1369
95	1030	3515	4545	302	830	1132
96	728	2685	3413	226	681	907
97	502	2004	2506	166	537	703
98	336	1467	1803	117	416	533
99	219	1051	1270	80	319	399
100	139	732	871	54	238	292
101	85	494	579	35	171	206
102	50	323	373	21	117	138
103	29	206	235	13	78	91
104	16	128	144	8	51	59
105	8	77	85	4	34	38
106	4	43	47	2	20	22
107	2	23	25	1	11	12
108	1	12	13	1	6	7
109	0	6	6	0	3	3
110	0	3	3	0	2	2
111	0	1	1	0	0	0
112	0	1	1	0	1	1
113						
114						

** Assuming 105 male births for every 100 female births (see page 373).*

Appendix D

Definitions

l_x are the number of survivors to age x of 100,000 live births of the same sex who subsequently experience mortality similar to that of the population of that sex in England and Wales in 1990–92.

d_x are the number dying between age x and $(x+1)$, described similarly to l_x, that is $l_x - l_{x+1}$.

q_x is the initial mortality rate between age x and $(x+1)$, that is, d_x / l_x.

μ_x is the force of mortality at age x, that is, $\frac{-1}{l_x}\frac{dl_x}{dx}$

and calculated as

$(11l_x - 18l_{x+1} + 9l_{x+2} - 2l_{x+3})/6l_x$ if $x = 1$ or 2, and

$(-l_{x-2} + 8l_{x-1} - 8l_{x+1} + l_{x+2})/12l_x$ otherwise.

T_x is the number of years that the survivors to age x collectively will survive, that is, $\int_0^\infty l_{x+t}dt$ and calculated as $l_x\,\mathring{e}_x$.

$\mathring{e}_x$ is the average expectation of life, the average number of years that those aged x will live thereafter, and calculated as

$$\mathring{e}_x = \sum_{t=1}^{w-x-1} \frac{l_{x+t}}{l_x} + \tfrac{1}{2} - \tfrac{1}{12}\mu_x$$

ω is the earliest age by which all the survivors are assumed to have died, so that $q_{\omega-1}$ is assumed to equal 1.

Appendix E

References

1 *Mid-year population estimates for England and Wales*. Monitor PP1 91/1, 93/2 and 93/3. OPCS.

2 **Shaw C.** The sex ratio at birth in England and Wales. *Population Trends* 57. HMSO (1989.)

3 *Australian Life Tables 1990–92*. Australian Govemment Publishing Service.

4 **Thatcher A R.** Trends in Numbers and Mortality at High Ages in England and Wales. *Population Studies* 46. University Press, Cambridge (1992.)

5 **Papaleonides P.** *Graduation by Smoothing Splines. Experiments with English and Greek Fertility Rates*. MSc in Actuarial Science Dissertation. City University London (1995.)

6 **De Boor C.** *A Practical Guide to Splines*. Springer Verlag, New York (1978.)

7 **Green P J** and **Silverman B W.** *Nonparametric Regression and Generalized Linear Models: A Roughness Penalty Approach*. Chapman and Hall, London (1994.)

8 **Reinsch C.** *Smoothing by Spline Functions*. Numerische Mathematik, vol 10, pp 177–183 (1967).

9 **Chadburn R G, Cooper D R** and **Haberman S.** *Actuarial Mathematics*. Subject D Core Reading. Institute and Faculty of Actuaries, Oxford (1995).

10 **McCutcheon J J.** Some Elementary Life Table Approximations. *Transactions of the Faculty of Actuaries*, vol 35, pp 297–301 (1977).

Appendix 2

Interim Life Tables, 1994–96

Interim Life Tables

Produced by The Government Actuary's Department

EXPECTATION OF LIFE

England & Wales, Males

Based on data for the years 1994–1996

Age x	m_x*	q_x†	l_x†	d_x†	e_x†
0	0.006911	0.006887	100000.0	688.7	74.37
1	0.000490	0.000490	99311.3	48.7	73.88
2	0.000305	0.000305	99262.6	30.2	72.92
3	0.000223	0.000223	99232.4	22.1	71.94
4	0.000196	0.000196	99210.2	19.5	70.96
5	0.000146	0.000146	99190.8	14.4	69.97
6	0.000157	0.000157	99176.3	15.5	68.98
7	0.000132	0.000132	99160.8	13.1	67.99
8	0.000158	0.000158	99147.7	15.7	67.00
9	0.000154	0.000154	99132.0	15.3	66.01
10	0.000149	0.000149	99116.7	14.8	65.02
11	0.000155	0.000155	99101.9	15.4	64.03
12	0.000186	0.000186	99086.5	18.4	63.04
13	0.000210	0.000210	99068.1	20.8	62.05
14	0.000271	0.000271	99047.3	26.9	61.07
15	0.000316	0.000316	99020.4	31.3	60.08
16	0.000388	0.000388	98989.1	38.4	59.10
17	0.000662	0.000662	98950.7	65.5	58.12
18	0.000772	0.000772	98885.2	76.3	57.16
19	0.000755	0.000754	98808.9	74.5	56.21
20	0.000830	0.000830	98734.4	82.0	55.25
21	0.000878	0.000877	98652.4	86.6	54.29
22	0.000801	0.000801	98565.9	79.0	53.34
23	0.000840	0.000840	98486.9	82.7	52.38
24	0.000845	0.000844	98404.2	83.1	51.43
25	0.000852	0.000852	98321.1	83.8	50.47
26	0.000853	0.000853	98237.4	83.8	49.51
27	0.000868	0.000868	98153.6	85.2	48.55
28	0.000899	0.000899	98068.5	88.1	47.60
29	0.000917	0.000917	97980.3	89.8	46.64
30	0.000935	0.000935	97890.5	91.5	45.68
31	0.001036	0.001036	97799.0	101.3	44.72
32	0.001000	0.000999	97697.7	97.6	43.77
33	0.001067	0.001066	97600.1	104.1	42.81
34	0.001120	0.001119	97496.0	109.1	41.86
35	0.001141	0.001141	97386.9	111.1	40.90
36	0.001212	0.001212	97275.8	117.9	39.95
37	0.001281	0.001280	97158.0	124.4	39.00
38	0.001380	0.001379	97033.6	133.9	38.05
39	0.001593	0.001592	96899.8	154.2	37.10
40	0.001715	0.001714	96745.5	165.8	36.16

* Crude mortality rate.

† See p 404 for definition.

Age x	m_x*	q_x†	l_x†	d_x†	e_x†
41	0.001843	0.001842	96579.7	177.9	35.22
42	0.001979	0.001977	96401.9	190.6	34.28
43	0.002216	0.002213	96211.3	213.0	33.35
44	0.002338	0.002336	95998.4	224.2	32.42
45	0.002549	0.002545	95774.1	243.8	31.50
46	0.002752	0.002748	95530.4	262.6	30.58
47	0.002917	0.002912	95267.8	277.5	29.66
48	0.003266	0.003260	94990.3	309.7	28.74
49	0.003767	0.003760	94680.7	356.0	27.84
50	0.004195	0.004186	94324.7	394.8	26.94
51	0.004592	0.004581	93929.8	430.3	26.05
52	0.005288	0.005274	93499.5	493.1	25.17
53	0.005894	0.005877	93006.4	546.6	24.30
54	0.006515	0.006494	92459.9	600.5	23.44
55	0.007286	0.007260	91859.4	666.9	22.59
56	0.008057	0.008025	91192.5	731.8	21.75
57	0.008943	0.008903	90460.7	805.4	20.92
58	0.009843	0.009795	89655.3	878.2	20.11
59	0.011085	0.011024	88777.1	978.6	19.30
60	0.012432	0.012356	87798.5	1084.8	18.51
61	0.013882	0.013787	86713.7	1195.5	17.74
62	0.015565	0.015445	85518.2	1320.8	16.98
63	0.017264	0.017117	84197.3	1441.2	16.23
64	0.019527	0.019338	82756.1	1600.3	15.51
65	0.021878	0.021641	81155.8	1756.3	14.80
66	0.024300	0.024009	79399.5	1906.3	14.12
67	0.027204	0.026839	77493.3	2079.9	13.46
68	0.030039	0.029595	75413.4	2231.8	12.81
69	0.032990	0.032455	73181.6	2375.1	12.19
70	0.037110	0.036434	70806.5	2579.8	11.58
71	0.040767	0.039953	68226.7	2725.8	11.00
72	0.044884	0.043899	65500.9	2875.4	10.43
73	0.050116	0.048891	62625.5	3061.8	9.89
74	0.053881	0.052467	59563.7	3125.1	9.37
75	0.059587	0.057863	56438.5	3265.7	8.86
76	0.065425	0.063352	53172.8	3368.6	8.38
77	0.072206	0.069690	49804.2	3470.9	7.91
78	0.079816	0.076753	46333.3	3556.2	7.47
79	0.086958	0.083334	42777.1	3564.8	7.04
80	0.096324	0.091898	39212.3	3603.5	6.64
81	0.104698	0.099489	35608.8	3542.7	6.26
82	0.115624	0.109305	32066.1	3505.0	5.90
83	0.125743	0.118305	28561.1	3378.9	5.56
84	0.137361	0.128534	25182.2	3236.8	5.24
85	0.148877	0.138563	21945.4	3040.8	4.94
86	0.161122	0.149109	18904.6	2818.9	4.65
87	0.173860	0.159955	16085.7	2573.0	4.38
88	0.187638	0.171544	13512.8	2318.0	4.12
89	0.205204	0.186109	11194.7	2083.4	3.88
90	0.225030	0.202271	9111.3	1843.0	3.65
91	0.237488	0.212281	7268.3	1542.9	3.45
92	0.269236	0.237293	5725.4	1358.6	3.25
93	0.287895	0.251668	4366.8	1099.0	3.11
94	0.309377	0.267931	3267.8	875.6	3.00
95	0.338095	0.289205	2392.3	691.9	2.92

* Crude mortality rate.
† See p 404 for definition.

Age x	m_x*	q_x†	l_x†	d_x†	e_x†
96	0.334192	0.286345	1700.4	486.9	2.91
97	0.335057	0.286980	1213.5	348.3	2.89
98	0.323296	0.278308	865.3	240.8	2.87
99	0.349376	0.297348	624.4	185.7	2.79
100	0.330693	0.283772	438.8	124.5	2.77
101	0.341654	0.291805	314.3	91.7	2.68
102	0.365385	0.308943	222.6	68.8	2.58
103	0.389474	0.325991	153.8	50.1	2.54
104	0.353448	0.300366	103.7	31.1	2.51
105	0.214286	0.193548	72.5	14.0	2.44

* Crude mortality rate.
† See p 404 for definition.

Interim Life Tables

Produced by The Government Actuary's Department

EXPECTATION OF LIFE

England & Wales, Females

Based on data for the years 1994–1996

Age x	m_x*	q_x†	l_x†	d_x†	e_x†
0	0.005364	0.005349	100000.0	534.9	79.58
1	0.000458	0.000458	99465.1	45.6	79.01
2	0.000267	0.000267	99419.5	26.6	78.05
3	0.000176	0.000175	99393.0	17.4	77.07
4	0.000129	0.000129	99375.5	12.8	76.08
5	0.000137	0.000137	99362.7	13.6	75.09
6	0.000126	0.000126	99349.1	12.5	74.10
7	0.000098	0.000098	99336.6	9.8	73.11
8	0.000090	0.000090	99326.8	9.0	72.12
9	0.000108	0.000108	99317.8	10.7	71.12
10	0.000109	0.000109	99307.1	10.8	70.13
11	0.000106	0.000106	99296.3	10.6	69.14
12	0.000111	0.000111	99285.7	11.0	68.15
13	0.000141	0.000141	99274.7	14.0	67.15
14	0.000182	0.000182	99260.6	18.1	66.16
15	0.000206	0.000206	99242.6	20.4	65.18
16	0.000239	0.000239	99222.1	23.7	64.19
17	0.000272	0.000272	99198.4	26.9	63.20
18	0.000288	0.000288	99171.5	28.6	62.22
19	0.000324	0.000324	99142.9	32.2	61.24
20	0.000289	0.000289	99110.7	28.7	60.26
21	0.000322	0.000322	99082.0	31.9	59.28
22	0.000298	0.000298	99050.1	29.5	58.29
23	0.000302	0.000301	99020.6	29.9	57.31
24	0.000305	0.000304	98990.7	30.1	56.33
25	0.000319	0.000319	98960.6	31.6	55.35
26	0.000354	0.000354	98929.0	35.0	54.36
27	0.000417	0.000417	98894.0	41.3	53.38
28	0.000381	0.000381	98852.8	37.6	52.40
29	0.000394	0.000394	98815.1	38.9	51.42
30	0.000437	0.000437	98776.2	43.2	50.44
31	0.000441	0.000441	98733.0	43.5	49.47
32	0.000547	0.000547	98689.5	54.0	48.49
33	0.000577	0.000577	98635.6	56.9	47.51
34	0.000612	0.000612	98578.7	60.3	46.54
35	0.000672	0.000671	98518.3	66.1	45.57
36	0.000723	0.000723	98452.2	71.1	44.60
37	0.000768	0.000767	98381.1	75.5	43.63
38	0.000883	0.000883	98305.6	86.8	42.66
39	0.000969	0.000969	98218.8	95.2	41.70
40	0.001074	0.001073	98123.6	105.3	40.74

* Crude mortality rate.

† See p 404 for definition.

Age x	m_x*	q_x†	l_x†	d_x†	e_x†
41	0.001212	0.001212	98018.3	118.8	39.79
42	0.001294	0.001293	97899.6	126.6	38.83
43	0.001446	0.001445	97772.9	141.3	37.88
44	0.001557	0.001556	97631.7	151.9	36.94
45	0.001751	0.001750	97479.7	170.5	35.99
46	0.001896	0.001894	97309.2	184.3	35.06
47	0.002036	0.002034	97124.9	197.5	34.12
48	0.002228	0.002226	96927.4	215.7	33.19
49	0.002454	0.002451	96711.6	237.0	32.36
50	0.002882	0.002878	96474.6	277.7	31.34
51	0.003126	0.003121	96196.9	300.2	30.43
52	0.003348	0.003342	95896.7	320.5	29.52
53	0.003806	0.003799	95576.2	363.1	28.62
54	0.004039	0.004031	95213.2	383.8	27.73
55	0.004550	0.004539	94829.4	430.5	26.84
56	0.004817	0.004806	94398.9	453.7	25.96
57	0.005402	0.005387	93945.3	506.1	25.08
58	0.005888	0.005871	93439.2	548.6	24.21
59	0.006592	0.006571	92890.6	610.4	23.35
60	0.007266	0.007240	92280.2	668.1	22.50
61	0.008170	0.008137	91612.1	745.4	21.67
62	0.009066	0.009025	90866.7	820.0	20.84
63	0.009998	0.009948	90046.6	895.8	20.02
64	0.011136	0.011075	89150.8	987.3	19.22
65	0.012783	0.012701	88163.5	1119.8	18.43
66	0.013954	0.013857	87043.7	1206.2	17.66
67	0.015455	0.015336	85837.6	1316.4	16.90
68	0.017535	0.017383	84521.1	1469.2	16.16
69	0.019337	0.019152	83051.9	1590.6	15.43
70	0.021604	0.021373	81461.3	1741.1	14.72
71	0.023671	0.023395	79720.2	1865.0	14.04
72	0.026306	0.025964	77855.2	2021.5	13.36
73	0.029096	0.028678	75833.8	2174.8	12.70
74	0.031454	0.030967	73659.0	2281.0	12.06
75	0.034830	0.034234	71378.0	2443.5	11.43
76	0.038591	0.037861	68934.5	2609.9	10.82
77	0.043362	0.042441	66324.6	2814.9	10.23
78	0.047766	0.046652	63509.6	2962.9	9.66
79	0.052625	0.051276	60546.8	3104.6	9.10
80	0.059149	0.057450	57442.2	3300.1	8.57
81	0.065940	0.063836	54142.1	3456.2	8.06
82	0.073863	0.071232	50685.9	3610.5	7.57
83	0.082427	0.079164	47075.5	3726.7	7.12
84	0.091590	0.087579	43348.8	3796.4	6.69
85	0.100661	0.095837	39552.3	3790.6	6.28
86	0.111537	0.105645	35761.7	3778.1	5.89
87	0.121102	0.114188	31983.7	3652.1	5.53
88	0.134962	0.126430	28331.5	3582.0	5.18
89	0.148567	0.138294	24749.6	3422.7	4.86
90	0.162057	0.149910	21326.9	3197.1	4.55
91	0.177146	0.162732	18129.7	2950.3	4.27
92	0.193483	0.176416	15179.5	2677.9	4.01
93	0.216903	0.195681	12501.6	2446.3	3.76
94	0.246081	0.219120	10055.2	2203.3	3.55
95	0.257628	0.228229	7851.9	1792.0	3.42

* Crude mortality rate.
† See p 404 for definition.

Age x	m_x*	q_x†	l_x†	d_x†	e_x†
96	0.276314	0.242773	6059.9	1471.2	3.28
97	0.287836	0.251623	4588.7	1154.6	3.18
98	0.298838	0.259991	3434.1	892.8	3.09
99	0.315957	0.272852	2541.3	693.4	3.00
100	0.324039	0.278858	1847.9	515.3	2.95
101	0.338690	0.289641	1332.6	386.0	2.91
102	0.309074	0.267704	946.6	253.4	2.90
103	0.303062	0.263182	693.2	182.4	2.80
104	0.347085	0.295759	510.8	151.1	2.60
105	0.311912	0.269831	359.7	97.1	2.53

* Crude mortality rate.
† See p 404 for definition.

Appendix 3

Index-linked Government Stock rates, 1995–98

Index-linked Government Stock

Over five years, inflation 5%, as at first working day of each month

	Over 5 years
1995	
3 January 1995	3.88
1 February 1995	3.88
1 March 1995	3.88
3 April 1995	3.86
1 May 1995	3.80
1 June 1995	3.55
3 July 1995	3.76
1 August 1995	3.65
1 September 1995	3.54
2 October 1995	3.67
1 November 1995	3.68
1 December 1995	3.52
1996	
2 January 1996	3.51
1 February 1996	3.57
1 March 1996	3.74
1 April 1996	3.76
1 May 1996	3.71
3 June 1996	3.85
1 July 1996	3.82
1 August 1996	3.76
2 September 1996	3.72
1 October 1996	3.47
1 November 1996	3.63
2 December 1996	3.45

	Over 5 years
1997	
2 January 1997	3.59
3 February 1997	3.53
3 March 1997	3.44
1 April 1997	3.62
1 May 1997	3.58
2 June 1997	3.68
1 July 1997	3.60
1 August 1997	3.55
1 September 1997	3.55
1 October 1997	3.26
3 November 1997	3.11
1 December 1997	3.08
1998	
2 January 1998	3.01
2 February 1998	3.06
2 March 1998	2.96
1 April 1998	2.85
1 May 1998	2.79
1 June 1998	2.63
1 July 1998	2.63
3 August 1998	2.55
1 September 1998	2.42